Rehear

# Rehearsal from Shakespeare to Sheridan

TIFFANY STERN

CLARENDON PRESS · OXFORD

*This book has been printed digitally and produced in a standard specification in order to ensure its continuing availability*

# OXFORD
UNIVERSITY PRESS

Great Clarendon Street, Oxford OX2 6DP
Oxford University Press is a department of the University of Oxford.
It furthers the University's objective of excellence in research, scholarship,
and education by publishing worldwide in
Oxford New York
Auckland Cape Town Dar es Salaam Hong Kong Karachi
Kuala Lumpur Madrid Melbourne Mexico City Nairobi
New Delhi Shanghai Taipei Toronto
With offices in
Argentina Austria Brazil Chile Czech Republic France Greece
Guatemala Hungary Italy Japan South Korea Poland Portugal
Singapore Switzerland Thailand Turkey Ukraine Vietnam

Oxford is a registered trade mark of Oxford University Press
in the UK and in certain other countries
Published in the United States
by Oxford University Press Inc., New York

ISBN 978-0-19-922972-7

# Acknowledgements

This study could not have been completed without the help of many people and institutions. My first and profoundest debt is to my uncle Patrick Tucker whose questions about Shakespearian rehearsal led me to write a thesis on the subject, and whose Original Shakespeare Company has been a constant source of inspiration. I also wish to express my deep gratitude to Peter Holland who supervised my PhD at Emmanuel College, Cambridge, and encouraged me to believe that details about historical rehearsal were recoverable when many people thought they were not; I am indebted to him for his wise advice and encouragement then and now. Ian Donaldson provided last-minute guidance, and in a rather unconventional Ph.D. viva, my thesis examiners Emrys Jones and Richard Luckett gave me much useful comment. David Mikosz and Martin Tucker were scrupulous and diligent readers and saved me from countless errors; David knows how much in debt I am to him for other kindnesses. For other help, both academic and personal, I thank my fellow graduates in Renaissance Literature, particularly Jason Scott Warren, David Jays, Raphael Lyne, Gavin Alexander, Subha Mukherji, James Cannon, and Damian Nussbaum, as well as other important friends, Maria Pilla, Josh and Jafi Lehrer-Graiwer, Richard Howells, Waheguru Pal Sidhu, Mary Laven, Gerard Breen, Dean Kolbas, and Jago Kitcat. Stefan Hoesel-Uhlig translated Renaissance German documents for me and kindly hunted down a useful reference in Munich. To Benjamin Griffin I owe a great deal: his advice, references and sharp editorial eye have helped me on countless occasions; his friendship and the friendship of Arkady Ostrovsky shaped my time at Cambridge intellectually as well as socially. The process of turning the Ph.D. into a book was completed at Merton College, Oxford, where I was elected to a Junior Research Fellowship in 1997. There I have had many privileges, not least those of regular conversations with John Carey, Richard McCabe, and Richard Rowland, and, during their time as visiting fellows,

Bryan Magee, Randall Martin, George Rousseau, and Paul Saltzman. Amongst the many supportive friends I have found at Merton, Suzie Clark, Senia Paseta, Galin Tikhanov, and Sam Eidinow deserve particular mention. Over the last three years, Sos Eltis, Pascale Aebischer, Paige Newmark and Pierre Hecker have kept up my enthusiasm for the drama; Kate Bennett, Sam Kessler, and Neil McDonald my enthusiasm for literature in general; while Marcin Walecki and Piotr Szymczak helped shape a new interest in Polish literature and culture. An unlikely association with the quantum computation department has influenced my life in many ways. Portions of the work on rehearsal could not have been completed without the kind guidance of Artur Ekert, who taught me how to use computers—and what 'entanglement' really means. I am fortunate in having, through Artur, met many physicists; Vlatko Vedral in particular has helped me through some difficult times, as has his wife Ivona Dragun. The staffs of The Cambridge University Library, The Bodleian Library, The British Library, The London Library, The Folger Shakespeare Library in Washington DC, and the Huntington Library in Los Angeles rendered valuable assistance at various stages of the project, and academics working in those libraries also helped to direct the research. I am especially grateful to suggestions made during Folger tea by Peter Blayney and Alan Nelson. My final acknowledgement is to my family, particularly my parents Geoffrey and Elisabeth Stern, my brother Jonty Stern, and my grandmothers Betty Tucker and Rose Stern, whose love, encouragement, and moral support have seen me through this project and many others. This book is dedicated, with affection, to the memory of my grandmother, Rose Stern, and to my parents.

# Contents

# Conventions and References

Many of the plays I refer to have not been reprinted since the seventeenth or eighteenth century, and some are in manuscript. I generally quote from manuscript or first editions, even when modern texts exist, as, for my purposes, prefatory matter and addenda often edited away are of vital importance. Recent editions have generally been consulted, however, and can be found referenced in footnotes and the Bibliography. Details of publication are supplied for texts printed after 1900; for texts published before then, only the date is given.

Prefatory matter, prologues, and epilogues are often not included in the system of page numbering. When this is the case, I refer to page by signature. A certain amount of expansion of contractions etc. has been silently performed when quoting old-spelling texts, but substantive emendations are bracketed; texts written in italics have been reversed. Titles which admit of various different spellings are given in the form used by the edition quoted.

Dates of performance are taken from Alfred Harbage and S. Schoenbaum, *Annals of English Drama: 975–1700* (London, 1964), and from W. B. Van Lennep *et al.*, (eds.), *The London Stage, 1660–1800, A Calendar of Plays* etc., 5 parts in 11 vols. (Carbondale, Ill.: 1960–69). My use of the 1964 edition of *Annals* is intentional: see Anne Lancashire's review of the third edition in *Shakespeare Quarterly*, 42 (1991), 225–30. Quotations from Shakespeare are from the *Norton Facsimile* of the First Folio (New York, 1968), unless otherwise specified. For reference purposes Shakespeare quotations use the Through Line Numbering of that facsimile, unless, again, another text is specified.

The abbreviations used are listed on the following page.

# Abbreviations

| | |
|---|---|
| CUP | Cambridge University Press |
| *DUJ* | *Durham University Journal* |
| *ELN* | *English Language Notes* |
| *HLB* | *Harvard Library Bulletin* |
| *MLN* | *Modern Languages Notes* |
| *MLR* | *Modern Language Review* |
| *MP* | *Modern Philology* |
| *MSC* | *Malone Society Collections* |
| *OED* | *Oxford English Dictionary* |
| OUP | Oxford University Press |
| *PQ* | *Philological Quarterly* |
| *REED* | *Records of Early English Drama* |
| *RES* | *Review of English Studies* |
| *ShakS* | *Shakespeare Studies* (USA) |
| *SSu* | *Shakespeare Survey* |
| *SP* | *Studies in Philology* |
| *SQ* | *Shakespeare Quarterly* |
| TLN | Through Line Numbering (*Norton Facsimile*) |
| *TN* | *Theatre Notebook* |
| *TRI* | *Theatre Research International* |
| *TS* | *Theatre Survey* |
| *YES* | *Yearbook of English Studies* |

I

# Introduction

Like many of us, Bernard Shaw was fascinated by the idea of
Shakespeare in rehearsal. 'What', he asked, 'would we not give
for the copy of Hamlet used by Shakespear at rehearsal, with the
original stage business scrawled by the prompter's pencil?'[1] He
was projecting a revealing prompt-book depicting the staging
and perhaps some of the guiding 'concepts' employed in
Shakespeare's production. The underlying assumption behind
this desire was that Shakespearian rehearsals had been detailed,
prescriptive, Shavian.

In fact both Alexander Pope, writing in the early eighteenth
century, and Edmond Malone, editing Shakespeare some years
later, claimed to have seen Shakespearian prompt-books.
Neither was much affected by the experience. Pope noted
tantalizingly that in 'the Quarto' (he did not say which) 'several
of those . . . passages were added in a written hand, which are
since to be found in the folio'; Malone, examining prompt
markings on a Quarto of *Romeo and Juliet,* recorded that 'the . . .
directions in this copy appear to be of a very old date, one of
them being in the ancient style and hand—"*Play musicke*"'.[2]
Pope and Malone were not surprised that there was little
information about Shakespeare's staging in the prompt-books,

---

[1] Preface to *Plays Unpleasant* in Bernard Shaw, *Collected Plays with their Prefaces,*
revised 1930, 7 vols. (London, 1970), i. 28. Shaw printed separate 'rehearsal copies'
of his plays; subsequent copies reflect changes undergone in rehearsal—see F. E.
Lowenstein, *The Rehearsal Copies of Bernard Shaw's Plays* (London, 1950).

[2] William Shakespeare, *The Works,* ed. Alexander Pope, 6 vols. (1723), i. p. xvii.
The Quarto had 'the parts divided with lines, and the Actors' names in the margin',
for which reason Pope identified the book as a playhouse text rather than a printer's
copy; *Supplement to the Edition of Shakspeare's Plays Published in 1778,* ed. Edmond
Malone, 2 vols. (1780), i. 26n. A 1599 Quarto of *Romeo and Juliet* containing the
same music cue is referred to in Edward A. Langhans, *Restoration Promptbooks*
(Carbondale, Ill., 1981), 41. That copy, which is presumably the one referred to by
Malone, was actually marked up for production during the Restoration.

as prompt-books in their own time likewise provided only minimal directions. For, between the sixteenth and eighteenth centuries, there was no 'director' or 'producer' in charge of production, and therefore no need for prompt-books to disclose more than the words to be spoken and the entrances to be cued. The 'Shakespearian' prompt-books reflected a way of preparing plays for the stage that eighteenth-century writers instinctively understood, and Shaw could not even imagine correctly.

The rise of the 'director' towards the end of the nineteenth century brought about a fundamental change in the organization of the theatre as a whole. But at the same time that new theatrical practices distanced the contemporary theatre from its past, literary interest in the historical theatre began to flourish. Stage-centred theatre-criticism, which argued that the specific, material conditions that affected production, also affected texts themselves, became a major area of critical study in the 1920s and has remained so ever since. Writers such as E. K. Chambers, W. W. Greg, W. J. Lawrence, C. W. Wallace, and Muriel Bradbrook believed that Shakespeare could only be properly understood in the context of the theatre for which he wrote; Allardyce Nicoll and Montague Summers examined Restoration and eighteenth-century theatrical conditions to see how they affected the drama of Congreve, Shadwell, and Dryden. Nowadays it is usual to edit texts with reference to the stage on which they were performed: the Oxford *Complete Works*, for instance, aims at 'recovering and presenting texts of Shakespeare's plays as they were acted in the London playhouses which stood at the centre of his professional life'; while the newest Arden editions present Shakespeare's 'literary texts' against the 'cultural texts' that shaped their production.[3] But the break in theatrical tradition seems to have resulted in a habit of unwittingly imposing present theatrical practice onto the past, so bringing about extraordinary misreadings of vital passages. How often does one come across the claim that Hamlet's advice to the players—to imitate exactly his enunciation of the text, and to

---

[3] William Shakespeare, *Complete Works: Compact Edition*, ed. Stanley Wells and Gary Taylor (Oxford, 1988), p. xxxix; general editors' preface to *The Arden Shakespeare: Third Series*, quoted from Jonathan Bate's edition of William Shakespeare, *Titus Andronicus* (London, 1995), p. xiii.

depict the 'passions' with careful attention to the rules that
govern gesture and pronunciation—is the best counsel that can
be given to a modern actor?[4] Nowhere is the tendency to
conflate modern and past theatrical practice more marked
than in the field of rehearsal; many—if not most—editors,
theatre historians, and literary critics impose on the past a
mythical period of regular group rehearsal that is very much
in the twentieth-century style. This is used as a catch-all to
contain and explain papers that cannot otherwise be made sense
of. So Martin Holmes's solution for the absence of an audience
in the Van Buchel–De Witt drawing of the Swan Theatre
(*c.*1596) is that the picture illustrates a rehearsal; while David
Bradley's explanation for the existence of the Dulwich 'platts' is
that rehearsals can be directed from them while the 'boke' is
away with the Master of the Revels.[5] In the prompt-book of
*Believe as You List*, when the part of Demetrius is assigned in the
text to three different actors, the solution suggested by T. J.
King is that 'Knight [the prompter] is trying them out in
rehearsal'.[6] 'Revision studies' particularly rely on assumptions
about the role of the author in the preparation of a play that
simply will not stand up against the facts. Looking for reasons to
explain why there are traces left over from performance in some
texts, or why some single plays exist in good-but-different
forms, modern editors have 'created' a period of regular
ensemble rehearsal overseen by the author: texts can then be
said to have changed and developed during that process.
Fredson Bowers perhaps started the trend, arguing that Elizabethan texts should be edited bearing in mind the revision that
they must have undergone during group rehearsal—'no play is
produced at present without a great deal of adjustment during
rehearsal both in large and in small matters, and we have no
right to assume that conditions were essentially different in the

---

[4] See e.g. John Barton, *Playing Shakespeare* (London, 1984), 6; and Michael
Pennington, *Hamlet: A User's Guide* (London, 1996), 84. This speech was so little
valued historically that it was cut out of productions of *Hamlet* during the late
Restoration and early 18th c., and was not restored until the time of Garrick—see
Thomas Davies, *Dramatic Miscellanies*, 3 vols. (Dublin, 1784), iii. 48.

[5] Martin Holmes, 'A New Theory about the Swan Drawing', *TN* 10 (1955), 80–
3; David Bradley, *From Text to Performance in the Elizabethan Theatre* (Cambridge,
1992), 89, 91.

[6] T. J. King, 'The King's Men on Stage: Actors and their Parts 1611–32', in G. R.
Hibbard (ed.), *The Elizabethan Theatre IX* (Waterloo, 1981), 28.

Elizabethan theatre'.[7] Without discussing rehearsal directly, Stanley Wells and Gary Taylor shaped their edition of Shakespeare's *Complete Works* around processes that are supposed to have arisen out of it. Their text is founded on the assumption that there were several collaborative group rehearsals before performance which were 'directed' by Shakespeare: 'Shakespeare must have been confident that he could influence the production process by word of mouth—probably as, indeed, a figure equivalent to that of the modern director', maintains Wells.[8] Taylor in *Reinventing Shakespeare* posits the theory that '[Shakespeare's] text . . . evolves under the pressure of . . . rehearsal by actors', a hypothesis he repeats in *Shakespeare Reshaped*, where he also claims that his edition intends to embrace the textual changes that took place between 'the evolution of the text' and its first performance (so assuming the text was fluid in preparation, and fixed by the time it reached the stage, a notion questioned in this book).[9] Scott McMillin and Sally-Beth MacLean in their ground-breaking study of the Queen's Company similarly presuppose that a series of group rehearsals would have been the normal place in which to establish cuts and revisions.[10] A belief in the ensemble revision of plays ties in well with modern theories about 'socialised texts', but is dependent on the idea of ensemble theatrical production.[11]

In fact, Shakespeare's texts are known for their unfinished business, their spiky edges, for a Luce that may be a Nell (*The*

---

[7] Fredson Bowers, *On Editing Shakespeare and the Elizabethan Dramatists* (Philadelphia, 1955), 113.

[8] Stanley Wells, *Re-editing Shakespeare for the Modern Reader* (Oxford, 1984), 57. See also his introduction to Shakespeare, *Complete Works*, p. xxxvi.

[9] Gary Taylor, *Reinventing Shakespeare* (London, 1989), 336; Gary Taylor and John Jowett, *Shakespeare Reshaped* (Oxford, 1993), 236. Jonathan Bate furthers the idea with his suggestion that Shakespeare's acting roles were probably confined to cameos, allowing him to give 'most of his energies in rehearsal to "directing" the company, showing them how to translate his words into stage actions', *The Genius of Shakespeare* (London, 1997), 7.

[10] Scott McMillin and Sally-Beth MacLean, *The Queen's Men and their Plays* (Cambridge, 1998), 114–16.

[11] Expressed in Stanley Wells and Gary Taylor, *William Shakespeare: A Textual Companion* (Oxford, 1987), 15; Taylor, *Reinventing*, 336; Stephen Orgel, 'The Authentic Shakespeare', *Representations*, 21 (1988), 1–27 (7). The phrase 'socialised text', used more than once by Taylor, comes from Jerome J. McGann's *Critique of Modern Textual Criticism* (Chicago and London, 1983). McGann is there denigrating the idea that authors have sole authority for their texts, and suggesting that their authority is shared by printer, publisher, editor, and other people involved in the production of a piece of literature; he is not addressing the question of revision.

*Comedy of Errors*), a Nell that may be a Doll. The latter occurs in
*Henry V*, where Pistol's wife is called Nell at HV, 522 and Doll at
HV, 2976. Taylor, in his edition of that play, makes a list of
'dramatic alterations which could have arisen during rehearsal'
while retaining the Nell–Doll ambiguity because it occurs in the
'bad' Quarto and so 'clearly survived into the play', a fundamental contradiction which chit-chat between actor and author
in rehearsal does not appear to have resolved.[12] Ideas about
rehearsal-revision are extended to other Elizabethan and Jacobean texts. T. J. King conjectures that the additional eleven-line
speech given to Memphonius in the manuscript of the *Second
Maiden's Tragedy* was added 'probably at rehearsal'; William
B. Long assumes that 'minor cutting' in the text of *John a Kent
and John a Cumber* reflects 'rehearsal decisions'.[13] The prompt-
book for *Sir Thomas More* was held back, claims Scott McMillin,
to incorporate 'improvisations which rehearsal had proved either
necessary or delightful':[14] the modern 'exploratory' nature of
rehearsal is thus also assumed to have shaped the text. The idea
of rehearsal-revision, though it has not yet swept through post-
Elizabethan literature in the same way, still informs editions of
later texts. John Ross, in his introduction to *The Recruiting
Officer*, complains that 'the Q1 text had probably not even
received the benefit of testing in rehearsals'.[15]

A brief look at 'modern' rehearsal illustrates where some of
these ideas come from. Usually in England and America about
four weeks are spent in rehearsal for a production, a play
generally receiving about 120–60 hours of rehearsal in all.[16]
Though known collectively as 'rehearsal', a number of different
kinds of event actually take place during the preparation

---

[12] William Shakespeare, *Henry V*, ed. Gary Taylor (Oxford, 1982), 264 n.

[13] King, 'The King's Men', 26; William B. Long, 'John a Kent and John a
Cumber: An Elizabethan Playbook and its Implications', in W. R. Elton and
William B. Long (eds.), *Shakespeare and Dramatic Tradition: Essays in Honor of
S.F. Johnson* (Newark, Del., 1989), 139.

[14] Scott McMillin, *The Elizabethan Theatre & the Book of Sir Thomas More* (Ithaca
and London, 1987), 38.

[15] George Farquhar, *The Recruiting Officer*, ed. John Ross (London, 1991),
p. xxxv.

[16] Hugh Morrison, *Directing the Theatre*, 2nd edn. (London, 1984), 80; John
Miles-Brown, *Directing Drama* (London, 1980), 122, 143, 160. This compares
unfavourably to Continental practice, where up to three months of rehearsal is not
unusual.

period: private rehearsal, partial rehearsal, group rehearsal, dress rehearsal, and technical rehearsal. Of those five, the last two happen just before a play is performed; the other three take place throughout the preparation process, and largely constitute it.

'Private' rehearsal, in which an actor is rehearsed alone in his part, is the rarest form of modern rehearsal and, when it happens at all, it is very private indeed. When Richard Burton performed the title role in John Gielgud's 1964 production of *Hamlet*, a 'closed' rehearsal was called for the two which the rest of the cast was 'asked not to attend'. Anxious to hear what advice Gielgud had to offer, Richard Sterne crept into the rehearsal room two hours beforehand, draped himself in a cloth, and hid under the platform, where he stayed for the next six hours: this was the only way he was able to witness the event.[17] No other actor in the play was individually rehearsed in this way, nor is there any indication that Burton was given more than one such practice.

Partial rehearsal (rehearsal of specific scenes at which only the relevant actors are present) together with full-group rehearsal (at which all the actors are present) takes up most of the preparation period. This time is dedicated to creating a performance by means of improvisation, character analysis, textual analysis, and experimentation: it is exciting, taxing, and, often, emotionally draining. Actors are encouraged to make discoveries about the play (or make the director's discoveries about the play), but are also sometimes required to make discoveries about themselves. The emotions exposed during this process contribute to the bonding between actors that occurs in rehearsal, which in turn is held to bring about close ensemble performances. The idea of 'finding' (rather than manifesting) a characterization is one of the primary aims of rehearsal, and this requires improvisation and experimentation, the object being to explore different ways and means for 'expressing the vaguest or profoundest imaginings, and for discovering the minutiae of behaviour'.[18] This

---

[17] Richard L. Sterne, *John Gielgud Directs Richard Burton in Hamlet* (New York, 1967), 6.

[18] Morrison, *Directing*, 48. Morrison here represents a conventionalized, normative, 20th-c. notion of the skills and processes involved in rehearsal. His sentiments are the same as those expressed earlier in the century by David W. Sievers in 'The Play Rehearsal Schedule and its Psychology', *Quarterly Journal of Speech*, 30 (1944), 80–4 (82).

characterization is developed with reference to other characters, and to the full story of the play: it can, for instance, be necessary for actors to watch scenes in which they do not perform.[19] New plays are often rehearsed in the presence of the authors who wrote them. This leads, at its best, to collaboration between playwrights, actors, and directors: modern playwrights frequently do refer to the way their texts have been altered and refashioned over rehearsal. Tom Stoppard thanks Peter Wood, the director of *Jumpers,* for his 'insight and inventiveness . . . throughout rehearsals'; the changes to his *Travesties* made during rehearsal and performance are documented by Philip Gaskell.[20] Edward Albee explains that he cuts lines in rehearsal; Robert Anderson lets Elia Kazan (his director) partially reshape his plays.[21] In rehearsals of old plays, a search is made to find a way of performing the lines that is both appropriate and new: a production aims to be unique, and specifically relevant to the players who act in it.[22]

The world of modern rehearsal is at times frighteningly directionless, at times joyously creative. Privileged insiders who have attended rehearsals often suggest that the audience, who only see a play in production, have missed out. For it is in rehearsal that discoveries are made, rehearsal is 'the giving birth' of performance, as Peggy Ashcroft put it, and performance is simply, claims Letzler Cole, 'the after-image of processes set in motion—explored, nourished, made fit for growth, realised— during the "work" of rehearsal'.[23] Many books about famous productions are actually concerned less with the performances themselves than with the process that brought them about.[24] Cole and Shomit Mitter examine specific directors by looking at the way they manage rehearsals; Stanislavsky, a director famous for his rehearsal practice, is usually discussed in terms of the way

[19] Morrison, *Directing,* 101.

[20] Tom Stoppard, *Jumpers* (London, 1972), 11; Philip Gaskell, *From Writer to Reader* (Oxford, 1978), 246–61.

[21] Jeane Luere (ed.), *Playwright Versus Director: Authorial Intentions and Performance Interpretations* (Westport, Conn., 1994), 24, 33–5.

[22] Morrison, *Directing,* 80.

[23] Susan Letzler Cole, *Directors in Rehearsal* (New York and London, 1992), 6, 2.

[24] For instance, Max Stafford-Clark, *Letters to George: The Account of a Rehearsal,* (London, 1989); Leon Rubin, *The Nicholas Nickleby Story* (London, 1981); David Selbourne, *The Making of A Midsummer Night's Dream* (London, 1982).

he prepared his plays, rather than in terms of the (not always successful) final result.[25]

Rehearsal involves intense, emotional, other-worldly 'moments': Hugh Morrison talks of the day when the indefinable 'It' happens and the production suddenly starts to cohere; Max Stafford-Clark elevates the rehearsal-world into a place where 'magic and creation can happen'.[26] Directors often suggest dissatisfaction that the 'magic' of rehearsal has to be submitted to the humdrum nature of performance, and sometimes compensate by turning the performances into pseudo-rehearsals. Gielgud used minimal scenery in his 1964 *Hamlet* and told his actors to wear day clothes and perform the play 'as if it were the final run-through'; the film *Vanya on 42nd Street* is a full production of *Uncle Vanya* in the form of a rehearsal, the actors wearing casual clothes, and drinking their 'vodka' from styrofoam beakers.[27] The dress and technical rehearsals that cap partial and group rehearsals are seldom specifically addressed even in books about rehearsal, because they happen when much of the creative process is over: they are necessary largely for practical reasons, and the performance to come is not shaped and developed by them.

Modern rehearsal takes the form it does because of the 'producer' (these days often called the 'director'), who is in charge of productions but (generally) not a performer in them. This figure did not come to be a regular part of production until the late nineteenth century (*OED*'s first recorded use of 'producer' meaning 'the person who produces a dramatic performance', is 1891). Producer-directors are considered artists in their own right: critics refer to Peter Brook's famous *Midsummer Night's Dream*. In the cinema, the supremacy of the director has been taken a step further—films are generally advertised by director's name only (without reference to the screen-writer's name)—*Schindler's List* and *Jurassic Park* are Spielberg films, *North by Northwest* and *Psycho* are Hitchcock classics. And it is

---

[25] Shomit Mitter, *Systems of Rehearsal* (London, 1992). See Norris Houghton, *Moscow Rehearsals* (London, 1938), and S. D. Balukhaty (ed.), *The Seagull Produced by Stanislavsky*, trans. David Magarshack (London, 1952).

[26] Morrison, *Directing*, 105; Stafford-Clark, *Letters*, 140. See also Peter Hall, *Diaries*, ed. John Goodwin (London, 1983), 143.

[27] Sterne, *John Gielgud*, 13.

telling that in the theatre the title 'director' has been lifted from the cinema to replace 'producer'—theatre 'directors' seem in their very name to lay claim to the overpowering rights that film directors have.[28]

Around the same time as the rise of the producer, the word 'ensemble' came into regular theatrical use (hitherto it had been used only in music).[29] 'Ensemble' implies shared preparation, shared ideals, and a form of theatrical 'democracy' between actors in production; modern theatrical companies often display their ensemble nature in their names—Joint Stock, Common Stock, Shared Experience, Cheek by Jowl. The group aims of modern rehearsal are, of course, stressed by this. Max Stafford-Clark writes of 'the collaborative nature of the theatre'; and Peter Brook, in an angry moment, accuses the actors rehearsing *A Midsummer Night's Dream* of 'developing techniques, but no shared understanding of the play's meaning'.[30]

At the same time that group rehearsal under a director became important, the kind of plays that required a large quantity of group rehearsal started to be written. This is not the place to discuss in which order these events happened, merely to observe that complex plays were produced, which, like Chekhov's *The Cherry Orchard*, need, as Elinor Renfield (a director) declares, 'time and care' in order 'to crack [their] code'.[31] Code-cracking is understood to be part of modern rehearsal, and naturally it has been applied backwards onto older texts, particularly to the plays of Shakespeare. Peter Brook felt that *A Midsummer Night's Dream* contained 'depths' that could only be 'plumbed' through the '*Sturm und Drang*' of the rehearsal process', while John Russell Brown writes of companies rehearsing Shakespeare and learning to 'respond to demands' made by the text that they had not previously recognized.[32] Theatre people often state

[28] Suggested by David Bradby and David Williams in *Director's Theatre* (London, 1988), 3.

[29] The word seems to have come into regular theatrical use in about 1910—see George Taylor, *Players and Performances in the Victorian Theatre* (Manchester, 1989), 102—though *OED* does not record its theatrical sense until 1938.

[30] Stafford-Clark, *Letters*, p. vii; quoted in Selbourne, *Making of A Midsummer Night's Dream*, 95.

[31] Cole, *Directors in Rehearsal*, 11.

[32] Selbourne, *Making of A Midsummer Night's Dream*, 65; John Russell Brown, 'The Nature of Speech in Shakespeare's Plays', in Marvin and Ruth Thompson (eds.), *Shakespeare and the Sense of Performance* (Newark, Del., 1989), 52.

that they are directed by Shakespeare through the 'instructions' he leaves in his plays, helped by the actual 'director' who serves as his mouthpiece. John Barton explains that if an actor follows 'the clues' he will find 'that Shakespeare himself starts to direct him', while Ann Pasternak Slater elaborates on the kind of instruction Shakespeare can offer in *Shakespeare the Director*.[33] Modern rehearsal is made to seem to be answering the demands of earlier texts.

In fact, before the twentieth century, before the rise of the director and the interest in ensemble production, performances were readied in another way. From the sixteenth to eighteenth centuries, different plays were put on every few days, sometimes every day, during the theatrical season, meaning that often an actor had to learn or relearn a part during the day for the evening's performance. For this reason, the stages of rehearsal were skewed quite differently: the emphasis of preparation was on 'private' or 'individual' rehearsal (also called 'study'), during which the actor worked on his or her own 'part' for performance. These 'parts' consisted of the individual actor's lines only, each speech preceded by a short 'watchword' or 'cue' of the last one to four words of the previous speaker's lines: actors would listen for the cue, and say the speech that they had learnt followed it. So roles were learnt in isolation not only from other performers, but from the rest of the play. Hence the number of plays that suggest actors know their parts, but do not know which parts other actors are playing (about to perform John Marston's *Antonio and Mellida*, actors ask one another 'whome act you?' and 'what dost thou play?'[34]); hence, too, the anecdotes about actors performing in plays whose story is unfamiliar to them: 'Mr. Raymur had never read the play, nor seen it: However . . . he . . . accepted the character, and . . . performed it literally perfect'.[35] For a new play, private 'study' took up most of the rehearsal period, during which actors focused on the action, emphases, and passions demanded by their separate parts, learning to manifest their character by applying to it the verbal and physical set-pieces required.

[33] Barton, *Playing Shakespeare*, 13; Ann Pasternak Slater, *Shakespeare the Director* (Sussex, 1982).
[34] John Marston, *The Plays*, ed. H. Harvey Wood, 3 vols. (London, 1934), i. 5.
[35] Tate Wilkinson, *The Wandering Patentee*, 2 vols. (1795), i. 174.

Parts were often practised in the presence of an 'instructor' who was either author, prompter, manager, or friend to the actor, and who helped further to prescribe the rules that limited verbal and gestural range. Aaron Hill taught Jane Cibber by marking on her part 'every accent and emphasis; every look, action and deportment proper to the character'; David Garrick taught Edward Cape Everard by 'reading' him his part with 'Now, sir, say *this* after me';[36] when Hamlet says 'Speake the speech . . . *as I pronounc'd it to you*' (*Ham.* 1849, my italics) he actually means just that. Once established, the method of playing was fixed not just for that particular production, but for all subsequent productions. New actors being trained to perform established roles were taught to mimic precisely the manner in which the part had first been acted: rehearsal was only necessary to ensure that the actor had 'correctly' received a part, and young players were harshly judged against their 'originals'— though '[Colley Cibber] values himself, as a good Copy of *Dogget* in the Part of *Nykin*', in fact '[he] appears too vigorous and robust in some Places, which *Dogget* kept under in a lower Key'.[37] The way actors received and responded to parts rather than full plays had a strong effect both on the way they conceived of their roles, and on the way texts changed in general, for alterations might be made on the part when it was removed from the body of the play: rehearsal and text here (as elsewhere) meet, and in this book I will argue that the one needs to be written about in terms of the other.

As well as affecting the way actors performed, parts also affected the way plays were written. Plays were designed to function quite strongly as separable units, each part containing within itself information as to how it should be enacted. Divided back down into parts, plays reveal an internal logic of prose and verse, long and short sentences, changing modes of address, that are somewhere between literary points and lost stage directions. A sudden change from prose to verse in a player's part can reveal, for instance, the moment when a character is supposed to fall in love.

Playwrights, even if involved in some of the individual instruction, had neither the time nor the opportunity to teach

[36] Thomas Davies, *Memoirs of the Life of David Garrick*, 2 vols., 2nd edn. (1780), i. 137; Edward Cape Everard, *Memoirs of an Unfortunate Son of Thespis* (1818), 17.
[37] *The Laureat* (1740), 40.

all the actors separately. By the start of group rehearsals, therefore, they were only partly in charge of what the actors were
doing, with little chance of significantly modifying or changing
already established ways of speaking and performing the text. In
addition, many authors were encouraged not to attend group
rehearsal and, when they did so, frequently found important
decisions had already been made by manager and prompter: the
theatre and the playwright were often in opposition to one
another. Lines were sometimes cut in group rehearsal, and
verbal changes were occasionally made there (as often as not
against the author's will), but the most significant moments for
overall revision were pre-rehearsal (when managers 'corrected'
texts before agreeing to mount them), during 'study' (when
individual actors changed their 'part' away from the text), and
after the first performance. As actors brought to group rehearsal
a finished performance, the occasion thus functioned like dress
rehearsals today, happening after the important decisions have
been made. Collective rehearsals were thus the most dispensable
part of play preparation: each age has examples of plays put into
performance without any group rehearsal at all.

Performances reflected the way plays had been prepared. The
prompter was something like a conductor, bringing into harmony actors who were largely familiar only with what they had
to do individually; he prompted words, timing and basic
blocking:

> Of their go-off, come on, he points the sides,
> By margin letters of P.S. O.P.
> Stage properties, stage business, music, band,
> Of stage arcana the prompter keeps the key.[38]

But the performance also reflected the individual state of
preparation amongst the players, in that it was not unusual for
an actor to fall out of character when not speaking—as when
Mrs Cibber, while acting Ophelia in the play scene of *Hamlet*,
'rose up three several times, and made as many courtesies, and
those very low ones, to some ladies in the boxes'.[39] Naturally
this method of rehearsing and performing affected the way

---

[38] John O'Keeffe, *Recollections of the Life of John O'Keeffe*, 2 vols. (1826), ii. 422.
'P.S.' is 'prompt side', 'O.P.' is 'opposite prompt'.
[39] *The Theatrical Review* (1763), 213.

audiences watched a play as well as the way the play was acted and revised.

The idea of the 'willing suspension of disbelief' was not articulated until 1817, when Samuel Taylor Coleridge came up with the phrase, which he used to describe the way people read poetry—only later still was it applied to the theatre.[40] Historically, the relationship of audience to actor was, before the advent of the darkened auditorium, not only closer but also more equal. Actors reacted and responded to the audience on their level, answering the regular (and expected) heckling, but also making points *in propria persona* about the nature of the performance itself:

In the last Scene of the pantomime from the Galleries some hissing; some crying off! off! &c till M[r] King address'd the Audience as follow [*sic*]: Ladies & Gentlemen. If this Token of your disapprobation proceeds from the Mad Scene being left out, give me leave to Assure you; many Applications have been made to the Managers to have it omitted.[41]

Audiences were actively involved not simply in approving or condemning a play, but in revising it; during the seventeenth and eighteenth centuries (and perhaps earlier), representative members of the audience, sometimes referred to under the generic name 'Mr Town', would demand specific changes to be made to the text after first performance. As authors were, from 1620 (or perhaps 1600) onwards, generally paid by receiving the revenue for second or third days, they were more-or-less bound to accede to the audience's wishes. The first day was in this way singled out as the 'rehearsal' of the written play (not of the actors);[42] it was one of the main occasions for full-play revision, and it always attracted a particularly critical audience. Opening days were generally charged at double the price of other days.

Plays seem to have been watched, as they were performed,

---

[40] Samuel Taylor Coleridge, *Biographia Literaria*, ed. George Watson (1817; London, 1975), 169.
[41] Richard Cross and William Hopkins, *Diary 1747–1776: Drury Lane*, 13 vols., Folger Library MS, W. a. 104, for 6 Feb., 1763–4.
[42] See George Colman, *Polly Honeycombe* (1760), p. vi: 'The first night's representation . . . like most other first nights, was nothing more than a Publick Rehearsal.'

with the emphasis at least as much on parts as on the whole. Audiences who had attended to see a particular performer sometimes applauded when the player left the stage until the curtain was brought down 'without suffering the whole to be regularly finished', and sometimes went home when the lead actor in a tragedy 'died'[43]: one reason, perhaps, why tragedies traditionally save almost all the deaths for a blood-bath in the last act. Part-oriented response is reflected in the way the audience might, for instance, take objection to single characters in plays as well as to plays themselves, and in the preponderance of actor-focused criticism over much of the period. Playwrights frequently claim in their prefaces that a sense of the play as a whole cannot be formed in performance, and can be gathered only by reading the text.[44]

The process of learning a play therefore had a bearing both on the way it was performed and on the way it was revised; and part-based rehearsal leaves clear, identifiable traces on plays for which there are two differing authoritative versions. Though it is usually imagined that, in the case of 'good' texts, one full play has been revised to become another full play, in fact, it can often be seen that some parts in plays have altered more substantially and quickly than other parts: that revision has happened along actors' parts rather than being equal throughout the play. In *Hamlet*, for instance, clown parts (Osric, Rosencrantz, Guildenstern) change most, and five major performers have parts that are altered substantially (Hamlet, Gertrude, Claudius, Horatio, Laertes), while other parts are virtually untouched. A variety of parts, as it seems, were written flexibly. In addition to this, some actors changed their parts more readily than others, as one of the few ways for performers to counteract prescriptive rehearsal (particularly in the case of inherited roles) was to change their parts internally: revision was the actors' chief manner of individualizing their performances. Sometimes revisions were one-offs, but sometimes they became elements of the plays themselves, and were handed on to the next generation of actors, 'there not being a performance in a whole season . . . in which there is not something or other introduced by the actor'.[45]

---

[43] William Cooke, *Memoirs of Samuel Foote*, 3 vols. (1805), i. 86; V. C. Clinton-Baddeley, *It'll be Alright on the Night* (London, 1954), 43.

[44] See Peter Holland, *The Ornament of Action* (Cambridge, 1979) 120.

[45] George Stayley, *The Life and Opinions of an Actor*, 2 vols. (1762), i. 184.

Deaths of old actors, acquisitions of new actors with new skills, the way old and new actors were prepared for the stage, can be seen to affect single parts within plays. Desdemona sings in the Folio text of *Othello* (the song is absent from the 1622 Quarto), probably reflecting the fact that the company did not always have a good singing boy to perform major female roles.[46] *Othello*, that is to say, is changed along a 'part' to accommodate the skills of a particular actor; plays could be altered along individual strands.

Actors working from cued parts, who were also typecast because of their heavy acting-schedule, seem often to have had an across-play acting personality. That is to say, they performed more-or-less the same role from play to play; they tended not to see each play as an individual whole, but rather to treat their own stretch of text as one long, continuous, consistent acting part. The effect is that different plays performed by the same company at about the same time hold hands with one another: an actor's character-traits and verbal tricks can be seen to follow through from one part to another over plays. This raises questions about the individuality of the text itself, and about the extent to which each play should be considered in terms of other productions in performance at the same time. It also highlights the importance of specific actors and the texts that were written for them.

Extraordinarily, though much has been written on the nature of the theatre, the nature of acting, and the nature of performance between the sixteenth and eighteenth centuries, the subject of rehearsal has never been specifically addressed. No book has been written on the subject, though many have been written about theatrical processes that arise from it (performance and acting theory), and textual processes (revision) that relate to it. Up until now, facts about rehearsal had been thought impossible to find: knowledge of historical rehearsal was thought to have been lost to us. So, for instance, Peter Thomson maintains that 'we know nothing of rehearsal practices in the Elizabethan theatre'; while Judith Milhous and Robert Hume,

---

[46] F. W. Sternfeld, *Music in Shakespearean Tragedy* (London, 1963), 79. For the suggestion that Desdemona's song is revised out of the Quarto because a boy's voice broke earlier than expected see E. A. J. Honigmann, *The Texts of 'Othello' and Shakespearian Revision* (London, 1996), 39–40.

writing on the Restoration theatre, say that 'what happened during rehearsals' is still an open question.[47] Presumably it is for this reason that rehearsal between 1576 and 1760 has not inspired a single article (Hogan's seven-page 'An Eighteenth-Century Prompter's Notes' briefly examines rehearsal between 1760 and 1794[48]).

Elizabethan rehearsal is seldom even mentioned by scholars, though assumptions about it lie behind two short pieces which ask whether Shakespeare 'produced' his plays, the very phrasing of the question implying a fundamental misunderstanding of the way the theatre worked at the time.[49] The conclusions reached in the articles—that Shakespeare did (Hart), and did not (Klein), produce his plays—are both equally defensible: some but not all playwrights saw their plays to the stage, but the question only has relevance if the process of 'production' is thought to be especially important in the life of a play, and neither Hart nor Klein attempt to consider what 'producing' itself was, historically. In books about the Elizabethan theatre, rehearsal is breezily passed over after writers have briefly identified themselves with one of the two schools of thought on the matter: that there was scarcely any rehearsal at all, and that intensive rehearsal took place on a daily basis.[50] Rehearsal between 1660 and 1747 is discussed over two or three pages in each of the three *London Stage* parts for the period (the last two parts do not specifically address it).[51] *The London Stage* does not set out to do more than present raw material to the theatre scholar, and its useful selection of rehearsal anecdotes and complaints comes from different times, different theatres, and different kinds of sources; individual and group rehearsal are not differentiated, neither is

[47] Peter Thomson, *Shakespeare's Professional Career* (Cambridge, 1992), 88; Judith Milhous and Robert D. Hume, *Producible Interpretation* (Carbondale, Ill., 1985), 35.
    [48] Charles Beecher Hogan, 'An Eighteenth Century Prompter's Notes', *TN* 10 (1955), 37–44.
    [49] Alfred Hart, 'Did Shakespeare Produce His Own Plays?' *MLR* 36 (1941), 173–83; and rejoinder, David Klein, *MLR* 57 (1962), 556–60.
    [50] For the first, see Peter Thomson, *Shakespeare's Theatre*, 2nd edn. (London, 1992), 60; Michael Hattaway, *Elizabethan Popular Theatre* (London, 1982), 51; for the second see Andrew Gurr, *The Shakespearean Stage*, 3rd edn. (Cambridge, 1992), 209; Taylor, *Reinventing*, 3.
    [51] W. B. Van Lennep et al. (eds.), *The London Stage, 1660–1800: A Calendar of Plays* etc., 5 parts in 11 vols. (Carbondale, Ill., 1960–69).

rehearsal of new and stock plays. David Thomas devotes a few pages of his valuable documentary history to rehearsal letters and anecdotes, again from various different provenances, again without analysis.[52] The two pages given over to rehearsal in the single volume of the *Revels History of Drama*[53] that addresses the topic simply rehash *London Stage* material. Judith Milhous and Robert Hume assign a section of *Producible Interpretation*[54] to Buckingham's fictional play *The Rehearsal*, concluding that rehearsal in the Restoration was not dissimilar to rehearsal these days (p. 63), that acting was 'at times down-right Stanislavskian' (p. 66), and that there is 'little barrier between seventeenth-century plays and twentieth-century assumptions about performance and meaning' (p. 69), a conclusion not suggested by the evidence already gathered by Milhous in her excellent *Thomas Betterton and the Management of Lincoln's Inn Fields*.[55] Some anecdotal material about rehearsal from the later eighteenth century has been gathered by V. C. Clinton-Baddeley, mostly for its entertainment value.[56] W. J. Lawrence, who in *Old Theatre Days and Ways* discusses over ten pages 'old-time rehearsing' between the seventeenth and nineteenth centuries, shows a fundamental grasp of the subject even as he leaps from century to century, country to country, in his observation that 'harmonious team-work' was not generally thought important at any time during the period.[57] Kalman A. Burnim examines rehearsal under Garrick in chapter 3 of *David Garrick, Director*,[58] providing the most comprehensive depiction of historical rehearsal published to date. Title aside, Burnim actually shows how a variety of different people were in charge of the rehearsal process, and also makes the important point that plays were differently valued: some were given careful rehearsal, others were not. He is, however, unclear about the precise distinction between individual and group rehearsal, and his suggestion that

---

[52] David Thomas (ed.), *Theatre in Europe: Restoration and Georgian England, 1660–1788* (Cambridge, 1989), 160–5; 391–3.
[53] John Loftis *et al.* (eds.), *The Revels History of Drama in English, v. 1660–1750*, (London, 1976), 143–4.
[54] Milhous and Hume, *Producible Interpretation*.
[55] Judith Milhous, *Thomas Betterton and the Management of Lincoln's Inn Fields* (Carbondale, Ill., 1979).
[56] Clinton-Baddeley, *Alright on the Night* (London, 1954).
[57] W. J. Lawrence, *Old Theatre Days and Ways* (London, 1935), 55.
[58] (Carbondale, Ill., 1961).

new plays received many careful rehearsals is, as he himself points out, not backed up by the actual evidence he has unearthed. As so very little has been written on rehearsal, almost any modern text that addresses the subject comes in for my criticism, including some of the tremendous works of theatrical scholarship that I have relied on for other information in my study.

Much more data than has been assumed survives about rehearsal from 1576 to 1780. Sources are diverse and scattered, however—there is no single logical place to look for material concerning theatrical practice. For the sixteenth century I gathered information from account books, prompt-books, court records, academic records, overseas records, legal documents, plays-within-plays, letters, play prefaces, prologues and epilogues; for the seventeenth and eighteenth centuries I was able to bolster official records with more colourful anecdotal material—actors' biographies, letters and anecdotes, contemporary diaries and newspapers, prompters' diaries and prompt-books. The body of evidence gathered, spanning over two centuries, shows that there was remarkable historical consistency in the nature and practice of rehearsal, later chapters confirming suggestions made in earlier chapters and vice versa. The material produced shows how rehearsal in the past was unlike rehearsal now, and why: because its priorities were different. And this inevitably means that there are certain questions that I cannot reply to. I cannot, for instance, say how many full and how many partial rehearsals were held for a single play before staging—but that is because a specific answer does not exist. Plays were, as a rule, put on when ready, since, if a play was shown to be unready, it was held back for more rehearsals. Even 'readiness' itself was a flexible idea: as plays could be accepted or rejected by the audience during their first performance, they were often further rehearsed only after having been 'approved' by the audience; if not approved, they could be dropped without too much time having been wasted on getting them up. Because of the disparate material I deal with, I tend to reach general conclusions rather than specific ones: I cannot, for instance, say what Shakespeare himself personally did in rehearsal—but I can show what was and was not within the range of possibilities.

My aim in writing this book has been to produce a lasting

reference work. For that reason, I do not take an overtly modern *approach* to the topic of rehearsal, which would date more quickly than the factual material provided here: this book is an unashamedly historical account of rehearsal and its ramifications, not a work of editorial or performance theory, though many of the issues I highlight about the construction of plays in and by the theatre problematize the text in ways that will be of interest to the theoretician.

The account begins with provincial and academic rehearsal in the early modern period: this provides the background for the early professional theatre examined in Chapter 2. The following chapters are all chronological; each covers the lifespan of a famous actor-playwright—in this way the book is divided into obvious theatrical 'eras'. Actors are discussed in sections on rehearsal, actor-training, pronunciation, gesture, acting style, and performance; theatre managers are represented by sections on managerial control; theatre prompters by sections on prompters in rehearsal and performance; playwrights are a focus throughout. For each period the way in which performers received their parts is examined, with questions asked about what they did during private 'study', who was and was not present during their separate rehearsals, and who was and was not present during their group rehearsals. The book explains the delicate balance struck at different historical periods between manager, author, prompter, and actor; it gives an idea of the power of managers and prompters and how it increased over time. An attempt is also made to show when new acting traditions came into being, who was responsible for them, and how they were disseminated and taught. And, by covering two centuries' worth of material, the book illustrates the way rehearsal developed, so giving a different angle on developments within performance and acting styles over time. *Rehearsal from Shakespeare to Sheridan* thus has something to offer to the theatre historian who wants to know what happened in the theatre; to the director or actor interested in mounting an 'original' production; to the theoretician who is exploring the complex issue of theatrical 'authorship'; and to editors interested in textual mutability and textual change.

Chapter 2, 'Rehearsal in the Theatres of Peter Quince and Ben Johnson', begins with a lexical examination of the range of meaning 'rehearsal' had during the early modern period. University and provincial rehearsal are then explored as a way of showing how non-professional theatres before and during the Renaissance put on their plays; this provides the background for a study of the early public theatre in the next chapter.

Chapter 3, 'Rehearsal in Shakespeare's Theatre', covers roughly the years 1570–1640, though references to earlier practice are sometimes given, for the professional theatre emerged out of the earlier strolling-player tradition. An attempt is made to determine the amount of rehearsal likely for any public-theatre production by a statistical consideration of the number of plays generally mounted during a season, while what rehearsal itself consisted of is investigated in sections which discuss the two initial 'readings', the distribution of parts, the 'study' period, the group rehearsal, and performance. Throughout, the roles of those people important to the rehearsal process (the author, manager, book-keeper, and actor) are given particular attention. Finally suggestions are made as to the ways in which performance responded to this kind of rehearsal—this includes an examination of the effect of 'parts' and of first-day revision (the 'rehearsal' of the text) on the text.

Chapter 4, 'Rehearsal in Betterton's Theatre' concerns the years 1640–1710—the 'Restoration period'. For this chapter Buckingham's play *The Rehearsal* provides an initial focus, distanced as it is from actual English rehearsal by its author's familiarity with the French method. The early Restoration theatre is investigated, with a look at what it inherited from Elizabethan performance practice, and what it borrowed from the Continent; then rehearsal itself, from the distribution and learning of parts, to the group rehearsal and production of plays, is addressed. The focus is on both amateur authors, who were generally excluded from the preparation of their plays; and on professional authors, who are shown losing power to the manager and the actors. The nature of extant texts and the effect the first night has on textual stability is, again, examined.

Chapter 5, 'Rehearsal in Cibber's Theatre' (1710–40) is devoted to eighteenth-century theatrical innovation. This chapter explores how the different theatres in operation over this period also have different attitudes to rehearsal, and highlights the distinction between what theorists were starting to think about rehearsal, and what rehearsal itself consisted of. The rehearsal play, it is argued, had solidified into a genre that inherited much of what it did, not from the nature of actual rehearsal itself, but from the format laid down by Buckingham. The same elements of rehearsal are established, from reading to performance, but the managers are shown to have become more powerful, particularly with respect to the revision of plays. The prompter, too, is seen to be taking on a role of increasing importance in the production of plays, so that rehearsal is presented as a forum in which texts are 'de-authored', even when the author attends the occasion.

By the time of Chapter 6, 'Rehearsal in Garrick's Theatre— and Later' (1740–80) rehearsal plays are shown to have become formulaic, so that they have almost nothing to do with contemporary rehearsal. Garrick is investigated, with sections exploring the 'new' acting he helped to establish, and the 'old' ways of rehearsing he continued to favour. Production from casting to textual alteration is studied; authors are shown to have seldom attended rehearsal at all, and to have been encouraged not to take up their right to 'read' their own plays. The new idea promoted in part by Garrick, that actors might 'interpret' rather than manifest their parts, meant that texts were often twisted to become fashionably 'sentimental', and had the result of further removing the emphasis of performance away from the full play onto its parts. Textual change is addressed and single actors' parts are illustrated to have had, frequently, a longer life than whole texts. First-night revision is revealed once more to have been usual practice. A brief conclusion looks towards rehearsal at the close of the eighteenth century.

## 2

# Rehearsal in the Theatres of
# Peter Quince and Ben Jonson

### REHEARSAL LEXICALLY

Many words that are now specific theatre property—or that at least have a particular meaning when referred to in a theatrical context—were still being established in the fifteenth and sixteenth centuries, as the theatre was itself being established. As late as Thomas Rawlins's *The Rebellion* (performed 1629–39), the question as to what one does with a play is the subject of dispute between the three tailors who fancy themselves as actors—do you 'do it', 'act it', or 'play it' (5.1)?[1] Legal documents list a superabundance of words to describe 'a play', including 'enterlude, Commodye, Tragidie, matter, or shewe'.[2] And indeed 'a play' might also be 'an exercise'; an actor might be 'a comedian', 'a player', or 'a histrione'; a performance might be 'a show', 'an exhibition', or, as will be considered later, 'a rehearsal'. These words were sometimes interchangeable (*The Historie of Iacob and Esau* is called a 'wittie Comedie or Enterlude' on its 1568 title-page), and sometimes carried a different shade of meaning ('tis no Play neyther, but a shewe' says Will Summers deprecatingly in Thomas Nashe's *Summers Last Will*).[3] The way terms were applied could vary according to the playwright or the company concerned. This is particularly true of the word 'rehearsal'; and as the kinds of theatrical events

---

[1] Thomas Rawlins, *The Rebellion* (1640), I1ᵇ: 'Doe; what doe? Act, act, you foole you, do said you, what doe? . . . Play a play a play, ha, ha, ha; O egredious nonsensicall wigeon.'
[2] Lansdowne MS quoted in *Malone Society Collections: I.ii*, ed. W. W. Greg (1908, Oxford, 1964), 175.
[3] Thomas Nashe, *The Works*, ed. R. B. McKerrow, 2nd edn., rev. F. Wilson, 5 vols. (Oxford, 1958), iii. 235.

meriting the ascription 'rehearsal', or, alternatively, 'repetition' or 'trial' are various, it is necessary to define the term itself.

When Thomas Heywood explains that he has 'derived' the antiquity of actors and acting, 'from the first Olympiads', he means it literally: he has taken the word 'tragedy', for instance, back to its Greek roots meaning 'goat-song', and then forward again into the seventeenth century, bolstered with classical respectability.[4] This is more significant than at first sight it appears since Elizabethan theatre was forever justifying itself by reference to historical precedent—James Burbage the actor-entrepreneur makes this clear in his choice of the Roman name 'Theatre' (and the Roman circular design) for his 1576 play-house. Generally, though, the tribute the early public theatre paid to classicism was little more than lip-service; playwrights were interested in the classical theatre only in so far as it gave authority to what they were doing. But this duality does result in a wealth of confusion in Latin-English glosses of the time: Thomas Thomas's *Dictionarium Linguae Latinae et Anglicanae* (1587) renders 'scena' first in Roman terms ('the front of the theater'), then in Elizabethan ('the place where players make them readie, being trimmed with hangings, out of which they enter upon the stage').[5] As this example shows, the words to be defined in Latin glossaries are provided by the classical stage, though the definitions themselves would often change to embrace contemporary Elizabethan concepts (or the personal feelings of the lexicographer).[6] Compare John Rider's *Bibliotheca Scholastica* (1589) definition of 'tragedy'—'to make a matter much worse than indeed it is', to Elisha Coles's 'tragedies' in *An English Dictionary* (1676)—'lofty plaies, treating of Great and Bloudy exploits'.

Neither 'rehearse' nor 'repeat' is defined specifically in relation

[4] Thomas Heywood, *An Apology for Actors* (1612), D1[b].

[5] For the extent to which Latin dictionaries used classical rather than contemporary sources in determining their choice of words see D. T. Starnes, *Renaissance Dictionaries* (Austin, Tex., 1954).

[6] Tetsuro Hayashi, *The Theory of English Lexicography 1530-1791* (Amsterdam, 1978), 9, maintains that Latin was already treated as a 'dead' language in the dictionaries, and that therefore it was not modified to embrace 'contemporary' concepts. But Jürgen Schäfer illustrates the reverse in his *Early Modern English Lexicography: I* (Oxford, 1989), 2. He shows that early English dictionaries chose to use Latin (rather than foreign language) dictionaries as base texts, because Latin definitions better reflected modern English ideas.

to the theatre in the glossaries, though a particular theatrical vocabulary does seem to have existed in contemporaneous plays. By comparing two Latin-English glosses of the time, John Rider's *Bibliotheca Scholastica* (1589) and Thomas Thomas's *Dictionarium Linguae Latinae et Anglicanae* (1587) however, a fairly full indication of the range of meaning acquired by the verb 'to rehearse' can be reached, suggesting that its primary connotation is 'to recite', which is sometimes equivalent to our contemporary usage of 'rehearse', sometimes a reference more particularly to the arts of rhetoric, and sometimes a synonym for 'to perform'. 'Edisero', for instance, is 'to declare, tell, or rehearse', in which a rehearsal is a one-time telling, but 'renarro' is 'to tell againe, to rehearse, to repeate', where rehearsal denotes something that happens more than once. In plays, characters are frequently asked to 'repeat' or 'rehearse' a letter that has just come into their hands, meaning not to read it a second time, but to read it a first time: that is to say, rehearsal did not necessarily signify a re-hearing or recurrent event. Henry Hexham's *Copious English and Netherduytch Dictionarie* (1648) draws a distinction between 'verhalen', 'To repeate, to mention, to Rehearse, or to Fetch' and 'Een dingh dickwils verhalen ofte herseggen', 'to rehearse a thing often'; and Randle Cotgrave's *A Dictionarie of the French and English Tongues* (1611) displays a similar ambivalence between 'a repetition, a rehearsall' which might happen any number of times, and 'repeté', 'asked or called backe . . . fetched, again', which seems to be limited to one time. Lastly the verb might extend into performance. This is illustrated by a 1630 poem that bemoans the fate of the poor actors who 'Behold their Benches bare, though they rehearse | The terser *Beaumonts* or great *Ionsons* verse'.[7]

In practice the verb 'to rehearse' had clear links with specific events that were non-theatrical in themselves but that fed into the early theatre. One of these took place in the school-room where children learnt to 'rehearse', 'repeat' or 'say over' their lessons—in other words, to reproduce the lesson precisely as it had been taught.[8] Imitation was the basis of education, and the master's 'correct' recitation was supposed to be copied directly: the struggling teacher Spoudeus of John Brinsley's *Ludus Litera-*

---

[7] In an introductory poem to Davenant's *Just Italian*, in William Davenant, *The Works*, 3 vols. in 1 (1673), ii. 442.

[8] Ian Michael, *The Teaching of English* (Cambridge, 1987), 269.

*rius* has 'directed' his pupils 'how to pronounce, [by] vttering the sentences oft before them'.[9] Pupils then 'rehearsed' back their lesson (Cloris checks whether Clarindo has learnt properly the speech she has taught him, with 'Shall I repeate the same again to thee? | Or els wilt thou rehearse it vnto mee?'[10]). This is what is happening in Thomas Heywood's *How a Man May Chuse a Good Wife from a Bad*, when the pompous schoolmaster Aminadab tells his pupils to 'rehearse your parts', a request that sounds strangely theatrical, as, up to a point, it is.[11] For it was in this sense of imitation or mimicking that 'rehearsal' was to take on an especially significant theatrical connotation.

'Rehearse' was also a noun. *OED* dates the first use of 'reherse' (meaning 'rehearsal') at 1490 (though it is recorded in Coventry regularly from 1450[12]). Later the noun 'rehearsal' took over, and it too had a different heritage that played into the theatre term. Its church application was to a particular kind of sermon preached on the Sunday after Easter which repeated ('rehearsed') the most salient points from the preceding four sermons of Easter week: a 'rehearsal sermon'. Anthony Munday quotes comments he has heard made by 'Mr Spark in his rehersal sermon at Paules Crosse'; and John Hoskins published a rehearsal sermon about the idea of repetition, explaining why the congregation should not 'be grieued to heare the same things' more than once.[13] This raises two points. One, that a 'rehearsal' could consist of important bits rather than a whole; the other, that a 'rehearsal' could be not a practice, but an event itself.

## BACKGROUND

The professional theatre was established only in 1567, when the first fixed theatre was erected in London. Before then the acting tradition had been maintained by country, university, and school

---

[9] John Brinsley, *Ludus Literarius: Or The Grammar School* (1612), 50.
[10] Samuel Daniel, *Whole Works* (1623), 274.
[11] Thomas Heywood, *How a Man May Chuse a Good Wife from a Bad* (1602), C3[b].
[12] *REED: Coventry*, ed. R. W. Ingram (Manchester, 1981), 190.
[13] Quoted in E. K. Chambers, *The Elizabethan Stage*, 4 vols. (Oxford, 1923), iv. 208; John Hoskins, *Sermons Preached at Pauls Crosse . . . Part 3: . . . the Conclusion of the Rehearsall Sermon . . .* (1615), 31.

performers and by strolling players; collectively they contributed to the newly established theatre, and, for some time, performed in tandem with it. But amongst themselves each variety of acting troupe varied in attitude to the others: each had its own place and reputation. William Gager, writing dramatic entertainments for Oxford students, reacts with righteous fury to the suggestion that university actors be compared to common players: 'I denye that we are to be termed *Scenici* or *Histriones*, for cum*m*inge on the Stage once in a yeere . . . As he is not a wrastler, that sometyme to prove his strencthe, tryethe for a fall or two.'[14] Actors in plays are put into context at the earliest opportunity— whether they be 'country comedians' (*Quinborough*, 5.1); 'Tragedians of the City' (*Ham.* 1375); or 'my Lord cardinalls' players' (*Thomas More*, 4.1). Every English variety of acting company had different methods and abilities, but each also connected on a basic level. Examining the records of the players on the periphery, in the universities, schools, and provinces, helps establish the rules that governed the early professional stage, and builds up a pattern of what to look for in the scanty public theatre accounts. So this chapter will explore what contemporaneous sources from the non-professional theatre reveal about the concepts of rehearsal in theory and practice; in the process it draws on what is known of medieval practice, since the Elizabethan theatre arose out of the theatre of its immediate past.

PROVINCIAL REHEARSAL

*Mayors' rehearsals*

One specific theatrical application of the time for the term 'rehearsal' was the mayor's rehearsal—this accounts for the most regular use of 'rehearsal' during the Renaissance. The occasion concerned not the practice and approval of actors but the practice and approval of texts, as will be recounted below; this 'rehearsal' occurred *after* performance.

Strolling players setting up a stage in a new town were obliged,

---

[14] F. S. Boas, *University Drama in the Tudor Age* (Oxford, 1914), 235.

according to a 1559 proclamation, to give a private performance to the local mayor and his council of the play or plays
they intended to act; local performers also had to perform in
front of the mayor before putting their entertainment on
publicly.[15] These performances were called 'rehearsals' no
matter how long the plays in question had been in repertoire;
'rehearsal' in this sense clearly meant 'recital', for what was
'rehearsed'—perhaps 'auditioned' might be a more comprehen-
sible word—was the piece itself, which was being tested for
suitability. If there were several plays on offer, the mayor would
choose which of them, if any, he deemed appropriate for
presentation: Chester accounts record money 'Spent . . . to
heare two plays before the Alder men to take the best'.[16] Texts
might at this 'rehearsal' also be changed, for plays were 'at the
libertie and pleasure of the mair with the counsell of his
bretheryn to Alter or Assigne' the characters 'as they shall
think necessary or conuenyent'.[17] The purpose of a mayor's
rehearsal is described by R. Willis in his *Mount Tabor*:

> In the city of *Gloucester* . . . when Players of Enterludes come to towne,
> they first attend the Mayor to enforme him what noble-mans servants
> they are, and so to get license for their publike playing; and if the Mayor
> like the Actors, or would shew respect to their Lord and Master, he
> appoints them to play their first play before himselfe and the Aldermen
> and Common Counsell of the city.[18]

The *REED* accounts are full of testimonies to just such occasions:
Chester offers 'at rehearsinge before mr major ijs vjd'; York
documents record 'in expensis factis hoc Anno super Maiorem
Aldermanyos et alios quam plures de Consilio Comere in festo
corporis christi videntes & Interludentes ludum in hospicio com-
muni Guyhall ex consuetudine' ['on expenses incurred this year by
the mayor, the aldermen and very many others from the council of
the Chamber on the feast of Corpus Christi who were seeing and
observing the play in the lodging belonging to the Common

---

[15] This process is described in full in Gerard Eades Bentley, *The Profession of
Player in Shakespeare's Time* (Princeton, 1984), 189.
[16] *REED: Chester*, ed. Lawrence M. Clopper (Manchester, 1979), 105. Mayors,
like university teachers, playwrights, and actors, were exclusively male during this
period: in this chapter they will all be referred to using the male pronoun.
[17] Ibid. 33.
[18] R. Willis, *Mount Tabor* (1639), 110.

Guildhall according to custom'].[19] And a mayor's rehearsal—that goes terribly wrong—is depicted in Thomas Middleton's *Mayor of Quinborough* (5.1). There the players who arrive at the mayor's house are actually 'Cheaters'; they gain their easy entrance, however, by what seems like a legitimate request for 'your Worships favour | And leave to enact in the Town-Hall'.[20]

Mayors' rehearsals were essentially superseded in the 1620s, when licences were issued giving professional companies royal permission to perform around the country at will.[21] London troupes as a result no longer always bothered to present productions to local mayors before playing, a fact that caused resentment in the countryside, and perhaps fuelled some of the civic opposition to travelling players. Other troupes continued to visit the mayor, but only to show him that they had the Master of the Revels' licence to perform. So Richard Head and Francis Kirkman record of a ragbag playing company that 'The first thing they did when they came to a Town, was to acquaint the Mayor thereof with their intent, producing their Patent which authorized them'.[22] But even the simple showing of a patent indicates a truth about all mayors' rehearsals: that however performance-like 'rehearsals' might seem to have been, their purpose was primarily a textual one: it was the words of the play not its production that had to be approved. This 'rehearsal' had no connection to the preparation of players, happening long after the performance itself had been established.

### How plays were prepared

The word 'amateur' did not exist in Elizabethan England, and was not to come into being for another 250 years (its first

---

[19] *REED: Chester*, 78, see also 78, 91; *REED: York*, ed. Alexandra F. Johnston and Margaret Rogerson (Manchester, 1979), 187 (trans., 802), see also, 259, 265, 267, (trans., 1539), 808, 810. A performative rehearsal of this kind before an 'overseer' or 'judge' was believed to have a classical precedent: Thomas Newman's *Eunuch* in *The Two First Comedies of Terence* (1627), 58, renders Terence's 'Magistratus cum ibi adesset, occepta est agi' (literally, 'when the magistrate had come, we began to act it') with the English 'The Ouerseers come, the Actors drew | To the rehearsall'.

[20] Thomas Middleton, *The Mayor of Quinborough* (1661), 62, 70. Though sometimes called *Hengist, King of Kent*, I will refer to this play using the title under which it was first published.

[21] Andrew Gurr, *The Shakespearian Playing Companies* (Oxford, 1996), 375.

[22] Richard Head and Francis Kirkman, *The English Rogue*, Part 4 (1671), 194.

recorded use, according to *OED*, is 1784). The term 'amateur' only has pejorative force in a system that promotes 'professionals', and the first completely professional companies and theatres were not established until the reign of Queen Elizabeth. To call any early modern performers 'amateur' is therefore misleading, particularly in view of the fact that the boys who performed publicly insisted that, though they were trained high-class entertainers, they were emphatically not professionals. To be 'a player' was a socially questionable position, and implied no superiority in acting; 'the mechanicals' in *A Midsummer Night's Dream* are not, therefore, being criticized for being amateurs. They are criticized because they are 'hempen home-spuns', 'rude mechanicals'—this is social criticism, not theatrical criticism.

Mystery and morality cycles were forbidden under Elizabeth, and strolling players without a patron were condemned as 'Roges Vacaboundes and Sturdy Beggars'.[23] Elizabethan drama had to have official sanction or no sanction, for the government feared the traditional loyalties embodied in local religious cycles. As a result, the rise of the fully professional, secular, and commercial theatre of Elizabethan London coincided with the decline of the local acting tradition in the rest of England:[24] a company such as that presented in *A Midsummer Night's Dream* was no longer allowed to function. This did not, however, lead to the complete elimination of country acting: local tradesmen might still gather together to put on plays with each other for their own amusement, though not for public performance, which is perhaps the nearest approach to 'amateur' acting that was made during the period. What was played was half-way between a group rehearsal and a performance. The Porter introducing the play *Narcissus* asks the 'youths' to repeat the play they had been 'gabling tother day . . . by the well there'.[25]

What kind of performers, then, lie behind *A Midsummer Night's Dream*'s mechanicals? Are they, as has been suggested, caricatures of the country actors of Shakespeare's youth, their play *Pyramus and Thisbe* a burlesque of an earlier dramatic

---

[23] Chambers, *Elizabethan Stage*, iv. 270.
[24] See Louis A. Montrose, 'A Kingdom of Shadows', in David L. Smith, Richard Strier, and David Bevington (eds.), *The Theatrical City* (Cambridge, 1995), 72–3.
[25] *Narcissus*, ed. Margaret C. Lee (1893), 4.

style?[26] Against the context of other provincial troupes, this seems unlikely. The mechanicals' production has little in common with the well-prepared and extremely proficient Coventry cycles; but it also does not resemble the other extreme—the completely primitive drama of the illiterate. In *A Midsummer Night's Dream*, every actor can read; in some country towns rehearsals were necessary simply to teach the actors what their lines were. A 1584–5 record gives an account of 'the speech of mr Robert brerwood Maior . . . made [i.e. written] by mr William Knight . . . and by the sayd maior learned by hart & by him pronounced: for although he could nether write nor read yet was of exelent memory'.[27] For some rustic performances no attempt was made even to memorize the lines before performance. Richard Carew in his *Survey of Cornwall* describes a 'guary' in which the uneducated actors, incapable of learning their parts at all, were prompted on stage 'by one called the Ordinary, who followeth at their back with the booke in his hand, and telleth them softly what they must pronounce aloud'.[28]

As Peter Holland explains, the kind of acting group depicted in *A Midsummer Night's Dream* never actually existed at all: the classical play put on by Quince and his company is unlike anything that their counterparts ever performed, for though groups of workers did mount productions, they never, to our knowledge, presented English versions of classical stories. The mechanicals as a performing group are a fictional idea.[29] As a fiction they can comfortably include elements of the drama of Shakespeare's youth muddled in with elements of contemporary Elizabethan practice—as indeed seems to have been the case. In Elizabethan terms, they are given court sanction for their performance like any professional troupe (they have been selected from an official list of those thought to be most 'fit through all *Athens*, to play in our Enterlude before the Duke and Dutches' (*MND* 273));[30] their subprofessionalism should be

[26] Suggested by Clifford Davidson in 'What hempen home-spuns have we swagg'ring here?: Amateur Actors in *A Midsummer Night's Dream* and the Coventry Civic Plays and Pageants', *Shakespeare Studies*, 19 (1987), 87-99.
[27] *REED: Chester*, 142.
[28] Richard Carew, *The Survey of Cornwall* (1602), 71.
[29] William Shakespeare, *A Midsummer Night's Dream*, ed. Peter Holland (Oxford, 1995), 90-2.
[30] It was common for playwrights to give their players-within-plays either the legal

borne in mind, for too much concentration on what has been seen as the amateur nature of the players has led critics to doubt how sincerely to judge their theatrical method.[31] There is no reason why their rehearsal should not be regarded as broadly true-to-life, in so far as it needs to be so.

The preparation of *Pyramus and Thisbe* is telescoped in time— the performers have only a day to learn their parts, and actually hold just one, fragmentary rehearsal (though there is also reference to a rehearsal in front of the Master of the Revels that, logically, cannot have taken place at any time). But in other respects the rehearsal process mirrors the standard for higher-class provincial production. The first thing to happen is that the 'parts' are distributed to be learnt separately at home ('con them', says Peter Quince, 'by too morrow night', *MND* 361). These 'parts' consisted of a 'cue' of a few words followed by the relevant actor's speeches—hence the term 'part': each actor received only a fragment, a 'part' of the play. Much theatrical by-play is made of the idea of 'cues' and 'parts' later on in *A Midsummer Night's Dream* when Flute fails to understand how to use his 'part' of 'Thisbe'—he muddles in his cues with his own lines and repeats 'all [his] part at once, cues and all' (*MND* 912–13). Quince calls for a single general group rehearsal to be held after the parts have been committed to memory—and then the performance takes place. Accounts of carefully prepared country plays record much the same process: the distribution of 'par-cells'[32] (individual parts) to the prospective actors being fol-lowed by a period of private learning (conning)—in York the actors are 'to haue ther part*es* fair wrytten & deliue*re*d theym [in tyme] soo that they may haue leysure to ku*n*ne euery one his part'.[33] It is only after the parts have been learnt that Quince or

---

right to perform, or punishment for performing illegally—in this way the theatre could not be accused of popularizing theatrical law-breaking. So the three tailor-actors in Rawlins's *Rebellion* have been specifically chosen to play for the king; the actors in Middleton's *The Mayor of Quinborough*, on the other hand, are rogues and vagabonds; while the actors in Marston's *Histriomastix*, who claim to be professionals belonging to Sir Oliver Owlet (but who do not have official recognition), are caught and punished within the play.

[31] Bernard Beckerman, *Shakespeare at the Globe* (New York, 1962), 122-4, draws attention to the speed with which tradesmen without theatrical training became professional troupes of actors—Quince and his fellows are not dissimilar in back-ground to ordinary Elizabethan acting companies.     [32] *REED: Chester*, 66.
[33] *REED: York*, 353. See also *Malone Society Collections: VII.* ed. Giles E. Dawson

the York players hold a group rehearsal; in the county records, group rehearsal, often over breakfast, directly precedes performance as the final veneer on an almost-ready play. Indeed in provincial inventories, collective rehearsal emerges as, literally, a cakes and ale event—to which we are indebted for the knowledge that it happened at all, for its traces survive in accounts recording costs incurred for food: 'Item spent at the first rehearse at the brekefast of the companye'; 'for kakes at our general reherse ijs'; 'for Ale to our generall reherse xs'.[34] Tradesmen had to work for most of the day, and probably breakfast (which took place at 6.30 a.m.[35]) was the only free time they had for dramatic activity.

Most records of country performances for annual plays suggest that from two to three events known as 'rehearsal' took place—two regularly in Coventry up to about 1565;[36] three are recorded occasionally elsewhere.[37] Final rehearsal was, however, separated from the others by the title 'general'—'a general rehearse'—which suggests that the first one to two rehearsals were 'partial'; indeed, the term 'general' denoting a special last, full-company rehearsal, continued in use until the eighteenth century.[38] The few records that make clear who attended rehearsals also indicate that the first and second rehearsals did not always involve all the actors—as in Chester where a 'sonday morninge' was given over to 'the hearinge of the Docters & litle God'.[39]

Unsurprisingly, more time was spent on preparing a production of a completely new play, than in getting up an old one. Whether the extra rehearsals were general, partial, private, or a mixture of all three, cannot be established, but *The Destruction of Jerusalem* required 'ffyve Reherses', and in Provence for the

(Oxford, 1965), 203-4: 'the Above bovnden *par*ties have taken vpon them to be players in y$^e$ stage playe . . . And have receyvyd players Speachys or *par*tes in the seyd playe . . . they & eu'y of them [must] learne befo⟨re⟩ the seyd feaste of pentecost theire *par*tes before lymytted & be redye then to playe the same|And further do at eu'y tyme of the rehearse of theseyd playe com to Romny aforesedy & Rehearse theire seyd *par*tes.'

   [34] *REED: Coventry*, 229; *REED: Chester*, 85, 91.
   [35] Sidney Lee and C. T. Onions (eds.), *Shakespeare's England*, 2 vols. (Oxford, 1917), ii. 134.
   [36] See *REED: Coventry*, 72, 139, 150, 156, 160, 163, 165, etc.
   [37] *REED: Coventry*, 220, 229, 237, 246, 250, etc. Halliwell-Phillipps reckoned on three as a rule of thumb, quoted 573.
   [38] See R.B.S. Esq., *The Critick Anticipated* (1779), 3: 'Did you make a *general* call for the attendance of all the performers this morning?'
   [39] *REED: Chester*, 78.

sumptuous *Mystère des Trois Doms* there were 'seven rehearsals at least'.[40] Quince in *A Midsummer Night's Dream* presents what seems to be a fusion between what I take to be a 'general rehearse' ('we will do it in action, as we will do it before the Duke', *MND* 817), and a partial rehearsal ('sit downe . . . and rehearse your parts', *MND* 884).

The position of 'master' or 'manager' of productions that Quince holds also has its parallel in country accounts. Clifford Davidson pits *A Midsummer Night's Dream* against the *REED* records for Coventry, and shows how Quince is equivalent to a 'pageant master'. That figure in turn seems to be met by John C. Coldewey's 'property player' who was in charge of overseeing productions in Chelmsford, his job involving making arrangements for the construction of the stage, keeping accounts, designing scenery, ordering property and rehearsals. Similarly, account books for Kent show a character in charge of managing rehearsals known as a 'Devysor'; while morality plays were overseen by a leading actor/stage-manager, usually the player who performed Vice.[41] Though specific details about the nature of the job of manager with respect to rehearsal are hard to find, two important facts emerge—one is that the manager was sometimes but not always the playwright; the other is that he could revise the text of the play he was mounting (even if he were not its author). In Anthony Munday's play *John a Kent*, Turnop becomes manager for a theatrical production, and his job involves making casting decisions (Hugh the Sexton wants to 'say the speeche I made my selfe' but, although he is the playwright, he is made to submit to Turnop's managerial authority), and adapting the text (it is 'newly corrected' by Turnop).[42]

[40] *REED: Coventry*, 303; Glynne Wickham, *Early English Stages 1300-1600*, 3 vols. in 4 (London, 1959-81), i. 304. The French seem in general to have rehearsed more than the English, as is pointed out by William L. Tribby, 'The Medieval Prompter', *Theatre Survey*, 5 (1964), 71-8 (75). Though the records for players in Chelmsford discovered by John C. Coldewey, 'That Enterprising Property Player', *TN* 31 (1977), 5-12, show that 'preparation' for plays in Essex began from three to five weeks before production (p. 6), in fact all that seems to have been set in motion at that stage was the hiring of builders and painters, and the construction of the stage: there is no indication that more rehearsal took place in Essex than elsewhere.

[41] Davidson, *MSC: VII*, 208; David Bevington, *From 'Mankind' to Marlowe* (Cambridge, Mass., 1962), 79-82.

[42] Anthony Munday, *John a Kent and John a Cumber*, facs. ed. Muriel St Clare Byrne (Oxford, 1923), 12, 14.

Similarly in records for Kent a 'Mr Gibson' revised over the St George play for Lydd productions between 1526 and 1532, accounts indicating that he was sent the 'olde play boke' for correction, and then went to Lydd to see (and perhaps oversee) the preparation.[43] Gibson made his revisions privately, away from the production, in London; Quince, who is manager (and, perhaps, author) of *Pyramus and Thisbe*, also makes alterations to the text, deciding to add the character of Moonshine to the play; he too makes those alterations in private some time between rehearsal and performance.

In all, for country players, the preparation period seems to have lasted for about a month, and consisted of the distribution of separate parts for private study, followed by one to two rehearsals which may well have been 'partial', and concluding with a 'general' full company rehearsal. The business side of the production was overseen by a manager who also had the right to make revisions to the text, even if he had not written it.

### ACADEMIC REHEARSAL

Polonius 'plaid once i'th' Vniuersity'(*Ham.* 1953) and is not ashamed of the fact, for universities drew a great distinction between their own highly prepared occasional productions and the disreputable performances of public 'players': 'As I . . . thinke the Prohibition of common Stage Players verie requisite,' writes the Earl of Leicester, 'so would I not have it meant thereby that the Tragedies, Comedies and shews . . . set forth by the Universitye men should be forbedden.'[44] Acting was part of the education process, for most students would find employment in the Church or the law, both of which required a certain standard of rhetorical ability. The preparation of plays was therefore tolerated as necessary 'for the emboldening of . . . *Iunior* schollers . . . It teacheth audacity to the bashfull Grammarian . . . it not onely emboldens a scholler to speake, but instructs him to speake well.'[45] William Gager, who wrote

---

[43] Davidson, *MSC: VII*, 199-200.
[44] Boas, *University Drama*, 192.
[45] Heywood, *Apology*, C3[b].

plays for students of Christ Church, Oxford, argues that the performances of scholars should be sanctioned as 'We Doe it . . . to trye their voyces and confirme their memoryes; to frame their speeche; to conforme them to convenient action'.[46] In some Cambridge colleges, acting in plays was an educational requirement: the statutes of St John's demanded that pupils take part in 'at least six dialogues or festival or literary spectacles', while Queens' College asked professors to instruct students in two plays per year in order to polish their acting and speaking skills:

Et ne inventus nostra exercitata forsa ad alia pronunciando ac gestu rudis et invrbana maneat Volumus vt grece linguae professor et etiam examinator quotannis inter 20. / Decembris diem et quadragesime initium in aula collegij duas commedias siue tragedias curent agendas.

And, lest our youth, trained perhaps in other respects, remain crude in pronunciation and gesture and unpolished, we wish the professor of the Greek language and also the examiner to be responsible for putting on two comedies or tragedies every year between the twentieth day of December and the beginning of Lent.[47]

Similar provisions were made in schools: pupils at Westminster performed an annual play to become better 'accustomed to proper action and pronunciation', and in Norwich Grammar School 'schollers' were to learn 'som lerned dyalog and commodie or two commodies at the least'.[48] There is also evidence for dramatic activity in King's at Canterbury, Ipswich, Wells, Louth, Ludlow, Beverley, Kettering, Winchester, Eton, Merchant Taylors', and St Paul's.[49]

In educational establishments 'rehearsal', in which the arts of rhetoric could be taught and practised, was considerably more important than performance; preparation periods for single performances were therefore long and intense. In Christ's College, Cambridge, 1552–3, there is an account for coals for the 'sondrie' rehearsals 'between christenmaas and fastingham',

---

[46] Boas, *University Drama*, 23-36; a 'pretty boy' with an epilogue is inserted into *Summers Last Will* 'to get him audacity', *Nashe*, iii. 293.

[47] *REED: Cambridge*, ed. Alan Nelson, I vol. in 2 (Manchester, 1990), 712, 205 (trans., 1130); see also 147.

[48] Quoted in William A. Armstrong, 'Actors and Theatres', *SSu* 17 (1964), 191-204 (197); *REED: Norwich*, ed. David Galloway (Manchester, 1984), p. xxxi.

[49] Paul Whitfield White, *Theatre and Reformation* (Cambridge, 1993), 105.

a six-week rehearsal period; at Christ Church, Oxford, in 1566, Richard Edwardes stayed two months ('qui duobus fere mensibus in Academia mansit') to ready his *Palamon and Arcyte*; Thomas Pestill, involved in a production of *Valetudinarium* at Queens' College, Cambridge (1637–8), stabled his horse there over twenty-seven consecutive nights—suggesting that there was a four-week rehearsal period for the play; at Clare College, Cambridge, the making of fires in the 'acting chamber' over seven weeks shows rehearsals beginning in the middle of January for a single performance on 8 March.[50] The regularity of the coal supply and the need for stabling suggests not simply that there was a long rehearsal period, but that there was intensive rehearsal within that period. For frequent 'preparation' was highly valued: Gager defended the 'honest preparation' of Oxford plays; and in a collective letter, six Heads of Cambridge Houses, together with the Vice-Chancellor and Master of Trinity, express their fury at the idea that their scholars be made to perform before they are ready—writing to the Vice-Chamberlain they ask for two things: 'some further limitacion of time for due preparacion, And liberty to play in latyn'.[51] Rooms in Cambridge colleges were set aside specifically for 'rehearsals'; they were known variously as 'acting' or 'repeating' chambers: 'for a chalder of coles for the repeating chamber' (Trinity College Senior Bursar's Accounts, 1614); 'for firing of ye acting chamber' (from a 'Sheet of accounts', 1615).[52] Performances themselves happened elsewhere on makeshift stages, erected for the purpose and then taken down again: rehearsal rooms were permanent, stages were temporary.[53] Tellingly, the Comödianten in *Der Bestrafte Brudermord* (a German version of *Hamlet* bearing traces of seventeenth-century production), who have been transmuted from 'the Tragedians of the City' (*Ham.* 1375) to university actors ('seyd ihr nicht vor wenig Jahren zu Witenberg auf der Universität gewesen . . . ?'), make specific reference to their rehearsal practice:

---

[50] *REED: Cambridge*, 178, 1210; Boas, *University Drama*, 100; Alan H. Nelson, *Early Cambridge Theatres* (Cambridge, 1994), 35, 74.
[51] Boas, *University Drama*, 238, 323. See also 232.
[52] *REED: Cambridge*, 519, 530.
[53] See Nelson, *Cambridge Theatres*, 36.

HAMLET. Konnt ihr uns nun wohl diese Nacht eine Comodie präsentiren? [Could you perform a play tonight?]

CARL. Ja, Ihro Hoheiten, wir sind stark und exercirt genug. [Yes, your Highness, we are both numerous and well rehearsed enough.][54]

But what took place over this lengthy preparation period? 'Rehearsal', here as for country players, seems to have signified a couple of different events, one being the private learning of a part at home with or without an instructor, another being public collective practice before performance. So 'rehearsals' in one sense began when pupils received their separate 'parts'—the book or roll of papers containing the lines they were to speak and, for a cue, a maximum of a sentence of the speech preceding each of their lines (one such university part, known as the part of 'Poore', survives; it is a cued script written into a blank book in the early seventeenth century).[55] Parts having been separately received, were also separately learnt: a 'boy' in the university play *Return from Parnassus* is accused by the stagekeeper of 'sitting vp all night at cards, when you should be conning your part'—he should have spent his evening alone studying his lines, rather than in company.[56] And although major roles might be taught or 'instructed', this too happened separately, away from the other actors or the full text. In 1614 Dr Preston, 'a rigid puritan', was asked 'for his assistance in preparing' his pupil, 'Mr Morgan', for the part of a woman: he was asked to coach not the play *Ignoramus*, but one student who was to perform in it. Preston declined, as he did not conceive, he said, that anyone 'intended Mr. *Morgan* for a player'.[57]

Depictions of what happened in instructed private rehearsal show the teacher to have been highly dictatorial. Richard Zouche's *The Sophister* (4.3) includes a scene in which Ambiguity guides Ignoratio in the correct pronunciation of a letter from Falacie. Ignoratio speaks the text, and Ambiguity 'directs' his speaking by gagging him like a choirboy until he is forced to 'improve' his enunciation:

---

[54] *Der Berstrafte Brudermord* in Albert Cohn, *Shakespeare in Germany in the Sixteenth and the Seventeenth Centuries* (1865), 263.
[55] Described and transcribed in *MSC: XV*, ed. N. W. Bawcutt (Oxford, 1993), 113-69.
[56] *The Three Parnassus Plays*, ed. J. B. Leishman (London, 1949), 218.
[57] George Ruggle, *Ignoramus*, ed. John Hawkins (1777), p. xxiii.

Now, how canst thou speak?
                    [*He pronounces some of Falacies Letters.*
It must be lowder . . . open like an Oyster . . .
                    [*He goes on pronouncing*
Oh that we had some Peble-stones, such as *Demosthenes* used;
    but hold . . .
Spare my fingers [*He gags him*], but while I tell a hundred.[58]

Thomas Tomkis' *Lingua* (4.2) gives another depiction of instruction, again showing it to be a continuation of the teaching-
through-imitation of the schools. Here Phantastes instructs
Comedus in how to perform his actions, not by talking to him
about the part, but by offering him a model to copy:

COMEDUS. *quid igitur faciam? non eam ne nunc quidam cum accusor ultro?*
PHANTASTES. Phy, phy, phy no more action, lend me your baies, doe it
    thus. *Quid igitur, &c.*
        [*He acts it after the old kinde of Pantomimick action.*[59]

Actors might be brought together on stage only once after
memorizing their texts before performance itself, as an anecdote
told by Edmund Gayton makes clear. He recalls a university
production in which two actors had both independently studied
their parts of ghosts. Neither, however, was prepared to see the
other on the stage at the single 'tryall' that preceded the
performance:

two Scholars there were in this Spanish Tragedy (which was the story
of *Petrus Crudelis*) whose parts were two Ghosts or Apparitions of some
Noble Personages, which that Bloody Prince had Murder'd. These two
at the Repetitions spoke their lines very confidently, insomuch, that the
Judges thought they would be very good Ghosts; but when the tryall
night came, that the Play was to be presented to some few friends
before the publicke exhibit, and then these two Scholars were put out of
their blacks into white long robes, their Faces meal'd, and Torches in
their hands, and some flashes of Sulphur made at their entrance; just as
they put their heads through the hangings of the Scene coming out at
two severall sides of the Stage, they shook so, and were so horribly
affrighted at one anothers ghastly lookes, that no force of those behind
them, could get them to advance a foot forward toward the stage, or
speak a word of their Parts.[60]

[58] Richard Zouche, *The Sophister* (1639), G4ᵃ.
[59] Thomas Tomkis, *Lingua* (1602), H3ᵃ.
[60] Edmund Gayton, *Pleasant Notes upon Don Quixote* (1654), 94-5.

The two actors had established their roles in isolation from the rest of the text, and, seemingly, without being very clear about the events of the story itself. Confronted with the 'spectacle' and the theatrical ensemble, their individually perfected performances collapsed. This reliance on cued parts rather than on any knowledge of ensemble performance explains how it is that Will Summers in Nashe's private play *Summers Last Will*, can threaten to 'put you besides all your parts' by acting 'the knaue in cue': one false or missed cue and an entire production could grind to a halt, no one knowing what to speak next.[61]

The designation of parts, and perhaps also the final rehearsal ('tryall'), seems generally to have been overseen by one person, though several different teachers helped with 'instruction'. Leland, in *Poetic Encomia*, bears witness *To Stephen Gardiner*: 'Et cum stet docto te fabula docta chorago | comica tum scenis parta corona tuis' ('And since the learned play depends upon you, the learned manager, | Then the crown for comedy (is) brought forth by your stages').[62] When Queen Elizabeth visited Cambridge in 1564, Roger Kelke, Master of Magdalene, was 'specyallye appoynted' by the Vice-Chancellor and Heads of Colleges 'to set fourth & to teache suche y^e Playes as should be exhibited before her Grace'; when she visited Oxford in 1566 Richard Edwardes was invited to supervise the training of Christ Church actors; similarly when Albertus Alasco, Prince Palatine of Siradia, was to visit Christ Church in 1583, George Peele was asked up from London to superintend theatrical arrangements.[63] If the playwright were alive, he might supervise his own production, though this was not invariably the case. At Trinity, Cambridge, in 1642, a payment is made 'to Mr Willis for D^r Cooleys Comedy' (Cowley's play *The Guardian*), which was, perhaps as a result, got up so badly and with such speed that 'it could neither be revised or perfected by the author, nor learnt without-Book by the Actors, nor set forth in any measure tolerably by the officers of the College'.[64] Even if they were not involved in mounting the play itself, playwrights tended to have had a hand in the instruction

---

[61] *Nashe*, iii. 236.
[62] *REED: Cambridge*, 94.
[63] Boas, *University Drama*, 91, 100, 180.
[64] G. C. Moore Smith, *College Plays Performed in the University of Cambridge* (Cambridge, 1923), 22; Abraham Cowley, *The Complete Works* (1656), 11^b.

process. Repudiating the charge that in his *Ulysses Redux* two boy
actors kiss each other, Gager writes that 'I have enquyred of the
partyes themselues, whether any suche action was vsed by them,
and thay constantly denye it; sure I ame, no suche thinge was
taught.'[65] One university playwright involved in the daily teaching
of his actors as an instructor, is depicted by the German Johannes
Rhenanus: 'Was aber die *actores* antrifft, werden soche (wie ich in
England in acht genommen) gleichsam in einer schule täglich
*instituiret*, daß auch die vornembsten *actores* deren orter sich von
den Poëten müßen unter wayßen laßen' ('But as regards the
*actors*, they are daily *instructed* in (as it were) a school, as I've seen
myself in England, where even the most refined *actors* are obliged
to let the poets instruct them').[66] Rhenanus' passage is often
quoted as a description of rehearsals in the Elizabethan public
theatre,[67] but it occurs in the introduction to *Speculum Aestheticum*
(1613), a translation of Thomas Tomkis' Trinity College, Cambridge, play *Lingua*, so renowned for its academic qualities that, as
Gayton explains, '*Lingua*, that learned comedy of the contention
betwixt the five senses . . . is not to be prostituted to the common
stage'.[68] Almost certainly Rhenanus is writing about academic
productions—his introduction concerns the English 'high style',
and he is probably making a direct reference to the preparation of
*Lingua* itself.[69]

[65] Boas, *University Drama*, 217.

[66] W. Creizenach, *Die Schauspiele der englischen Komödianten* (1889). School
acting lessons consisted of a teacher 'instructing' a pupil in pronunciation and
gesture through imitation as described; it would seem that this is also taking place
in the universities. Brinsley, *Ludus Literarius*, 214, recommended that schoolteachers
should instruct pronunciation and gesture up to a certain point, but continued, 'For
more exquisite knowledge and practice hereof, I leaue it to the Vniversities, which are
to perfect all those faculties which are but begun in the Grammar Schooles.'

[67] It is used out of context to describe 'Shakespearian' rehearsal in Alfred Hart,
'Did Shakespeare Produce His Own Plays?', *MLR* 36 (1941), 173-83 (173); and
rejoinder, David Klein, *MLR* 57 (1962), 556-60 (556).

[68] Gayton, *Pleasant Notes*, 271.

[69] 'High style' is discussed in Ernst Höpfner, *Reformbestrebungen auf dem Gebiete
der Deutsche Dichtung des XVI. und XVII. Jahrhunderts* (1886), 39. *Lingua* was first
performed in 1607, and regularly repeated thereafter. Chambers, *Elizabethan Stage*,
iii. 498, states that Rhenanus was probably in England in 1611, giving as his source
Philipp Losch's *Johannes Rhenanus* (1895). In fact Losch (ch. 3) is unable to establish
either when Rhenanus was in England, or what he saw. He does indeed suggest that
Rhenanus might have accompanied the young prince Otto on a journey to Holland
and England in 1611, but qualifies this by observing that Rhenanus is unacknow-
ledged in the prince's English travel account, and that, in any case, there are records
showing him to have been in Germany during at least part of that time.

Schools, which put on plays for the same academic reasons as the universities—to train young scholars in the arts of action and gesture—sometimes completed their rehearsals with a performance in front of the queen. So Richard Mulcaster, a master at the Merchant Taylors' School, annually presented plays to the court 'in whiche his scholers wear only actors . . . and by that meanes [he] taughte them good behaviour and audacitye'.[70] But children's performances became so popular in their own right that enterprising choir-masters and teachers started to set up boy acting companies in London. The children of the Chapel Royal who had performed plays under Richard Edwardes in the 1560s, were established in a playhouse at Blackfriars in 1576; the choirboys of St Paul's who had put on dramatic performances at court from about 1520, started, under Sebastian Westcott, playing in a theatre attached to the cathedral in about 1575.[71] The boys performed in public for gain, but denied being professional players, using the argument that they only mounted productions for educational reasons. In this way they were able to keep their status as 'private' companies, which both gave them the social cachet that the 'public' companies did not have, and kept their plays out of reach of the Master of the Revels, whose remit was to oversee public performances only.

The Blackfriars' and Paul's companies were subject to inhibitions on playing during the 1580s, but both started performing again at the turn of the century. During the years in which they acted, the children had a reputation for their educated, elegant style; in John Marston's *Antonio's Revenge* (1.5) one boy is made to taunt the cheap ranting of the adult professionals:

> . . . would'st have me turn rank mad,
> Or wring my face with mimic action;
> Stampe, curse, weepe, rage . . . ?
> Away tis apish action, player-like.[72]

The boys thus kept up the pretence that they were above public performances, even in the very act of putting them on. As late as the accession of King James, the two principal boy troupes still

[70] Quoted in Edwin Nungezer, *A Dictionary of Actors* (New Haven, 1929), 390.
[71] David Mann, *The Elizabethan Player* (London, 1991), 111.
[72] John Marston, *The Plays of John Marston*, ed. H. Harvey Wood, 3 vols. (London, 1934), i. 83.

shied away from accepting the title of mean acting companies, calling themselves rather 'the children of' (in other words, 'the boy choristers of') Paul's, Blackfriars etc., in order to maintain their 'private' exclusivity.[73] This leads to some confusion in interpreting plays written for boy companies, which often stress the fact that the audience is watching a rehearsal—indeed, boy performances were often called 'rehearsals'.[74] Professional players had recourse to the same argument to protect their performances from detractors: public 'rehearsals', they claimed, were necessary to ensure that the actors would be ready for eventual private performance in front of the queen. But writers producing plays for the boys took the argument one step further. In Marston's *Antonio and Mellida* (1599), written for the début of the new Paul's Company, the players enter onto the stage *'with parts in their hands: having cloakes cast over their apparell'*—they appear to be undressed and unready to perform. They proceed to discuss the problems they have with the play itself: they can 'say' their parts, but are 'ignorant in what mould we must cast our Actors'. Their problems stem largely from the fact that they do not know which roles the other members of their company are playing (Galeazzo: 'Well, and what dost thou play?'; Balurdo: 'The fool . . .'). So the induction clearly maintains that the boys have only been individually prepared so far—in this way the play situates itself as something like the university 'tryall', the single group rehearsal before real performance. Of course, a scripted induction cannot be taken at face value; its purpose here is probably to soften the audience in advance, on the off-chance that the things do not go as well as they should for the new young company (as is the epilogue, with its insistence that 'What imperfection you have seene in us, leave with us, & weele amend it'[75]). In *Jacke Drum's Entertainment* (1600), similarly, the Tyer-man enters to

[73] Michael Shapiro, *Children of the Revels* (New York, 1977), 1.
[74] Reavley Gair, *The Children of Paul's* (Cambridge, 1982), 84, 94-5. The Blackfriars building itself had both courtly and 'rehearsal' associations: Wickham, *Early English Stages*, ii. 124, explains that Blackfriars had contained the official rehearsal room when it was owned by the Revels' Office in 1547. He believes that Richard Farrant visited the building during this period. If that is so, then perhaps Farrant hoped to purchase the courtly 'rehearsal' image along with the right to perform his boys there.
[75] *Marston*, i. 5-7, 63. Fully discussed in John Marston, *Antonio and Mellida*, ed. W. Reavley Gair (Manchester, 1991), 44-5.

tell the audience that the play cannot proceed as the author has snatched away the prompt-book and will not let the children out onto the stage. Finally a boy actor comes on to explain that the playwright has not been bad tempered so much as loath to have the play performed 'Wanting a Prologue, & our selves not perfect'; 'What hoe,' exclaims the Prologue to *Wily Beguilde* some years later, 'where are these paltrie Plaiers? stil poaring in their papers and neuer perfect?'[76] By resolutely insisting that their performances were simply 'rehearsals' for their 'real' performances in court and by performing only two or three times a week (separating themselves from adult players who needed to perform daily to support themselves), the boys gave themselves the mystique of court players.[77] And their 'rehearsal' is shown to be so near to performance as to be, literally, indistinguishable from it; though these rehearsal-performances also illustrate what the received image was of the 'tryall' or final group rehearsal: lines imperfectly remembered, slightly hesitant actors, and the confusion of ensemble playing resulting from the fact that only individual rehearsal has hitherto taken place.

In fact as the boys did not perform daily, they potentially had more rehearsal time than adult actors. The suggestion that they were less prepared—that they, perhaps, disdained to be more prepared—but were somehow still extremely proficient, only made them look better against the lumbering professionals. In reality, the children were given regular instruction, though, as ever, the teaching happened for the most part privately and not on ensemble occasions. Ben Jonson, whom John Aubrey praised for being 'an excellent instructor', made a point of flaunting, in the mouths of his child actors, the (almost intrusive) educational role he had maintained. In his *Cynthia's Revels* the two boys each claim to have studied the same prologue with Jonson; one was taught it 'first', but the other wants to say it because 'the Authour

---

[76] *Marston*, iii. 179; *Wily Beguilde* (1606), A2ª.

[77] See Mark Eccles, 'Martin Peerson and the Blackfriars', *Shakespeare Survey*, 11 (1958), 100-6 (104), who points out that William Strachey used to receive his part of the profit from the plays 'sometymes once, twyce, and thrice in a weeke'. He uses this evidence to argue against the idea put forward by Chambers, Wallace, and, latterly, Gurr (*Companies*, 31, 359), that the Blackfriars' company performed only once a week up until about 1610. All refer to the epilogue of *Eastward Hoe*, 'May this attract you hither once a week'; Eccles points out that other plays could still have been acted within the week.

[thinks] I can speake it better'; Meere-craft in *The Devil is an Asse* (2.7.56–77) explains that if he had a 'witty boy' like Dick Robinson (a boy player in the King's Company for which the play was written) he would be able to 'instruct' him 'to the true height'.[78] Like a university teacher, Jonson extended his care for his favourite pupils into matters of general education: 'Nid field' (the child actor Nathan Field) 'was his Schollar & he had read to him the Satyres of Horace & some Epigrames of Martiall.'[79] In writing mostly for boy players, tutoring them carefully, and harping frequently on his classical heritage ('he was better Versed & knew more jn Greek and Latin, than all the Poets jn England and quintesence[th] their braines'[80]), Jonson seems to have been trying to position his dramatic activities within the academic tradition, perhaps as part of his plays-as-literature campaign. Certainly he liked to call himself 'master' of his plays, suggesting both command and pedagogic authority over his productions: 'these Master-*Poets* . . .' sighs the stagekeeper when 'Jonson' is unkind to him.[81]

Other people beside the playwright also helped to instruct the child actors—in particular, the 'manager' who ran their company. In 1581 the Earl of Leicester explained that William Hunnis intended 'to practise the Queen's children of the Chapel . . . in like sort as [Richard Farrant] did for the better training them to do her Majesty's service'; in his 1608 Paul's-Cross sermon William Crashaw condemned Edward Pearce, the master in charge of Paul's boys, as one who '*teacheth children to play,* and, by so doing, made himself '*not an instructor, but a . . . destroyer of children*'.[82] A variety of people had a hand in the instruction process; even with one person technically 'manager' of a production, a number of different theatrical practitioners prepared the actors.

Exactly how long the children had to see their performances to the stage seems to accord with the time given to university productions: in *The Knight of the Burning Pestle*, the Citizen

---

[78] Benjamin Jonson, *The Works,* ed. C. H. Herford and P. and E. Simpson, 11 vols. (Oxford, 1925-52), iv. 35; John Aubrey, *Brief Lives,* ed. Oliver Lawson Dick (1949; London, 1962), 334; *Jonson,* iv. 35.

[79] *Conversations* in *Jonson,* i. 137.

[80] Ibid. i. 149.

[81] Ibid. iv. 13; vi. 508.

[82] Shapiro, *Children,* 15; Gurr, *Companies,* 345.

asks for a play 'of my owne trade' and the Prologue replies that 'you should have told us your minde a moneth since' (1.1)—this month, though, would have included the writing as well as preparation of the piece, and other plays would also have been mounted over the same period of time.[83]

University and school rehearsal, then, consisted of a period of individual learning in isolation from the other players, but often in the presence of a teacher. In this way it equates to the period of private study time given to literate country players. More than one teacher might be involved in the individual instruction of actors, though there was clearly a master 'in charge' of the general production—again, this mirrors country production. Despite the fact that boys' plays sometimes suggest that there has been no collective rehearsal, at least one full, often performance-like, group rehearsal or 'tryall', equivalent to the last 'general' rehearsal, seems to have been normal.

[83] Francis Beaumont and John Fletcher, *The Dramatic Works*, ed. Fredson Bowers, 9 vols. (Cambridge, 1966-1994), i. 12.

# 3

# Rehearsal in Shakespeare's Theatre

## BACKGROUND

Although the public theatre had nearly a century of existence before being foreclosed by Parliament in 1642, it lacked clear rules of procedure. Between 1567 and 1642, the rough limitations of this chapter, there were no permanent stage rules, for the professional theatre was creating itself as it went along. Philip Henslowe's so-called *Diary*—the only surviving day-to-day record of theatrical performances (limited to seven scattered periods between the years 1591 and 1597 at the Rose Theatre)— does at least illustrate some basic facts about Elizabethan production over the prolific 1590s, when different plays were performed almost every night, a great number of new plays were mounted every year, and the 'life' of a play in its original form was generally short. This contrasts with the careful maintenance of a limited repertoire that typified other and earlier forms of English theatre. Stock repertoires had been built up by the 1630s which meant that fewer new plays needed to be mounted each year in the professional theatre—but as the procedure of putting on a different entertainment every evening continued to be usual, what had by then become the established mode of preparation probably did not change at root.[1] This chapter explores rehearsal from the establishment of the early

---

[1] Exceptions include *A Game at Chess*, performed for nine days in a row in Aug. 1624 before being banned; *Holland's Leaguer*, performed for six days in 1631; and the three-day run of *The Late Lancashire Witches* in Aug. 1634. Each play was likely to be banned as soon as the authorities discovered its true import and was continuously performed in the meantime; each of these runs is presented as being exceptional. Gurr, *Companies*, 21, argues that from the 1630s onwards short runs became the norm. With five playhouses to provide variety, a play could, he claims, comfortably run for a week or longer at one playhouse. In fact, as Chs. 4–6 will show, competition between playhouses tended to lead to shorter runs; and runs of over six days did not anyway become normal until the establishment of the author's sixth-day benefit in the 1690s.

professional theatre to its closure. William Shakespeare, a figure of importance in his own time, and central importance subsequently, was an actor and writer for the Chamberlain's (later King's) Company; he was actively involved in the playhouse from about 1590 to 1616, and is, when possible, made a focus.

The public theatre evolved out of the travelling theatre, and remained intimately connected to it. In the early 1560s various privileged troupes of strolling players had been allowed to put on plays at court and in London on a regular basis; eventually they were bold enough to erect London theatres to perform in: the early theatres in London were set up as fixed booths for travelling players. The Globe (1599) and Fortune (1600) were the first theatres to be established solely for use by London-based, officially sanctioned companies; until the turn of the century, theatre companies played in London as a supplement to their travels.[2] Even after this, however, London troupes had to return to strolling whenever plague or politics closed the theatres. As a consequence, the early professional theatre had to remain compatible with travelling practice.

Though there are not too many records relating to the preparation of productions for strolling players, enough survive to make apparent what seems to have been the usual procedure. In the first half of the sixteenth century strolling players seem generally to have studied new plays at their patron's house just before Christmas. Anthony Hall was given board for four weeks at Rutland's household in 1542 while 'lernyng a play to pley in Christemes'; similarly, Bale rehearsed *Three Laws* from his living at Bishopstoke for Christmas 1551, as is clear from the accusation levelled by 'a papist' at one of his players: '[he called him] a heretyke and knave because he had begonne to studie a parte in suche a Comedie as myghtely rebuked the abhomynacyons ... of the Bishopp of Rome'.[3] It is telling that the events here are

---

[2] Gurr, *Companies*, ch. 2 and 3.

[3] Quoted in Suzanne R. Westfall, *Patrons and Performance* (Oxford, 1990), 127; John Bale, *The Complete Plays*, ed. Peter Happé, 2 vols. (Cambridge, 1985), i. 6. Christmas was generally the time for preparing and performing plays for patrons. The accounts for the Clifford family include a sum of money 'paid to the younge men of the toun being his lᵖs tenants & servants, to fit them for acting plays this Christmas'—see John Tucker Murray, *English Dramatic Companies, 1558–1642*, 2 vols. (London, 1910), ii. 152. At the Inns of Court all 'comedies called enterludes' were stopped by an order of the bench in 1550, except during the times of solemn Christmas—see E. K. Chambers, *Medieval Stage*, 2 vols. (Oxford, 1903), ii. 194.

described in terms of 'studying' or 'learning' plays (words that apply, as will be shown, to private preparation); *REED* accounts give no indication that further rehearsal of any kind ever took place on the road (except for the 'rehearsals' in front of the mayor).[4] The professional London theatre seems to have adopted a modified version of this system of holiday preparation. The theatre was seasonal, and happened in 'terms' and 'vacations', terminology borrowed from the inns of court which provided many of the audience;[5] during vacation time, the lack of spectators and the presence of summer plagues tended to force companies to leave the capital and take to the road. While away from London, troupes could perform a few stock plays repeatedly in different towns; no variety of rehearsal was necessary. However, just before the new theatrical season started up again in the capital, there seems to have been a period during which new plays were prepared and old ones perhaps 'refreshed'. It is wise to steer clear of the nebulous word 'rehearsal' at this stage, and simply establish that certain periods of the year seem to have been set aside for concentrated work on new productions. J. Leeds Barroll suggests that members of the King's Company bought country houses near London specifically in order to have places where the troupe could gather to ready their plays when the theatres were shut; he instances Augustine Phillips, who had a house in Mortlake in 1604, from where the King's Company

---

[4] Jerzy Limon, *Gentlemen of a Company* (Cambridge, 1985), 46, claims that in Germany the half-English Brandenburg company were given four days for 'rehearsal and "other preparations"' before performing in Gdansk, but the text from which he derives this information, Johannes Bolte's *Das Danziger Theater in 16. und 17. Jahrhundert* (1895), 446–64, only mentions 'der extruction vnd praeparation vnßers theatri' and simply refers to the erection of the stage. *REED* editions for Lancashire, Devon, Gloucestershire, Norwich, Cumberland, and Westmorland contain no reference to 'rehearsals' at all, and though it is necessary to be wary of concluding too much from this (records tend to be made only when specific financial or legal matters are concerned), rehearsals hardly emerge as a matter of key importance. Mayors' rehearsals are described in Ch. 2.

[5] See Thomas Middleton, and Thomas Dekker, *The Roaring Girle* (1611), A3[a]: 'Now in the time of sprucenes, our plaies followe the nicenes of our Garments, . . . fit for the Times and Tearmers'; Thomas Nabbes, *The Bride* (1640), A4[b]: 'Vacation Still: so little custome comes'; Samuel Harding, *Sicily and Naples* (1640), A1[a]: 'some Players braine new drencht in sacke | Do's clap each terme new fancies on its [the play's] backe'; Dekker, *Worke for Armourers* in Thomas Dekker, *The Non-Dramatic Works*, ed. Alexander B. Grosart, 5 vols. (New York, 1963), iv. 96: '*Tearme* times, when the *Two-peny Clients*, and *Peny Stinkards* swarme together to heere the *Stagerites*'.

came to perform at Wilton over the summer.[6] This tallies with Roslyn Knutson's observation that each theatrical season opened with plays from the season before—from which she concludes that 'continuations' were used to provide daily productions until the company had completed getting up their new plays.[7] Henslowe's 'diaries', the source for Knutson's statistics, do indeed suggest that the bulk of new plays were staged just after vacations, over the late summer, or around Christmas— though records relating to production expenses and 'readings' to the company also show that some level of continuous preparation will have been necessary throughout the year to cover the few new plays that were mounted during the season.[8]

## MASTER OF THE REVELS' REHEARSAL

There was, however, one particular kind of 'rehearsal' easy to confuse in written accounts with the preparation of plays. This was the Master of the Revels' rehearsal, which was, in many ways, similar to the mayors' rehearsal of the previous chapter. It was, that is to say, a primarily text-based event, that succeeded rather than preceded performance.

Before the professional theatre was established, the primary task of the Master of the Revels had been to prepare dramatic performances for the court. These he[9] readied from scratch, gathering his own troupes of actors together and teaching them plays. William Baldwin's *Beware the Cat* (1570) starts with just such an occasion: 'I was at Court with Master Ferrers, then master of the King's Majesty's pastimes, about setting forth certain interludes, which for the King's recreation we had devised and were in learning.'[10] When the professional theatre

---

[6] J. Leeds Barroll, *Politics, Plague, and Shakespeare's Theater* (Ithaca, NY, 1991), 112.

[7] Roslyn Lander Knutson, *The Repertory of Shakespeare's Company 1594–1613* (Fayetteville, Ark., 1991), 38.

[8] Literary and production expenses are usefully tabulated in Neil Carson, *Companion to Henslowe's Diary* (Cambridge, 1988), 103–17.

[9] The male pronoun is correct for the Master of the Revels, actors, playwrights, and holders of other theatrical offices in this chapter.

[10] William Baldwin, *Beware the Cat*, ed. William A. Ringler Jr. and Michael Flachman (San Marino, Calif., 1988), 5.

came into being, however, the Revels' job was redefined. He still had to find entertainments to amuse the royal household, but he no longer had to mount them himself—he needed to do no more than pick a few select productions out of the plays already fully prepared and in performance on the London stage.[11] His method was to demand to see a private run-through, known as a 'rehearsal', of such plays as had been successful in the public theatre over the previous year, a 'rehearsal' being, in effect, an 'audition' of the performance in question. So accounts concerning this kind of 'rehearsal' depict the Master of the Revels overseeing many plays—but only choosing a few of them for the queen: costs are recorded 'for . . . examynynge and Rehersinge of dyvers plaies and Choise makinge of x of them to be showen before her Maiestie at Christmas'.[12] The selection made, more events known as 'rehearsal' might take place, during which the actors worked on the changes demanded by the Master of the Revels, and brought their production up to royal standards. There is never any suggestion that the Master of the Revels attended these 'rehearsals'—indeed, when an account is recorded for expenses incurred during the actors' 'sondry rehersalls afterwarde [after Tilney's rehearsal] till to be p<sup>r</sup>sented before her Ma<sup>tie</sup>', the occasion is defined by the Master of the Revels' absence.[13]

The consequence of this new method of providing plays for the court was that the Master of the Revels ceased to be intimately connected to the theatre in the way he had been when he prepared productions himself; he became a critic and judge, and his 'rehearsal' came to be regarded as a potentially negative occasion in which texts might be deselected or altered.

---

[11] One exception to this is the Queen's Company, a group made up out of good actors from different companies. Tilney appears to have been responsible for selecting the actors—the Revels accounts have a note dated 10 Mar. 1583 ordering him 'To chose out a companie of players for her majestie'—see Gurr, *Companies*, 58. W. R. Streitberger, *Edmond Tyllney* (New York, 1986), 7, suggests that Tilney also rehearsed this company.

[12] Albert Feuillerat, *Documents Relating to the Office of the Revels in the Time of Queen Elizabeth*, (Louvain, 1908), 326; see also T III 71. In this way, N. W. Bawcutt's important new publication of the records of Sir Henry Herbert, *The Control and Censorship of Caroline Drama* (Oxford, 1996), is questionable when it briefly attributes to Herbert the job of 'supervising' rehearsals prior to performance (p. 27), for the court rehearsals Herbert may have occasionally overlooked were given well after the original performance had taken place.

[13] Feuillerat, *Documents*, 326.

So it is that in *A Midsummer Night's Dream*, Philostrate (Q), or Egeus (F), the Master of the Revels, is critically portrayed.[14] He has seen *Pyramus and Thisbe* 'Rehearst' ('which made mine eyes water', *MND*, 1864), but he uses his rehearsal-knowledge to do down the play before performance, even though he had initially selected the actors and set them to the trouble of preparing.[15] Another potentially negative Revels' rehearsal occurs in Anthony Munday and Henry Chettle's *The Downfall of Robert, Earl of Huntington*. Ingeniously, the play presents a group rehearsal for court performance taking place in front of a judge, without making clear who the judge is. Eltham reminds Skelton, the play's supposed author, that

> the king himselfe
> . . . bid mee take great heede
> Wee faile not of our day, therefore I pray
> Sende for the rest, that now we may rehearse.[16]

The actors gathered, Skelton motions towards 'all these lookers on', and we realize that by sleight-of-hand we, the audience, have been transformed into a collective Master of the Revels potentially more critical than the king himself—'I will perswade the King: but how can you | Perswade all these beholders to content?'[17] This is a cunning device, for there is no suggestion that the play, which is thoroughly public theatre in its nature, was ever performed in court;[18] yet by the time the story has fallen short of its tragic conclusion, we have been elevated into a nobleman-censor, and flattered away from being overcritical.

Over time, the job of Master of the Revels became increasingly textual in nature. In addition to overseeing plays for the court, Edmund Tilney was asked to 'approve' all public theatre plays before performance, banning unsuitable scripts, providing

---

[14] Penry Williams, 'Shakespeare's *Midsummer Night's Dream*: Social Tensions Contained' in David L. Smith, Richard Strier, and David Bevington (eds.), *The Theatrical City* (Cambridge, 1995), 59.

[15] Quince and his men have been chosen from an official list of those regarded as most 'fit through all *Athens*, to play in our Enterlude before the Duke and Dutches' (*MND* 273), just as Tilney was given the job of selecting the actors to make up the Queen's Company.

[16] Anthony Munday and Henry Chettle, *Downfall of Robert, Earl of Huntington*, facs. ed. John C. Meagher (Oxford, 1965), A2ª.

[17] Munday, *Downfall*, L2ᵇ.

[18] Harold Jenkins, *The Life and Work of Henry Chettle* (London, 1934), 145.

'licences' for suitable ones, and censoring blasphemy and political intrigue from the ones that were in between. His 1581 patent, reissued to Sir George Buc in 1603, and again to Sir John Astley in 1622, stated that actors had 'to present and recite before our said servant' all their plays before public performance.[19] But even in the 1580s Tilney was incapable of seeing all the many plays concurrently ready for production on the London stage. Instead he asked companies to bring their manuscripts in for inspection, so that he only actually watched plays being considered for specific court occasions[20]—or rather, his 'rehearsal' was, generally, a silent reading that did not require the presence of actors. As a result, there are accounts of how the Master of the Revels 'perused, & neccessarely corrected & amended' plays,[21] but no accounts of his making performance suggestions. By the time Henry Herbert came to office in 1623, his duties, still described as 'Rehersalles and makinge choice of playes and comedies and reforminge them'[22] were actually, as the records show, almost exclusively to read plays. Like mayors' rehearsals, courtly rehearsals were about words and scripts, not performance.

### PREPARING A PLAY FOR THE STAGE

*Number of days to produce a play*

In fact 'rehearsal' as the collective practice for a performance is seldom referred to, largely because of the way in which plays were actually brought to the stage. The permanent theatre serviced a London audience small and regular enough to require

---

[19] Gerard Eades Bentley, *The Profession of Dramatist in Shakespeare's Time* (Princeton, 1986), 148.

[20] Bentley, *Dramatist*, 149.

[21] Feuillerat, *Documents*, T III 71. Richard Dutton, *Mastering the Revels* (London, 1991), 34, states that 'perusing' in this context means 'seeing a performance of the play rather than simply reading the play-book'. As proof he quotes Heywood's *Apology for Actors*, in which the palace of St John's is described as the place 'where our Court playes have beene in late daies yearley rehersed, perfected, and corrected'—a passage that offers no reason for reinterpreting the word 'perusal'. But either way, concern with textual suitability rather than acting suitability underlies the choice of this word.

[22] *MSC: XIII*, ed. W. R. Streitberger (Oxford, 1986), 85.

a continuous supply of new plays, and to expect even the old plays to 'change' frequently to provide new entertainment. So the number of plays handled by the early professional theatres was extraordinary. The Admiral's Company in their 1594–5 season performed six days a week, and offered thirty-eight plays in all, of which twenty-one were new; few plays remained in the repertory for more than a year.[23] In January 1596, the same (Admiral's) Company played on every day except Sunday and presented fourteen different plays. Of these, six were only ever given one performance.[24] The next month their new play, Chapman's *The Blind Beggar of Alexandria*, first performed on 12 February, was followed by a play they had not performed for 140 days, Marlowe's *Dr Faustus*. During the 140 days that intervened between one *Faustus* and the next, the Admiral's Company had played 107 performances of twenty-one other works. In other words, a constant stream of new plays met a constant stream of old ones that had to be relearnt. This startling programme is not dissimilar to practice abroad: from the late 1580s the two permanent playhouses in Madrid were each supplied with three or four plays a fortnight for much of the year, and a run-of-the-mill play generally did not last longer than between about three and five performances.[25]

From about 1612 until the theatres were closed in 1642, fewer new plays were required, as there was, by this time, a bank of acceptable old plays in existence that were suitable for revival.[26] Malone suggests that the King's Company was offering something in the region of two, three, or four new plays a year between 1622 and 1641 and this seems to be confirmed by the Harbage and Schoenbaum *Annals*; during the same period companies would also have been performing about thirty to forty of the old plays that were in their repertoire.[27] But adaptations were frequent, and also had to be relearnt, though they did not count as new productions—so there was still a

[23] Andrew Gurr, *The Shakespearian Stage 1574–1642* (Cambridge, 1992), 103; Knutson, *Repertory*, 51–2, 73.

[24] Bentley, *Dramatist*, 33.

[25] Malveena McKendrick, *Theatre in Spain 1490–1700* (Cambridge, 1989), 72.

[26] Bentley, *Dramatist*, 15.

[27] See Malone's 'Life of the Poet and an Enlarged History' in William Shakespeare, *The Plays and Poems*, ed. J. Boswell, 21 vols. (1821), iii. 153, 166; Keith Sturgess, *Jacobean Private Theatre* (New York and London, 1987), 60.

substantial amount for Jacobean actors to memorize: 'Lente vnto
. . . Thomas deke*rs* for his adicions in owld castell the some of xs'
reads an entry in Henslowe's diary; in Middleton's *Mayor of
Quinborough* the strolling players try to advertise their old play by
claiming that 'the Cheater' now has more tricks 'And gulls the
Clown with new additions' (5.1).[28]

Time had to be spared for the constant learning and relearning
required of the actors—an actor might have to learn a new role
every two weeks, while keeping thirty or forty others in his
head.[29] So the number of days given over to preparing a new
play in the professional theatre is a vexed issue. *Civil Wars Part
1*, for instance, was given to the Admiral's Company on 29
September 1598, and staged five weeks later, on 4 November.
That means that there were potentially five weeks to get the play
up. In fact, though, a new play, *Pierce of Winchester* received its
first performance in between, on 21 October, and throughout
there were daily performances of other plays.[30] This argues the
difficulty of determining the number of group rehearsals given to
a single play, even when its preparation period is established.
Beckerman, making his calculations from Henslowe's diaries,
concludes that the time between purchasing a script and
performing it extended from three to fifty-one days, the average
duration being something over twenty days.[31] Neil Carson
demurs: from his exhaustive study of Henslowe's diaries he
suggests that the normal preparation time for a new play was
two weeks, but also offers clear examples of plays that were put
into performance with what he calls 'exceptional haste', after
nine, six, and three days' preparation.[32] Knutson, reading the
same diaries, settles for a full three weeks.[33] Even when analysing
the same accounts, scholars cannot reach compatible conclu-

---

[28] *Henslowe's Diary*, ed. R. A. Foakes and R. T. Rickert (Cambridge, 1961), 216;
Thomas Middleton, *The Mayor of Quinborough* (1661), 63. Roslyn L. Knutson,
'*Henslowe's Diary* and the Economics of Play Revision for Revival, 1592–1603', *TRI*
10 (1985), 1–18, argues against the idea that plays were automatically revised after
they had been in production for a number of years. According to her reading of
Henslowe's accounts, plays were only revised for specific commercial reasons, and
the 'normative preferred practice' was to leave texts alone.
[29] Bernard Beckerman, *Shakespeare at the Globe* (New York, 1962), 130.
[30] Peter Thomson, *Shakespeare's Professional Career* (Cambridge, 1992), 93.
[31] Beckerman, *Shakespeare*, 10.
[32] Carson, *Companion*, 73–4.
[33] Knutson, *Repertory*, 35.

sions about the length of time set aside for the company's 'rehearsal', largely because of their tendency to favour examples suggesting that preparation took up many days over those that suggest that preparation took up only a few days. In fact, to calculate averages in such a situation makes no sense: the number of days during which the actors *could* have rehearsed is not the same as the number of days they *did* rehearse; an equal number of collective rehearsals could be given to a play over a month or three days—if the number were small. Writing about the production of collaborative texts, Carson refers to the 'surprising' haste with which plays were 'rushed into production' (mounted in under two weeks), and explains how several of the playwrights whose timetables obliged them to be elsewhere, would have been unable to attend during most of the 'rehearsal period'. He writes from the assumption that there was (ideally) a substantial amount of time set aside for group rehearsal, and that authors wanted to be involved in the rehearsal process; his surprise comes from the fact that his evidence suggests the reverse.[34] The preparation period suggested by an Elizabethan play itself is under seven days: Sir Oliver Owlet's Company in John Marston's *Histriomastix* (2.1) decide to give their play out 'for Friday' (within the week), although it has not even been fully written.[35] Owlet's company is, of course, on one level made up of a set of impostors, but Posthaste, the company poet, is a parody of Anthony Munday (or, it has even been suggested, of Shakespeare); the play also depicts the Elizabethan public theatre.[36] The following chapters show that plays could be allotted a varying amount of time for preparation depending on when they were put on within the theatrical season, and that different kinds of play were allotted different portions of preparation time: more for a tragedy; less for a farce.

Information from abroad does not greatly clarify the matter. The better class of Spanish actors seem to have 'rehearsed' on a daily basis (in season), as is suggested by a Spanish contract of 1612, and by Agustin de Rojas who complains that 'from nine till

[34] Neil Carson, 'Collaborative Playwriting: The Chettle, Dekker, Heywood Syndicate', *TRI* 14 (1989), 13–23.
[35] John Marston, *The Plays of John Marston*, ed. H. Harvey Wood, 3 vols. (London, 1934), iii. 260.
[36] See Anthony Caputi, *John Marston, Satirist* (New York, 1961), 95.

twelve' every morning the Spanish *comedias* 'are constantly rehearsing' (*Viage Entretenido*).[37] But what exactly is taking place so regularly is ambiguous: it is unclear whether de Rojas is referring to individual or group rehearsal. Records for the Italian court theatre are more explicit: there actors prepared their parts regularly in private, but only attended group rehearsal when specifically called to do so.[38] So in a dialogue about the Italian theatre written *c*.1556–66 Massimiano asks to see a rehearsal of the playwright Veridico's new piece. 'Not to-day, sir', answers Veridico, 'I gave no instructions for the actors to meet to-day. To fetch them now would be . . . almost impossible.'[39] A similar attitude is certainly suggested in the one Elizabethan document that specifically addresses the subject, Robert Dawes's contract. Unlike the Spanish agreement, this contract states neither time nor place for the play's 'rehearsal' (even though it does stipulate regular playing times). Dawes, both an actor and a sharer in the Admiral's Company is commanded to 'attend all suche rehearsall, which shall the night before the rehearsall be given publickly out', implying that group rehearsal did not take place on a regular basis, but was announced beforehand as necessary, a suggestion that occurs again in a letter from Sir Henry Wotton, who writes that one of the King's Company has just learnt he has to 'repeat' a play the following afternoon, and therefore 'cannot be at home to receive me'.[40]

The demands of the Elizabethan theatre in season were tremendous. With daily performances, each of a different play, actors had to learn or relearn their lines either during the day, or as soon as the day's performance ended. Naturally that had to be their priority. Situations existed in which plays no longer in repertory had to be revived, the actor being obliged to (re)learn a

[37] In Hugo Albert Rennert, *The Spanish Stage in the Time of Lope de Vega* (New York, 1909), 147, 159.

[38] For the influence of formal Italian theatre on English production, see F. S. Boas, *University Drama in the Tudor Age* (Oxford, 1914), 134; the nature of Italian courtly theatrical production is discussed in Richard Andrews, *Scripts and Scenarios* (Cambridge, 1993). *Commedia dell' arte* players had a single rehearsal before their (largely extemporized) performances—see Andrea Perrucci, *Dell' arte rappresentativa, premeditata ed all' improvviso* (1699), trans. in A. M. Nagler, *A Source Book in Theatrical History* (New York, 1952), 257–9.

[39] Allardyce Nicoll, *The Development of the Theatre* (London, 1927), 255.

[40] *Henslowe Papers*, ed. Walter W. Greg, 3 vols. (London, 1907), iii. 124. Gerard Eades Bentley, *The Jacobean and Caroline Stage*, 7 vols. (Oxford, 1941–68), ii. 552.

script for performance the following day; with so little time to learn or relearn parts for performance, it is unlikely, in these instances, that there was any collective rehearsal at all. The Chamberlain's Company resurrected Shakespeare's *Richard II* for the Earl of Essex overnight, though it was 'old' complained Augustine Phillips 'and long out of use'.[41] Retired plays were dragged out of obscurity at the last minute to amuse the queen ('Burbage . . . Sayes ther ys no new playe that the quene hath not seene, but they have Revyved an olde one, Cawled *Loves Labore lost* . . . to be playd to Morowe night');[42] and Hamlet himself suggests '*The murther of Gonzago* . . . wee'l ha't to morrow', adding 'You could for a need study . . . some dosen or sixteene lines, which I would . . . insert in't' (*Ham.* 1577).

For revivals of stock plays, or repetitions of plays within the season, there is no suggestion that 'refresher' rehearsals took place. The idea that the actor has only just learnt which stock play he is to perform in is common enough practice to be dramatized by Massinger who has Aesopus in *The Roman Actor* (1.1) wondering 'What doe wee acte to day?'[43] Though bills were set up 'upon postes certaine dayes before' to tell the audience what plays to expect,[44] circumstances would some-times force the actors to put on a play they had not prepared for at all (having intended to perform another): Edmund Gayton recalls a restless crowd who dithered as to what they wanted, 'sometimes *Tamerlane*, sometimes *Jugurth*, sometimes The Jew of *Malta*, and sometimes parts of all these' so that at last the players were 'forc'd to . . . put off their Tragick habits and conclude the day with the merry milk-maides'; an Italian diplomat heard the groundlings insist that the play of their choice be performed the next day; and in 1633, Sir Henry Herbert 'sent a warrant . . . to suppress *The Tamer Tamd*, to the King's Players, for that afternoone; . . . They acted *The Scornful Lady* instead of it'.[45] But little preparation was actually

[41] E. K. Chambers, *The Elizabethan Stage*, 4 vols. (Oxford, 1923), ii. 205.
[42] E. K. Chambers, *William Shakespeare*, 2 vols. (Oxford, 1930), ii. 332.
[43] Philip Massinger, *The Plays and Poems*, ed. Philip Edwards and Colin Gibson, 5 vols. (Oxford, 1976), iii. 21.
[44] John Northbrooke, *Spiritus est vicarius Christi in /terra/* (1577), 74.
[45] Edmund Gayton, *Pleasant Notes upon Don Quixote* (1654), 271; E. K. Chambers, 'Elizabethan Stage Gleanings', *RES* 1 (1925), 182–96 (186); Bawcutt, *Censorship*, 182.

necessary for a revival, as nothing new would be specifically added to the production unless it underwent a revision. The 'ideal' of a play was that play in its original production, and all subsequent performances were supposed to grope their way back to it. This is illustrated by the second part of the anonymous university play *Return from Parnassus* which depicts certain real-life characters including Richard Burbage, the famous lead actor of the Lord Chamberlain's Company. 'Burbage' thinks he has found an apprentice to perform the part of Hieronimo in *The Spanish Tragedy*, and starts to hand on to him the *method* of playing the role: 'obserue how I act it and then imitate me' (4.3). Another character who appears in the play is 'William Kempe', the fool for the Lord Chamberlain's Company; he too finds a trainee—'Thou wilt do well in time, if thou wilt be ruled by . . . my selfe'.[46] Both actors give private instruction as to how to perform the relevant part; both offer a formula for the role as they themselves play it: the performance they give is a fixture to be observed and copied. John Downes, a Restoration prompter, was for this reason able at least to claim that his players had directly inherited Shakespeare's 'action'; he traces the performance of certain roles (not always accurately) back through generations of teaching to Shakespeare himself.[47] Because inherited parts were taught through imitation, a member of an audience could realistically claim to know a play as well or better than the (new) actors performing it. Marston's *The Malcontent* passed from the Queen's Revels to the King's Company, and William Sly plays an irritating spectator who has seen the old company perform the play 'often', and offers to give the actors 'intellegence for their action' out of his experience.[48] As companies remained more or less constant,[49] preparation for stock plays was only essential for new actors—and they could be individually taught their parts without the whole group losing a

---

[46] *The Three Parnassus Plays*, ed. J. B. Leishman (London, 1949), 341. The author probably saw the Lord Chamberlain's company perform either in London or in Cambridge—see Boas, *University Drama*, 343–4. See also the prologue to Thomas Jordan's *Money is an Asse*, performed *c.*1635, published 1668: 'Had every Actor been some others Ape, | Seen his part Plaid before him, . . . | We had been Children, not to Act the Play', *A2*ᵃ.

[47] John Downes, *Roscius Anglicanus*, ed. J. Milhous and R. D. Hume (London, 1987), 55, 51.      [48] *Marston*, i. 141.

[49] Sturgess, *Jacobean Private Theatre*, 59.

valuable morning's private study as a consequence. So it is necessary to sort out how precisely time was divided over the three-day to five-week preparation period—how plays were read and distributed to the actors, how parts were learnt and studied—before it is clear how much time was left for collective 'rehearsal'.

## Reading

For the author the rehearsal process began with one kind of reading, for the actors it began with another. Robert Daborne, the playwright, sends a letter to Philip Henslowe concerning the piece that he is in the process of completing: 'one Tuesday night if y$^u$ appoynt J will meet y$^u$ & mr Allin & read some, for J am vnwilling to read to y$^e$ generall company till all be finisht.'[50] In other words, Daborne will give a private reading in advance of a more public reading. This illustrates the two readings involved in the acceptance and preparation of a play. The first reading was low key, private, and often given before one, or a small group, of the actor-sharers; this was the reading in which the play itself was 'auditioned' for suitability. During the audition-reading, the playwright did no more than offer the substance of his play for approval; the company, if they were interested, would then pay him to finish it (or sell the plot on to someone else to finish it). Samuel Rowley has 'hard fyue shetes of a playe of the Conqueste of the Jndes' and decides to promote it ('I dow not doute but it wyll be a verye good playe'); similarly Shaa has 'heard their booke and lyke yt'.[51] Conversely, John Jones relates how the company 'upon a slight and half view of [my play], refused to do it'; and Nicholas Rowe, writing in the early eighteenth century, tells an unlikely story about a judgemental Elizabethan playreading involving Ben Jonson:

the Persons into whose Hands [Jonson's play] was put . . . were just upon returning it to him with an ill-natur'd Answer . . . when *Shakespear* luckily cast his Eye upon it, and found something so well

---

[50] Greg, *Henslowe Papers*, iii. 70.
[51] Ibid. iii. 56, 49. Sometimes this involved nothing more than showing the outline to the players. Foakes and Rickert, *Henslowe's Diary*, 85 records how money is lent by Henslowe to Ben Jonson 'vpon a boocke w$^{ch}$ he showed the plotte vnto the company'.

in it as to engage him first to read it through, and afterwards to recommend Mr. *Johnson* and his Writings to the Publick.[52]

The second type of reading took place when the playwright, having completed his approved play, read it in front of the full company. Henslowe records money 'lent . . . vnto the company for to spend at the Readynge of that boocke at the sonne in new fyshstreate'.[53] Daborne several times refers to such readings: on one occasion he suggests that he will give his new play a group reading, on another that he will read 'the old Book' to the company (presumably an old text he has worked up).[54] These occasions introduced the story of the play to the players, and also gave the playwright a chance to speak the text in the manner in which he wished to hear it performed—the nearest, perhaps, he might get to having any 'directorial' influence over the production. Postehaste, the playwright in Marston's *Histriomastix* (2.1), reads out his text highlighting the passion so strongly that it overtakes him. Announcing the words of Dame Vertue '*My Sonne thou art a lost childe*', which he carefully points out to the actors is 'a passion', ('note you the passion?'), he is so overcome with emotion that he has to give over the play: 'read the rest sirs, I cannot . . . for teares.'[55]

A third kind of reading might follow (or perhaps substitute for) the second. This was when the actors themselves had a read-through of the play before taking each part home to learn. In Italy the playwright Veridico gets his actors 'to read the whole play in order that they . . . may learn the plot, or at least that portion which concerns them, impressing on all their minds the nature of the characters they have to interpret. Then I dismiss them and give them time to learn their parts.'[56] Again, the importance of the reading is that it is one of the few occasions during which the actors can learn the plot—and even then, Veridico implies that they are not obliged to know the full story. Group-reading, perhaps of this kind, was sometimes practised by the Admiral's Company, as is

[52] Bentley, *Dramatist*, 80; William Shakespeare, *The Works*, ed. Nicholas Rowe, 6 vols. (1709), i. pp. xii–xiii. The story is itself dubious, but shows how judgemental readings were understood to have taken place in the 16th c.

[53] Foakes and Rickert, *Henslowe's Diary*, 88.

[54] Greg, *Henslowe Papers*, iii. 72, 81.

[55] *Marston*, iii. 259.          [56] Nicoll, *Development of the Theatre*, 266.

indicated by a record of money 'Layd owt for the companye when they Read the playe of Jeffa for wine at the tavern'.[57] The reading to the actors/by the actors constituted the introduction of the play to the players, and could be denoted a collective rehearsal. Following the reading, casting would take place, after which the author would receive the balance of the purchase money for his play, and sometimes it was at this stage that his part in the production came to an end: Daborne does not seem to have had any further part in the preparation of his plays; collaborative playwrights were generally not involved in mounting their plays at all.[58] Playwrights who were also actors or who had a financial attachment to a company however, might continue to take a part in the preparation of their plays. Actors, after the reading, received their 'parts' and settled down to learn them in private.

## Parts and study

An actor's part contained his own lines and the one, two, three, or (occasionally) four words that preceded each of his speeches. The one professional-theatre part that survives from before the Interregnum—that of Orlando for Robert Greene's *Orlando Furioso*—gives some idea about just how much (and how little) a Renaissance actor had to go on. The part contains no indication to whom any speech is directed, nor does it give the name of the speaker of the cue; it is also without character notes either in scribal or actor's hand (though both hands are present on the text). What it does contain are a few property notes— 'enters w^th a mans legg'; some action notes—'he walketh vp & downe', '⟨he⟩ singes', 'he whistles for him'; and notes concerning other people whose actions will affect Orlando—'A. begins to weepe'.[59] Lacking as it is in information, the part is nevertheless clearly archetypal: professional theatre parts from the next two centuries are almost identical in form.[60]

---

[57] Foakes and Rickert, *Henslowe's Diary*, 201.

[58] See Neil Carson, 'Collaborative Playwriting', 13–23.

[59] *Two Elizabethan Stage Abridgements: 'The Battle of Alcazar' and 'Orlando Furioso'* ed. W. W. Greg (Oxford, 1922), 152, 156, 158.

[60] Recently there has been some question as to whether the university part of Poore which names the speaker and has longer cues is an example of what parts had

The actor's cued part was given a variety of names. It might be called 'part' or 'parcell'—both titles that acknowledge it as a segment of something larger; or it might be called 'scroll' or 'roll' (from which the word 'role' perhaps derives)—titles that suggest that the fragment is being treated as a self-contained whole: players did not necessarily feel the need to know more than their words and cues. And in many ways parts had a complete life separate from the text they were segments of—actors might well be given parts to learn even before a play was fully written, as Daborne's letters show.[61]

'Parts' were then 'studied', a word defined as 'the action of committing to memory one's part in a play' (*OED* sig. 6b); this meaning is selectively acknowledged by critics writing about Renaissance theatre, and yet its ramifications are seldom considered. Actors in the professional and non-professional theatre alike studied alone, away from their fellow players: as Stephen Gosson put it in his polemic *The Ephemerides of Phialo*, 'the Player so beateth his parte too him selfe at home, that hee giues it right gesture when he comes to the scaffolde'; indeed, when Bustofa in Beaumont and Fletcher's *Maid in the Mill* is interrupted learning his part he tries to get rid of his visitor with 'will you not give a man leave to con?'[62] Frequently actors comment on their own individual state of study, rather than on the rehearsals they have attended—implying that they are prepared, even if other actors are not. The first of the two quarrelling boy actors in Ben Jonson's *Cynthia's Revels* declares that he has the most right to speak the prologue as 'I . . . studied it first'; the prologue for a new actor preparing to play the eponymous Jew of Malta informs the audience that 'if none here gainsay it | The part he hath studied,

come to be like by the 1630s. But surviving 17th- and 18th-c. professional partbooks or 'sides' as they were then called, also give cues of generally no more than four words, and do not as a rule name the speaker of the cue line. See descriptions of forty odd surviving partbooks from the 18th c. documented in Edward A. Langhans, *Eighteenth Century British and Irish Promptbooks: A Descriptive Bibliography* (New York, 1987). Other surviving parts are discussed in following chapters. The extra 'help' for the actor of the part of Poore makes sense in the context of a single, one-off university production by non-professionals. Poore is described and transcribed in *MSC: XV*, ed. N. W. Bawcutt (Oxford, 1993), 113–69, and discussed in David Carnegie, 'Actors' Parts and the "Play of Poore"', *HLB* 30 (1982), 5–24.

[61] Greg, *Henslowe Papers*, iii. 69.

[62] Stephen Gosson, *The Ephemerides of Phialo* (1579), 159; *The Maid in the Mill* in Francis Beaumont and John Fletcher, *Comedies and Tragedies* (1647), 4A3ᵃ.

and intends to play it'.[63] One apocryphal story even tells of Cromwell's strange ability at quick-study: he took on the part of the King in *Lingua* at the last moment, and 'imployed' the 'little time' he had to learn it so well, that 'it seemed, that it was Infused into him'.[64] Ideally, of course, study was capped by group rehearsal: 'Each take his part' as Menander says, 'and study to reherse | That none may stumble at an easy verse' (John Stephens, *Cinthia's Revenge*, 4.8);[65] in *Midsummer Night's Dream*, Snug hopes to receive his written role as soon as possible 'for I am slow of studie' (*MND*, 330)—he wants to be sure he has time to learn his part before the group rehearsal. On the other hand, clowns, who were expected to extemporize, often stressed the fact that they were poor of study, the implication being that they were putting on an unscripted, extemporized performance. There is no suggestion here that collective rehearsal has made up for lack of other preparation. William Kempe, the clown of the early Shakespeare plays, is depicted in John Day's *Travailes of Three English Brothers,* where he describes himself as 'somewhat hard of Study' but offers to act extempore; in Richard Brome's *Antipodes*, the clown Byplay, who cannot 'be perfect in a thing | He studies' is said to be funnier with his extemporization than the rest of the company with their flawless performances.[66]

Critics, not correctly weighing the constancy of meaning that 'study' bore in the theatre from the Elizabethan period until at least the eighteenth century, have run into several basic errors. When Daborne writes that the actors 'ar now studijng' a play that he has not yet completed—he means just that: not that the players are rehearsing the play, but that they are learning their parts.[67] Similarly, when Herbert, Master of the Revels,

[63] *Jonson*, iv. 35; Thomas Heywood, 1633 prologue to *The Jew of Malta* in Christopher Marlowe, *The Complete Works*, ed. Fredson Bowers, 2 vols. (Cambridge, 1973), 261.

[64] S. Carrington, *The History of the Life and Death of His Most Serene Highness, Oliver, Late Lord Protector* (1659), 3.

[65] John Stephens, *Cinthia's Revenge: or Mænander's Extasie* (1613), P2[a].

[66] John Day, *Works*, ed. A. H. Bullen, 2nd edn., rev. Robin Jeffs (London, 1963), 370; Richard Brome, *The Dramatic Works*, ed. R. H. Shepherd, 3 vols. (1873; New York, 1966), iii. 256.

[67] Greg, *Henslowe Papers*, iii. 69. Scott McMillin in his excellent *The Elizabethan Theatre & the Book of Sir Thomas More* (Ithaca, NY, and London, 1987), 37, misreads Daborne when he claims that the records show plays put into rehearsal 'while the authors were still completing the text or making final revisions'.

admonishes Mr Knight the book-holder, with 'The players ought not to study their parts till I have allowed of the booke', and later tells him to 'purge ther parts as I have the booke', he too is referring to the process of study: the players are learning scripts before they have been officially approved (they subsequently have to return their parts for 'purging' and minor changes—giving them very little time to learn the alterations and rehearse the play before it is performed).[68] These instances also illustrate that considerable time between the completion of a play and the first performance was spent in 'study'; indeed, the patent that set up the King's Company in 1603 is framed in terms of 'studying' rather than 'rehearsing', giving the company the right to perform any plays 'theie have alreadie studied or hereafter shall use or studie':[69] there are many more references to Renaissance 'study' than to Renaissance 'rehearsal'.[70]

After individual study, group preparation was a luxury, not a necessity, as plays make clear. Bustofa, who is 'studied in my part' of Paris in a play about the three graces (Beaumont and Fletcher, *Maid in the Mill*, 2.1), is not sure whether something has gone wrong when Gerasto joins their scene and snatches 'Venus' away: 'Ha? what follows this? has carried away my sister *Venus*: | He never rehears'd his part with me before'.[71] Plays often indicate that an actor has privately learnt his role, but does not know what parts his fellow actors are playing ('what part play you?'), or whom he is supposed to be addressing ('you must . . . learn to know, to whom you are to speak').[72] This also, of course, shows why at least one general rehearsal was a good idea—with a script that did not indicate 'to whom you are to speak' external guidance about basic interaction with the other actors was extremely useful. Just before the 'rehearsal' in Anthony Munday and Henry Chettle's *The Downfall of Robert, Earl of Huntington*, for instance, Skelton reminds little Tracy (who is to play Maid Marion), '*Robin* is your loue: Sir *Thomas* mantle yonder, not Sir *Iohn*'.[73]

Having parts with cues rather than a whole play meant that

[68] Bawcutt, *Censorship*, 183, 182.      [69] Quoted in Gurr, *Companies*, 113–14.
[70] For instance, Chambers, *Elizabethan Stage*, contains no references to Renaissance rehearsal apart from rehearsals in front of the Master of the Revels.
[71] Beaumont and Fletcher, *Comedies and Tragedies*, 4A4[b].
[72] Munday, *Downfall*, A2[a]; Cosmo Manuche, *The Just General* (1652), 30.
[73] Munday, *Downfall*, A2[b].

actors learnt their own fragment in isolation from the story that surrounded it. For this reason, they did not have a natural sense of the play as a whole; a fact that was reflected both in the way they performed when together, and, I will argue, in the way they revised their lines. Authors wrote for learning of this kind, and the parts they produced contained the information players needed for solo practice. For instance, in *Twelfth Night* 1.5, Olivia conceives a passion for Viola (at this point disguised as a boy, Cesario). Divide the play down to 'recreate' Olivia's cued part, and the actual moment at which the love is engendered is clear: the moment when Olivia's part switches from prose to verse (ironically with the words 'Your Lord does know my mind, I cannot loue him', (*TN* 549), the very words with which Olivia denies her love for Orsino). The transformation from prose to verse marks a change in the pace and tempo of the scene, but it is also an actor's stage direction, visually obvious from the arrangement of speeches on the part. 'Actual' stage directions indicating similar occasions—like the notorious '*Isabella fals in loue with Rogero when the changers speak*' in Marston's *Insatiate Countesse* (2.1)—are simply other ways of conveying the same information in Renaissance texts.[74] The same device is used in *Much Ado about Nothing*. Beatrice breaks out of prose and into poetry when she hears Benedict confess his passion for her: 'What fire is in mine eares? Can this be true?' (*MA* 1198). Benedict's 'love' creates love in Beatrice, just as had been predicted. And, from the actor's point of view, the arrangement of the text tells 'Beatrice' just when to discover her own love for her sparring-partner. Other acting directions can also be seen in actors' parts—for instance, in the exchange between the terms 'you' and 'thou', formal and informal modes of address that direct the actor as to the nature of the relationship being explored on stage.[75]

Plays frequently glance at the mechanics of cued parts in metatheatrical moments—'your speech being ended, now comes in my cue', says Captain Bonvile in Thomas Heywood's *The*

---

[74] *Marston*, iii. 22.

[75] For these, and other cued-script observations, see *The Shakespeare's Globe Acting Editions* of Shakespeare's folio plays, privately produced by Patrick Tucker and Michael Holden (London, 1990– ). These are also the only editions to provide parts for Shakespeare's plays.

*Royall King and the Loyall Subject*; Dr Makewell in John Clavell's *The So[l]ddered Citizen* declares that 'all's fitted, | If you be perfect, in yo$^r$. Cues, and action'.[76] The cueing system allowed players to act a play with knowledge only of their own parts, and therefore made it possible to put on productions with minimum preparation. Difficulties would arise, however, when a cue was missed: one false or absent cue could bring an entire performance to a standstill, no one knowing what to say next. Plays that concern mounting productions or reciting speeches show a weary familiarity with the problem. In James Shirley's *The Humorous Courtier* Deppazi has learnt a speech of love to say to the Countess, but is completely thrown when she ends her sentence with the 'wrong' word: 'I beseech your grace, speake your part right, | "Oblivion" is my qu. I doe remember.'[77] On the other hand, Russell in Thomas Middleton's *A Fair Quarrel* (1.1) keeps giving the servant his cue of 'ha, ha, ha', and keeps being ignored: 'Ha, ha, ha. | Thats the rascalls qu, and he has mist it . . . Ha, ha, ha, theres his qu once again.' The servant's final, cynical comment on arrival is 'My maister laughes, that's his qu to mischiefe.'[78] That actors were dependent on cued parts rather than on the story of the text, was also the stuff of standard playhouse banter at the time. Young Gudgen in Lodowick Carlell's *The Fool would be a Favourit* is acting in a play that is halted when its unappreciative audience decides to leave. Knowing only his cues, he fails to understand what is going on:

MAN. Master, Master, rise, rise.
YOUNG GUDGEN. That's not my cue, he's out.
MAN. The Princesse is gone.
YOUNG GUDGEN. Gone is not my cue neither.[79]

'Study' did not always happen in complete isolation—for the word referred both to private learning and learning with a teacher. It did not, however, tend to involve either the rest of

[76] Thomas Heywood, *The Royall King, and the Loyall Subject* (1637), C1$^a$; John Clavell, *The So[l]ddered Citizen*, ed. John Henry Pyle Pafford and W. W. Greg (Oxford, 1936), 74.
[77] James Shirley, *The Humorous Courtier*, ed. Marvin Morrillo (New York, 1979), 142.
[78] Thomas Middleton, *A Fair Quarrell* (1617), B4$^b$.
[79] Lodowick Carlell, *Two New Playes. viz. The Fool would be a Favourit . . . Osmond, the great Turk* (1657), 74.

the text or the other performers: when Alphonso helps the illiterate Medice study his part (in Chapman's *The Gentleman Usher*, 1.1), he is careful to shelter him from the other players; he makes sure that 'None but my selfe, and the Lord *Medice*' get to know the words of the speech before performance. Similarly in Middleton's *Your Five Gallants*, the boy is depicted as having studied with Fitsgrave but no one else (Taylbee: 'Is the boy perfect?' Fitsgrave: 'That's my credit sir, I warrant you').[80]

Tutored study was often called 'instruction'—the same word that was used in educational establishments, though, confusingly, the word 'rehearsal' might also be applied to it. Again, much as in schools and universities there were a number of different people involved in instructing the actors for every production, meaning that there was no single, unifying teacher. Artesia in Cosmo Manuche's *The Just General* (3.1) favours working with the playwright—'The Poet may instruct you',[81] but anyone could set up as an instructor. Domita in Philip Massinger's *The Roman Actor* (3.2) claims regally to know such a lot about performance that she herself has 'beene instructing | The Players how to act'.[82] Professional actors were naturally also involved in the instruction process. Boy players in adult companies were apprenticed to a sharer rather than to the company itself, and part of the job of that sharer was to teach the art of acting.[83] More generally, established actors instructed secondary actors: in Richard Brome's *The English Moore* (4.2) Arnold and Buzzard are 'Busy at rehearsal practising their parts', Arnold teaching Buzzard to play an idiot boy; in John Gee's *New Shreds*, though there is only one performer on the stage, there are

---

[80] George Chapman, *The Plays of George Chapman: The Comedies*, ed. Allan Holaday and Michael Kiernan et al., (Urbana, Ill., 1970), 145; Thomas Middleton, *Your Five Gallants* [1608], I2[b].

[81] Manuche, *General*, 30.

[82] Massinger, iii. 131.

[83] Gerard Eades Bentley, *The Profession of Player in Shakespeare's Time, 1590–1642* (Princeton, 1984), ch. 5. Players maintained guild memberships to certain 'trades', simply as a way of ensuring that they could take on apprentices (they were not legally allowed to do so as actors)—see Stephen Orgel, *Impersonations* (Cambridge, 1996), 61–4. G. W. Body in 'Players of Interludes in North Yorkshire in the Early Seventeenth Century', *North Yorkshire County Record Office Publications*, 3 (1976), 95–130 (103), relates how Thomas Pant, apprentice cordwainer under Robert and Christopher Simpson, took his masters to court for not teaching him his trade but training him 'for these three yeres in wandering in the country and playing of Interludes'.

'diverse others within the tiring-house that take a great deale of paines . . . to instruct the Actor'.[84] Burbage and Kempe's role as instructors in *Return from Parnassus* has already been discussed. Some players and some playwrights became recognized, established instructors; some were even so reputed for their ability to teach acting that they helped out for important theatrical occasions outside the playhouse. After Mulcaster, the respected schoolteacher-instructor, had left the Merchant Taylors' School, the boys had to apply for assistance when they needed to learn speeches for state visits. At one point 'by reason that the Company doubt their Schoolmasters and Scholars be not acquainted with such kind of entertainment' Ben Jonson was invited in to 'teach' a boy a speech to welcome the king; Heminges was brought in on another occasion 'for . . . direction of his boy that made the speech to His Majesty'; George Peele was sent to Christ Church, Oxford, to instruct the university actors; Munday was hired to 'direct' speeches that he had written for the court:

it is ordered that m^r Chamberlen shall pay vnto m^r Anthony Monday who was imployed for the devising of two speeches to be delivered to the Prince and for directions when my Lord Maior and Aldermen attended the prince the some of seauen and ffortie shilling*es* by him disbursed for diuers necessaries concerning the same preparacõn and ffowre pownd*es* six shillinges and ffowre pence for his paines and labour taken in the same     (5 June 1610)[85]

Instruction from the author of a play *amongst others* was relatively normal (Damplay in Jonson's *The Magnetic Lady* significantly asks a boy actor 'where's one o' your Masters, Sirrah, the Poet?'[86]). The playwright, though, was hardly in a position to teach every single actor his separate part; moreover, an actor might specifically object to being give authorial tuition. This happens in Richard Brome's *The Court Begger*, where Court-wit the writer assumes that Citwit's wife and boy will speak his passages 'as i'le instruct you', but Citwit refuses on the grounds that 'you have an ill tone to instruct in . . . you give your words no

[84] *Brome*, ii. 55; John Gee, *New Shreds of the Old Snare* (1624), 21.
[85] T. H. Vail Motter, *The School Drama in England* (London, 1929), 112; Boas, *University Drama*, 180; MS Corporation of London Records Office, Repertories of the Court of Aldermen, Re 29, fol. 233^r.
[86] *Jonson*, vi. 508.

grace'.[87] Nevertheless, a Theatrical Miscellany preserved at the Folger Shakespeare Library contains a portrait of 'the player' drawn in 1630, and headed 'The Poet only is his Tyrant'.[88] The poet a tyrant, and the actor his puppet—or, often, his parrot— were both commonplaces. Robert Greene calls actors 'Puppits . . . that speake from our mouths'; on another occasion his Tully tells Roscius (the actor) that 'of thy selfe thou canst say nothing', and warns him to 'disdain not thy tutor'; Samuel Rowlands's *Letting of Humours Blood* (1600) includes a poem addressed to poets, asking 'Will you stand spending your inuentions treasure, | To teach Stage parrets speake for pennie pleasure'?[89] That the poet created and the actor merely imitated are such ritual insults that it is easy not quite to realize what these statements portray about the nature of poet–actor instruction. If the actor is a puppet then he follows the motions of the author exactly; if he is a parrot, then not only is he copying the words of his poet, he is also copying his verbal emphases and cadence. On closer inspection it becomes clear that what a playwright did, if he had the chance to offer individual tuition, was what all the other instructors did: give a complete performance of the pronunciation and gestures required by the part, to be imitated by the actor. So John Davies, whose *Scourge of Folly* indicates that he was friendly with Shakespeare, Ben Jonson, Marston, and other contemporary playwrights, writes a poem to the actor asking:

> What *Peacocke* art thou prowd?
> Wherefore? because
> Thou *Parrat*-like canst speake what is taught thee.
> A *Poet* must teach thee from clause to clause
> Or thou wilt breake *Pronunciations* Lawes.[90]

When Hamlet tells his actor to 'Speake the speech . . . as I pronounc'd it to you' (*Ham.* 1849) (tellingly, 'as I taught thee' in Q1 [F2ᵃ], the 'thee' confirming that he refers to a single actor only), he means that he has 'instructed' the actor he is addressing—probably the one who is to speak his own 'dosen or

---

[87] *Brome*, i. 262.

[88] 'Theatrical Miscellany', Folger MS, T.b.1, 100.

[89] Robert Greene, *The Life and Complete Works*, ed. Alexander Grosart, 15 vols. (1881–86), xii. 144; viii. 132. 'To Poets' in Samuel Rowlands's *The Letting of Humours Blood in the Vaine* (1600), A3ᵃ.

[90] John Davies, *Microcosmos* (1603), 214.

sixteene lines' (*Ham.* 1577). The poet naturally taught action too. Edward Sharpham's *Cupids Whirligig* (1607) features the teacher Master Correction who declares that he has taken as many pains with his pupils 'as anie Poet whatsoeuer could have done, to make them answere vpon their Q. with good action, distinction, & deliberation'.[91]

Individual instruction meant that the entire learning process— even the discursive process—had happened by the time the group rehearsal was called: what an actor brought to rehearsal was not a part to be worked on, but a completed performance often bolstered by outside authority. At the same time, 'instruction' had left actors little opportunity to contribute anything of their own to their parts, and I will argue that they sometimes counteracted this by modifying their lines in performance, using extemporization and textual change as means of asserting themselves in their parts against the constraints of enforced action. Individual instruction gave mixed authority to the playwright involved in the production: it allowed him to settle particular performances but not all performances, so that he was responsible for threads running through the play (as were other instructors), but not responsible for the action of the whole. In fact no play can be linked conceptually to a single person—which explains why lexicographers had such difficulty determining who precisely was in charge: Rider's *Bibliotheca Scholastica* (1589) divides responsibility for a production between 'a writer or maker of comedies' (*comicus*); 'The master of the play' (*designator*); and 'He that setteth forth plaies' (*choragus*).[92]

Before leaving the actor, there is one more question that must be looked at: whether players performed many varied roles, or had one standard acting 'line'—contemporary texts, confusingly, seem to hint at both, and the matter is important, for acting a variety of parts requires more preparation than repeatedly acting one part in different plays. When Fernando asks 'what parts dost use to play?' (Middleton, *The Spanish Gipsie*, 4.2), or Thomas Heywood suggests that 'Actors should be men pick'd out

---

[91] Edward Sharpham, *Cupids Whirligig* (1607), I4ᵃ.

[92] The theatrical hierarchy in the classical theatre itself consisted of '*domini*' (the 'masters' of the troupe), '*conductores*' (who undertook a contract to produce the play) and '*choragus*' (the property-manager who hired out the costumes). See W. Beare, *The Roman Stage* (London, 1950), 158.

personable, according to the parts they present', or Ben Jonson writes of the death of 'Salomon Pavey', a boy player famous for his portrayal of old people, they are all claiming that there was a kind of typecasting in operation in the Elizabethan theatre.[93] On the other hand, there are also those suggestions that 'one man in his time playes many parts' (*As You Like It*, 1121); or that a single actor may have performed 'A foole, a coward, a traytor or cold cinique' (*The Roman Actor*, 4.2).[94] One problem is that some minor parts that 'want individuality' might be divided between several hirelings—as is the case in Massinger's *Believe As You List*, a play written for the King's Company. As the original cast list shows, a number of characters in Massinger's play are split between performers—the part of Demetrius, for instance, is played by 'Pattrick' and 'Rowland' when he is to speak, and 'Balls' when he is silent.[95] Nevertheless, a fair amount of typecasting does seem to have taken place amongst more major players, hinted at by the generic names so often initially given by playwrights to characters in their plays—'bastard', 'king', 'steward', 'nurse', 'fool', 'old lady' etc.—and so often meticulously removed by editors.[96] Such titles are matched by the division of actors in *Hamlet* into 'he that playes the King', 'the aduenturous Knight', 'the Lover', 'the humorous man' and 'the Clowne' (*Ham*. 1366). Certainly costumes on Henslowe's lists seem to be generic or symbolic, arguing for the existence of stock characters with stock dress. Probably, as Gerard Eades Bentley has suggested, there was some kind of typecasting in existence that was not completely consistent.[97] T. J. King makes the reasonable suggestion that the most important consideration in casting was not the type of role to be acted but the size of the part: the leading actors would get the largest roles.[98] Of course,

[93] Thomas Middleton, *The Spanish Gipsie* (1653), G3[b]; Thomas Heywood, *Apology for Actors* (1612), E3[a]; *Jonson*, viii. 77.

[94] *Massinger*, iii. 72. See also Thomas Overbury, *The Overburian Characters to which is added A Wife*, ed. W. J. Paylor (Oxford, 1936), 77.

[95] Philip Massinger, *Believe As You List*, ed. John Johnson (Oxford, 1927), pp. xxii, xxxiii.

[96] G. K. Hunter, 'Flatcaps and Bluecoats', *Essays and Studies*, 30 (1980), 25 n. Stock characters are not themselves proof for stock casting, but suggest a tendency towards typecasting in the theatre.

[97] Bentley, *Player*, 228.

[98] T. J. King, 'The King's Men on Stage: Actors and their Parts 1611–32' in G. R. Hibbard (ed.) *The Elizabethan Theatre IX* (Waterloo, 1981), 38.

this can be argued the other way round: the playwright writes the
largest part for the chief actor; there is certainly something to be
said for Baldwin's often criticized idea that 'the play was
regularly fitted to the company, not the company to the play'
(an idea acknowledged by *The Two Merry Milke-Maids* with its
insistence that 'every Writer must governe his Penne according
to the Capacitie of the Stage he writes too both in the Actor and
the Auditor').[99] As collected parts tended to be inherited *en
masse* from another actor, so they seem to have been regarded as
making up a coherent group: Joseph Taylor, for instance,
appears to have succeeded to Burbage's parts.[100] 'Inheritance'
might, of course, result in an actor having more than one distinct
acting 'line'; and a young boy whose 'line' was to play women
would have had to gather a new collection of adult male parts
when he grew up.[101] Acting within a 'line' and having a formula
that covered every performance made sense in a theatre in which
there was little preparation time: it is always easier to play
roughly the same part.

## Pronunciation and gesture

Study alone or in instruction consisted of establishing the correct
pronunciation and gesture for a play. Both were considered
separate entities following classical rhetorical tradition: Livy
relates that Livius Andronicus, when his voice gave way on
stage, employed a boy to sing for him, while he himself
concentrated on miming.[102] 'Action' (the physical side of
acting) included gesture and facial expression; 'pronunciation'
(the verbal side of acting) included the enunciation of words,
and the musical cadence in which they were spoken. Both were
taught at Cambridge, in the 'acting' (gesture) or 'repeating'

[99] T. W. Baldwin, *The Organization and Personnel of the Shakespearian Company* (Princeton, 1927), 197; *The Two Merry Milke-Maids* (1620), A2ª. *Iests to Make you Merry*, in Dekker, *Non-Dramatic Works*, ii. 282, depicts two emulous actors testing their superiority against each other by naming the 'good parts' they have been given.
[100] See Chambers, *Elizabethan Stage*, ii. 346.
[101] For a boy moving on to adult roles see Henry Glapthorne's 1639 'For *Ezekiel Fen* at his first Acting a Mans Part', in *The Plays and Poems*, ed. R. H. Shepherd, 2 vols. (1874), ii. 196. Peter Holland has shown how Restoration actors often had at least two distinct 'lines' in *The Ornament of Action* (Cambridge, 1979).
[102] Beare, *Roman Stage*, 211.

(pronunciation) chambers.[103] In performance the two were
separately evaluated by the audience—the Epilogue to Massinger's *Emperour of the East* worries whether the actor 'Hath giuen
you satisfaction, in his art | Of action and deliuery'.[104] Foreign
audiences could be diverted by the action of English actors
whose words they did not understand; and an audience for
whom there were no corrective spectacles for short-sight could
be entertained by what they heard—'sit in a full Theater, and
you will thinke you see so many lines drawne from the
circumference of so many eares, whiles the *Actor* is the
*Center*.'[105] As these two arts were separate, so they were separ-
able: an audience might 'say, | They only come to heare, not see
the Play, | Others to see it only, there have beene . . .'[106]

Heywood recommends that actors should either 'know how to
speake' or be able to 'speake well, though they vnderstand not
what'; either can 'by instructions be helped & amended'.[107] Rules
of pronunciation are set out clearly in school books and books on
oratory, and most acknowledge that actors use similar arts, some
with a sneer ('parasiticallie as stage plaiers vse'), and some with
muted praise ('In the substance of external action for most part
orators and stage-players agree').[108] Pronunciation involved
cadenced speech based on the identification and emphasis of
tropes; schoolboys were 'taught carefully, in which word the
Emphasis lyeth'; actors learnt 'to speake their parts emphatically
and to the life' (Richard Brome, *The Court Begger*, 2.1).[109]

The other skill was 'action'—the mimetic gestures that accompanied the words of a play. That there were conventions for
manifesting certain emotions is clear from the texts that try to
define what they are. The 'country man' who wrote *The Cyprian
Conqueror* (*c*.1633) gives a preface explaining the requisite
gestures for his play: 'in a sorrowful parte, yᵉ head must hang
downe; in a proud, yᵉ head must bee lofty; in an amorous, closed

[103] *REED: Cambridge*, 519, 530.
[104] *Massinger*, iii. 488.
[105] See Limon, *Gentlemen*, 1; Overbury, *Overburian Characters*, 76.
[106] Henry Glapthorne, *Ladies Privilege* (1640), A3ᵇ.
[107] Heywood, *Apology*, E3ᵃ.
[108] Abraham Fraunce, *The Arcadian Rhetorike* (1588), facs. ed. R. C. Alston
(Menston, 1969), 17ᵇ; Thomas Wright, *The Passions of the Mind in General* (1604),
179.
[109] John Brinsley, *Ludus Literarius* (1612), 213–14; *Brome*, i. 215.

eies, hanging downe lookes, & crossed armes, in a hastie, fuming, & scratching y$^e$ head &c'.[110] In such passages as this, it is, of course, difficult to sort the 'rules' from the 'conventions'. Clearly some stage actions simply mimicked social behaviour of the time, while others were contrived and required an audience capable of 'reading' them. The two are, in fact, separated in the famous manuals for the deaf, John Bulwer's *Chirologia* and *Chironomia* (1644): *Chirologia* shows the 'Natural' (instinctive) language of the hand, and *Chironomia*, the 'Art' or rules that govern 'Manuall Rhetorique'. But it is also clear that some stage action was artificial enough for actors to be able to do it 'wrongly'—which was why it had to be taught:

> But most men ouer-act, misse-act, or misse
> The action which to them peculiar is;
> And the more high the part is which they play,
> The more they misse in what they do or say.[111]

And as with pronunciation, 'correct' action consisted of using gestures to highlight important words: William Kempe, a schoolteacher, recommends that pupils of the age of 12 should learn 'the . . . gesture fit for euery word, sentence, and affection', or as Heywood put it, 'fit his phrases to his action, and his action to his phrase, and his pronuntiation to them both',[112] or as Hamlet recommended, 'Sute the Action to the Word, the Word to the Action' (*Ham.* 1865). How important this 'action' was is illustrated by the passage in *Titus Andronicus* in which Titus, who has cut off his own hand, is forced to rely on words alone without the requisite gestures: 'how can I grace my talke', he laments, 'Wanting a hand to giue it action?' (*TA* 2301).

Jonson carefully instructed boy players in speaking and gesture, and the results he achieved were particularly impressive. Robert Herrick goes so far as to imply that the whole of the acting profession ceased to function properly after Jonson's death, either in terms of action or pronunciation:

---

[110] BM MS Sloane 3709, fol. 8r, quoted Gurr, *Shakespearian Stage*, 100.
[111] 'To honest-gamesome Robin Armin' in John Davies, *The Complete Works,* ed. A. B. Grosart, 2 vols. (1878), ii. 60.
[112] William Kempe, *The Education of Children in Learning* (1588), G3$^a$ (sig. mislabelled C3$^a$); Heywood, *Apology*, C4$^b$.

After the rare Arch-Poet JOHNSON dy'd,
. . . men did strut, and stride, and stare, not act.
Then temper flew from words; and men did squeake.
Looke red, and blow, and bluster, but not speake.[113]

Late in life Jonson had to deal with the King's Company, who were less pliant than his boy actors. He had, by this time, had a stroke, and their lack of subservience, combined with his inability to control all that they did, led him to condemn the production after his play was badly received: *The New Inne* was, according to its title-page, 'A COMŒDY . . . neuer acted, but most negligently play'd, by some, the Kings Seruants'. The insult is in the suggestion that the formalities of properly learnt and established gesture, 'action', were above these performers—they simply 'played'.

The interpretation of a text into the appropriate pronunciation and gesture involved breaking the script down into relevant 'passions' (the emotional stuff of tragedy): a term often used to describe the art of acting at the time was 'passionating'. Actors' skill was tested by their ability to illustrate 'the passions', love, grief, horror, fear etc., as Hamlet makes clear when he asks the player to perform 'a passionate speech' as a way of giving the court 'a tast of your quality': 'weele have a speech straite, come give us a tast of your quality, come a passionate speech' (*Ham.* 1476). Later, when he gives the player some serious acting advice, he frames it in terms of dealing temperately with 'the verie Torrent, Tempest, and (as I may say) the Whirle-winde of Passion' (*Ham.* 1853). The whole idea of performing the passions badly is sent up by Falstaff in *1 Henry IV*. Preparing to play-act the part of Henry IV in a game with Hal, Falstaff tries to give the appearance of passion rather than act it, demanding 'a Cup of Sacke' in order to redden his eyes so that 'it may be thought I haue wept, for I must speake in passion, and I will doe it in King *Cambyses* vaine' (*1HIV 1341*). Reading a part into changeable passions goes some way towards explaining the high emotional charge of plays at the time; the respect for speedy transitions between one passion and another gives a reason for the rapidity with which emotions suddenly change in some of the most famous tragedies: Othello's and Leontes' sudden jealousy;

---

[113] Robert Herrick, *The Poetical Works*, ed. L. C. Martin (Oxford, 1956), 150.

Lear's sudden rage.[114] The application of pronunciation and gesture in private study and instruction to parts meant that the actor was focused entirely on the words in his text; his performance came from what he himself was saying, without reference to the things said to him or about him by other people.

### The group rehearsal

Group rehearsal(s) ideally capped the preparation period, though the question remains open as to how many preceded a new play. Dawes is asked to attend 'all suche rehearsall' that is 'given publickly out', and clearly this rehearsal is 'general' (it is announced to the whole company) and important (fines of 12 pence are levied for not attending it).[115] Such rehearsal is mentioned again in a contract drawn up by Henslowe and Jacob Meade with Nathan Field's company, to 'pay vnto them all suche somes of monny as shall com*m*e vnto their hand*es* v[ppon receipt of] any forfectures for rehearsall*es* or suche like payment*es*'.[116] The plural might suggest more than one rehearsal—or the possibility of more than one rehearsal—though evidence is mixed on the subject. *Histriomastix* (4.1) depicts a group rehearsal at which a fine is imposed—Posthaste the poet will have to pay 12 pence for arriving late. In *Histriomastix*, this is both the first and the only general rehearsal the actors will have; and certainly stress on a final, singular kind of rehearsal is given by Sir Henry Wotton when he writes of the new play 'which they are to repeat to-morrow in the afternoon' in preparation for acting it 'publicly . . . on Wednesday'.[117] Both university and provincial players had as a rule only one general rehearsal, and I am inclined to think that the same is roughly true also of the public theatre. Plays that have subplots involving mounting a drama from scratch, though dubious individually as sources, are collectively lax in their attitude to full company rehearsals. There is no group rehearsal for the internal plays in Kyd's *Spanish Tragedy*; Jonson's

[114] Fully discussed in ch. 1 of Joseph R. Roach's *The Player's Passion* (Newark, Del., 1985).
[115] Greg, *Henslowe Papers*, iii. 124. Though this fine is light in comparison to the £40 charged for taking costumes out of the theatre.
[116] Greg, *Henslowe Papers*, iii. 24. I have conjecturally supplied the missing words.
[117] Bentley, *Jacobean and Caroline Stage*, ii. 552.

*Cynthia's Revels*; Beaumont and Fletcher's *Maid in the Mill;* Chapman's *The Gentleman Usher*, or Carlell's *The Fool would be a Favourite*; and in Shakespeare's *Midsummer Night's Dream*, and Marston's *Histriomastix* one rehearsal only is held, and that is not completed. Brome's *A Jovial Crew* (5.1), has performance seemingly preceded only by 'study', though the actors are told the story they are going to play in; Middleton's *Your Five Gallants* includes a single collective rehearsal.[118] In short, there is no evidence to indicate that more than one group rehearsal was normal. Two points must however be made here. One is that a system of instantly changeable repertory meant that if a play proved unready for performance, another could always be put on in its place: a play thus did not necessarily receive a fixed amount of group rehearsal, but as much as was appropriate (or possible). The other is that the appropriate number of collective rehearsals necessary could occasionally be as little as none. The time of the year when the play was got up would also have made a difference. Holidays certainly allowed the opportunity for more general rehearsal, and it may be that plays prepared over the vacation were better practised than those prepared within the season. How general even 'general rehearsal' ever was is another question: it is unclear whether minor hirelings attended group rehearsal; walk-ons did not—Killigrew told Pepys that as a child he would go to the Red Bull and 'when the man cried to the boys, "Who will go and be a divell, and he shall see the play for nothing?"' he would take the role and get into the play free.[119]

Partial rehearsals which seem to equate to the provincial players' one or two 'reherses' did also take place. In Chapman's *The Widdowes Teares* Laodice is attending more rehearsals of her segment with Hylus than Argus thinks necessary—'Pray *Venus* my yong Ladie | *Laodice* haue not some little prick of *Cupid* in her, shee's so | diligent at's rehearsall' (3.2).[120] And partial rehearsals of group 'moments'—songs, dances, sword-fights, and slapstick—were all that it was absolutely *necessary* to rehearse before a production, as another Chapman play, *The*

---

[118] Middleton, *Your Five Gallants*, I1a–I2b; *Brome*, iii. 437: 'I'll undertake . . . these *Players* . . . in a device which they have already studied.'

[119] Samuel Pepys, *The Diary*, ed. Robert Latham and William Matthews, 11 vols. (London, 1970–1983), iii. 243–4. For a list of stage 'mutes' see 'Shakespeare's Supers' in W. J. Lawrence, *Those Nut-Cracking Elizabethans* (London, 1935), 44–58.

[120] Chapman, *The Plays*, 513.

*Gentleman Usher* (1.2), illustrates. There each actor has learnt his separate part, Medice under the instruction of Alphonso, the others alone. Their questions to one another before performance again illustrate that no collective rehearsal has been held (Bassiolo: 'Are all parts perfect?' Sarpego: 'One I know there is.' Lasso: 'And that is yours.' Sarpego: 'Well guest in earnest Lord'), but the boys who need to sing the song are heard rehearsing their bit together (*'Re mi fa sol la?'*), earning the congratulations of Lasso: 'O they are practising; good boyes, well done'. Similarly in Middleton and Rowley's *The Changeling* Lollio and Alibus divide their rehearsal of the mad dances, Alibus being sent off to 'looke . . . to the madmens Morris', Lollio being 'let . . . alone with the other [the fools].'[121]

## Time of group rehearsal

Group rehearsals could not have been held in the evening—at least on the public theatre stage—for the same reason that performances could not: it would be dark. Nor does testimony suggest that there was any practice after the play, all indications being that the actors went straight to dine in the taverns afterwards: Gayton refers to the people who court the players 'to re-act the same matters in the Tavernes' after performances; the Drawer in Nathan Field's *Amends for Ladies* apologizes for the fact that the Gentlewomen have not yet arrived, explaining that '[Besse Turnups] beleeues they | sup with the Players' (3.4).[122]

For the couple of hours preceding performance, there could be no rehearsal on the stage, as the theatres were already filling with people. John Holles wrote to the Earl of Somerset about a trip to the Globe in 1624 'w*h*ich hows I found so thronged, y*a*t by scores yei came away for want of place, thou as yet little past one'.[123]

[121] Thomas Middleton and William Rowley, *The Changeling* (1653), G2[b].
[122] Gayton, *Pleasant Notes*, 140; Nathan Field, *Amends for Ladies* (1618), E3[b]. See also Wentworth Smith, *The Hector of Germany* (1615), H4[a].
[123] William Ingram, 'The Early Career of James Burbage' in C. E. McGee (ed.) *The Elizabethan Theatre X* (Waterloo, 1983), 66; Gayton in *Pleasant Notes*, 14 refers to 'the sleeper in the empty Theater; who coming before the Play, or Auditors, dream'd of the passages, and laugh'd, clapp'd, hiss'd, and stamp'd, as if the Players had been enter'd'. See also T. Fairman Ordish, *Early London Theatres* (1894; London, 1971), 59.

There is, however, a reference to an afternoon rehearsal in the letter by Sir Henry Wotton quoted earlier.[124]

Generally, though, breakfast time seems to have been the most available period of the day for rehearsal, just as it had been for the provincial players. Edwin Booth, who provided the stolid writer of the Variorum *Othello* with his own flamboyantly thespian 'actor's copy' of the play, is responsible for glossing the Duke's 'At nine i'th'morning, here wee'l meete againe' (1.3.308) with the footnote 'Probably the hour of rehearsal in Shakespeare's time'; however as that is in fact the rehearsal hour that the Spanish actors kept, he may even be correct.[125]

*Place of general and partial rehearsals*

At St Johns Palace, London, plays were put on for the Master of the Revels in a special room 'where the Rehersalls be made'; similarly in Cambridge, special permanent rehearsal rooms were allocated in Trinity College and Clare.[126] At Trinity College the rehearsal room became the tiring chamber during actual performances, and the same seems to have been true in reverse in the public theatre, where tiring rooms could double as rehearsal chambers: Ben Jonson's 'repeating head' has gone all to pieces in the tiring room; and in the anonymous *Lady Alimony* (1.3) complaints are made about a 'proud . . . Fellow' who has just come into the tiring room and so 'disturbs' the actors' 'preparation'.[127] Tiring rooms were small, however, and the type of rehearsal that occurred in them may have taken the form only of 'instruction'. Some kind of collective rehearsal on the stage itself before performance would make practical sense: perhaps Holmes is right in his suggestion that the Swan drawing, with its full stage and empty auditorium, illustrates a group rehearsal in progress.[128]

---

[124] Bentley, *Jacobean and Caroline Stage*, ii. 552.
[125] William Shakespeare, *A New Variorum Othello*, ed. Horace Howard Furness (1886), 78; Rennert, *The Spanish Stage*, 159.
[126] Feuillerat, *Documents*, T III 71; Alan H. Nelson, *Early Cambridge Theatres* (Cambridge, 1994), 43, 74.
[127] *Jonson*, vi. 281; *Lady Alimony* (1659), A4[b].
[128] Martin Holmes, 'A New Theory about The Swan Drawing', *TN* 10 (1955), 80–3.

REHEARSAL, WRITING, AND REVISION

*The book-holder (prompter)*

Proper names inserted in manuscript into prompt-books are usually those of hired men, and the explanation for this seems to be that the book-holder was responsible for the allocation of minor parts, an idea put forward by the reliable Bentley, as well as by the more wayward King.[129] Authorial stage directions such as that in *Alcazar* (3.1) which states 'manet Stukley and another' do not so much show, as has been argued, that the playwright is indifferent as to which actor plays which small part, but that he recognizes where his own preserve ends and the book-holder's begins.[130] The prompter had a minor involvement in casting. He was also a potential instructor, indicated in a roundabout way in John Ford's *Broken Heart*, when Prophilus avoids repeating his old vows or studying new ones, with the declaration that should he do so, 'I should but repeat a lesson | Oft conn'd without a prompter'.[131] When, in the Prelude to *Thorny Abbey*, the Prompter makes an attempt to tell the audience the full story of the play, he relates what he has gathered from the actors' 'studied parts': he seems to know parts, not the production.[132] That same play gives a brief picture of what the book-holder might do in individual rehearsal.

PROMPTER. Sirrah! go on: *We're to present you—*
FOOL. I won't have't non-sence *We're to present you*—but I'le hav't *I am to present you.*[133]

Here the fool is shown, interestingly, appealing for authority to change his lines from the prompter. And indeed at the time the prompter seems to have been recognized as being as much a reformer of the text, as a teacher of it. Edward Knight, book-

---

[129] Bentley, *Player*, 84, King, 'The King's Men' in *Elizabethan Theatre IX*, 22.

[130] Bernard Beckerman, 'Theatrical Plots and Elizabethan Stage Practice' in W. R. Elton and William B. Long (eds.), *Shakespeare and Dramatic Tradition: Essays in Honor of S. F. Johnson* (Newark, Del., 1989), 118.

[131] John Ford, *The Broken Heart* (1633), C1ᵇ-C2ᵃ.

[132] William M. Baillie (ed.), *A Choice Ternary of English Plays* (Binghamton, NY, 1984), 45. Baillie gives a late Commonwealth date for this prologue, but as theatres were closed during the time of Cromwell, the prologue probably continues to reflect Renaissance practice.            [133] Baillie (ed.), *Choice Ternary*, 44.

holder for the King's Company, was asked to 'purge' the actors' parts by the Master of the Revels, Henry Herbert, who also thanked him for amendments that he had already made to '[save] mee labour'.[134] In the prompt-book of Massinger's *Believe as You List* there are clear marks of deletion made by the book-holder, who has also revised over what he takes to be errors in the text itself; in the *Thomas More* manuscript, the reviser is again apparently the book-keeper, for he marks up the prompt-book with casting suggestions (Scott McMillin interprets this as 'tolerable evidence' that the revisers cast minor characters in the play as they worked[135]). As the book-holder had charge of the prompt-book, these revisions will have been given the authority of a place in the acting text, and will have been included in the parts that were handed out to actors. His revisions, therefore, will have been sanctioned by such group or partial rehearsal as there was, and by performance. Before performance, then, the prompter was involved in casting, probably helped out with instruction, and was undoubtedly a small-scale reviser of the text.

## *The manager*

Professional theatre plays were, like university and country plays, under the charge of a 'manager', but this figure was nothing like a director. A manager was not involved with a play intellectually or conceptually, but was in charge of practical matters: his job was, variously, to teach actors, to oversee finances, to make travelling arrangements, to 'represent' the company as its public face, to take responsibility for costumes, and—often—to revise texts before performance.

In professional touring groups there was usually a 'lead player' who made arrangements and did a certain amount of teaching: James Burbage, who was a leading member of the Earl of Leicester's Company, before establishing The Theatre in London, seems to have overseen productions in this manner.[136] This continued in the professional theatres, despite

[134] Chambers, *Shakespeare*, i. 117; Bawcutt, *Censorship*, 183.
[135] Chambers, *Shakespeare*, i. 117; McMillin, *Elizabethan Theatre*, 42.
[136] Ordish, *Early London Theatres*, 50.

the fact that companies were run in very different ways: some
worked on a system that was more 'democratic'—the King's
Company, for instance, was run by a group of sharers; some—
such as boy companies—were run by autocratic impresarios;
between the two were companies like the Admiral's at the Rose—
adult players who were dependent on a financier | theatre-
owner.[137] As Andrew Gurr illustrates, companies run by 'sharers'
became rarer: they were replaced by landlord-managers such as
the ex-players Christopher Beeston and Richard Gunnell, or
their leading players took charge. At the same time, Gurr also
points out that even Henslowe had taken advice from two of the
principal sharers in his company over theatrical matters,[138] and it
seems clear that from the very first each company had one or
two principal actors to be its public representatives. These
representatives, like Restoration/eighteenth-century actor-managers, were also regular instructors in their respective companies. John Heminges, for instance, was 'Player and
Housekeeper' to the King's Company, received court payments, paid the Master of the Revels, and at the same time
was referred to in a jokey epigram as 'God' over Burbage
('Fear not Burbage, heaven's angry rod | When thy fellows are
angels and old Heminges is God').[139] In 1607, the Merchant
Taylors' School obtained Heminges's services to help train the
boys for a performance in front of King James (see above, 'Parts
and Study'); Joseph Taylor, who, with John Lowin, succeeded
Heminges, was similarly treated as an expert in instruction when
he was described by John Pory as 'the prime actor at the Globe'
and asked to teach 'action' to Henrietta Maria and her ladies.[140]
In 1637 the Lord Chamberlain warned the Stationers' Company
that before printing plays they should get written certificates of
approval from various named authority figures within theatrical
troupes: Lowin and Taylor for the King's Company, Christopher
Beeston for the King's and Queen's Young Company, or 'such
other persons as shall from time to time have the direction of
those companies'.[141]

These managerial figures seem particularly to have been
involved in actor-training; several of them eventually formalized

[137] Gurr, *Companies*, 9.                    [138] Ibid. 90.
[139] *MSC: II.iii*, ed. W. W. Greg (Oxford, 1931), 369; Bentley, *Player*, 151, 155.
[140] Motter, *School Drama*, 112; Bentley, *Player*, 61.          [141] Ibid. 163.

their manner of educating actors by running their own training
theatres. Richard Gunnell, an ex-actor, and William Blagrave,
deputy to the Master of the Revels, built a playhouse and set up a
boy company, the King's Revels, which functioned like a nursery
to the Blackfriars Theatre. It was finally taken over by Richard
Heton, who himself provided an ambitious set of papers in which
he laid out the powers he wanted to have: he intended to 'select,
order, direct, set up and govern' his company of actors.[142]
William Beeston set himself up as 'Governor & Instructer' for a
group that became named the 'Beeston Boys' after him, taking on
apprentices 'to instruct them in the quality of acting and fitting
them for the stage'.[143] He was later described by Brome the
playwright in his *Court Begger* as the man

by whose care and directions this Stage is govern'd, who has for many
yeares . . . directed Poets to write and Players to speak till he traind up
these youths here to what they are now. I some of 'em from before they
were able to say a grace of two lines long to have such parts in their
pates then would fill so many Dryfats.[144]

But another aspect of the managerial function is made clear by
the way Beeston treated his playwrights. Like the country
managers, Beeston took it upon himself to revise what the
poets produced. When Henry Herbert complained to Beeston
about 'impersonations of lords and others of the court' in James
Shirley's *The Ball*, Beeston promised him that 'many things
which I found faulte withall should be left out, and that he
would not suffer it to be done by the poett any more, who
deserves to be punisht'.[145] Herbert also records how an old play
was 'new written or forbisht by Mr. Biston'.[146] The job of
adaptor was also taken on by Taylor, the actor-manager for

[142] Sturgess, *Jacobean Private Theatre*, 63; Bentley, *Player*, 173.

[143] Gurr, *Shakespearian Stage*, 65; Bentley, *Player*, 144.

[144] *Court Begger* in *Brome*, i. 272. The 'instruction' that Beeston offered became
transmuted into the directorial duties of his successor Davenant whose job was 'to
govern, order, and dispose of [the actors] for action and presentments'—see Bentley,
*Player*, 142. Brome's Davenant figure (*Court Begger*, II.i) declares that he will
'procure a Patent for my selfe to have the onely priviledge to give instructions to
all the actors in the City, (especially the younger sort) the better to enable them to
speake their parts emphatically and to the life'—see *Brome*, i. 215. For an identification of 'Court-wit' with Davenant see Martin Butler, *Theatre and Crisis 1632–1642*
(Cambridge, 1984), 220.

[145] Bawcutt, *Censorship*, 177.                                  [146] Ibid. 174.

the King's Company after Heminges. He is thanked for what he has done to Fletcher's *Faithful Shepherdess* in the 1634 edition of that play: he has 'cur'd' the play from 'her courser rents, | And deckt her new with fresh habiliments . . .'[147]—in other words, he has revamped the play by revising it and revamped the performance by giving the play new costumes. The managerial task, as later, was actually a glorified version of the prompter's task: to ready the actors for the play, and the play for the actors.

*The author*

The poet's name did not feature on playbills for the Elizabethan theatre: he was not publicly of particular importance. Not until 4 March 1698/9 did Dryden record that he had seen an author's name in a bill—'a new manner of proceeding, at least in England'.[148] Nevertheless, playwrights were often involved with the preparation of their plays on some level. Middleton perhaps lost a Cambridge Fellowship ('his deponent . . . thinkethe he hath') in order to spend his time 'in London daylie accompaninge the players'.[149] A non-actor poet such as Middleton, was, presumably, bound to his production by a financial incentive of some kind—either having a legal contract with the acting company, or waiting on the promise of revenue from a benefit performance.

Almost all playwrights with any say in production at all were concerned with the casting of major characters. Particularly the first time a play was performed, the author was useful; even authors who were not men-of-the-theatre (and Bentley defines only fourteen as being completely 'professional'[150]) seem to have been given the first shot at casting the play. This initial participation made sense, for generally an author had written for a particular company, and had certain actors in mind for each part. 'Your Poets take great paines to make your parts fit for your mouthes' declares *Ratseis Ghost*; Gayton similarly jokes about

[147] Bentley, *Jacobean and Caroline Stage*, ii. 552.
[148] John Dryden, *The Letters*, ed. Charles E. Ward (1942; New York, 1965), 113.
[149] G. Phialas, 'Middleton's Early Contact with the Law', *SP* 52 (1955), 186–94 (192). Middleton's attitude towards his position is illustrated in his *Spanish Gipsie* G3ᵃ when Sancho, introducing his group of strolling players to Fernando, counts his number as nine. 'Nine!' replies Fernando, ' . . . you are ten sure'. 'That's our Poet,' explains Soto, 'he stands for a Cipher.'        [150] Bentley, *Dramatist*, 37.

'the Poets of the Fortune and Red Bull', who 'made their lines proportionable' to the tear-throat actors.[151] Well-behaved actors, as Middleton depicts them, 'submit always to the Writers wits' and do not 'envy one another for best parts' (*No Wit/Help like a Womans*, 3.1). There were plenty of actors who were not quite so humble: Donella in Shirley's *The Bird in a Cage* (4.2) wonders if the princess's companions will 'quarrell About the parts, like your spruce Actor'; while the epilogue to Massinger's *Emperour of the East* complains that 'The maker did conferre his Emperours part' on the main actor by force.[152] The acceptance of playwrights as casting authorities was widespread enough to be commonplace; Sir Walter Raleigh, in a theatrical metaphor in which God is 'the Author of all our tragedies', also allots Him the job of appointing us 'all the parts we play', in as impartial a manner as possible (*History of the World*).[153] But the author does not always come best out of the process. Signior Multecarni, a parody-poet based on Ben Jonson[154] in John Suckling's *The Sad One* (4.5), tries to arrange the doubling between two of the actors without thinking through the consequences for the play:

MULTECARNI. Well, if there be no remedy one must act two parts;
   *Rosselio* shall be the Fool and the Lord,
   And *Tisso* the Citizen and the Cuckold.

---

[151] *Ratseis Ghost* (1605), A3[b]; Gayton, *Pleasant Notes*, 24.

[152] *No Wit/ Help like a Womans* (1657), 78; James Shirley, *The Bird in a Cage* (1633), G4[b]. Massinger, iii. 488. 'Maker' is 'playmaker', a word that preceded 'playwright' but means exactly the same thing. OED quotes the first recorded use of 'playwright' as 1687, though in fact 'Play-Rights' are referred to in Thomas Goffe's *The Careles Shepherdess* (1656), 6. For actors quarrelling about casting, see also *Histriomastix* (4.1) in Marston, iii. 283; *MND* (347); Munday, *John a Kent*, 12. In Rawlins, *Rebellion*, I2[a–b], the Third Taylor tries to force his fellow actors to cast him not only as the Ghost, but also as Heironimo and Horatio in *The Spanish Tragedy*; For dissatisfaction with parts see Marston, i. 7–8 and James Shirley, *The Dukes Mistris* (1638), K4[b]: 'I have but plaid the part, which | Was most against my *Genius*, of any that ever I | Acted in my life'.

[153] Quoted in Thomas B. Stroup, *Microcosmos* (Lexington, Ky., 1965), 10. Hart in 'Did Shakespeare Produce', 177, imagines that he has a piece of 'direct evidence' to show that a playwright had no involvement with his production. He quotes Robert Armin's introduction to *The History of the Two Maids of Moreclack*: 'I would have againe inacted Iohn myselfe but . . . I cannot do as I would'. The explanation for this, as David Wiles, *Shakespeare's Clown* (Cambridge, 1987), 142, points out, is that when Armin published the work in 1609, the theatres were closed in a plague scare and the King's Revels company had gone bankrupt—neither Armin nor anyone else was able to act at the time.

[154] John Suckling, *The Works*, ed. L. A. Beaurline (Oxford, 1971), p. ix.

1 ACTOR. That cannot be, Signior, you know,
One still comes in, when the other goes out.
MULTECARNI. By *Jove* 'tis true; let me see,
We'll contrive it, the Lord and the Userer,
The Citizen and the Polititian,
And sure they never are together.[155]

Perhaps authorial involvement was not always appreciated by the actors.

Over time, the necessity for authorial participation in productions decreased: at the Rose towards the end of century, the Admiral's Company revived plays whose authors had been dead for some years.[156] But given that revivals were supposed to be as like the original as possible, a poet, having helped out once to set the play going, would never, anyway, be needed again; besides, the 'manager' could always prepare every aspect of the play from the beginning. Such would have been the case when Henslowe bought *The Wise Man of West Chester* (probably *John a Kent*) from the Lord Admiral's Company without the knowledge of its author, Munday.[157]

After casting, which often seems to have been decided during the 'reading', the playwright's involvement in production might, like Daborne's, come to an end. In that case either the manager or an 'attached' playwright would see the play to the stage. *The Traytor*, for instance, was described in the seventeenth century as a tragedy that 'was suppos'd to be *Shirly*'s, but he only usher'd it on to the Stage; The Authour of it was one Mr. *Rivers*': Shirley took on the job of playwright-in-charge for Rivers's text.[158] 'Attached' authors naturally kept up their involvement with their own plays, giving instruction to the major performers as described above. Affectionately looking back at the earlier stage from after the Interregnum, Richard Flecknoe writes of the ideal authors (Shakespeare, Jonson, Beaumont, and Fletcher) and their consummate, subservient actors (Burbage and Alleyn): 'It was the happiness of the Actors of those Times

---

[155] *Suckling*, 26.
[156] David Bradley, *From Text to Performance in the Elizabethan Theatre: Preparing the Play for the Stage* (Cambridge, 1992), 1.
[157] Bentley, *Dramatist*, 83.
[158] See Milhous and Hume, 'Attribution Problems', 5–39; *The Gentlemen's Journal*, Apr. 1692, 21.

to have such Poets . . . to instruct them, and write for them; and no less of those poets to have such docile and excellent Actors to Act their playes.'[159]

Playwrights who were very involved also took over practical aspects of the performance, accepting the role otherwise held by the manager. Details of this are easier to find for boy productions than adult ones, possibly because boys were more carefully prepared. Certainly in Jonson's *Cynthia's Revels* the boys ironically relate that they have specifically not had the attention of the playwright in the following instances: 'to prompt vs aloud, stampe at the booke-holder, sweare for our properties, curse the poor tire-man, raile the musicke out of tune'.[160] These are the very actions that Jonson engages in by his own admission in *The Staple of Newes*. Gossip Mirth describes 'the Poet' having a fit of hysterics:

he is within . . . i' the Tiring-house . . . rowling himself up and downe . . .
He doth sit like an vnbrac'd Drum with one of his heads beaten out;
For, that you must note, a *Poet* hath two heads, . . . one for making, the other repeating, and his repeating head is all to pieces; . . . hee hath torne the booke in a *Poeticall* fury, and put himselfe to silence in dead *Sacke*'[161]

A few pieces of sideways information seem to imply that Shakespeare, like Jonson, was 'on hand' as Gurr carefully phrases it, when *2* and *3 Henry VI* and *Richard III* were staged. The 'bad' Quarto stage directions that indicate that Somerset died under the Castle inn-sign in *2 Henry VI*, and that Clifford was wounded with an arrow in the neck in *3 Henry VI*, both suggest that extra-textual information was given to the actors by someone who knew the Holinshed source well; as does the fact that Richard III had 'his hand continual on his dagger' (as an epitaph in praise of Burbage's performance has it), also a detail from Holinshed.[162] The last instance shows no more than

---

[159] Richard Flecknoe, *Love's Kingdom . . . with a short Treatise of the English Stage* (1664), G6[b]. Flecknoe has dubious authority: he had become bitter about the Restoration theatre when almost all his plays were rejected, and is clearly painting an idealized picture of the past in his *Treatise*; nevertheless he may also have had access to information about the Elizabethan theatre lost to us—his assertion that Shakespeare instructed players is backed up by Downes, *Roscius*, 51, 55; that Jonson was a good instructor is maintained by John Aubrey, *Brief Lives*, ed. Oliver Lawson Dick (1949; London, 1962), 334.
[160] *Jonson*, iv. 40.     [161] Ibid. vi. 281.     [162] Gurr, *Companies*, 271.

that Burbage was individually rehearsed by the author; the first two, however, suggest Shakespeare's practical input into the performance. Shakespeare and Jonson, in all probability, oversaw whatever collective rehearsal there was. Yet were this to have been the case, what would it mean? Being in charge of collective rehearsal meant, as suggested by Jonson above, taking charge of properties, of music, of clothes—it meant 'managing' the production. The author's 'creative' contributions, as should now be clear, were made largely during individual instruction.

And yet, as has also been established, individual instruction involved numerous different people. So how could authors 'direct'? In fact, playwrights, unable to convey too much by word of mouth, seem to have enwrapped their 'direction' into the form in which they wrote their plays in the first place: they produced texts that, divided in parts, would bring about the action required in performance—without the actor necessarily needing to understand what is going on. One instance of this is the 'premature' or 'false' cue—the part that apparently gives the actor who is to speak his cue too early. 'Premature' cues bare all the hallmarks of deliberate scripting—in that the surrounding text anticipates and provides for them. Shakespeare's *Merchant of Venice*, 3.3 (*MV* 1704) contains a clear example of premature cueing. Solanio's first cue for the scene is 'have my bond'; his part as received for that cue will have looked something like this:

*Solanio*
——————————————————————haue my bond.
    It is the most impenetrable curre
    That euer kept with men.

Shylock's preceding speeches include four premature cues before the real one. So that each time 'Solanio' heard the cue, he will have tried to respond, and each time Shylock will have cut him short with demands that he shut up: 'I will not hear thee speak'. Indeed, reading the text without an awareness of the cueing system makes Shylock's speech nonsense: why does he keep demanding silence when he is the only one talking? 'Have my bond' was Solanio's cue, and whenever the actor heard that formula he will have tried to put in with his response. Here is the passage, with the premature cues in italics:

SHYLOCKE. Ile *haue my bond*, speake not against my bond,
   I haue sworne an oath that I will *haue my bond*:
   Thou call'sdt me dog before thou hadst a cause,
   But since I am a dog, beware my phangs . . .
   Ile *haue my bond*, I will not heare thee speake,
   Ile *haue my bond*, and therefore speake no more.
   Ile not be made a soft and dull ey'd foole,
   To shake the head, relent, and sigh, and yeeld
   To Christian intercessors: follow not,
   Speaking, I will *haue my bond*.
SOLANIO. It is the most impenetrable curre
   That ever kept with men.

*(MV* 1690–1705)

Weighed down with the irritation and embarrassment of repeated false cues, the actor playing Solanio will have been wrought to a pitch of uncompromising anger by the time he was actually permitted to speak. The interruption and the shouting down are provided for by the part, and the anger required, rather than being 'directed' in advance, is created in performance.[163]

Another set of two—perhaps three—false cues along the same lines occurs in a conversation in Shakespeare's *Romeo and Juliet* (1.3) between the Nurse, Juliet, and Juliet's mother (the 'Old Lady'). The premature cue for the 'Old Lady' and for Juliet is 'and said I' on hearing which 'Old Lady' is to say 'Inough of this, I pray thee hold thy peace', and Juliet is to say 'And stint thou too, I pray thee *Nurse*, say I':

NURSE. . . . for euen the day before she broke her brow, & then my
   Husband God be with his soule, a was a merrie man, tooke vp the
   Child, yea quoth hee, doest thou fall vpon thy face? thou wilt fall
   backeward when thou hast more wit, wilt thou not Iule? And by my
   holy-dam, the pretty wretch lefte crying, *& said I*: to see now how a
   Iest shall come about. I warrant, & I shall liue a thousand yeares, I
   neuer should forget it: wilt thou not Iulet quoth he? and pretty foole it
   stinted, *and said I.*

---

[163] Premature cues of the same tenor occur in *Jovial Crew* (5.1), *Brome*, iii. 433. Throughout the scene Martin continually tries to say something to Justice Clack, and, throughout, Justice Clack speaks over him: '*CLACK:* . . . Provided, I say (*as I said before*) that she be safe, that is to say, uncorrupted, undefiled; that is to say—*as I said before*. *MARTIN:* Mine intent, Sir, and my onely way—*CLACK:* Nay, if we both speak together, how shall we hear one another? *as I said before.* Your intent, and your onely way, you would ha' said, was to run away with her . . .'.

OLD LADY. Inough of this, I pray thee hold thy peace.

NURSE. Yes Madam, yet I cannot chuse but laugh, to thinke it should leaue crying, *& say I:* and yet I warrant it had vpon it brow, a bumpe as big as a young Cockrels stone? A perilous knock, and it cryed bitterly. Yea quoth my husband, fall'st vpon thy face, thou wilt fall back-ward when thou commest to age: wilt thou not Iule? It stinted: *and said I.*

JULIET. And stint thou too, I pray thee Nurse, say I.

(*Rom.* 387–405)

One last Shakespearian example, full of internal ironies, is the rehearsal of the mechanicals in *A Midsummer Night's Dream* (3.1). Bottom is playing Pyramus, and his cue is 'never tyre', so that the Bottom/Pyramus actor's part for this point in the scene will have been:

*Pyramus*

————————————————- never tyre:

If I were faire, Thisby, I were onely thine.

And here is the full text of the scene:

THISBE. . . . As true as truest horse, that yet would *never tyre*,
Ile meete thee Piramus, at Ninnies toombe.

QUINCE. Ninus toombe man: why, you must not speake that yet; that you answere to Piramus: you speake all your part at once, cues and all. Piramus enter, your cue is past; it is *never tyre.*

THISBE. O, as true as truest horse, that yet would *never tyre:*

PYRAMUS. If I were faire, Thisby, I were onely thine.

(*MND* 908–17)

Keen Pyramus wrongly enters three times on his cue of 'never tyre'; indeed, the very words with which Quince chides him for neglecting his cue, 'your cue is past; it is never tyre', give him another premature cue. After Quince's 'never tyre', both Thisbe and Pyramus, who now both have 'never tyre' as their next cue, will start speaking. The whole section is, of course, dedicated to making jokes about silly mechanicals who can't understand how to use the cueing system. The premature cueing device was standard and can be found in the work of many playwrights. *The London Prodigal*—not a Shakespeare play, despite its title-page—includes an exuberant figure of fun called Oliver whose heavy Devonshire accent makes him extremely difficult to

understand. His interlocutors ignore half of what he says, or, as
in the following extract, simply try to stop him short: his part is
filled with premature cues that will ensure no one hears him,
though:

*Oliver*

—————————————————— to work upon.
Work thy plots *upon me*, stand a side, work thy foolish
plots *upon me*, chill so use thee, thou wert never so
used since thy dam bound thy head, work *upon me?*
—————————————————— let him come.
Zyrrha, zyrrha, if it were not for shame, chee would a
given thee zutch a whister poop under the ear, chee
would have made thee a vanged another at my feet:
*stand a side* let me loose, cham all of a vlaming fire-
brand; *stand aside.*
—————————————————— your friends sake.
A vig for all *my vreens*, do'st thou tell me of *my
vreens?*
—————————————————— purse and person.[164]

Parts suggest that though entrances tended to be cued by the
prompter, exits were cued in texts and, again, could be given
'prematurely'. One example of an early exit cue is given to the
Ghost in *Hamlet*, 1.1 (*Ham.* 65):

*Ghost*

—————————————————— Charge thee, speake.
[*Exit the Ghost*

Here is what happens in the full text:

HORATIO. What art thou that usurp'st this time of night,
   Together with that Faire and Warlike forme
   In which the Majesty of buried Denmarke
   Did sometimes march: By Heaven I *charge thee speake.*
MARCELLUS. It is offended.
BARNADO. See, it stalkes away.
HORATIO. Stay: speake; speake: I *Charge thee speake.*
[*Exit the Ghost*
(*Ham.* 59–66)

---

[164] *The London Prodigall* in M$^r$. *William Shakespear's Comedies, Histories, and
Tragedies . . . The third Impression* (1664), 4.

In terms of the 'story', the ghost, his throne 'usurped' by his brother, takes offence at Horatio's ill choice of words and stalks away. But in terms of managing the scene, the actor playing the ghost never needs to be told when or why to start his exit—or even that he is 'offended'. The text itself does that; the actor's movements will have been clear to him without his having to know what else was going on in the scene.

Playwrights seem to have written in such a way that the appropriate action would simply happen in performance; they wrote for a part-based system of acting. Nor does it seem likely that actors, trained to perform from parts, would have 'learned' through performance to ignore premature cues—the parts told them to speak at the 'wrong' time (because the 'wrong' time was the 'right' time) and their scripts obliged them to continue to do so.

THE NATURE OF PERFORMANCE

Naturally the performances themselves reflected the way plays had been rehearsed. But they were also continuations of the rehearsal process, for, technically, all public performances were 'rehearsals', a fiction the theatre appealed to as necessary, but for reasons different from those of the boy players. Legally, public performances were practice for eventual private performance in front of the queen: regular playing, it was claimed, was the only way actors could 'attaine . . . dexteritie and perfection . . . the better to content her maiestie'.[165] The formula was used to shield playing companies from angry puritans, and in times of trouble, actors and their protectors would dredge it up: Sir Francis Walsingham, writing on behalf of the players, reminds the Lord Mayor that 'without frequent exercise of such plaies as are to be presented before hir majestie, her seruants cannot conueniently satisfie hir recreation' (1583).[166] Legal references to public performances, presumably for the same reason, tend to be instinct with the vocabulary of rehearsal, and verbs like

---

[165] Quoted in Chambers, *Elizabethan Stage*, iv. 287.
[166] Ibid. iv. 296; see also 331.

'practise' abound: 'Licence hath been graunted unto two companies, to use and practise stage playes, whereby they might be the better enhabled and prepared to shew such plaies before her Majestie' (1598 Privy Council Minute).[167] Out-of-season practices are even presented as substitutes for performances, suggesting that otherwise performance could stand in the stead of regular, full-company rehearsals, since they both serve the same purpose:

To Iohn Hemyngs one of his ma[tes] plaiers . . . in the behalfe of himselfe and the reste of his Company by way of his ma[tes] rewarde for their private practise in the time of infecc*i*on that thereby they mighte be inhabled to performe their service before his ma[tie] in Christmas hollidaies 1609.

To Iohn Heminges . . . and the reste of his companie beinge restrayned from publique p\l/ayinge w[th]in the Citie of London in the tyme of infecc*i*on duringe the space of sixe weekes in which tyme they practised pryvately for his Ma[tes] service.[168]

As audiences could accept or reject plays after the first day, actors may well have had a resistance towards serious rehearsal, at least until it was clear that the production had 'taken'—prologues speak of unready actors who will, if the the play is approved, 'mend' their acting.[169] Inductions for the public theatre do not, like those for the boy theatres, make the pretence of apologizing for the fact that the actors may be unready; instead they flaunt it: 'Do I not looke pale, as fearing to bee out in my speech?' asks one Prologue. Two successive Prologues do not know their lines in Goffe's *The Careles Shepherdess*: 'Pox take the Prompter' cries the first; the second *'being out, looks in his hat, at which an Actor plac't in the Pit laughs'*.[170] Plays of the time self-referentially relish jokey references to underrehearsal: Depazzi in Shirley's *The Humorous Courtier,* tries to remember a set speech that he has been taught in order to woo the countess:

---

[167] Ibid. iv. 352.

[168] *MSC: VI,* ed. David Cook and F. Wilson (Oxford, 1962), 47, 48.

[169] See e.g. *The Loyall Subject* in Beaumont and Fletcher, *Comedies and Tragedies,* 3G[b], : ''tis fit we should aske, . . . | How you approve our action in the play. | If you vouchsafe to crowne it with applause . . . you give us cause | Hereafter with a generall consent | To study, as becomes us, your content'.

[170] Thomas Heywood, *The Foure Prentises of London* (1615), A4[a]; 'Praeludium' to Goffe, *Careles Shepherdess,* 7–8, thought to be by Brome—see Richard Brome, *The English Moore,* ed. Sara Jayne Steen (Columbia, Mo., 1983), 6.

'Why your cheekes are, as they are, death, I ha forgot | This tis
when you won't come t'rehearsall' (4.1); Artesia in Cosmo
Manuche's *Just General* turns on Delirus who has just tried to
kiss her, exclaiming 'You are abominably out . . . you | . . . must
go con your Part anew, and learn to know, to whom you are to
speak' (3.1).[171] Functionaries of the theatre therefore had the
important task of bringing together unready, or only individually
ready actors, and fusing them into a group performance.

### Book-holders in performance

In *A Source Book in Theatrical History*, A. M. Nagler reproduces
three medieval pictures containing prompters or *régisseurs*: the
mid-fifteenth century *Mystère de Sainte Apolline*; *Weingartenspiel*
(1539); and Hubert Cailleau's *Valenciennes director* (1547).[172]
With their books the *régisseurs* prompted the actors; with their
sticks they guided them as with a conductor's baton (in Mons in
1501 they were known by the title *conducteurs de secrets*[173]). The
parallels between a prompter and a modern-day orchestral
conductor are marked: both 'direct' during performance, uniting
a set of people working only from cued parts separately learned
(a player in an orchestra is not given a full score—just the music
for his or her particular instrument). Though by the Renaissance
the prompter no longer stood in the middle of the stage with his
baton—as in the medieval period—his role in performance
remained that of conductor, unifying actors who had learnt
their roles away from their fellows.

Surprisingly, the Elizabethan book-holder was not very highly
thought of. In Goffe's *Careles Shepherdess*, book-holding is
equated to door-keeping and candle-snuffing—both low and
unskilled professions; the book-holder Edward Knight is
ranked with the rest of 'the Kinges Ma[ties]: servantes in their
quallity of . . . necessary attendantes' in a warrant.[174] Yet Knight
is also frequently referred to in letters from Herbert, the Master
of the Revels; given what little information there is about

---

[171] James Shirley, *The Humorous Courtier* (1640), F3[b]; Manuche, *Just General*, 30.
[172] A. M. Nagler, *A Source Book in Theatrical History* (New York, 1952), 50–1.
[173] Gustave Cohen, *Le Livre de conduite du régisseur . . . pour le mystère de la Passion* (Paris, 1925), p. xii.
[174] Goffe, *Careles Shepherdess*, 6; Bawcutt, *Censorship*, 158.

sixteenth- and seventeenth-century actors, and who played which part, it is amazing how often we know not only the name but also character details about the book-holder. In *Summers Last Will*, Will hears '*Dick Huntley*' the book-holder telling the players to 'Begin, begin'; John Taylor used to know 'one *Thomas Vincent* that was a Book-keeper or prompter at the Globe play-house'; John Crouch in *Man in the Moon* (1649) writes about 'Peters' who was '*Book-holder* at the Bull-play-house'.[175] A book-holder occasionally appears in an induction, for he inhabits a strange, semi-fictional world, standing both within and without a play, allowed to become part of its fabric. When in Brome's *Antipodes* (3.8) a voice emanates from behind the curtain prompting 'Dismisse the Court', Letoy responds, 'Dismisse the court, cannot you heare the prompter?'[176] Whether the prompter's commanding bell and whistle (a feature of seventeenth- and eighteenth-century theatre) existed before the innovation of movable scenery is a moot point; it was certainly used to herald changes of scene in masques, for Jonson refers to Inigo Jones's 'whistle, and his men': in this instance at least, the prompter's devices also stage him, making his presence fully audible to the audience.[177]

Factual and fictional accounts both contain references to people who take on one element of the book-holder's job for an evening. Lord Robert Dudley, for instance, helped out in a university production in 1563-4:

whyle [Dido] was a handling, the Lord Robert, Steward to the Universitie, and Master Secretarie Cecil, Chancellor, to signifye their good wille, and that things might be orderlye done, vouchsafed to hold both books on the scaffold themselves and to provide also that sylence might be kept with quietness.[178]

Plays also provide 'casual book-holders', like Aesopus in *Roman Actor*, who prompts Caesar's entrance; and the Duke of Castile in *Spanish Tragedy* (4.3), to whom the king gives a copy of the play, commanding 'you shall be the booke-keeper. | This is

[175] *Nashe*, iii. 233; John Taylor, *Works*, 3 vols. (1630), iii. 70; Leslie Hotson, *The Commonwealth and Restoration Stage* (Cambridge, Mass., 1928), 15.

[176] *Brome*, iii. 292.

[177] 'An Expostulacion w^th Inigo Iones', in *Jonson*, viii. 402. 'Scenes' were a new device, and only spectacular productions—masques and court performances—will have used them.    [178] *REED: Cambridge*, 231.

the argument of that they show'.[179] Such passages suggest that anyone might be the book-holder, an idea not easy to reconcile with the enormous effect book-holders had on production. The solution may lie in the fact that there were two parts to the book-holder's duties, roughly equivalent to those of the medieval *régisseurs*: one, book-holding itself during performance—prompting cues of entrance and missed speeches; the other, preparing for performances and 'conducting' them on the stage—marking up prompt-books, writing plots, readying actors, instituting action. The first anyone could do; the second required particular skills. It is even possible that the titles 'prompter' and 'book-keeper/holder' actually stood for two different people as well as two different tasks—which would account for the fact that there seem to be two prompt-books ('both books') in the Lord Robert Dudley quotation above. Early dictionaries of the time describe the 'choragus' as variously 'A keeper of . . . apparell' and 'the setter foorth of the playes' (suggesting that the tyre-man and book-holder could on occasion be one and the same) and draw a distinction between these directorial duties and the simple 'monitor', another translation of 'prompter', but this time simply 'he that telleth the players their parte'.[180] By 1664 the 'choragus' had come to be an obviously key figure in productions: 'A setter forth or the Master of plays'[181]—the book-holder had crept up in importance to become that 'master' that Ben Jonson had so proudly claimed himself to be. This dichotomy goes partway to explain why the book-holder was technically not very highly thought of, though so prominent in performance.

In *Lady Alimony* the book-holder is jokingly named 'Siparius', a word that means curtain; more specifically, 'a courtaine or veile drawne when the players come vpon the stage' (Thomas, *Dictionarium,* 1587). Almost certainly this is a reference to the book-holder's position during performance, behind a curtain that divided some part of the tiring room from the stage. From here he could listen to the performance—and watch it too through a slit in the material.[182] For the prompter needed to

[179] *Massinger*, iii. 79; Thomas Kyd, *The Spanish Tragedy* (1592), K3[a].

[180] Thomas Thomas, *Dictionarium Linguae Latinae et Anglicanae* (1587).

[181] Francis Gouldman, *A Copious Dictionary in Three Parts* (1664).

[182] The prompter almost certainly occupied the same space, variously described as behind the 'hangings', 'curtains', or 'arras', that was taken up by a playwright on the first day. From there an author could both hear what was going on—'the Poet

hear what was going on, so that he could help actors who forgot their lines—'Pox take the Prompter' cries the actor who is 'out' for his prologue; 'I pray you holde the booke well,' Will Summers warns the book-holder in *Summers Last Will*, 'we be not *non plus* in the latter end of the play.'[183] A player who missed a cue might be lost as to which speech he was supposed to give, and the prompter would then have to start him off: in *Hide Parke* (3.2) Mistress Caroll asks whether Mr Fairefield wants a 'prompter to insinuate | The first word of your studied Oration'.[184] The book-keeper also needed to be in a position to see the action, for he cued not only entrances but also timing and blocking. One prologue asks for silence because 'I heare the players prest, in presence foorth to come'; indeed, the 'play-house book-keeper' who 'would . . . stampe and stare . . . when the actors misse their entrance', is the stuff of theatrical comedy.[185] As the person responsible for prompting the timing of stage action the book-keeper is casually referred to in *Othello*—'Were it my Cue to fight, I should haue knowne it | Without a Prompter' (*Oth.* 301); in Brome's *Antipodes* the book-keeper with his 'Dismisse the Court' is also responsible for ending scenes and clearing the stage.[186] In other words, the prompter was directing basic blocking during the play's enactment. And this means, from the actors' point of view, that items of a play that might otherwise have had to be learnt in collective rehearsal, did not actually have to be known in advance of production; much of what was necessary for performance would be prompted within performance itself.

There seem to have been other people responsible for helping the prompter—in particular, call-boys and stage attendants. In the tiring house the 'blue-coated Stage-keepers' referred to in the

stands listning behind the arras | To heare what will become on's Play' (James Shirley, *The Dukes Mistris* (1638), K4<sup>b</sup>), and watch the performance—'he standes peeping betwixt curtaines' (Francis Beaumont and John Fletcher, *The Woman-Hater* (1607), C3<sup>b</sup>). The 'new' Globe's claim that regular prompting cannot have happened on the stage because it is impossible to hear the actors from the tiring room is not met by the many references in plays to receiving or offering prompts; it seems to be based on misunderstanding where the prompter was situated.

[183] Goffe, *Careles Shepherdess*, 7–8; *Nashe*, iii. 290.
[184] James Shirley, *Hide Parke* (1637), F2<sup>a</sup>.
[185] Nathaniel Woodes, *The Conflict of Conscience* (1581), A2<sup>b</sup>; Lewis Machin, *Every Woman in her Humour*, ed. Archie Mervin Tyson (London, 1980), 203.
[186] *Brome*, iii. 292.

prologue to Thomas Nabbes's *Hannibal and Scipio* make sound-effects like 'the . . . horrid noise of target fight' from backstage; a stagekeeper opens Jonson's *Bartholomew Fair*, and a tire-man has a role in Jonson's *Cynthia's Revels*, and Marston's *Malcontent*.[187] The 'plat' or 'plot' that hung in the tiring house—a plan containing a scene-by-scene account of entrances and exits—was almost certainly prepared for call-boys rather than for actors, as is sometimes claimed. Plays, full as they are of metatheatrical references, never mention actors using the plot; moreover, as Bradley points out, references such as 'enter . . . the red faced fellow' do not seem to have been designed for actors to see.[188] The plots of *Seven Deadly Sins* and *Fortune's Tennis* are both in the hand of the book-holder concerned with *Thomas More*; and the phrasing of descriptions of action within plots often recalls prompt-book stage directions: plots seem to have been abstracted from prompt copies—and the prompter will hardly have duplicated information he already had for himself.[189] With their use of terms such as 'manet' (which Greg calls an apparently useless convention), the plots in fact give backstage people who can hear but not see the performance a picture of what is happening on the stage, and an impression of the time-sequence of the action. In the eighteenth century there was even a 'stage tradition that [Shakespeare's] first office in the theatre was that of prompter's attendant; whose employment it is to give the performers notice to be ready to enter'.[190]

## Actors and parts in performance

Though not much has been recorded about the actor in performance, what little there is suggests something that will clearly emerge over the following chapters: that many actors, having learnt to deal primarily with their own parts in private study, had not learnt to think of the play as a unity. So there are indications that one actor did not always keep in character while another was performing: Letoy in Brome's *Antipodes* accuses one

---

[187] In Thomas Nabbes, *Hannibal and Scipio* (1637), A3b.
[188] Bradley, *Text*, 79.      [189] Greg, *Dramatic Documents*, 73–90.
[190] *Supplement to the Edition of Shakspeare's Plays Published in 1778*, ed. Edmond Malone, 2 vols. (1780), i. 67.

player of losing interest 'when you have spoke', and turning to the audience, 'Not minding the reply'; indeed, Burbage was singled out for praise for 'never falling in his Part when he had done speaking; but with his looks and gesture, maintaining it still'.[191] Big-headed actors might self-consciously direct their performances away from the players they were with, rather than towards them 'for applause-sake', like the man described by John Stephens, who 'When he doth hold conference vpon the stage; and should look directly in his fellows face . . . turnes about his voice into the assembly'.[192] But audiences too had a tendency to watch in a part-focused way. *Cynthia's Revels* contains a description of a '*Neophyte*' who is interested only in one performer and his part, not in the play itself. So he waits for the entrance of his 'idoll', and, in the mean time 'repeates . . . His part of speeches, and confederate iests, | In passion to himself'.[193] Richard Baker claims that Alleyn and Burbage could make any play pleasing 'where their Parts had the greatest part', and a telling commonplace book judges Shakespeare's plays in terms of 'parts' that make them up, so that Othello and Iago are described as '2 parts well penned' and Hamlet is 'an indifferent good part for a madman'.[194]

Additions and cuts traceable to actors in plays are often clearly made on part-based lines. In the 'bad' (1600) Quarto of *Henry V*, a number of performers seem to have been responsible for small alterations to their parts, some of them space-fillers (Fluellen's 'looke you' and 'God's plud'), some of them additional cheap laughs ('ancient Pistoll' is repeated many times—presumably because 'Pistoll' sounded like 'pizzle'). But the actor playing Pistoll has apparently been more free with his text than other actors—in that his part has changed more, gaining some entire new lines like 'Keepe fast thy buggle boe' (2.3), and 'couple gorge' (4.6). Similarly Harold Jenkins believes that some of the *Hamlet* Folio additions—Hamlet's free-standing 'O vengeance' for instance—are traceable specifically to Burbage, who altered his part to include extra revenge-tragedy rants in his

---

[191] *Brome*, iii. 259; Flecknoe, *Love's Kingdom*, G7ᵃ.
[192] *Essayes and Characters* (1615), 297.
[193] *Jonson*, iv. 91.
[194] Richard Baker, *Theatrum Redivivum* (1662), 34; Gamini Salgado, *Eyewitnesses of Shakespeare* (London, 1975), 47.

speeches.[195] Part-based learning is reflected also in muddled speeches. For example, all any actor actually needed to remember to make a play itself work were his cues: the central area of any oration could be busked, which again happens in 'bad' *Henry V* (1.2.47) where the King remembers the framework of his Salic law speech, but makes rubbish of the actual body.[196] But this introduces a larger issue: that textual change was not in its nature uniform. In production some 'parts' altered more substantially and more quickly than others.

An example of this happening can perhaps be seen in the two texts of *Othello*, one of which makes 'Desdemona' a singing part, the other of which does not. Revisions of a number of different kinds have happened in the play, but the song revision seems to have been made to match playhouse exigencies: depending on the date of the two texts, it was either added because a singing boy had been acquired, or removed because a singing boy's voice had broken.[197] Either way, it is a part revision—a revision along a

---

[195] See William Shakespeare, *Hamlet*, ed. Harold Jenkins (London, 1982), 62. Though the claim is often discredited, there are other suggestions that revenge features were interpolated by Burbage into Shakespeare's text. For instance, an epitaph for Burbage bemoans: 'No more young Hamlet, though but scant of breath, | Shall cry "Revenge" for his dear father's death'—quoted in full in J. Payne Collier, *Memoirs of the Principal Actors in the Plays of Shakespeare* (1846), 52. Hamlet does not cry out for 'revenge' in any extant copy of the play—though significantly he does 'schwör . . . die Rache' in *Der Berstrafte Brudermord* (Albert Cohn, *Shakespeare in Germany in the Sixteenth and the Seventeenth Centuries* (1865), 252), a play that may include lines remembered from early productions. As Burbage is particularly famous for his 'Revenge', we must at least consider that he inserted the phrase into Shakespeare's play; it certainly featured in the ur-Hamlet as recalled by Thomas Lodge in *Wits Miserie* (1596), in which 'y$^e$ ghost . . . cried so miserably at y$^e$ Theator . . . Hamlet, reuenge' (quoted in Stanley Wells and Gary Taylor, *William Shakespeare: A Textual Companion* (Oxford, 1987) 398).
[196] See William Shakespeare, *Henry V*, ed. Gary Taylor (Oxford, 1982), 21. One *Hamlet* in-joke seems to stem from the practice of acting from cued parts. Talking to Reynaldo, Polonius loses his train of thought (or, it would seem, his place in his speech): 'Polonius: And then Sir does he this? He does: what was I about to say? I was about to say somthing: where did I leaue? Reynaldo: At closes in the consequence: At friend, or so, and Gentleman. Polonius: At closes in the consequence I marry, He closes with you thus' . . . (*Ham.* 942–8). Michael Pennington in *Hamlet: A Users Guide* (London, 1996), 60, is not the first to suggest that this is the record of the actor himself forgetting his lines. But he goes on to comment on the fact that 'Reynaldo' does not help out his fellow actor by telling him what to say next, only prompts him with what he has said already. The nature of cued parts of course explains this: actors possessed only their own lines; all 'Reynaldo' could do was to remind 'Polonius' where he had left off in his speech.
[197] Discussed in E. A. J. Honigmann, *The Texts of 'Othello' and Shakespearian Revision* (London and New York, 1996), 14–16, 39–40.

particular strip of text. The same seems to have happened in *Twelfth Night*, which was clearly written with a singing Viola in mind: at the play's opening Viola believes that it is her high voice and choral skills that will get her a place in Orsino's house ('Thou shalt present me as an Eunach to him, | It may be worth thy paines: for I can sing, | and speake to him in many sorts of Musicke' (*TN* 109)). But in the comedy as we have it, songs have been revised away from Viola (probably, again, because the boy's voice had broken) and given to Feste: a two-part revision, involving the recalling and rewriting of essentially two parts rather than the full play—Orsino's part still involves his request for Viola to sing 'one verse' of 'That old and Anticke song' (*TN* 886).[198] Specific parts, that is to say, may be found to alter more than others, to meet the requirements of the playhouse. When plays of the time advertize that they have been revised and altered, they often emphasise either that single parts have been increased in size, or that single parts have been added to the text—the 1615 Quarto for Kyd's *The Spanish Tragedy* has been 'Newly . . . enlarged with new Additions of the *Painters* part'.

Some actors' parts habitually changed more significantly and more frequently than others. Clowns and fools in particular, seem to have had more fluid texts; the fool was a minor original, and did in miniature what a playwright did in large, a point often made at the time. *Lady Alimony* refers back to the period 'when | the Actor could embellish his Author, and return a Pean | to his Pen in every accent'; Letoy remembers when 'fooles and jesters spent their wits, because | The Poets were wise enough to save their owne | For profitabler uses' (*Antipodes*, 2.2).[199] After a hysterical outburst of extempore rhyming (a fool's skill) Hamlet asks Horatio whether this may not earn him 'a Fellowship in a crie of Players' (*Ham.* 2149). Aubrey's chief heroes of extemporization are Jonson and Shakespeare—'A Grace by Ben Johnston extempore, . . .'; 'at the Tavern at Stratford . . . [Shakespeare] makes . . . this extempore Epitaph'; Greene's 'country author' in *A Groatsworth of Wit* (1596) shows his skill by making 'a plaine rime extempore'.[200] So linked are

---

[198] See W. W. Greg, *The Shakespeare First Folio, Its Bibliographical and Textual History* (Oxford, 1955), 361.

[199] *Lady Alimony*, A3[b]; Brome, iii. 260.

[200] Aubrey, *Brief Lives*, 334; Greene, xii. 132.

fool and playwright in matters of verbal creativity that Malone in
1790 tells an anecdote in which Shakespeare is challenged by a
blacksmith theme-giver to define the difference between a youth
and a young man. He is said to have replied, 'Thou son of fire,
with *thy face like a maple,* | The same difference as between a
scalded and a coddled apple.' This is, in fact, simply a version of
a Tarlton jest: 'Gentleman, this fellow, with this face of map-
ple, | Instead of a pippin, hath thrown me an apple.'[201] Tradition
gives the playwright and the clown the same creative gifts;
clowns seem to have been expected to embellish and even
partially write their texts—authors are linked in this way with
the very element of their plays over which they have no control,
another fact that raises questions about the nature of 'authorship'.

It is, for instance, a 'bad' Quarto quality to have an enlarged
humorous or fool section—comic interpolations seem to have
been introduced into the quarto of Greene's *Orlando Furioso*;
and in the manuscript for *John of Bordeaux* the clown's part is
swollen out of normal proportion to the rest of the play.[202] Fools
added their own punch-lines into each play they were in,
irrespective of whether it was appropriate, as is made clear in
('bad') 1603 Quarto 1 *Hamlet* when Hamlet rails against the
clown who has 'one sute | Of ieasts'—a single set of jokes—that
serves him for every production (3.2.50).[203] In the Spanish plays
of P. Pedro Pablo Acevedo, the main texts are in Latin and the
rustics' parts are in colloquial Spanish[204]—the clowns' sections
are clearly colloquial, and seem to have been more changeable as
a result. In England there was, perhaps, a playhouse system for
indicating in a text which parts were changeable and which were
fixed. For instance, in both quartos of *Romeo and Juliet,* the
Nurse's part (but no other) is sometimes printed in italics: in the
manuscript underlying at least one of the texts (one may have
corrupted the other) the nurse's part clearly looked visually
different from the other parts. Italics were often employed in
play manuscripts (and printed texts) to indicate 'removable'

---

[201] Chambers, *Shakespeare*, ii, 273–4.
[202] Alfred Hart, *Stolne and Surreptitious Copies* (Melbourne, 1942), 67; *John of Bordeaux*, ed. William Lindsay Renwick (Oxford, 1936), p. viii.
[203] William Shakespeare, *The Tragicall Historie of Hamlet* (1603), F2ᵃ.
[204] See McKendrick, *Theatre in Spain*, 52.

fragments like songs, letters, prologues, and epilogues; perhaps they also indicated malleable or less solidly rooted parts. Hamlet's (Folio) objection to the clown's defilement of a play by speaking 'more than is set down for him', in no way signifies that Shakespeare's plays are free of this; indeed that very passage is so differently represented in the 'bad' 1603 Quarto (quoted above) there is an ironic possibility that it may itself be interpolated. Other texts also assume that certain parts might be constructed more loosely than others. When Donella prepares a play in Shirley's *Bird in a Cage* she gives her women the parts of 'Ladies whom the King leaves to keepe [Eugenia] Company', instructing them to 'entertaine what humor you please'. Cassiana and Katerina, surprised at the freedom given them, exclaim 'This is our owne parts indeed', to which Donella replies 'Yee will play it the more naturally'.[205] This is matched by stage directions as, for instance, '*Enter Forrester, missing the other taken away, speake any thing, and Exit*'; '*Iockie is led to whipping ouer the stage, speaking some wordes, but of no importance*'.[206]

The fool was, on certain occasions, supposed to entertain the audience with his skills at extemporization; one of his jobs was to fill with banter unexpected 'gaps' that for some reason occurred in performances. So the second-rate clown in *Pilgrimage to Parnassus* is thrust on stage and told either to 'saie somwhat for thy selfe, or hang & be *non plus*' (674); at the Red-Bull Play-house 'it did chance that the Clown . . . being in the Attireing house, was suddenly called for upon the Stage, for it was empty'.[207] In such instances they are asked to 'fool' rather than to reflect the play they are in, by, for instance, holding 'interlocutions with the audience', a way that Byplay in *The Antipodes* explains has been 'allow'd | On elder stages' and Letoy agrees, 'Yes in the dayes of *Tarlton* and *Kempe*' (*Antipodes*, 2.2).[208] Kempe himself concurs in *Travails of Three English Brothers*, where he declares that he will gladly 'put out the sacke of witte I ha' left' in an 'extemporall merriment', but finds studying difficult.[209]

Robert Armin, the replacement fool for the Chamberlain's

[205] Shirley, *Bird*, G4[b].

[206] *The History of the Tryall of Cheualry* (1605), E4[a]; Thomas Heywood, *The Second Part of King Edward the Fourth* (1599), Y2[b].

[207] *Parnassus Plays*, 129; Thornton S. Graves, 'Some References to Elizabethan Theatres', *SP* 19 (1922), 317–27 (322).

[208] *Brome*, iii. 260.                                    [209] *Day*, 370.

Company after the departure of Will Kempe, was a more serious
fool and less famous for speaking out of turn; he may or may not
have extemporized. He seems to have been supposed not to;
that, at least, is suggested by his title-page to *Quips upon
Questions* (1600): 'True it is, he playes the Foole indeed; | But
in the Play he playes it as he must'. But interestingly, as a fool,
particularly as a replacement for Kempe, he needed at least to
*appear* to be extemporizing. His scripted lines give every sign of
being filled with his pet phrases, so his own personal verbal tick
'all is one' ('Thus' he writes in his *Nest of Ninnies*, 'fooles
thinking to be wise, become flat foolish, but all is one') occurs
in *Twelfth Night* ('But that's all one our Play is done', (*TN*
2578)).[210] In his personal writings too, Armin muddles his stage
and real characters: with Dogberry-like 'boldness' he relates that
he is one who 'hath been writ down an ass in his time'.[211] There
is a special trading going on between Armin's *Nest of Ninnies*
(1608) and Shakespeare's *Historie of the life and death of King
Lear* (published in the same year): a 'cinnik' is one who (says
Armin) 'Lets the cart before the horse';[212] a phrase recalling (or
prompting) the Fool (assumed to have been played by Armin),
who encapsulates Lear's back-to-front world with the question
'may not an Asse know when the cart drawes the horse'.[213] If he
did not extemporize on the stage, then Armin may have had a
hand in writing his own parts. There is certainly a similarity
between his way of portraying fooling, and fooling in the plays in
which he performs. For instance, his relation of a fool–king
conversation is redolent of lines in *Lear* :

what is the cleanliest trade in the world? Marry, sayes the king, I think a
comfit-maker, for hee . . . is attired cleane in white linnen . . . No,
*Harry*, sayes *Will*, you are wide. What say you then, qth the king? mary,
sayes *Will* I say a durt-dauber. Out on it sayes the king, that is the
foulest, for hee is durty up to the elbows. I sayes *Will*, but then he
washes him cleane againe . . . I promise thee *Will* saies the king thou

---

[210] *A Nest of Ninnies* 1608), B1[a]; facs. in Robert Armin's *Collected Works*, ed.
J. Feather, 2 vols. (New York, 1972). This same phrase is also in many of the
'additional' lines of Fluellen in Shakespeare's 'Bad' *Henry V* (1600), D1[a]: 'but its all
one, | What he hath sed to me, | looke you, is all one', suggesting both that Armin
performed that role, and that he did in fact extemporize a little.
[211] *Italian Taylor*, A3[r]; facs. in Armin, *Works*.          [212] Armin, *Nest*, G4[b].
[213] William Shakespeare, *Historie of the life and death of King Lear* (1608), D1[b]

hast a prety foolish wit, I, *Harry*, sayes he it will serue to make a wiser man than you a foole me thinks.[214]

Some plays create or anticipate moments or gaps when extemporization will become necessary in response to the audience. In *Love's Labour's Lost* Holofernes warns Mote—about to perform Hercules in *The Nine Worthies*—that should the crowd become restless and start to hiss, he should 'cry Well done *Hercules*, now thou crushest the Snake' (*LLL* 1870). And indeed the actors are put to a spirited defence of themselves and their characters ('I will not be put out of countenance', *LLL* 2560), just as they are in *The Taming of the Shrew*, and *The Mayor of Quinborough*. The audience freely allowed themselves to banter with characters known for their extemporization. One jest-book story tells of a spectator who rudely pointed at Tarlton in the middle of a performance. Tarlton responded by thrusting two fingers back, so making horns at the interrupter. 'The captious fellow . . . asked him why he made hornes at him. No, quoth Tarlton, they be fingers: 'For there is no man, which in love to me, | Lends me one finger, but he shall have three.'[215]

Additions might be physical as well as verbal. In a highly gestured theatre, non-verbal byplay could significantly affect the way the audience responded to a drama: fools like Tarlton and Reade were famous for the facial additions they made to their parts. When an English play travelled to Germany, it was a Pickleherring (fool) that was taken on to translate it; he then simply worked his way into the text, becoming an integral part of it. In a German *Midsummer Night's Dream*,

Pickleherring punches Bully Bottom in the neck, then Bully Bottom knocks him over the head with the wall; they get hold of each other by the hair and pull each other about on stage, so that the wall comes to pieces entirely. Peter Quince tries to separate them. (Andreus Gryphius, *Freunden und Trauer-speile auch . . . Herr Peter Squentz Schimpff-Spiele*, 1658).[216]

Plays in performance seem, as later, to have been modified verbally or physically by certain actors as a way of personalizing

---

[214] Armin, *Nest*, F3ᵃ.

[215] *A Nest of Ninnies*, ed. M. Zall (Lincoln, 1970), 92.

[216] George W. Brandt (ed.), *German and Dutch Theatre 1640–1848*, (Cambridge, 1993), 66.

them, for an actor, having learnt his part parrot-fashion, had no other obvious input into his own performance. Revised texts sometimes incorporated these actors' additions: the 'few songs', added to Heywood's *Rape of Lucrece* 'by the stranger that lately acted *Valerius*'; the speeches 'penned by others', and 'pronounced in stead of some of the former speeches' in Thomas Hughes's *The Misfortunes of Arthur*.[217] And not only was the kind of revision in which individual actors were involved part-based; post-performance theatrical revision was also frequently part-based.

Of the two 'good' texts of *Hamlet*, Quarto 2 (1604) is thought to descend from a manuscript (pre-performance) text, and the Folio from a post-performance one.[218] The Folio, that is to say, is a revision of the second Quarto. And yet it is a revision that has a markedly different character from the adaptation of *King Lear*, a point made by Eric Rasmussen.[219] Rasmussen compares *Lear* and *Hamlet* cuts, and observes that in *Lear* the reviser cancelled the ends of speeches and scenes; he also, in several instances, reattributed speeches. The result is a 'full-play' revision—so many cue lines have been altered that the prompt-book would have needed to be written out again from scratch, all actors' parts would have had to be returned to the prompter, and new parts written out with new cue-lines to be relearnt by the actors. Amendments of this significance would only make practical sense when major recasting was about to happen—in that it would be enormously difficult for actors to relearn familiar parts with considerable verbal differences and new cues. The *Hamlet* revisions, which Rasmussen calls 'surgery', on the other hand, make sense in terms of actors' parts, and can almost all be traced to the exigencies of cued scripts, as can the major additions.

*Hamlet* cuts are, for the most part, not full-play, so not all the actors would have had to return their parts for rewriting when the alterations were made. The Ghost's part, for instance, remains unchanged (there is an additional 'swear' traceable to

[217] Thomas Heywood, *Rape of Lucrece* (1608), K2ᵃ; *Early English Classical Tragedies*, ed. John W. Cunliffe (Oxford, 1912), 293.

[218] William Shakespeare, *Hamlet*, ed. G. R. Hibbard (Oxford, 1987), 67–130.

[219] Eric Rasmussen, 'The Revision of Scripts', in John D. Cox and David Scott Kastan, (eds., *A New History of Early English Drama* (New York, 1997), 441–60 (445).

actor's interpolation); Reynaldo's part is the same (again, there is the addition of a word or two, attributable to actor's interpolation); Polonius and Ophelia too are basically unaltered. Only certain parts would clearly have had to be recalled for over- or re-writing: Hamlet, Gertrude, Claudius, Horatio, Laertes, Rosencrantz, Guildenstern, Osric. The last three are 'comic'— there is, as discussed above, a general tendency for comic parts in plays to change particularly quickly.

The revisions that are made to the parts are, in most cases, cuts of passages that occur in the middle of speeches. This makes cue-script sense: revise a speech in its centre and the cues are not affected; moreover, for cuts of this kind, the revision could be marked on the scroll itself, saving the necessity of writing out a new part. So, in *Hamlet*, 3.4.152:[220]

HAMLET. O throwe away the worser part of it,
  And leaue the purer with the other halfe,
  Good night, but goe not to my Vncles bed,
  Assune a vertue if you haue it not,
  ~~That monster custome, who all sence doth eate~~
  ~~Of habits deuill, is angell yet in this~~
  ~~That to the vse of actions faire and good,~~
  ~~He likewise giues a frock or Liuery~~
  ~~That aptly is put on to~~ refraine night,
  And that shall lend a kind of easines
  To the next abstinence, ~~the next more easie:~~
  ~~For vse almost can change the stamp of nature,~~
  ~~And either the deuill, or throwe him out~~
  ~~With wonderous potency~~: once more good night,
  And when you are desirous to be blest,
  Ile blessing beg of you, for this same Lord
  I doe repent; but heauen hath pleasd it so
  To punish me with this, and this with me,
  That I must be their scourge and minister,
  I will bestowe him and will answere well
  The death I gaue him; so againe good night
  I must be cruell only to be kinde,
  This bad beginnes, and worse remaines behind.
  One word more good Lady.

(Q2, I4$^{a-}$b; *Ham.* 2540)

[220] The text shown here is the 1604 Quarto marked with the Folio 'cuts'. Act, scene, lines are keyed in to Hibbard's edition of *Hamlet* for ease of reference.

Other within-speech cuts occur after 1.2.60, 3.2.205, 3.4.72, 3.4.73, 3.4.190, 4.1.39, 4.7.88, 4.7.99; four other, slightly more questionable within-speech cuts occur at the following places (they have been attributed, perhaps with cause, to eye-skip in the print-house): 2.2.210; 2.2.393; 2.2.320; 5.1.100.

There are only three occasions on which ends of speeches are cut, so affecting the cue line. Hamlet's 'This heauy headed reueale east and west | Makes vs tradust, and taxed of other nations' (1.4.16) goes, but that particular cut may well be traceable to historical circumstance: King James had married a Danish wife, and extended reference to the swinish drunkenness of the Danes will have consequently become inappropriate. In other words, this may have been an enforced cut, parts aside—though it is also the case that the speech is followed by the entrance of the Ghost, and the entrance itself (rather than Hamlet's last lines) works equally well as the cue for Horatio's next speech, 'Look, my Lord, it comes'. Two other speeches only are cut at their ends: Horatio's at 1.4.53, and the Player Queen's at 3.2.160 (the latter has been attributed to Folio error[221]).

Other kinds of cut are made in dialogue when two people are speaking, so that what is lost is a question and its reply; a speech and its repost. In this way, the second actor in the dialogue loses both speech and preceding cue, which is, again, easier for the cue-script actor: he never hears the cue, so he never gives the speech. At 4.3.26 the result is:

HAMLET. . . . . your fat King and your leane begger is but variable seruice, two dishes but to one table, that's the end.
~~KING. Alas, alas.~~
~~HAMLET. A man may fish with the worme that hath eate of a King, & eate of the fish that hath fedde of that worme.~~
KING. What doost thou meane by this?

(Q2, K2ᵃ; *Ham.* 2686)

More usual is the practice of cutting three speeches, so that the second speaker loses both cue and response, and the original speaker is made simply to continue speaking at a point slightly further along in his part. One cut of this kind occurs at 4.7.69, another at 1.1.147:

---

[221] Shakespeare, *Hamlet*, ed. Hibbard, 359.

HORATIO. . . . this I take it,
Is the maine motiue of our preparations
The source of this our watch, and the chiefe head
Of this post hast and Romeage in the land.
~~BARNADO. I thinke it be no other, but enso;~~
~~Well may it sort that this portentous figure~~
~~Comes armed through our watch so like the King~~
~~That was and is the question of these warres.~~
~~HORATIO. A moth it is to trouble the mindes eye:~~
~~In the most high and palmy state of Rome,~~
~~A little ere the mightiest Iulius fell~~
~~The graues stood tennatlesse, and the sheeted dead~~
~~Did squeake and gibber in the Roman streets~~
~~As starres with traines of fier, and dewes of blood~~
~~Disasters in the sunne; and the moist starre,~~
~~Vpon whose influence Neptunes Empier stands,~~
~~Was sicke almost to doomesday with eclipse.~~
~~And euen the like precurse of feare euents~~
~~As harbindgers preceeading still the fates~~
~~And prologue to the Omen comming on~~
~~Haue heauen and earth together demonstrated~~
~~Vnto our Climatures and countrymen.~~

[*Enter Ghost*

But soft, behold, loe where it comes againe . . .

(Q2, B2^b; *Ham.* 121)

Sometimes there are signs that revisions may have originated in the separate parts and then been transferred onto the full text—rather than vice versa. So Horatio in 5.2 has three sequent speeches cut that are scattered in the scene itself. His 'part', that is to say, will have been crossed in this manner:

——————————————————————— this water fly?
No my good Lord.
——————————————————————— ~~Sir.~~
~~Ist not possible to vnderstand in another tongue, you will~~
~~doo't sir really.~~
——————————————————————— ~~Of Laertes.~~
~~His purse is empty already, all's golden words are spent.~~
——————————————————————— the carriages?
~~I knew you must be edified by the margent ere you had~~
~~done.~~
——————————————————————— for's turne.
This Lapwing runnes away with the shell on his head.

His first two cancelled speeches occur in a conversation that is cut in the folio, but Horatio's last cut speech is stranded in uncancelled text:

COURTIER. . . . Three
    of the carriages in faith, are very deare to fancy, very responsiue to
    the hilts, most delicate carriages, and of very liberall conceit.
HAMLET. What call you the carriages?
~~HORATIO. I knew you must be edified by the margent ere you had done.~~
COURTIER. The carriage sir are the hangers.

(Q2, N2<sup>b</sup>-N3<sup>a</sup>; Ham. 3615)

One last kind of cut is whole-scene, which, again, makes easy cue-script sense: the entire passage is simply erased from each of the parts concerned. After 4.4.8 a scene is removed, bringing about cuts in the parts of Hamlet, Rosencrantz and the Captain. Another obvious cut is whole-part: in 5.2 the walk-on Lord is revised away, occasioning also a cut in the part of Hamlet with whom he has a dialogue.

On three occasions the Folio makes substantial 'additions' to the text: at 2.2.238–67, 2.2.333–58, and 5.2.69. In the first two instances, the characters concerned are Rosencrantz, Guildenstern, and Hamlet; in the last the characters concerned are Hamlet, Horatio, and Osric. Each of the actors playing these parts coincides with the list of actors receiving cuts to their parts: the parts would, anyway, have had to be given up for alteration, and in the specific instances of Rosencrantz, Guildenstern, and Hamlet, entire new parts would almost certainly have had to be written out. Horatio's minimal alterations, however, might have been squeezed onto his role; and Osric's new lines could have been pasted onto his part as they more or less fill the space occupied by lines that are revised out. This makes cued-part sense: the revisions and alterations are so arranged as to necessitate as little writing of new parts as possible. So the revisions in *Hamlet* may offer a clue as to how plays were formally shortened and revised after performance—along part lines. Revisions in *The Second Maiden's Tragedy,* which are of a similar kind,[222] show part-based revision to have been normal.

[222] Rasmussen, 'Revision', 445.

The tales of yearning authors doing their best to check up on players during production are traceable to the fact that most substantial revision or alteration of parts happened after performance. Brome, who had been Jonson's servant, makes reference to 'Poeticke furies' who threaten an actor's life for changing a syllable of the text (*The Antipodes*, 2.1) in what would seem to be a barbed account of the poetical terrorism exercised by his master.[223] Jonson clearly judged and condemned actors in performances, going up to the 'Gallery, when | your Comedies and Enterludes haue entred their Actions' and making 'vile and bad faces at euerie lyne'.[224] Bishop Hall similarly depicts poets sitting 'in high Parliament'

> . . . watching euery word, and gesturement,
> Like curious Censors of some doughtie geare,
> Whispering their verdit in their fellowes eare.
> Wo to the word whose margent in their scrole,
> Is noted with a blacke condemning cole.
> But if each periode might the Synode please,
> Ho, bring the Iuy boughs, and bands of Bayes.
> (*Virgidemiarum*, 1.3)[225]

But if the actors did change the text, there was little a poet could do about it. When a complaint was made to Chapman that lines officially censored in his play were being spoken on the stage, he replied that he had no power to stop the actors in performance:

I have not deserv'd what I suffer by your Austeritie, yf the two or three lynes you crost were spoken; My vttermost to sup=presse them was enough for my discharge; To more than wch, no promysse can be rackt by reason; I see not myne owne Plaies, Nor carrie the Actors Tongues in my Mouthe.[226]

Herbert refers to a similar occasion on which his injunctions were disregarded on the text itself of the *Martir'd Soldier*. The play had been reallowed with reformations 'which were not observed, for to every cross they added a stet of their owne'.[227] Actors also

---

[223] *Brome*, iii. 257.

[224] *Satiromastix* in Thomas Dekker, *The Dramatic Works*, ed. Fredson Bowers, 4 vols. (Cambridge, 1964), i. 382.

[225] Joseph Hall, *The Poems*, ed. Arnold Davenport (Liverpool, 1969), 15.

[226] A. R. Braunmuller, *A Seventeenth-Century Letter-Book* (Newark, Del., 1983), 246. This also indicates that Chapman was in charge of his production.

[227] Bawcutt, *Censorship*, 143.

added lines, as those spoken in *The Magnetic Lady* but not passed by Herbert, testify. Herbert records that he was 'discharged . . . of any blame' for the corrupt text, when 'the whole fault of their play' was laid 'upon the players'; but he assumed the worst when *The Winter's Tale* was handed to him to be reallowed because the original book had been lost. He demanded Heminges's word 'that there was nothing profane added or reformed'.[228] The complaint that a poet cannot ultimately control performance is made several times by Dekker: in his epilogue to *The Roaring Girle* he (or, perhaps, Middleton) asks that his play be excused 'for such faults, as . . . negligence of the Actors do commit'; in *The Whore of Babylon* he expostulates:

let the Poet set the note of his Nombers, euen to *Apolloes* owne Lyre, the Player will haue his owne Crochets, and sing false notes . . . The labours therfore of Writers are as vnhappie as the children of a bewtifull woman, being spoyld by ill nurses[229]

Similarly, Brome, who in *The Antipodes* (2.1) had made a playwright declare that he would not threaten 'the Actors life' simply for adding or taking away a syllable,[230] ironically accuses his actors of just that, with clear fury, at the end of the Quarto text of 1640 to the same play. He explains to the reader that 'You shal find in this Booke more than was presented upon the *Stage*, and left out of the *Presentation*, for superfluous length (as some of the *Players* pretended)'.[231] As actors' textual change, planned and unplanned, happened in or after performance, it is performance itself that emerges as a major forum for revision. The first performance particularly offered an opportunity for cuts and adaptations to be made, for it was the audition-like 'rehearsal' of the text.

---

[228] Bawcutt, *Censorship*, 165, 142.

[229] *Dekker*, iii. 101; ii. 497–8. Dekker has 'set the note of his Nombers' which suggests he has rehearsed the actors, even though he 'apparently had not witnessed the production'—see Cyrus Hoy, *Introductions, Notes, and Commentaries to Texts in 'The Dramatic Works of Thomas Dekker'*, 4 vols. (Cambridge, 1980–1), ii. 308.

[230] *Brome*, iii. 257.

[231] *Brome*, iii. 339. For similar alterations made with the author's consent, see Humphrey Moseley's epistle to Beaumont and Fletcher, *Comedies and Tragedies*, A4ª: 'when these *Comedies* and *Tragedies* were presented on the Stage, the *Actours* omitted some *Scenes* and Passages (with the *Authour's* consent) as occasion led them'; and *The Duchess of Malfi*, in John Webster, *The Works*, ed. David Gunby, David Carnegie, Antony Hammond *et al.*, 2 vols. (Cambridge, 1995), i. 467: 'The perfect and exact Coppy, with *diverse things Printed, that the length of the Play would* not beare in the Presentment'.

*First performance*

As is clear from mayors' and Revels' 'rehearsals', performative 'rehearsals' implied not actors' preparation, but textual revamping. At first performances in the theatres, similarly, the plays themselves were 'rehearsed' as before the mayor and the Revels: they were 'tested' for approval by the people. Two plays from the Admiral's 1594–5 season were performed only once; new plays were tested against poor returns, so that if 'it . . . pleas'd not the Million' (*Ham.* 1481), 'it' was dropped. This was no surprise to eighteenth-century theatre-historians, who still followed the same practice: 'The custom of passing a final censure on plays at their first exhibition is as ancient as the time of [Shakespeare]'.[232] In fact, in the time of Shakespeare (and later), first days were separated from other days by the use of legal terminology: the play was 'tried' and the audience was the judge, 'trial' clearly being a trial of the play itself, as prologues and epilogues make clear when they plead for leniency towards the playwright, generally depicted as trembling behind the curtains to await the audience's decision.[233] If successful, the play was deemed to have passed its trial—'these Playes haue had their triall alreadie, and stood out all Appeales'; 'it hath past the Test of the Stage'.[234] 'Tryall', was also what university players called their last rehearsal before performance; the 'trial' was a particular state of production different from other performances, and particularly rehearsal-like in nature. But the fact that a special vocabulary was used

---

[232] *Supplement*, ed. Malone, i. 46.

[233] See also the manuscript epilogue to Brome's *English Moore,* reproduced in Sara Jayne Steen's edition of that play, 157. In several epilogues the playwright is described as being in a place where he can see but not be seen. In Henry Glapthorne's *Ladies Priviledge* (1640), J2ᵃ, the author 'betwixt hope and Feare | Stands pensive in the Tyring-house to heare | Your Censures of his *Play*'; in James Shirley, *The Cardinal* (1652), F3ᵇ, the Epilogue relates of the playwright, 'I do know | He listens to the issue of his cause'.

[234] Heminges and Condell, 'To the great Variety of Readers,' in William Shakespeare, *The First Folio*, A3ᵃ; Heywood, 'Epistle to the Reader', in John Cooke's *Greenes Tu Quoque* (1614), A2ᵃ. See also 'The Description of a Poet' in William Fennor, *Fennors Descriptions* (1616), B2ᵃ–B3ᵃ: 'Sweet Poesye | Is oft convict, condem'd, and judg'd to die | Without just triall, by a multitude | Whose judgements are illiterate, and rude'; *The Novella* in *Brome*, i. 104: 'Hee'll bide his triall, and submits his cause | To you the Jury'; Thomas Nabbes, *Totenham Court* (1638), A3ᵃ: 'That you should authorize [the play] after the *Stages* tryall was not my intention'; John Ford, *The Ladies Triall* (1639), K4ᵇ: 'The Court's on rising; tis too late | To wish the Lady in her fate | Of tryall now more fortunate'.

to describe the first performance also illustrates how the occasion somehow affected the way the play was subsequently considered. One issue was that the audience were asked to approve or disapprove a play by their cries of 'aye' or 'no' at the end of the initial performance, so determining whether the play would live or die, as articulated by the epilogue to Walter Mountfort's *Launching of the Mary*:

> Yf then this please (kinde gentlemen) saye so
> Yf yt displease affirem yt wth your No.
> your, I, shall make yt liue to glad the sire
> your, No, shall make yt burne in quenchles fire.[235]

A play that was 'damned' after the initial showing was not usually performed again. Examples of damned productions include Jonson's *New Inne*, 'squeamishly beheld, and censured' by the 'hundred fastidious *impertinents*, who were there present the first day'; Fletcher's *The Faithfull Shepheardesse*, 'scornd' by its original audience; also Jonson's *Sejanus*; Beaumont's *Knight of the Burning Pestle*; Webster's *White Divel*; Fletcher's *Monsieur Thomas*; Massinger's *Emperour of the East*.[236] So 'passing' the

---

[235] Walter Mountfort, *The Launching of the Mary*, ed. John Henry Walter (Oxford, 1933), 124. For the subsequent two centuries, the audience would continue to be asked to give their response to the first night with 'aye' or 'no'. See Ch. 6, 'First performance'. Prologues and epilogues often refer to their first-day status, and to awaiting the audience's judgement. See, for instance, the epilogue to James Shirley's *The Sisters* (1652), E6a: 'you [the audience] | May save or kill, my lif's now in your hands'.

[236] *Jonson*, vi. 395–7; John Fletcher, *The Faithfull Shepheardesse* [1609], A2[b]. See the introductory poem to Ben Jonson's, *Sejanus His Fall* (1605), A3[b]: 'I view'd the peoples beastly rage, | Bent to confound thy grave, and learned toile, . . . this Publication setts thee free: | They for their ignorance, still damned bee'; Francis Beaumont, *Knight of the Burning Pestle* (1613), A2[a]: 'this unfortunate child . . . was . . . exposed to the wide world, who for want of judgement . . . utterly rejected it'; *The White Divel* in Webster, *Works*, 140: 'it wanted . . . a full and understanding Auditory'. John Fletcher's *Monsieur Thomas* (1639), A2[a], 'did participate | At first presenting but of common fate' because out of the audience 'but a few | What was legitimate, what bastard, knew'; William Singleton declares in an introductory poem to *The Emperour of the East* in Massinger, iii. 406: 'What I haue read . . . I dare crowne | With a deseru'd applause, how ere cri'd downe | By such whose malice will not let 'em bee | Equall to any peece'. Glapthorne, *Ladies Priviledge* (1640), A3[b], refers to spectators who 'for shortnesse force the Author run, | and end his Play before his Plot be done'; 'THE uncivil ignorance of the People, had depriv'd' William Davenant's *The Just Italian*, of life, had not the Earl of Dorset 'stept in to succour it' (William Davenant, *The Works*, 3 vols. in 1 (1673), ii. 440). The Epilogue to William Shakespeare's *The Second part of Henrie the fourth* (1600), L1[b], 'was lately here in the end of a displeasing play, to pray your patience for it and to promise you a better.'

trial with 'approval', as explained in terms of the applause received on the first day, was very important. It is, hardly surprisingly, extolled in printed plays; 'a general applause' is the converse of a 'damnation', and claiming to have made it through the 'trial' with honour gives the readers a guide as to the quality of a play: 'it hath past the Test of the stage with . . . generall . . . applause' is a standard title-page encomium.[237] As these examples show, a play grew in desirability after having been moulded by the playhouse and sanctioned by the spectators in performance; and it was the 'approved' performing text that had come about by the second day that was taken to be the 'real' or stable play, the play in the form that a potential buyer would wish to have it; play prefaces emphasize to the reader that they have been 'tried' and 'tested', broadcasting that they are post-performance and post-first-day scripts.

That the first performance was a playtext's 'rehearsal' partly explains why Henslowe charged double for first performances: both to make as much money as possible in case the piece was never performed again, and to make the first-day audience feel exclusive—they were the people 'who the Poet and the Actors fright, | Least that [their] Censure thin the second night'.[238] But the special nature of the first performance also suggests something about the revision process that, again, emerges more clearly in the following centuries. Certainly by the Restoration a habit had formed of revising plays directly after the first night, in the light of the audience's criticism, for that audience was going to affect the attendance of the author's 'benefit' night—the night on which the playwright would receive a substantial portion of the revenue from the performance as payment. When benefit performances were first established is hard to

---

[237] Cooke, *Greenes Tu Quoque*, A2[a]. See also Thomas Heywood, *The Golden Age* (1611), A2[a]: 'my Booke . . . hath already past the approbation of Auditors'; James Shirley, *The Wedding* (1629), A3[a]: 'It hath passed the Stage'; Rawlins, *Rebellion*, A2[a]: 'This Tragedy had at the presentment a generall Applause'; *The Picture* in Massinger, iii. 195: 'The Play in the presentment found . . . a generall approbation'; *The City Madam* in Massinger, iv. 19: 'this Poem was the object of . . . Commendations, it being . . . censured by an unerring Auditory'; John Kirke, *The Seven Champions of Christendome* (1638), A3[b]: 'it received the rights of a good Play, when it was Acted, which were Applauses & Commendations'.

[238] See Knutson, *Repertory*, 25; Henry Harington, 'On Mr. JOHN FLETCER'S [*sic*] ever to be admired Dramaticall Works', Beaumont and Fletcher, *Comedies and Tragedies*, f4[b].

identify, but as the flexibility of the 'trial' text is connected to them, it is worth running over the surviving evidence for their existence during the Renaissance.

The earliest direct reference to authorial benefits occurs in 1611, when a prologue deals critically with the kind of playwright who cares for nothing provided that 'hee *Gaines,* | A Cramd *Third-Day*'; benefits are mentioned again by Daborne in 1613 who declares that he and Tourneur will have for their *Bellman of London* 'but twelv pownds and the overplus of the second day'.[239] But Davenant in *Playhouse to Be Lett* maintains 'You Poets us'd to have the second day' as far back as 'the times of mighty *Tamburlane* | Of conjuring *Faustus,* and the *Beauchamps* bold' (the time of Marlowe and Heywood—before 1600).[240] By the late 1620s and thereafter until the closure of the theatre, second-performance 'benefits' were a usual method of payment: Brome's contract with Queen Henrietta's Company gives him a weekly wage with, in addition, 'the benefit of one day's profit of playing such new play as he should make'; Malone, reading Herbert's original office book (now lost), found that 'between the years 1625 and 1641 [dramatists'] benefits were on the second day of representation'.[241] In plays of the 1630s and 1640s, references to second-day benefits are numerous; they frequently occur in prologues and epilogues, so making clear also the fact that prologues and epilogues were only spoken before the benefit performance (i.e. they were only spoken on the opening day): 'Profit he [the playwright] knowes none | Unles that of your Approbation, | Which if your thoughts at going out will pay, | Hee'l not looke further for a *Second Day*' [perf. 1634–5?]; 'He's One, whose unbought Muse did never feare | An Empty second day, or a thinne share' [perf. 1637–8]—a reference to the two systems of payment operating at the time; 'the next night when we your money share, | Hee'll shrewdly guesse what your opinions are' [perf. 1638].[242]

---

[239] *If this be not a Good Play, the Devil is in it,* in *Dekker,* iii. 121; W. W. Greg, *Henslowe Papers,* 3 vols. (London, 1907), iii. 75.

[240] *Davenant,* ii. 76.

[241] Quoted in Bentley, *Dramatist,* 128; 132.

[242] Prologue to *The Scholars* in Francis Beaumont, *Poems by Francis Beaumont* (1653), 79; Jasper Mayne, *The Citye Match* (1639), B1ᵃ; *The Unfortunate Lovers* in William *Davenant,* ii. 165. See also Shirley, *Cardinal* (1652), F3ᵇ: 'when without a clap you go away, | I'l drink a small-beer health to his second day' (perf. 1641);

From the institution of the benefit onwards, it became imperative for a playwright to ensure that spectators would not damn the play before 'his' night; one way of doing this was to accede to their revision requirements. As a 1632 epilogue explains: 'By the Poet, Sirs, | I'm sent to crave a Plaudit . . . his promis'd Pay | May chance to faile, if you dislike the Play'.[243] From significantly early on in the history of the theatre, prologues and epilogues can be seen inviting first-performance spectators to indicate for 'correction' the bits that do not please them. So the Prologue to *Foure Prentises*, played between 1592 and 1600, 'would willingly amend' errors, though he begs the audience to overlook what they can; while the Prologue to *Lovers Melancholy*, played in 1628, asks that the '*true Critick*', defined as being someone who can both 'judge' and, significantly, 'mend' plays, let pass the 'Sceanes and Stile' as they are.[244] Massinger in *The Guardian*, played in 1633, wishes to know what his errors are, so that he can 'bestow | His future studies to reform from this | What in another might be judg'd amiss'; but Sir John Denham throws his work back in the teeth of critical spectators: 'you that discommend it, mend the Play' (played in 1641?).[245] Play prefaces and introductory poems collectively show that

Shirley, *The Sisters* (1652), A3ᵃ: 'a Play | Though ne'r so new, will starve the second day' (1642); prologue to *The Whisperer* reproduced in John Tatham, *Ostella* (1650), 111: 'Our *Author* likes the *Women* well, and says . . . on *his Day* . . . leave them not behind' (perf. c.1640–50); Henry Harington, 'On Mr. JOHN FLETCER'S [*sic*] . . . Dramaticall Works', in Beaumont and Fletcher, *Comedies and Tragedies*, f4ᵇ: 'You who the Poet and the Actors fright, | Least that your Censure thin the second night'; John Tatham, *The Fancies Theater* (1649), (\*)7ᵃ: 'I shall deeme thee worthy praise, | . . . When Fancie in thy *Theater* doth play, | And wins more credit than a second day'. Allusions from the 1650s to benefit nights are referred to in Bentley, *Dramatist*, 134. The pleas made by prologues and epilogues to treat a trembling author well, and not to censure a play too harshly, are themselves only relevant for initial performances. Often prologues refer to the first-performance status of the plays they front: for instance in Beaumont and Fletcher, *Comedies and Tragedies*, the Prologue to *The Spanish Curate*, H1ᵇ, comes 'To tell ye . . . we have a Play, | A new one too, and that 'tis launched to day'; similarly that to *The Humorous Lieutenant*, 3T2ᵃ, explains: 'We have a Play, a new Play to play now'.

[243] *The Novella* in Brome, i. 179.
[244] Heywood, *Foure Prentises*, A4ᵇ; John Ford, *The Lovers Melancholy* (1629), A3ᵃ.
[245] *The Guardian* in Massinger, iv. 114; Sir John Denham, *The Sophy* (1642), A2ᵃ. See also *The Captaine* in Beaumont and Fletcher, *Comedies and Tragedies*, 2K1a: 'IF you mislike . . . this Play utterly, . . . as you goe by, say it was amisse; | And we will mend'; *Antonio* in Marston, i. 63: 'What imperfection you have seene in us, leave with us, & weele amend it'; Manuche *Just General*, A2ᵇ: the actors 'shall study [to] mend | Such faults as you shall say our Author pen'd'.

first-performance revision was thought of as normal; that a play on its opening was offered to the audience as a mutable text ready for improvement. The third impression of Beaumont and Fletcher's *Philaster* has a preface that makes this very clear. The play is likened to gold by the stationer who introduces it. Both are, as he explains, tested and 'refined' before receiving final approval: 'the best Poems of this kind, in the first presentation, resemble that all-tempting Minerall newly digged up, the Actors being onely the labouring Miners, but you [the audience] the skillful Triers and Refiners'.[246] Authors of plays that, for one reason or another, have not been tested in public, know to anticipate an adverse response from the potential readership, and apologetically hunt for excuses to justify themselves. Shirley's *The Court Secret* had been prepared for Blackfriars but was never performed there because of the closure of the theatres. Though the play therefore 'wanted that publique Seal which other Compositions enjoyed' explains the epistle (for the text has never been 'warranted by Applause') yet certain important readers have seen and 'allowed' it—it has, in a sense, been 'tried', at least by the people whose opinions matter.[247] Shakespeare's *Troilus* in its Quarto (b) form is much more defensive. Its haughty epistle explains how the play has never been 'stal'd with the Stage', or 'clapper-clawd with the palmes of the vulger'. But the real issue is that *Troilus* is an unperformed play, and the shift in tone at the end of the epistle manifests this. 'Refuse not', recommends the careful conclusion, 'nor like this the lesse, for not being sullied, with the smoaky breath of the multitiude'.[248]

There is, unsurprisingly, a good deal of evidence showing that the playwright was present for the first performance—as he

---

[246] Francis Beaumont and John Fletcher, *Philaster* (3rd impression, 1628), A2[b]. Richard Woolfall 'To his Friend the Author' in Lewis Sharpe, *The Noble Stranger* (1640), A3[a], jeers at potential 'Critick Readers', telling them that they are too late: the piece has already 'proved fortunate' at the theatre so that now 'I dare boldly say, | Who ere dislikes it cannot mend thy Play'.

[247] James Shirley, *The Court Secret, never Acted but prepared for the Scene at Black-Friers* (1653), A3[a–b].

[248] William Shakespeare, *The Famous Historie of Troylus and Cresseid* (1609), (π2a–b. The question as to whether the play had actually been privately performed is a complex one; no satisfactory solution has been found for the different information offered in variant Quarto title-pages and the Stationers' Register. Here I am specifically interested in the way the writer of the epistle presents his belief that the play has never been mounted.

needed to be to receive his criticism. Indeed, the poet's state of first-performance nerves as he waits to hear the 'result' of the test is the subject of a standard in-house joke, namely, that he cannot tell the difference between the opening of bottled ale and a hiss.[249] Sometimes playwrights were, like Jonson, publicly visible; usually they stayed backstage where they could not be seen by the spectators, but could help in production: when Epilogue in *Love's Riddle* 'forgets' his lines, he goes into the tiring house to be reminded of them by their maker.[250] For involved playwrights continued to take a business-like interest in performance, even sometimes doubling with prompter or call-boy in overseeing entrances and exits; a jokey epilogue is pronounced by Pollard, who is made to enter by being 'thrust on stage' by the author:

> I am coming to you, Gentlemen, the Poet
> Has help'd me thus far on my way, but I'l
> Be even with him[251]

Another advantage to being backstage was that the poet's person and his tremors were hidden as he waited to hear whether his play had 'passed': 'You'd smile to see, how he do's vex and shake, | Speakes naught but if the Prologue does but take, | Or the first Act were past the Pikes once, then— | Then hopes and Joys, then frowns and fears agen'; 'I've left him now | With's limber Hat, o'reshadowing his Brow, | His Cloke cast thus—to hinder from his ear, | The scornes and censures he may shortly hear'.[252]

First performances, then, were textual 'rehearsals', and seem, from at least the beginning of the seventeenth century (but quite possibly from before then) to have been the forum for audience-led revision. There is enough evidence to suggest that plays were often regarded as being flexible between first and second performance; a pre-performance text and a post-performance

---

[249] See Beaumont and Fletcher's description of a playwright's 'shakings & quakinges, towards the latter end of [his] new play' in *Woman-Hater* (1607), C3ᵇ: 'he standes peeping betwixt curtaines, so fearefully, that a bottle of Ale cannot be opened, but he thinks some body hisses'. John Stephens's *A base Mercenary Poet* in *Satyrical Essayes, Characters and Others* (1615), 292, describes the reverse situation: 'And when hee heares his play hissed, hee would rather thinke bottle-Ale is opening'.

[250] See *Satiromastix* in *Dekker*, i. 382; Abraham Cowley, *Love's Riddle* (1638), G4ᵃ.

[251] Shirley, *Cardinal*, F3ᵇ.

[252] Prologue to *The Scholars* in Beaumont's *Poems* (1653), 75; *Davenant*, ii. 384.

text might well be different, and, indeed, some of the texts that we have in two versions could well be the result of overnight revision rather than of the long reflective period of rewriting that has often been imagined.

### First performance and the audience

What kind of criticism was the audience able to give? References are limited, perhaps because playwrights often made the required alterations without demur: only unhappy authors articulate their first-performance grievances, and then only if they publish their texts. But there are one or two allusions that give a general sense of the nature of first-performance comment. The preface to Thomas Killigrew's *Pallantus and Eudora*, played by the King's Company in 1635, recalls that there was only one significant objection made against the story at its first showing. This was that 'Cleander', who in the play was a boy of 17, spoke words more suitable for a 30-year-old:

> But the Answer that was given to One, that cried out upon the *Monsterousnesse* and *Impossiblitie* of this thing, the first day of the Presentation of the Play at the *Black-Friers*, by the Lord Viscount *Faulkland*, may satisfie All Others . . . The Noble Person, having for some time suffered the unquiet, and impertinent Dislikes of this Auditor, when he made this last Exception, forbore him no longer, but . . . told him, Sir, *'tis not altogether so Monsterous and Impossible, for One of Seventeen yeares to speak at such a Rate, when He that made him speak in that manner, and writ the whole Play, was Himself no Older.*[253]

Another playwright who also details the objections made to his play, again finding it necessary to offer reasons why the text has not been changed for the audience, is Henry Burnell, who records how some people were 'offended' at the conclusion of his play 'in regard *Landgartha* tooke not then . . . the Kings kind night-imbraces. To which kind of people . . . I answer . . . that a Tragie-Comedy sho'd neither end Comically or Tragically'.[254] Jonson's *Every Man Out of His Humour*, on the other hand, broadcasts the fact that it has undergone revision immediately after the opening day. It 'had another *Catastrophe* or Conclusion,

---

[253] Thomas Killigrew, *Pallantus and Eudora* (1653), A2[a].
[254] Henry Burnell, *Landgartha* (1641), K1[a].

at the first Playing: which . . . many seem'd not to rellish . . .; and therefore 'twas since alter'd'.[255] The manuscript of Walter Mountfort's *The Launching of the Mary; or, The Seamans Honest Wife*, written in 1632, also bears distinct signs of first-performance revision. It has been formally censured by Henry Herbert, Master of the Revels, which slightly confuses the matter, but it contains a special second-performance prologue that explains how the play 'H'as been before the Tryers' and has subsequently 'lost a limb to save the rest'. The plural noun 'tryers' identifies the critics as the first-performance audience, 'tryers' referring to the people who attend the 'trial'. The specific second-performance prologue confirms this; Herbert's censorship appears to be confined mainly to oaths, whereas the revisions in the text are wide-ranging, including, for instance, cutting out insults to the profession of army captain: slights that are unlikely to have worried the Master of the Revels.[256]

CONCLUSION

Renaissance companies had to balance a heavy performance schedule against their need to rehearse. Their preference for saving full group rehearsals for the weeks in which they were not playing is evident; this means that there was probably less group rehearsal during playing time (which covered most of the rest of the year). Though three weeks seems to have been the usual length of time for preparing a play, there is no evidence to suggest that more than the traditional single group rehearsal was held within that period, as private learning ('study'), often with a teacher, was the most important part of preparation. For superior players this teacher was sometimes the playwright; major players instructed lesser players. 'Study' seems to have involved teaching a part by imitation; it was not a creative event, nor did it encourage textual exploration and discovery, so that there is little justification for claiming that texts were substantially revised by actors in preparation. On the contrary, actors' revision tended to

---

[255] Ben Jonson, *The commicall satyre of every man out of his humour* (1600), R3ᵃ.
[256] The manuscript is described in Evelyn May Albright, *Dramatic Publication in England, 1580–1640* (New York and London, 1927), 171–2; the second prologue is not reproduced in John Henry Walter's Malone society edition.

happen in performance itself, when the actor was free from teachers. In terms of readying a performance, group rehearsal was only actually necessary for parts of plays that could not be learnt alone—songs, sword-fights, quick changes etc.—and was therefore the most dispensable part of play preparation, especially as blocking, music, even, perhaps, some gestures, seem to have been conducted during performance by the prompter and his men.

The fact that performances were 'rehearsals' had textual ramifications, as rehearsals for the mayor or the Master of the Revels made clear. The kind of revision that had taken place before performance was largely private: it happened in the office of the Master of the Revels, and in the home of the prompter or manager as he modified or 'purged' a book. But revision in or as the result of a 'trial' performance seems also to have been an important part of the process of putting on a play.[257] Though much has been written on revision between productions, little consideration has been given to revision within productions, or as the result of a single performance. Yet some actors seem to have revised and altered their parts, sometimes for a single occasion, sometimes permanently, and full plays too seem to have sometimes been adjusted as a response to first-performance criticism.

### THE FUTURE OF THE RENAISSANCE THEATRE

In 1642 a pronouncement was made that put an end to the public theatre companies in London for the duration of the war; shortly afterwards, in 1644, the Globe was pulled down to make way for tenements.[258] But the Restoration theatre in many ways picked up from where the Renaissance theatre had left off. The new theatre companies studied, rehearsed, and performed their

---

[257] *Pace* Stanley Wells and Gary Taylor, who based their *Complete Shakespeare* on the premise of fluid rehearsal revision, followed by a relatively fixed first-performance text: 'We have regarded as authoritative virtually everything which happens to the text of a play in its evolution from initial idea to first performance . . . culminating in a collaborative public performance' (Gary Taylor and John Jowett, *Shakespeare Reshaped* (Oxford, 1993), 236).

[258] Gurr, *Shakespearian Stage*, 79; See Walter H. Godfrey and Sir Howard Roberts (eds.), *The Survey of London, Bankside Volume*, 22 (London, 1950), 78.

plays in much the same manner; they were equally uninterested in long-term textual permanence. They moved away from Shakespeare's theatre only when they tried to emulate it: in the fragments of the Elizabethan dramatic tradition which they dredged up or created, and imposed awkwardly on top of the late seventeenth- and eighteenth-century theatre—the motto of Drury Lane was said to have been the Globe's, 'Totus mundus agit histrionem' ('the whole world plays the player'—or, 'all the world's a stage').[259] The Restoration theatre showed a tendency to idealize and fictionalize the Elizabethan past, and to apply the result to its own theatre, while scorning and directly imitating Continental theatrical practice.

[259] But see Tiffany Stern, 'Was Totus Mundus Agit Histrionem Ever the Motto of the Globe Theatre?', *TN* 51 (1997), 122–7.

# 4

# Rehearsal in Betterton's Theatre

## BACKGROUND

In 1660, professional acting companies, having been disbanded during the Commonwealth, were shakily re-establishing themselves. At this early stage they had not yet settled on a formula for acting or presenting plays: should they take their methods from perceived Elizabethan precedent, or from the French theatre that had so entertained the exiled court? The powerful author-manager was a tradition seemingly offered by both: Molière depicts himself as a playwright in charge of rehearsal in *L'Impromptu de Versailles*, while idealized accounts of Elizabethan authorial 'instruction' accrued around respected Renaissance playwrights, particularly Jonson.[1] The little acting that had taken place during the Commonwealth seems to have relied on authorial management (without the framework of a professional theatre, this is hardly surprising): when a play was presented in 1651, first by Oxford students, and then by players, 'the Poet gave equal Instructions' to both.[2] The Restoration theatre was established with a belief that authors should be in charge of their productions: the actor Thomas Betterton in Charles Gildon's semi-fictionalized *Life* boasts that he and the actress Elizabeth Barry will talk to 'the most indifferent Poet in any Part we have thought fit to accept of'.[3] In form, authors had control over their plays—should they choose to exercise it.

---

[1] See Richard Flecknoe, *Love's Kingdom . . . with a short Treatise of the English Stage* (1664), G6ᵇ; John Aubrey, *Brief Lives*, ed. Oliver Lawson Dick (1949; London, 1962), 334. A 1660 production of *The Alchemist* asks how the actors can perform their roles without Jonson there to teach them 'Line by Line, each Tittle, Accent, Word'—see *Prologues and Epilogues of the Restoration*, ed. Pierre Danchin, 1 vol. in 2 (Nancy, 1981), I:i, 53.

[2] Charles Gildon, *The Lives and Characters of the English Dramatick Poets* (1699), 17.

[3] Charles Gildon, *Life of Mr. Thomas Betterton* (1710), 16.

A high percentage of early Restoration playwrights were courtiers and men of noble birth: no dramatist made a living in the theatre between 1660 and 1665.[4] These respected, powerful noblemen, with their ideas about how best to re-establish drama in England and their quantities of free time, were active in the production of their plays in a way that other and subsequent amateur writers were not. And from about 1668, professional playwrights, often with contractual 'attachments' to particular companies, started writing and overseeing the majority of new plays performed; their number was added to towards the end of the century by 'semi-professionals', often actors, who also wrote and produced their own plays.[5] Casual playwrights were no longer necessary, and often, no longer desirable.

As companies had, of necessity, begun by performing 'old plays', particularly those of Jonson, Shakespeare, Beaumont and Fletcher, so they had from the very start of the Restoration become accustomed to preparing productions without the help of an author, under the charge of actors and managers. This partly explains the difficulty that critics have in deciding who was responsible for the rehearsals of the time—some claiming that it was the author, some the manager, and some a senior actor.[6] But the issue is more complicated than this. The Restoration theatre, which had started by producing plays without authorial help, speedily learnt that it did not generally need authors—with the exception of the useful contractually attached professionals. The idea that the playwright was in charge of production was adhered to in form, but not in fact. With the institution of theatrical managers who wanted an active role in

---

[4] Robert D. Hume, 'Securing a Repertory: Plays on the London Stage 1660–5', in Antony Coleman and Antony Hammond (eds.), *Poetry and Drama 1570–1700: Essays in Honour of Harold F. Brooks* (London, 1981), 156–72 (168).

[5] Judith Milhous and Robert D. Hume, *Producible Interpretation* (Carbondale, Ill., 1985), 41–3. Allan Richard Botica, 'Audience, Playhouse and Play in Restoration Theatre' (unpublished doctoral thesis, University of Oxford, 1985), 102, divides playwrights into 'nobility and gentry', 'professional dramatists', and 'writers who had to balance their dramatic interests against the demands of their employment'. He calculates that between 1660 and 1700, 23% of playwrights came from the nobility or gentry, 28% were professionals, and 33% were 'amateur' (16% unknown).

[6] For the claim that actors supervised rehearsals see Joanne Lafler, *The Celebrated Mrs Oldfield* (Carbondale, Ill., 1989), 9. Milhous and Hume, *Producible*, 59, state both that the author '[took] most of the responsibilities we would regard . . . as directorial' and that 'Regular daily rehearsals were normally supervised by the manager', an inconsistency they do not reconcile.

the production of all plays (like William Davenant, and after him, Thomas Betterton), and with the growth in the importance and power of the actor—leading first to the rise of the actor-manager, and secondly, to a large number of actor-triumvirates (Betterton, Barry, and Bracegirdle in 1695; Cibber, Wilks, and Doggett in 1710)—the playwright's active presence became a hindrance instead of a help. The struggling, nervous theatre of 1660 wanted authorial instruction and assistance; the confident professional theatre of 1710 (the time-span of this chapter) emphatically did not. The need to train new actors (including adult women) from scratch at the beginning of the Restoration, and the part in that training process that managers, actors, and prompters necessarily took, drew the emphasis of all productions away from what playwrights could teach, towards what theatrical aficionados could teach. As a result, by the end of the century, even professional playwrights sometimes 'chose' to abnegate authority while amateurs who possessively retained nominal authority over their texts, were actually at the mercy of—at various different stages—professional playwrights, actors, and audience, and were frequently forced to revise their plays against their wills.

### RESTORATION THEATRE COMPANIES

The story of the Restoration theatre begins with two theatrical companies that merge, separate, and merge again repeatedly over the following decades, changing names and figureheads, but involving mostly the same actors. The details are complex, particularly when briefly summed up, as here, but the theatre itself—as opposed to its ownership—remained relatively constant in its production methods.

At the start of the Restoration there was a dependency on a perceived 'old school' of acting, maintained largely by the older generation itself, which consisted of such pre-Restoration actors as Charles Hart, Michael Mohun, and Robert Shatterell. Most of these performers began playing for Thomas Killigrew in 1660 as part of the King's Company, a troupe that deliberately linked itself to its illustrious Jacobean predecessors of the same name (Killigrew also claimed rights to the pre-Restoration King's

Company's repertory).[7] The younger generation of actors
largely fell to the lot of Sir William Davenant, and made up
the Duke's Men; they too were schooled in the ways of the past:
Davenant trained his actors in the pre-Commonwealth tradition
he had experienced in the 1630s, basing his method of playing
Hamlet (so he claimed), on the manner he had seen 'Mr. *Taylor*
of the *Black-Fryars* Company Act it', and handing on the mode
of acting Henry VIII as he 'had it from Old Mr. *Lowen*, that had
his Instructions from Mr. *Shakespear* himself'.[8] The Restoration
theatre seemed to be trying to take up from where the Caroline
theatre had left off.

The patents that allowed Davenant and Killigrew to run
theatres in London were offered in perpetuity and no more
were issued: from 1660 onwards only two companies were
legally allowed to put on plays in the capital. Killigrew managed
his company from 1660 to 1682; Davenant ran his from 1660
until he died in 1668. Davenant's company was then taken over
by Thomas Betterton, the actor; he was assisted, first by the
actor Henry Harris, then by the actor William Smith; he himself
remained manager until 1687. But in 1682 Betterton's company
merged with King's and so became the only company (known as
the United Company) operating in London. For legal reasons,
control of this company passed into the hands of Christopher
Rich and Thomas Skipwith, who were primarily financiers and
gave the management of the theatre over to actors; they ran their
'Patent' company from 1693 to 1709, but in 1695 Betterton,
along with Anne Bracegirdle and Elizabeth Barry, rebelled and
set up their own theatre in Lincoln's Inn Fields, where they ran
an actors' co-operative from 1695 to 1704, thus re-establishing
the two-company system in London. The Lincoln's Inn company ('Betterton's') was then managed by Sir John Vanbrugh,
architect and playwright, partly at Lincoln's Inn, and partly at

---

[7] See Judith Milhous, *Thomas Betterton and the Management of Lincoln's Inn Fields*
(Carbondale, Ill., 1979), 15–25.

[8] John Downes, *Roscius Anglicanus*, ed. J. Milhous and R. D. Hume (London,
1987), 51, 55. This is not actually possible as Taylor did not perform the part while
Shakespeare was alive—see p. 51 n. Davenant added to his claim to be performing
within the Shakespearian tradition, by asserting that he was, in fact, Shakespeare's
illegitimate son (Aubrey, *Brief Lives*, 177). W. R. Chetwood, *A General History of the
Stage* (1749), 21, adds 'The Features seem to resemble the open Countenance of
Shakespear, but the want of a Nose, gives an odd Cast to the Face'.

the Queen's Theatre in the Haymarket, a new venue built especially for operas. In 1708 both companies briefly merged again, but in 1709 Betterton's players went back to Queen's and Rich was expelled from Drury Lane. Then, in 1710, the two companies united once more under Colley Cibber, Thomas Doggett, and Robert Wilks. That same year, Betterton died.

Given their history of combining and separating, both companies' methods of readying plays for production will certainly have been similar. The compatibility of Davenant's and Killigrew's ideas about the preparation and performance of plays is borne out by the fact that the two ran a joint 'nursery' for training young actors in 1667.[9] So, in this chapter, information about productions will be taken from both companies; though the focus will be on any company of which Betterton was a member. This is because Betterton was a continuous presence in the Restoration theatre between 1660 and 1710, and influenced the stage in many different ways: he was not only the most famous actor of his time, but was also a manager, a playwright, and a 'theatricalizer' of texts. Moreover, Betterton's reflections on the theatre are, in part, preserved, in two different books— one, an early English acting manual in the form of a biography, Charles Gildon's *Life of Mr. Thomas Betterton* (1710); and one an early work of theatre scholarship (purportedly written by Betterton himself but in fact by Edmund Curll), *The History of the English Stage* (1741). Modern scholarship, unsurprisingly, has had more to say about Betterton than about any other theatrical Restoration figure.

## THE AUTHORITY OF BUCKINGHAM'S *THE REHEARSAL*

It is usual to claim that there is very little extant information about casting and rehearsal during the Restoration.[10] That is not strictly true, as this chapter will show; also questionable is the

---

[9] Robert D. Freeburn, 'Charles II. the Theatre Patentees and the Actors' Nursery', *TN* 48 (1994), 148–56 (150).

[10] See William Van Lennep, Emmett L. Avery, and Arthur H. Scouten (eds.), *The London Stage, 1660–1800: A Calendar of Plays*, 5 parts in 11 vols. part I: *1660–1700*, (Carbondale, Ill., 1965), p. cli; Milhous and Hume, *Producible*, 59.

assertion made by Judith Milhous and Robert Hume, that two Restoration plays, *The Rehearsal*, by George Villiers, the second Duke of Buckingham, and the anonymous *Female Wits*, offer 'the best sources' of information about rehearsals during that period.[11] In fact, Buckingham's *Rehearsal* provides confusing and contradictory information, partly fictional, partly based on a very specific kind of 'rehearsal', partly stemming from French theatrical practice, and partly illustrating the role Buckingham thought authors should have (rather than did have) in rehearsal. So *The Rehearsal* is both a hurdle and a starting-point; it is necessary to look at what the play says and why, before turning to real theatrical rehearsal in the period.

The *Rehearsal* was first written in 1664, but its performance was stopped when playhouses were closed on account of the plague. The anti-hero of this lost *Rehearsal* was called Bilboa, and was a parody of Robert Howard (writer of heroic plays) as the eighteenth-century 'key' to the text explains.[12] After 1667 *The Rehearsal* was revised and the hero renamed 'Bayes', a clear allusion to the poet laureate John Dryden, though references to Robert Howard still show through the palimpsest. After performance the play was further revised, and additions were made to heighten the Dryden parody, as the differences between the first Quarto (1672) and the third (1675) make clear.[13] So the text was, from its inception, changeable: it adapted to criticize new people and new ideas as convenient. This adaptability kept *The Rehearsal* in regular production for over a century—it was repeatedly performed, with new actors and writers as its target, until it finally dropped out of the repertory in favour of Richard Sheridan's *The Critic* in the late eighteenth century.[14] For this

---

[11] Milhous and Hume, *Producible*, 59–66, are the only scholars who have recently considered Restoration rehearsal at all, and consequently they come in for all my criticism. That I am also indebted to their scholarship is, I hope, clear.

[12] George Villiers, Duke of Buckingham, *The Rehearsal: a comedy. Written by his Grace, George late Duke of Buckingham. To expose some Plays then in Vogue, & their Authors. With a Key and Remarks* (1709), p. xii.

[13] See George Villiers, Duke of Buckingham, *The Rehearsal*, ed. D. E. L. Crane (Durham, 1976), p. x.

[14] John Mottley, *A List of all the English Dramatic Poets*, appended to Thomas Whincop's *Scanderbeg* (1747), 228, relates how 'Prunella', an interlude designed to ridicule popular Italian operas 'was introduced into the *Duke of Buckingham's Rehearsal*', when Richard Estcourt acted the part of Bayes for his benefit; Tate Wilkinson, in his *The Wandering Patentee*, 4 vols. (1795), i. 279, states simply that 'Bayes is always *ad libitum*'.

reason the play cannot be said to illustrate either one person, or
one moment in theatrical history, particularly as Bayes, the
parody-author, is clearly based on a number of people besides
Dryden and Robert Howard, including Howard's three brothers
Edward, William, and Henry; Robert Stapylton; Thomas Killigrew; Davenant; and perhaps even the Earl of Arlington.[15] The
range of people aimed at in the character 'Bayes' is confusing,
extending not only across several different playwrights (and a
politician?), but across several different *kinds* of playwright:
professional theatrical men, 'semi-professionals', skilled court
wits, and less skilled dabblers, whose rehearsal power, and
methods of rehearsing, differed accordingly.[16] The actual
rehearsing author behind Bayes is obscured by diverse layers
of different fictions; this can be explained by a fact that further
complicates the issue: Bayes was created by a group of authors,
all of whom had different levels of theatrical knowledge, for
Buckingham was helped (it is unclear how much) in writing *The
Rehearsal* by Thomas Sprat, Martin Clifford, Samuel Butler, and
probably also Edmund Waller and Abraham Cowley.[17] The
mishmash that went into writing what was, after all, a parody
of heroic drama, not of rehearsal practice, produced some

[15] See Dane Farnsworth Smith. *Plays about the Theatre in England from The
Rehearsal in 1671 to the Licensing Act in 1737* (London, 1936), 12, and George
McFadden. 'Political Satire in The Rehearsal'. *YES* 4 (1974), 120–8 (123).
McFadden's argument concerns the moment when Bayes returns to the stage with
a patch on his nose—thought, from Malone onwards, to refer to Davenant.
McFadden, arguing that Arlington, a political enemy of Buckingham's, wore a
black covering on his nose (Davenant did not) draws attention to the pictures that
accompany *The Rehearsal* showing Bayes 'with a black patch'. In fact the patch
illustrated in the black and white etching is described in the text as 'wet . . . brown
paper'; but as Bayes is a composite figure, both people could equally well be aimed at
in the parody—or neither, as the nose incident might have its origin in Molière's *Dom
Juan*.

[16] Davenant ran a theatre company: Dryden, later to become an 'attached' poet
with rehearsal duties, had had eight to ten plays performed by 1671; Robert Howard,
seven (one with Buckingham); and Edward Howard, four. Edward Howard is known
to have seen his plays to the stage: Villiers (Buckingham)'s *Rehearsal . . . with a Key*,
p. xix claims that some of Bayes's most crass and unhelpful comments—'he does not
top his Part'—are based on Edward Howard at rehearsal. Stapylton had had three
plays performed: Arlington, none.

[17] See George Villiers, Duke of Buckingham, *The Rehearsal*, ed. Montague
Summers (Stratford-upon-Avon, 1914), p. viii. Milhous and Hume, 'Attribution
Problems in English Drama'. *HLB* 31 (1983), 5–39 (27), conclude that the play was
written largely by Buckingham, with substantial assistance from Sprat and Clifford,
and ideas contributed by Buckingham's literary circle in general.

confusing inconsistencies. Most of the authors aimed at in Bayes's character were relatively powerful in the theatre, but the story of *The Rehearsal* makes Bayes an amateur who has never produced a play before (his others were rejected, as he explains in 2.2), and a low-class amateur at that, as his obsequious thanks for being graced by the 'honorable Title' of 'sir' illustrates. By awkwardly straddling professional–amateur, high-born–low-born lines, the figure of Bayes has perpetuated the myth amongst theatre historians (shown in this chapter to be effectively untrue) that all authors had roughly equal rights over the productions of their plays. *The Rehearsal* gives power and position to low-born amateur writers that they did not generally have.

Marsilia, the poetess of the anonymous *Female Wits* (1696),[18] represents the playwright Mary de la Rivière Manley. There is no doubt about this attribution—the preface to the play explains that 'the Lady whose Play is rehears'd, personates one Mrs. M——ly.' (A1[b]). For this reason *The Female Wits* is more likely than *The Rehearsal* to reflect actual theatrical experience (at least under Mrs Manley), especially as the play is thought to have been written by Drury Lane actors, particularly, it has been suggested, by Joseph Haynes, who had played Bayes in *The Rehearsal* for many years, and had also performed in some of Mrs Manley's productions.[19] If the play was indeed written by actors, then its depiction of rehearsal has theatrical authority; the factual elements of *The Female Wits* however are heavily overlaid by fictional ones, for the text self-consciously parrots *The Rehearsal*, as its dedication proudly broadcasts: 'though we must not presume to say it comes up to the Character of the Duke of *Buckingham*'s Works, yet it does not fall short of it' (A1[b]). In order to emphasize the similarity between Bayes and Marsilia, *The Female Wits* is pointedly structured along the same lines as *The Rehearsal*: it too features critical friends watching a trial play; it too concludes with the players performing a dance before going off to dinner; its author also loses (her) footing on the stage; and also removes the play in disgust to give it to 'the

---

[18] This date of performance is taken from *The Female Wits*, facs. ed. Lucyle Hook (Los Angeles, 1967), pp. i, xv.
[19] *Female Wits*, pp. xii–xiii; questioned by Milhous and Hume, 'Attribution Problems', 16.

other House'. *The Female Wits* naturally, as part of the mirroring process, inherits some of the fictions provided by *The Rehearsal*, and in many ways does not offer an independent source of information about actual theatre practice. This is not confronted by Milhous and Hume, who draw their conclusions about rehearsal from the moments of coincidence between the two plays, which are actually the least reliable (because most imitative) points. Amongst the 'fictional' aspects of both plays is the idea that the author was responsible for directing the dancing (which, Milhous and Hume footnote, 'may well have been a sore point').[20] There is no shortage of information about the professional dancing masters hired to instruct actors;[21] indeed the character Bayes was written for John Lacy, dancing master for the King's Company when *The Rehearsal* was performed, and this is doubtless the reason why a parody dance lesson is held in the play at all.[22] Marsilia too instructs the dancing—as part of her place within the Bayes tradition.

The kind of rehearsal depicted in both *The Rehearsal* and *The Female Wits* has a precedent in the English theatre, but a precedent of a very particular kind. The parody itself takes the form of a dress-rehearsal of a play, overseen by its agitated author and two of his acerbic acquaintances, all of whom comment throughout. This allows the 'real' watching audience both to see an entire play-within-a-play, and to hear a response to it: a 'rehearsal-format' play has to depict a full, group rehearsal, that is, in many ways, like a performance (as it is in fact a performance), but which allows for interjections. This was similar to a kind of rehearsal held for important plays. Evelyn records how he went to 'heare the Comedians con, & repeate' *The Adventures of Five Hours* in 1662, Thomas Shadwell appeals to the Duke of Newcastle, with 'your *Grace* saw this *Comedy* (before the Sting was taken out)', indeed, Brian Fairfax describes

---

[20] Milhous and Hume, *Producible*, 62–3.

[21] Thomas Shadwell in *The Sullen Lovers* (1668), A3ᵃ, carps against plays 'stuff'd full of Songs and Dances', declaring that in such cases the 'Composer and the Dancing Master are the best Poets'; Peter Motteux in *The Loves of Mars and Venus* (1696), 4, includes an 'entry of Dancing-masters, teaching their Scholars'; Thomas Brown in *The Works*, 4 vols. (1778–9), i. 193, claims that 'an author need not trouble himself about his thoughts and language, so he is but in fee with the dancing-masters'. Dancing was an integral part of many plays from about 1662–3 onwards— see *London Stage*, I, pp. cix–cx.

[22] Aubrey, *Brief Lives*, 288.

how Buckingham sometimes sought entertainment 'at rehearsals'.[23] When a play was more-or-less 'ready', special rehearsals sometimes took place to which the most influential and powerful members of the would-be audience were invited: a performative 'rehearsal' for gentlemen. Marsilia in *The Female Wits* (p. 23) is annoyed because only her friends have come to the rehearsal, whereas she was hoping for 'Knights, Squires, or however dignified, or distinguished'. First-night criticism, as I will show, was often condemning, and these special rehearsals were intended to flatter the critical, who were encouraged to offer their advice and corrections (to author and actors alike[24]), in a bid to win good opinion before performance. The hope would then be that positive rumours would circulate before the public performance of the play (the 'puff' was later instituted for the same reason): the Duke of Devonshire attended the rehearsal of *The Funeral* and, writes Richard Steele, a reason for the town's subsequent approbation of the play is 'that He permitted it'.[25] Rehearsals of this kind, involving a play almost ready to be staged (the play in *The Rehearsal*, for instance, is in its final rehearsal) are something between private performances and rehearsals. The nature of day-to-day rehearsal is not addressed in rehearsal-format plays.

The question still remains as to why Bayes, who was based on a variety of professional authors, should be presented as an amateur. The answer to this lies in Buckingham's French theatrical background. It has long been recognized that *The Rehearsal* is similar in form to Molière's play *L'Impromptu de Versailles* of 1663, and that almost certainly Buckingham adapted ideas from *L'Impromptu* when making his own play: Buckingham was inspired by French theatre, and tempted to imitate it.[26] Nor

---

[23] John Evelyn, *Diary*, ed. E. S. de Beer, 6 vols. (Oxford, 1955), iii. 348; Thomas Shadwell, *The Complete Works*, ed. Montague Summers, 5 vols. (1927; New York, 1968), i. p. lxxxviii; Brian Fairfax, *A Catalogue of the Curious Collection of Pictures of George Villiers, Duke of Buckingham* (1758), 37.

[24] See Patrick Fitz-Crambo, *Tyranny Triumphant* (1743), 8: 'when an ingenious Author had writ a good Play, the best of our noble Critics would attend a Rehearsal, to assist even a *Mohun* or a *Hart* to get up their Parts.'

[25] Richard Steele, *The Funeral* (1702), A2ᵇ.

[26] See J. E. Gillet, *Molière en Angleterre, 1660–1700* (Paris, 1913), 25–33. The idea is discussed fully in Smith, *Plays about the Theatre*, 10 and appendix A; and is again put forward in Villiers (Buckingham), *Rehearsal*, ed. Crane, p. vii. In fact, the exact relationship between *L'Impromptu* and *The Rehearsal* has to remain slightly open to

was he alone, for the English court, exiled to the Continent
during the Interregnum, had been tutored in French theatre; on
their return they did what they could to recreate it. Colley Cibber
may have attributed Charles II's questionable taste for comic
acting to the fact that he 'receiv'd his first Impression of good
Actors from the *French* Stage', but in the early days of the
Restoration, it was normal for the court to denigrate English
practices and promote French ones.[27] Samuel Pepys records an
occasion on which the king told his musicians to stop playing
Singleton's music in favour of French compositions 'which my
Lord says doth much out-do all ours'.[28] In fact, for as long as
possible, Charles II tried to maintain a direct connection with
French forms of theatre rather than English ones: John Evelyn
saw a (bad) French comedy at the Cockpit, Drury Lane in 1661;
by 1662 there was a French troupe in London entitled *Comédiens du Roy d'Angleterre*.[29] English playwrights submitted to the
king's interests: Roger Boyle, Earl of Orrery, started to write
heroic plays in couplets because 'I found his majesty relished
rather the French fashion of playes, than the English'; and
Dryden 'brought | Th'exactest Rules by which a Play is
wrought' from a combination of '*French* and *English* Theatres'.[30]
Unpractised at writing plays, authors did not seem to mind
turning to the French theatre for ideas and sources; between
1660 and 1671, approximately thirty-five foreign plays were
adapted or translated into English, of which over twenty were

question. Buckingham had a busy timetable for 1663, the year *L'Impromptu* was first
performed, and is unlikely to have seen the play in France, though he could well have
heard its story—King Louis XIV, for instance, knew the substance of *The Rehearsal*
shortly after it began playing in London: he taunted his minister Colbert with the
threat that 'he would be out of fashion' if he did not produce a comedy, as 'the chief
minister of state in England had gotten a great deal of honour by writing a farce'—
quoted in John Harold Wilson, *A Rake and His Times* (London, 1954), 166.
Buckingham cannot have read the text of *L'Impromptu* (unless he had access to a
manuscript copy), as it was not printed until the publication of Molière's *Œuvres
Complètes* in 1682.

[27] Colley Cibber, *An Apology for the Life*, ed. B. R. S. Fone (Ann Arbor, 1968), 89.

[28] Samuel Pepys, *The Diary*, ed. Robert Latham and William Matthews, 11 vols.
(London, 1970–83), i. 297.

[29] Sybil Marion Rosenfeld, 'Foreign Theatrical Companies in Great Britain in the
Seventeenth and Eighteenth Centuries', *Society for Theatre Research Pamphlet*, series
no. 4 (1955), 2.

[30] Quoted in Nancy Klein Maguire, *Regicide and Restoration* (Cambridge, 1992),
55.

French.[31] A self-conscious move was made to bring the English theatre in line with the French, physically, literarily, and musically—Betterton was sent to Paris to learn how French playhouses were constructed, and Dorset Gardens was built on his reports; later he visited France to research the musical requirements of the *tragédie lyrique*.[32] Throughout the early Restoration period, fragments of French theatre were lifted and welded into the English; *The Rehearsal* is, in some ways, as much a suggestion *about* rehearsal (based on French theatrical practice), as a reflection *of* it.

It is no surprise that Buckingham, who had himself lived for some time in France during the Commonwealth (he enlisted in the French army in 1654[33]), was steeped in French drama. He had made a point of studying the 'Decorum of *Foreign* Theaters' and watched impressive French performances put on 'under the Regulation of Monsieur *Corneille*'.[34] He spoke fluent French, in which he wrote bawdy poems, letters, and, significantly, plays. With the help of his French friend Charles Saint-Évremond, Buckingham tried to introduce the 'better' side of English theatrical literature into France. Together they wrote 'a Comédie à la manière des Anglois', *Sir Politick Would-Be*, a French version of Jonson's *Volpone*.[35] Conversely, Buckingham also collaborated with English friends, Edmund Waller, Thomas Sprat, Martin Clifford, Charles Sackville, Earl of Dorset, Sir Charles Sedley, and perhaps others (many of the same people, significantly, with whom he is said to have written *The Rehearsal*), to translate French plays, such as Corneille's *Pompée and Héraclius*, into his native tongue and so educate the English.[36] It was one of Buckingham's traits that he consciously borrowed from one theatrical culture in order to embellish and 'improve' the other.

Buckingham left no serious written account of his opinions of the English theatre, though the carping tone of *The Rehearsal* indicates what he thought of its playwrights. But Pierre Desmaizeneux records how Buckingham and Lord d'Aubigny discussed

---

[31] Ibid. 54.
[32] Peter Holland, *The Ornament of Action* (Cambridge, 1979), 3; Curtis A. Price, *Henry Purcell and the London Stage* (Cambridge, 1984), 13.
[33] Christine Phipps, *Buckingham: Public and Private Man* (New York, 1985), 7.
[34] Villiers (Buckingham), *Rehearsal... with a Key*, p. ix.
[35] Charles Saint-Évremond, *Sir Politick Would-Be*, ed. Robert Finch and Eugène Joliat (Geneva, 1978), 2.　　　　　　　　　　[36] Phipps, *Buckingham*, 10.

'the Dramatic Pieces of several Nations' with Charles Saint-Évremond, and how the latter subsequently turned the conclusions into his *Reflections on the English Stage*.[37] Saint-Évremond was in his own rights censorious,[38] and the extent to which the *Reflections* is indebted to his friends is unquantifiable, though it is telling that the only dedication in the book is 'Upon Operas: To the Duke of Buckingham'. The tone of *Reflections* at least reflects that of Saint-Évremond's cross-cultural conversations, and it is unmistakably critical, not only of the English manner of writing plays, but of the English manner of staging them—the coarse and primitive obsession with showing the audience 'bodies weltering in bloud', the general tendency to favour 'their senses upon the stage'.[39] Buckingham seems to have felt that the English theatre was deficient in a number of ways when compared with the French theatre, and, as elsewhere, he turned to literature—in this case, *The Rehearsal*—to make his opinions known and to offer instruction. For it was always Buckingham's practice to use his mockery as a teaching tool; indeed, his enemies claimed that he had a priestly need to prescribe, modify, and proselytize that was far from being humorous:

> Your zealous Care for Reformation
> Of Stage, and pulpitt, & y$^e$ Nation
> Show, you'd be preaching, wer't in fashion.[40]

Well-wishers of Buckingham, like Shadwell, enthused not about the ridicule of *The Rehearsal*, but about the improving effect that the play had: 'no man who has perfectly understood the *Rehearsal*, and some other of your Writings, if he has any

---

[37] Pierre Desmaizenaux, *The Life of Monsieur de St. Evremond* in Charles Saint-Évremond, *The Works . . . made English from the French Original*, 3 vols. (1714), iii. p. xl.

[38] His approval, when received, was something to boast of—see John Oldmixon, *Amintas* (1698), A1$^b$: 'Monsieur St. *Evremont*, who confesses he is not a perfect Master of the Tongue, says the delicacy of thought in the *Aminta* has touch'd him.'

[39] Charles Saint-Évremond, *Mixt essays upon tragedies, comedies, Italian comedies, English Tragedies and opera's, written originally in French* (1685), 4–5. Such conversations seem to have been taking place generally at court. John Loftis in Loftis *et al.* (eds.), *The Revels History of Drama in English, v. 1660–1750* (London, 1976), 8, suggests that the literary discussions represented by Dryden in his *Essay of Dramatic Poesy* (1668) reflect topics of conversation at court. 'If so, men of letters were preoccupied with a reassessment of English Drama . . . in the light of their expanded knowledge of continental drama'. Flecknoe in *Love's Kingdom*, G4$^b$–G5$^b$, also finds French theatre superior to English theatre 'because our Stage has stood at a stand this many years'. [40] Phipps, *Buckingham*, 337.

*Genius* at all, can write ill after it.'[41] Within the parody, behind the misguided, ill-timed intrusiveness of Bayes, Buckingham was presenting the pivotal role an author, irrespective of background, ought to have—and that he himself certainly always had—in the production of his plays. For the very idea of having an amateur playwright in charge of a production is a French one, not an English one; it was the French who admitted all varieties of author into rehearsal, including, as a 1673 account explains, 'l'autheur qui . . . n'est pas encore parvenu à ce haut degré de mérite et de réputation de quelques illustres'.[42] That Buckingham wished amateur writers to have a central role in preparing their plays for the stage will have been based partly on the importance he himself gave to the rehearsal process, and partly on his lack of altruism. Rehearsal was tough for actor and author alike, for there the inadequacies of a play were made manifest. In fact the internal play within *The Rehearsal* is not only shown to be terrible, but is condemned by the players before performance: 'the rehearsal' has ensured that the play is never staged. As a result of taking plays away from their amateur authors and giving them to competent professionals with rehearsal power (typical English Restoration practice), more bad plays were put into performance.

Contemporary comment shows that many considered Buckingham's careful preparation of his actors unusual. Enthusiasts praised his surprising devotion: Francis Lockier writes of the 'incredible . . . pains [Buckingham] took with one of the actors to teach him to speak some passages in Bayes's part in the *Rehearsal* right'; Thomas Brown records that when Lacy fell sick of the gout, 'His Grace himself' returned 'to instruct [Haynes] in the Nature of the Part'.[43] Little is known about the first, 1664, version of *The Rehearsal*, except that it 'had been several times *Rehears'd*'.[44] In part, this can be explained by the nature of the parody. Much of Buckingham's theatrical writing was based on sending up contemporary figures—Sir William Coventry, for instance, was aimed at in *The Country Gentleman*—and actors had to be carefully rehearsed in order

---

[41] Thomas Shadwell, *The History of Timon of Athens* (1678), A2[b].

[42] Samuel Chappuzeau, *Le Théâtre français* (1867), 54.

[43] Joseph Spence, *Observations, Anecdotes, and Characters of Books and Men*, ed. J. M. Osborn, 2 vols. (Oxford, 1966), i. 276; Tobias Thomas [alias Thomas Brown], *The Life of the Famous Comedian Jo Haynes* (1701), 5.

[44] Villiers (Buckingham), *Rehearsal . . . with a Key*, p. xii.

to imitate the targets effectively.[45] Buckingham himself was an
impressive mimic, and it is natural that he should have been
concerned to ensure that the humour of his writing was not lost
in a drab performance.[46] But it is telling that he never parodied
'rehearsal' itself in *The Rehearsal*: indeed, as his detractors were
quick to point out, Buckingham, in his own conscientious and
overbearing preparation of actors, displayed a strange kinship
with his anti-hero:

> But when his Poet John Bayes did appear,
> 'Tis known to more than half that were there,
> The greatest part was his own Character

> For . . . his Grace has Tormented the Players more,
> Than the Howards and Fleckno, and all the store
> Of Damn'd Dull Rogues they were Plague'd with before.[47]

Knowledgeable in the theory of the theatre, Bayes is only ham-
fisted when he tries to put his ideas into practice, a point Price
makes when he declares that the playwright's decision to write a
tune for the resurrection scene in 'Effaut flat' (F minor) was
intelligent and theatrically appropriate.[48] The *method* of rehearsing that was followed by Buckingham and depicted in
*The Rehearsal* is clearly more careful and author-based than
was normal in England at the time, but accords much more
closely to French rehearsal, in which the author, as a 1673
account explains, 'assiste ordinairement à ces répétitions, et
relève le comédien, s'il tombe en quelque défaut, s'il ne prend
pas bien les sens, s'il sort du naturel dans sa voix ou dans le

---

[45] See Sir Robert Howard and George Villiers, Duke of Buckingham, *The Country
Gentleman*, ed. Arthur H. Scouten and Robert D. Hume (London, 1976), 26.

[46] For Buckingham's counterfeiting skills see Anthony Hamilton, *Memoirs of the
Comte de Gramont*, trans. Peter Quennell (London, 1930), 138. Summers in his
edition of Villiers (Buckingham), *Rehearsal*, p. xi, suggests Buckingham taught Lacy
to reproduce Dryden's mannerism exactly, but characteristically offers no source for
his information. In fact Davies, *Miscellanies*, iii. 171, seems to have been the first to
'suppose [Lacy] endeavoured to resemble [Dryden] . . . in dress and deportment',
and is simply extrapolating from material about Buckingham's intensive rehearsal
practice.

[47] Reproduced in Phipps, *Buckingham*, 339. That Bayes is in fact a reflection of
Buckingham is a claim that the defensive Dryden also made: 'the author sat to
himself when he drew the picture, and was the very Bayes of his own farce'—see John
Dryden, *Of Dramatic Poesy*, ed. George Watson, 2 vols. (London, 1962), ii. 78.
Perhaps Buckingham lifted more than he had intended from *L'Impromptu*, in which
the burlesqued poet is indeed Molière.          [48] Price, *Henry Purcell*, 50.

geste'.[49] *The Rehearsal*, rather than offering a key to normal seventeenth-century practice, was, in design, more true to particular rehearsal-performances offered by the English theatre for important plays, and in nature more clearly aligned to French theatrical practices, heralded as appropriate by Buckingham (who imitated them). Both *The Rehearsal* and *The Female Wits*, but especially *The Rehearsal*, must be used with caution; whenever possible they will be referred to only when they are confirmed by other sources.

## PUBLIC THEATRE REHEARSAL

### Seasonal rehearsal

The theatrical year continued to be divided into 'terms' ending with a 'vacation'—the Inns of Court still provided many of the theatre's audience.[50] That the acting period was defined by the presence or absence of the more regular and impressive spectators both stresses the theatre's reliance on certain factions of its audience, and explains why the kinds of plays put on, and the times at which they were mounted, changed over the year.

The playing season lasted, as a rule, from September or October to June, during which time theatres would be operational six days a week, closing only for the week before Easter, on Fridays during Lent, when a member of the royal family died, or as a precaution against the plague.[51] Within a season, upwards of

---

[49] Chappuzeau, *Le Théâtre français*, 62.

[50] For connections between 'terms' and the inns of court in plays, see *The Playhouse to be Lett* in William Davenant, *The Works*, 3 vols. in 1 (1673), ii. 76: 'your busie Termers come to the Theatres, | As to their Lawyers-Chambers'; and *Female Wits*, 14: 'he . . . belongs to one of the Inns of Chancery . . . [and] sweats hard in Term-time'. For references to terms by name, see George Powell, *The Treacherous Brothers* (1690), A3[b]: 'I resolv'd the Town showd [*sic*] not . . . have a whole *Hillary-Term* with never a new *Play*'; '*Easter* term' is referred to in a 1670 epilogue to *Every Man in His Humour*, reproduced in Danchin, I:ii, 355. References to the vacation can be found in Richard Burridge, *A Scourge for the Play-Houses* (1702), 13, where 'poor Wretches of Actors, one part of the Year, when no Acting is, are forced to sharp and spunge about for Subsistance'; and *The Constant Nymph* (1678), A2[a], which was staged without 'Adornments' because 'it was Vacation-time, and the Company would not venture the Charge'. For the various social groups that made up the audience, see Botica, *Audience*, 60–84, *et passim*.

[51] *London Stage*, I, p. lxix. The most significant plague closure occurred in 1665, when theatres were shut for sixteen months.

fifty different plays were staged, of which probably about ten would have been new—that certainly was the case by 1700. But the hectic programme of the 1590s, when a different play was shown every day, was no longer followed. Short 'runs' had been established: new plays, provided they passed the first-night 'test', would perform for at least three nights in a row (up to the author's third-night benefit); with the introduction of the sixth-night benefit, they ran six nights in a row; while stock plays had runs of about eight to ten nights.[52] As time passed, however, the audience became more sophisticated—or more condemning, depending on the way one looks at it. As a result, runs of new plays became shorter, while stock plays had concomitantly longer runs: by 1703, 'Suddain Death's the Fate of Modern Plays, | For few we see, are Born to Length of Days'.[53] Restoration companies at their most competitive—for instance, mid-season 1695–6—might perform fifteen or more different plays within the month, and keep adding other productions during the season. The Duke's Company, when it was doing well in the 1670s, and Betterton's Company (its successor), flourishing in 1695, were both performing more than twenty new plays a year (the United Company of 1682, conversely, performed only three or four new plays annually).[54]

Rehearsals took place in the vacation for the season to come (one telling epilogue joshes with the 'gallants' for having been away in the country 'while we study or revive a play'[55]), and if the Restoration companies were like those of the Renaissance and the eighteenth century, then new plays were slowly added to the repertoire between September and November, so that more careful (and more frequent) rehearsal took place at the beginning of the season. Rehearsal at some level continued throughout, however, for a specific genre of plays were held back for special late-season presentation. When respectable Londoners left for the country in the summer, the nature and demands of the theatrical audience altered: the player in *Playhouse to be Lett* explains that 'men of judgement' have gone away to the country,

---

[52] Milhous and Hume, *Producible*, 37.

[53] Thomas Baker, *The Tunbridge-Walks* (1703), a1ª. See also *The Comparison between the Two Stages*, ed. Staring B. Wells (Princeton, 1942), 2: 'I am sure you can't name me five Plays that have indur'd six Days acting, for fifty that were dam'd in three'.                                        [54] Milhous, *Betterton*, p. ix.

[55] Aphra Behn, *The Widdow Ranter* (1690), A3ᵇ.

and it will therefore be pointless to perform a French translation, as the vacation audience 'Affect Commodities of lesser price'.[56] Such plays were presumably rehearsed as well as performed towards the end of the season, so that a level of continuous preparation should be assumed throughout the theatrical year.

Other, more specific rehearsals, were sometimes demanded by occasion. *Entr'acte* entertainment became increasingly popular, and songs, and particularly dances, were often inserted between the acts of old, known plays;[57] these too had to be rehearsed. Particularly intensive and careful preparation was required for court performances, though the time spent on such rehearsals was not wasted, as the publicity they generated heightened expectation for the play's 'public' appearance.[58] Plays for court might be required at any time of the year, again arguing that rehearsal took place throughout the season. The amount of time spent in preparing a single play, then, depended on a number of different factors: the success of the company (and whether it was in competition with another company), the time of the season, and the number of other plays to be studied. What is clear is that, with short play 'runs' as the norm, there was a potential for more rehearsal per play than there had been before the Interregnum; what is also clear is that a large proportion of the time set aside for readying a play for performance was still spent in private study rather than in group rehearsal, and that many plays were deemed to have been underrehearsed when they entered into production.

*Number of days to produce a play*

Shadwell mingled complaints about the performance of one of his plays with references to the almost catastrophic effect bad acting had had on Sir George Etherege:

the *Actors* (though since they have done me some right) at first were extremely imperfect in the Action of it . . . The last (*viz.*) imperfect

---

[56] *Playhouse to be Lett* in *Davenant*, ii. 75. Lacy in the prologue to *The Old Troop* (Danchin, I:i, 290) compares his own frivolous output to Dryden's—'Let Wits, and Poets, keep their own stations; | He writes to th'Tearms, and I to th'long vacations.'
[57] See *London Stage*, I, p. cix.
[58] See *London Stage*, I, p. lxx; and Eleanor Boswell, *The Restoration Court Stage* (1932, New York, 1966), *passim*.

Action, had like to have destroy[']d *She would if she could,* which I think
. . . is the best Comedy that has been written since the Restauration of
the Stage: And even that, for the imperfect representation of it at first,
received such prejudice, that, had it not been for the favour of the
*Court,* in all probability it had never [been] got up again.[59]

A look at Davenant's Company, and its Lincoln's Inn succes-
sors—the company generally accepted to have paid more attention to theatrical discipline[60]—reveals many complaints about
uneven performances. Pepys in his diaries twice mentions actors,
including Betterton, who corpse on the stage; Edward Howard's
*The Womens Conquest* had a 'misfortune' in that some of the
parts were 'ill and imperfectly performed'; Aphra Behn's *Dutch
Lover* was 'hugely injur'd in the Acting', having been 'done so
imperfectly as never any was before'; Stanford in Thomas
Shadwell's *The Sullen Lovers* finds that 'if I go to the Theatre
. . . either I find an Insupportable Play; or if a good one, ill
acted'.[61] Of course such objections must be taken in context: as
Elkanah Settle pointed out, disappointed authors whose plays
had been unsuccessful tended to blame the acting rather than
their own inability to write.[62] But sloppy acting was usual
enough to be at least a convincing explanation for a play's
failure, and a simple pragmatic reason partly explains this:
many actors would not learn a play properly until they knew
that it would 'take', not wishing to waste time on a production
that might only survive a night or so. Cibber, for instance, was
quizzical as well as admiring when he recorded seeing Robert
Wilks learn 'a Volume of Froth . . . in a new Play, that we were
sure could not live above three Days'; and Settle mentions often
having heard 'the Players cursing at their oversight in laying out
so much on so misliked a Play'.[63] Then again, actors had to
balance their instinct not to learn their lines fully until they were
sure a play would be successful, against a damned play's obvious
consequence—another play to be hurriedly got up. Nell Gwyn
'cursed, for having so few people in the pit' one evening, because

---

[59] Thomas Shadwell, *The Humourists* (1671), π2$^a$.
[60] Milhous, *Betterton*, 21.
[61] *Pepys*, viii. 421–2; Edward Howard, *The Womens Conquest* (1671), C1$^b$; Aphra
Behn, *The Dutch Lover* (1673), a1$^b$; Shadwell, *Sullen*, 4.
[62] Elkanah Settle, *The Empress of Morocco* (1673), A1$^b$.
[63] Cibber, *Apology*, 133; Elkanah Settle, *Ibrahim* (1677), a3$^b$.

she realized that she would have to learn (or relearn) a different set of lines for the next night.[64]

Bad performances naturally reflect back on the nature of rehearsal itself. If a play is obviously unprepared when it is brought to the stage, then the rehearsal and study that preceded it must have been inadequate, another complaint frequently made in prefaces. Moreover, if the amount of rehearsal given to a play was usually insufficient, then the early performances functioned on some level as substitute rehearsals: Henry Higden, for instance, described the first performance of *Wary Widdow* as 'but an imperfect Rehearsall'.[65] As ever, there was often a fine line between rehearsal and performance.

At various different stages in the life of the Restoration theatre, bad rehearsal practice was particularly noticeable. In the early days, when all actors were new to the trade, rehearsal seems generally to have been well attended, though Pepys complained that a 1661 production of *The Widow* by Killigrew's company was 'wronged' by actresses who did not know their lines (presumably Killigrew had hurried the female performers into action before they were ready, in order to beat Davenant in being the first to put women on the stage).[66] Over time, rehearsal attendance seems to have become selectively worse: whenever a new company was formed, or company structure changed in any way, firmer rules than ever were laid down stressing the importance of attending rehearsal and the fines that would be levied for absenteeism.[67]

As David Thomas points out, regular rehearsals were the product of a prospering theatre, and lack of rehearsal could be expected from a theatre that was doing badly.[68] He suggests that the careless presentation of Betterton's struggling company around the turn of the century is traceable to this; and indeed, David Crauford, in 1700, famously complained that the Patent Company could mount a play in twenty days that Betterton's could not even get rehearsed in six weeks:

---

[64] *Pepys*, viii. 463.

[65] Henry Higden, *The Wary Widdow* (1693), A4[a].

[66] See Betterton's fond recollections of early rehearsal in Gildon, *Betterton*, 15; Elizabeth Howe, *The First English Actresses* (Cambridge, 1992), 24.

[67] See Milhous, *Betterton*, 30–1; Allardyce Nicoll, *A History of English Drama*, 3 vols. (1923; Cambridge, 1952), i. 324.

[68] David Thomas (ed.), *Theatre in Europe: Restoration and Georgian England* (Cambridge, 1989), 164.

Mr. *Betterton* did me all the Justice I cou'd indeed reasonably hope for. But that Example he gave, was not . . . follow'd by the whole Company . . . Mr. *Bowman* . . . kept the first Character of my Play six weeks, and then cou'd hardly read six lines on't . . . I was oblig'd to remove it after so many sham Rehearsals, and in two days it got footing upon the other Stage. Where 'twas immediately cast to the best Advantage, and Plaid in less than twenty days.[69]

But Crauford's complaint is unusual, because struggling companies tended not to mount new plays. Whenever the theatre was doing badly, or the two companies joined together, stock plays flourished. So under the United Company, formed in 1682, theatrical competition disappeared, with the result that, as Matthew Prior quipped, 'Betterton of late so thrifty's grown, | [he] Revives old Plays, or wisely acts his own', and almost no rehearsal was necessary.[70] It was in fact during the prospering years, when lively competition between the two companies forced onto the stage more new plays than the actors had time to prepare, that most of the complaints about sloppy and underrehearsed performances were made. Doggett, writing of a 1696 production by Betterton's company, hoped that 'the judicious' would not condemn his play simply because 'it suffer'd in the Acting'; the title-page of James Drake's *The Sham Lawyer* (1697) offers the play 'As it was Damnably Acted at the Theatre Royal, Drury Lane'.[71] Peter Motteux writes about putting on a play in a week or less over that period, 'Nay, w'have had new ones studied for one Day'.[72]

That there had simply not been enough rehearsals before performance was recognized by both author and audience as inevitable: Pepys uncritically observed that 'for want of practice' the actors in Massinger's *The Bondman* (28 July 1664) 'had many of them forgot their parts a little', but went on to praise Betterton's performance; William Walker humbly, and again without any

---

[69] David Crauford, *Courtship A-la-Mode* (1700), A3ᵃ.

[70] Matthew Prior, 'A Satyr on the Modern Translators' in *The Literary Works*, ed. H. Bunker Wright and Monroe K. Speares, 2 vols. (Oxford, 1959), i. 19. Powell describes that same period of time as one when 'the reviveing of the old stock of Plays, so ingrost the study of the House, that the Poets lay dorment; and a new Play cou'd hardly get admittance'—*Treacherous Brothers*, A3ᵃ.

[71] Thomas Doggett, *The Country-Wake* (1696), A3ᵃ. In the season 1695–6 twenty-five new plays were mounted, the highest number during the Restoration—see *London Stage*, I, pp. cxxvii, clvi.

[72] Motteux, prologue to Mary Pix, *The Innocent Mistress* (1697), A2ᵃ.

great criticism, declared that he had no complaints 'of the Civility of the House, as to the Performing, only the want of Time and Rehearsals'.[73] The response was more vitriolic (but still not completely condemning) if rehearsals were judged to have been ill conducted. John Dennis suspected that his play's unfortunate reception was partly due to 'the Calamities which attended the Rehearsal, which were so numerous as never had befaln [*sic*] any Play in my Memory'.[74] Nevertheless, he then focused his criticism on the audience which, he felt, had been unnecessarily malevolent. Rehearsal was an important contributing factor to a play's success, but was not of paramount importance because, as will be seen, the emphasis of production continued to be on private study rather than on the few group rehearsals that capped it.

From Crauford's complaint it is obvious that there was no absolute rule that dictated the number of days required for theatrical preparation; there was, however, a 'hierarchy' of plays that roughly determined rehearsal time. George Powell speedily mounted his farce while acknowledging 'that . . . the other weightier, massier Sense, now in Rehearsal, and Study, cou'd not so easily be hammer'd into the Players Heads, nor got up fast enough'.[75] In an ideal situation, short plays, afterpieces, and farces were given between a week and a fortnight's preparation: ' 'tis a slight Farce, five days brought forth with ease'; 'to tell the Truth, the whole Play was . . . studied up in one Fortnight'.[76] Full plays seem to have taken roughly a month: George Farquhar, referring to a failed play, writes of 'the Loss of the Month in Rehearsing'; Crauford's *Courtship A-la-mode*, was, after setbacks, performed within twenty days; *The Tender Husband* was received by the company 'the latter End of March Anno 1705' and 'acted . . . the first time on 23 April, 1705'; Cibber's *A Woman's Wit* (1696) expected a première 'within a Month after the Parts . . . shall bee Distributed'.[77] Plays for court

---

[73] *Pepys*, v. 224; [William Walker], *Marry, or do Worse* (1704), A2[a].

[74] John Dennis, *Gibraltar* (1705), A2[a].  [75] Powell, *Brothers*, A3[b].

[76] Aphra Behn, *The False Count* (1682), 66; George Powell, *Bonduca* (1696), A3[b]. Of course, this is partly because farces were shorter than other plays—'Critics' insists, in Edward Ravenscroft's *The Italian Husband* (1698), A2[a], that a play with three acts must be a farce and cannot be a tragedy (which has five acts). This affords Ravenscroft the chance to explain why he is writing a three-act tragedy.

[77] *A Discourse upon Comedy* in George Farquhar, *The Works* (1660), i. 101; Crauford, *Courtship*, A3[a]; Leslie Hotson, *The Commonwealth and Restoration Stage* (Cambridge, Mass., 1928), 380; Nicoll, *English Drama*, i. 381–2.

and 'operas', which required much more preparation both of performers and scenery, were made ready over a number of months: *Albion and Albanius*, for instance, was got up over a four-to-six month stretch.[78]

## Reading

Designated members of each company seem to have chosen plays for representation: Davenant and Betterton for the Duke's and the United companies; senior actors for Killigrew and Rich. By 1704, Cibber was reading plays for the Patent Company.[79] Once accepted, a play was read publicly to the full company by the author. This reading was very necessary, as the private study (which followed the reading) was still essentially solitary: the reading was one of the few occasions during which the story of the play itself could be conveyed to the actors. Samuel Chappuzeau, writing about readings in the French theatre in 1673, explains that the first public reading to the actors served two purposes: for the author it was a way of presenting his play to the players 'avec le plus d'emphase qu'il peut', and offering, by the manner in which he read it, some performance notes; for the actors it was a chance to gauge the amount of use the author would be over the preparation period, and to criticize and try to 'improve' the play before they received their parts: 'les comédiens disent ce qu'ils ont remarqué de fâcheux, ou trop de longueur, ou un couplet languissant'.[80] Much the same process took place in England, where the actors clearly considered themselves 'judges' of the play, while the author was more concerned with the reading as a directorial training session. For instance, *A Comparison* describes a reading where 'a Dinner was bespoke at a Tavern for half a Score, at least that

---

[78] Milhous, *Betterton*, 48. Shadwell wrote his *Psyche* sixteen months before performance, as his preface makes clear, but that is no reason for Milhous's claim that the play was 'in the works' over that time. English 'operas', or semioperas as Roger North calls them, were spectaculars consisting of spoken and sung text and sumptuous scenery. They were extremely expensive to stage, and were only performed when time, money, an appropriate theatre, and composers were to hand. At their most popular, during the 1690s, five or six operas of this kind were put into performance a year—see *London Stage*, I, pp. cxxvi–vii.

[79] Milhous and Hume, *Producible*, 44.

[80] Chappuzeau, *Le Théâtre français*, 56.

number came to judge [the] Play'. During the reading 'most of 'em dropped off, but two remain'd to hear it out'.[81]

There are several testimonies to a group of actors having refused a play, which suggests that plays could be rejected not only after a private reading, but also after the reading to the company. Shadwell wrote to the Earl of Dorset to complain, first that the players had rejected his play, secondly that they were instead having 'a play of Dryden's read to them'; Susanna Centlivre had enormous difficulty in getting *The Busie Body* accepted as it had been received 'very cooly' when first 'offered to the Players'.[82] Actors' responses to a play largely depended on the playwright's histrionic talents in the reading—playwrights 'qui ont le récit pitoyable' injured their works by reading them, as Chappuzeau makes clear; Cibber famously compared Dryden and Nathaniel Lee as readers of their own plays, showing the different effect a good reading had on the actors:

When [Dryden] brought his Play of *Amphytrion* to the Stage, I heard him give it his first Reading to the Actors . . . the whole was in so cold, so flat, and unaffecting a manner, that I am afraid of not being believ'd, when I affirm it. On the contrary, *Lee*, far his Inferior in Poetry, was so pathetick a Reader of his own Scenes, that . . . while [he] was reading to Major *Mohun* at a Rehearsal, *Mohun* . . . threw down his Part, and said, Unless I were able to *play* it, as well as you *read* it, to what purpose should I undertake it?[83]

Old or stock plays were, no doubt, read by the manager or whoever was responsible for 'ushering the play to the stage', as was the case in 1730,[84] for a reading by an authority figure was always necessary: it was the only contact actors would have with the play as a whole until the collective rehearsal period—or performance. But given the different aims of reader and listener in the reading, the groundwork for actor–author clashes was laid out even at this initial stage.

---

[81] *Comparison between the Two Stages*, 8. See also Thomas Durfey, *Old Mode and the New* (1709), A2[b]: 'it was read and put to the Test before some of the best Judges the Stage has'. Readings, as in the Renaissance, continued to take place over drinks in the evening.

[82] *Shadwell*, ed. Summers, i. pp. ccxxix–ccxxx; Mottley, *List*, 189. See also Villiers (Buckingham), *Rehearsal*, ed. Crane, 19.

[83] Chappuzeau, *Le Théâtre français*, 57; Cibber, *Apology*, 67.

[84] Benjamin Victor, *The History of the Theatres of London and Dublin, from the year 1730 to the Present Time*, 2 vols. (1761), ii. 4.

*Parts*

Actors continued to receive parts (often called 'sides') after the reading, rather than full copies of the plays they were to perform in. The only surviving Restoration part, that of Trico in the play of *Ignoramus*, shows the cue system to be much the same as in the Renaissance, the cues themselves varying in length from one word (or even one syllable) to four words. Again, very little acting information is given in the part, which still does not indicate who speaks the cue line; it also lacks information about entrances and other stage business—actors will have continued to be heavily dependent on the prompter during performance.[85] Playing from parts imposed particular learning requirements: cues had to be learnt (Cibber 'sometimes gave the *Cues* so loosely that it was difficult to play with him'[86]), but internally the text could be varied without disturbing the other actors.

As in the previous century, the cueing system could be used to 'direct' actors, structuring moments of babble, and moments of formalized interchange. In Shadwell's *The Virtuoso*, Sir Formal Trifle tries to defend himself, but his words 'I am a person' are cue both to first and second Ribband-Weavers, one of whom is to mock 'A person . . .', one of whom is to cry 'Pox on you . . .'. The second Weaver's 'A person' is itself a cue back to Sir Formal, who will try to interject with his repeated 'Gentlemen—I am a person' prematurely, and will then find himself having to give his line once more when the 'real' cue is given out. Confusing—but confusing in a ritualized and scripted way:

SIR FORMAL. All this I can bear, if you will but hear me, Gentlemen—
*I am a person*—
2 WEAVER. *A person*, a Rogue! a Villain! a damn'd Vertoso! *A person!*
SIR FORMAL. I say, Gentlemen, *I am a person*—
1 WEAVER. Pox on you—we'll use you like a Dog—Sir—
SIR FORMAL. Quousque tandem effrenata jactabit andacia. This is a barbarity which Scythians would blush at.[87]

In plays of the time, the cueing system provides the same old metatheatrical jokes, imposing complicity between actors and audience at the expense of total absorption in a story:

[85] Langhans, 'A Restoration Actor's Part', *HLB*, 23 (1975), 180–5.
[86] Fitz-Crambo, *Tyranny*, 10.
[87] Thomas Shadwell, *The Virtuoso* (1676), 84.

THYESTES. It . . . sets me to a Reeling—
ATREUS. Reeling, that's my Cue.[88]

Similarly, the reality of the actor, the actor *as* actor, was partly what the audience were coming to see. Shared stage and auditorium lighting, and the close proximity of the stage, boxes, and pit, meant that there was less imaginary 'distance' imposed between audience and actor than now; the perceived personality of the actor behind the part was a source of constant fascination to the spectators. It is obviously the actors themselves who are uppermost in Critick's mind when he reports about a performance in which '*Wilks* (for I forget the Drammatick names) is marry'd to Mrs. *Rogers*'.[89] Epilogues and prologues taunt the audience with snippets of information about the 'real' nature of the performers who speak them: the flirtatious Nell Gwyn, the 'chaste' Mrs Bracegirdle.[90] And the audience responded by taking the kind of personal interest in specific actors that brings about a 'star' system. Elizabeth Pepys, wife to the diarist, for instance, was so enamoured of Betterton that she walked out of *Macbeth* when the great actor was too ill to play the part, and, as a dubious tribute to her hero, named her dog after him.[91] As Holland explains, the audience looked to and trusted the actors, and the actors in turn 'mediated' plays to the audience.[92] Actors thus had enormous power, for the standards of their performances were public comments on the parts they were playing. In order to be successful, therefore, playwrights were under an obligation to accede to performers' wishes.

The word 'part', then as now, meant both the written text assigned to a certain actor, and the character that that actor played. Actors were given the physical parts to keep at home, encouraging them to feel a sense of ownership over the lines themselves,[93] which was heightened by the fact that playwrights often fitted roles to particular actors—without whom, they claimed, their plays would be unperformable. So actors 'owned'

---

[88] John Wright, *Thyestes* and *Mock Thyestes* (1674), 138. See also William Wycherley, *The Country Wife* (1675), 66: 'SIR JASPAR: No, your Ladyship will tickle him better without me, I suppose, but is this your buying China, I thought you had been at the China House? HORNER: China-House, that's my Cue, I must take it.'

[89] *Comparison between the Two Stages*, 95.

[90] Examples are given in Howe, *First English Actresses*, 98–9.

[91] *Pepys*, viii. 483; Mary Edmond, *Rare Sir William Davenant* (Manchester, 1987), 150.    [92] Holland, *Ornament*, 56–60.    [93] Ibid. 65.

their parts, and plays 'depended' on their performances—
'Whenever the Stage has the misfortune to lose [Wilks]', wrote
Farquhar, 'Sir Harry Wildair may go to the Jubilee'.[94] As text
and actor were intimately connected, the first production
remained fixed as the ideal, and perhaps only, way in which a
play should be performed. Cast lists, attaching plays to the actors
who first realized the roles, further singled out the original run as
what the play was meant to be. A performance involving new
actors was necessarily less good than a performance with the
'real' cast: to Dennis it seemed 'absolutely impossible . . . that
any Actor can become an admirable Original, by playing a Part
which was writ and design'd for another Man's particular
Talent'.[95] Indeed, it was thought impossible for a play even to
survive a change of company without being substantially altered
in form. Cibber felt obliged largely to rewrite *A Woman's Wit*
when he gave it over to the Lincoln's Inn company; when he
then returned it to the Theatre Royal he had to change the text
once more 'to confine the Business of my Persons to the
Capacity of different people'.[96] Nahum Tate similarly was
forced to make 'a Retrenchment of whole scenes in the Action'
of *Cuckolds Haven* because the principal part could not be
performed by Nokes 'for whom it was design'd, and only
proper'.[97] And most plays were thought of as having a limited
lifecycle as a result: they were written for specific performers and
were therefore not for all time, but for a specific time—many,
which 'could not' be put on by other actors, were never repeated
after their first run.[98] Authors' dependency on their actors gave
the actors powerful status in the actor–author struggle; the
actors' 'right' to parts written for them gave them considerable
freedom in the way they manifested those parts on the stage.

If a play survived long enough for parts in it to be 'inherited'
by other actors, then the new actors were under a compunction

---

[94] Preface to *The Constant Couple* in George Farquhar, *The Complete Works*, ed.
Charles Stonehill, 2 vols. (Bloomsbury, 1930), i. 86. Similarly John Bankes's *The
Great Cyrus* 'was a good Play; but Mr. *Smith* having a long part in it, fell sick upon
the Fourth Day and Dy'd, upon that it lay by, and ne'er had bin Acted since'—
Downes, *Roscius*, 92.

[95] John Dennis, *The Invader of His Country* (1720), A5ᵃ.

[96] See Holland, *Ornament*, 73.

[97] Nahum Tate, *Cuckolds Haven* (1685), A1ᵃ.

[98] Milhous and Hume, *Producible*, 39.

to perform in, as near as possible, the same way as the first actors: originality of performance was not a goal, as is illustrated by one of the many occasions on which the two companies were at loggerheads—in this instance, both trying to upstage one another in their performance of William Congreve's *The Old Bachelor*. George Powell, attempting to win the audience away from Betterton's respected performance, wrote in the playbills that he would perform his part 'in Imitation of the Original'—he claimed that he would act, not the character 'Heartwell', but Betterton's performance of Heartwell: he would upstage the famous actor by *being* him.[99] Plays were, obviously, not encouraged to develop in revivals, and rehearsals for revivals were necessary only to ensure that the imitation was working, and the lines were learnt: the manner of preparing a play was always backward- rather than forward-looking. But this also meant that 'a performance' of a lasting play could easily outlive its actor; in this way, the 'part' was the actor's immortality, not the author's ('they who remember me in *Richard the Third*, states Cibber, 'may have a nearer Conception of *Sandford*, than from all the critical Account I can give of him'[100]). It is only natural that revision should have become the popular way of coping with 'old' plays that were to be revived—especially if there had been any change in ownership in parts since the first production. Dryden refers to the gusto with which actors alter texts when preparing them for another run, a process he calls 'Murd'ring Plays, which [the actors] miscal Reviving'.[101] But only in a revised and rewritten text could the new actors shake off the duty of methodically repeating the previous production: revised texts opened up the possibility of a 'new' performance. Much the same can be said of single, individual 'parts' which actors

---

[99] Cibber, *Apology*, 114. Powell also mimicked Betterton's Falstaff so closely that he copied 'those acute pains of gout' which sometimes 'surprized' Betterton in performance—see Davies, *Miscellanies*, i. 138.

[100] Cibber, *Apology*, 81–2.

[101] In a poem appended to George Granville's *Heroick Love* (1698), A4[b]. Statistics about the frequency with which plays are adapted have not yet been gathered, though see how often even stock plays by Cibber, Vanbrugh, Farquhar, and Congreve are revised. Peter Motteux explains how he reduced 'the most moving Part' of *The Unnatural Brother* 'acted 6 Months ago . . . into the Compass of one Act, with some Additions; yet without mutilating my Author's Sense', *The Novelty* (1697), A4[a]. In certain instances the play changed its nature altogether: Robert Howard and John Dryden's *The Indian Queen*, a 1664 tragi-comedy, resurfaced in 1695 as an opera.

could only personalize by embellishing. Either way, frequent revision was almost a requirement.


### 'Lines'

Actors tended to develop stereotyped characters (sometimes called acting 'lines', sometimes called 'casts') that they always played. This limited the amount they had to learn, for their education only had to teach them how to perform certain types of role. A description of the young David Garrick gives an example of the range of 'lines' on offer: he was so talented that he was excellent 'in every Cast of Playing': 'the King, the Clown, the Rake, the Fop, the Footman, or the fine Gentleman'.[102] Garrick was actually typical material for a lead actor (who had more flexibility of range). The rest had one or, at the most, two distinct lines, one tragic and one comic, neither of which necessarily affected the other.[103] These 'lines' might promote or hold back the actor concerned. Cibber suffered by being early typecast in an unprofitable line. He had imitated Doggett as Nykin in Congreve's *Old Batchelor*, and afterwards 'if I sollicited for any thing of a different Nature, I was answer'd, *That was not in my Way*'.[104] Actors became known for their 'lines', which were associated with their personalities in the minds of the audience—and often in fact. This gave the audience an expectation that the actors would be true to their perceived characters, rather than to the text they were performing, another reason why textual change was often necessary. Robert Wilks and Jane Rogers were a favourite romantic duo for a while, and they carried out details of their real-life love affair on the stage: 'when [Wilks] was obliged to perform the Part of a Lover with any other Woman, he did it after so careless a manner . . . [that] Mr. *Rich*, . . . was obliged to let Mrs. *Rogers* always act the Heroine in every Play where Mr. *Wilks* was the Hero.'[105] Trying a part not in one's line was not always to be recommended, as Sandford discovered. He

---

[102] Mottley, *List*, 237.
[103] Holland, *Ornament*, 80.
[104] Cibber, *Apology*, 116.
[105] *Memoirs of the Life of Robert Wilks* (1732), 29.

attempted an 'honest' role though he was known for playing villains; the audience felt cheated and damned the play 'as if the Author had impos'd upon them the most frontless or incredible Absurdity'.[106] More intelligent casting outside an actor's 'line' could, however, add a layer of complexity to a play.[107]

Such a system had its dangers, and militated against the idea of authorial instruction. Actors who had learnt their parts often felt that further lessons were not necessary; in particular, they grew to resent the attempts of playwrights to teach them parts that were along 'lines' they had maintained for years. Cibber found that several actresses, once they had had any acting success, were 'desirous of being left to their own Capacity' rather than be seen to need 'farther Assistance'; Betterton uses almost the same words to discuss young players' lax attitudes to instruction at the turn of the century.[108]

*Study*

'Ther was noe Play of myne Acted' writes Orrery to Sir Henry Bennett on 31 August 1664, 'they are now but Studyinge it; I hope within less than a Fortnight twill be on y^c Theatre' (it was first acted on 14 September); Dryden wrote to Walsh on 12 December 1693 about his play *Love Triumphant* 'which is now studying; but cannot be acted till after Christmasse is over'.[109] 'Study' occupied most of the rehearsal period, and these examples suggest that more than two weeks of the preparation period were spent, by the actors, in study.

During study a part was learnt and instructed as in the previous chapter. Again, the term 'rehearsal' might sometimes be used to include 'study', though the two are generally differentiated: Powell distinguishes between plays 'now in Rehearsal, and Study'; and Gildon recommends that actors 'always speak out in their private Study, and in *Rehearsals*'.[110] Lack of sufficient study-time for preparing a play was another complaint made by playwrights: the run of John Leanerd's *The Country*

[106] Cibber, *Apology*, 78.
[107] Holland, *Ornament*, 86–98.
[108] Cibber, *Apology*, 168; Gildon, *Betterton*, 15–16.
[109] Quoted *London Stage*, I, 83; Dryden, *Letters*, 62.
[110] Powell, *Brothers*, A3^b; Gildon, *Betterton*, 99.

*Innocence* ended abruptly because of 'a Mischance which happened to one, whose part was too considerable to be quickly studied'; Peter Motteux ironically observes that as the best actors were studying other plays at the time, he 'could not expect they would study mine', going on humbly to thank William Bowen who did succeed in learning his part 'while he was studying several others'.[111] One problem was that skilled actors too frequently thought (or realized) that they could get away with only short study: because Powell 'idly deferr'd the Studying of his Parts . . . to the last Day', writes Cibber, he had difficulty in retaining the 'Look of what he was meant to *be*' on the stage: he was presumably too busy trying to recall his lines.[112] This goes part of the way towards explaining what 'study' was supposed to establish—not just the lines, but the appropriate physical characteristics required by a part. Gildon's Betterton further explains the use of 'study'. He writes about the same period addressed by Cibber, when the young actors had taken to imitating Powell's lax attitude towards study. Whereas in the past study had been paramount, claims 'Betterton', now actors hope to learn their lines and establish their gestures in group rehearsal:

When I was a young Player under Sir *William Davenant*, we were . . . obliged to make our Study our Business, which our young Men do not think it their duty now to do; for they now scarce ever mind a Word of their parts but only at *Rehearsals*, and come thither too often scarce recovered from their last Night's Debauch; when the Mind is not very capable of considering so calmly and judiciously on what they have to study, as to enter thoroughly into the Nature of the Part, or to consider the Variation of the Voice, Looks, and Gestures.[113]

The quotation shows that study was not just for learning appropriate words, tones, and actions, but for settling the 'nature' of the part, which was then brought, ready-formed, to rehearsal. Nor was it appropriate to do one's study in group rehearsal itself, for, as Betterton makes clear, by the time actors came to rehearsal, they were expected to have finished their work on their parts: to leave study until rehearsal was to guarantee a bad performance. The actor's most important work was there-

---

[111] John Leanerd, *The Country Innocence* (1677), A3ᵃ; Peter Motteux *et al.*, *The Novelty* (1697), A4ᵃ.

[112] Cibber, *Apology*, 133; see also *Pepys*, viii. 430.

[113] Gildon, *Betterton*, 15.

fore supposed to be based on the part as received and not on the way that that part interacted with the text as a whole; indeed, an actor might practise far from the prompt-book and far from the theatre. One anecdote tells how John Verbruggen went out into some local fields to learn his part in Nathaniel Lee's *Theodosius*. There three highwaymen saw him

> walking all alone, making all the Gestures imaginable of Passion, Discontent, and Fury, a-casting up his Eyes to the sky, displaying his arms abroad . . . [and] expressing in a very passionate manner these Words of *Varanes*, in the Tragedy of *Theodosius* . . .
> *I charge thee not!—*

The highwaymen's pity was aroused by the man's distress; they approached him and begged him not to kill himself—to which he responded angrily, '*What a Plague is all this for? I arn't going to Hang, Stab, nor Drown my self for love; I arn't in love; I'm a Player only getting my Part.*' They then robbed him and went on their way.[114]

Study might be instructed by several people—the author, the manager, other actors, teachers from outside the theatre, and the prompter—all of whom shared the burden of helping the separate actors with their roles. Anne Oldfield, for instance, is praised by Cibber as being open to all forms of instruction from whatever quarter—she 'never undertook any Part she lik'd, without being importunately desirous of having all the Helps in it, that another could possibly give her'; Michael Mohun, Charles Hart, James Nokes, and Cave Underhill are described as 'wonderful Performers' because they 'would earnestly sollicit Instruction from anyone . . . able to inform them in any Thing relative to Acting'.[115] The theatre of the time is full of examples of managers delegating or sharing their rehearsal duties with their leading actors; Betterton, in his United Company, also paid his 'Housekeep[r]' an additional sum 'to teach to act'.[116] When Dryden in 1668 became a contracted playwright to the King's

---

[114] Captain Alexander Smith, *The History of the Lives of the Most Noted Highway-Men*, 2 vols. (1714), i. 90.

[115] Cibber, *Apology*, 168; Fitz-Crambo, *Tyranny*, 8.

[116] Thomas (ed.), *Theatre in Europe*, 51. The housekeeper was probably an old player. *The London Spy* (1703), 426, explains how the decaying Dorset Garden theatre has 'an old Superannuated Jack Pudding, to look after it' ('Jack Pudding', always an insult, was also the generic name for an English clown actor).

Company, he was also given a share in the company's business side: as a result he found himself arranging scenery and music, and, significantly, instructing players.[117] The theatre's emphasis on private study meant that instructors were desirable for each major actor—a job that no single person could fulfil.

Particularly in the early years, when all actors and playwrights were novices, outside instruction was valued, and the court wits seem to have been quite often involved in the process. Gildon's Betterton continues to recommend the actor to turn, in private study, to a friend who understands gestures and motion 'to correct your Errors, as you perform before him, and point out those *Graces*, which wou'd render your Action completely charming'.[118] So Pepys rehearsed Elizabeth Knepp backstage at the King's House Scene-Room, reading 'the Qu's to Knepp while she answered me, through all her part'.[119] Another famous casual instructor was John Wilmot, Earl of Rochester, who set out to teach Mrs Barry to be 'the finest Player on the Stage' in under six months, for a dare. To do this, he instructed Mrs Barry in essentially puppet-fashion—he made sure 'not to omit the least Look or Motion' in his lessons, and taught her 'the proper Stress' of the voice. But he did also spend time encouraging her to produce the feeling and 'humour' that 'the person she represented was supposed to be in'. This is presumably what Betterton meant by the 'nature' of the part; it consisted not in a kind of method acting based on identification with the character, but in the recognition of the appropriate emotions (the 'passions' and 'humours') required by the part, and the ability to tap into those emotions and manifest them physically.[120] Again, these instruction sessions took place from a part, so that the character played was determined without reference to other characters: Rochester's 'private Instructions' to Mrs Barry were given mostly at the actress's home, and, though he also 'made her Rehearse near 30 times on the Stage', he never invited the other actors to join her; even the public theatre space might be occupied by 'private' rehearsals.[121] This was not unusual, and explains the

---

[117] Maguire, *Regicide*, 193.    [118] Gildon, *Betterton*, 55.

[119] *Pepys*, viii. 463.

[120] For the nature of the 'passions' and for ways of depicting them, see Roach, *Player's Passion*, chs. 1 and 2. For the direct identification of 'passions' with 'character' in a part, see Davies, *Miscellanies*, iii. 121.

[121] Edmund Curll [pseud. Thomas Betterton], *The History of the English Stage*

points at which 'study' and 'rehearsal' can seem interchangeable and become confused. There were, for instance, occasions during which all the actors would gather in one room at the theatre, but continue to study privately rather than together. Often this was called 'rehearsal', but, though it admitted of the possibilities of instructive help from anyone present in the room, it was at root solitary. *The Spectator* (4 April 1711) depicts players rehearsing in this manner: 'one is sighing and lamenting his Destiny in beseeching Terms, another declaring he will break his Chain, and another in dumb-Show striving to express his Passion by his Gesture'; Richard Burridge similarly describes seeing Betterton's actors gathered together but working individually at 'getting' (i.e. 'learning') their 'Cues, or Parts'.[122]

Minor actors were not always given the opportunity to practise privately with an instructor. In that case, they were indeed reliant on the group rehearsal for clues as to how to act their part. In Buckingham's *Rehearsal*—which depicts a final rehearsal—three players discuss the fact that they have privately learnt their roles, but cannot fathom either the pronunciation required ('how it is to be spoken') or the gesture ('whether angry, melancholy, merry, or in love').[123] They have not been 'instructed', though the player of Volscius has (as becomes clear when Bayes 'over acts the Part', performing the blueprint role, over the performance of the actor).[124] The author therefore was confronted in group rehearsal with a set of actors variously studied: some had learnt their parts alone, some with others, and some with the author; some had not learnt their parts at all.

### Pronunciation and gesture

Pronunciation and gesture were broadly standardized, though comedy and tragedy seem to have used different levels of convention: actors could have quite different tragic and comic

(1741), 14–15. Rochester together with Buckingham, Wilmot, and the Earl of Dorset are described by John Dennis as the 'extraordinary men at Court' who helped establish 'dramatic judgement' in the early, struggling theatre—see Emmet L. Avery, 'The Restoration Audience', *PQ* 45 (1966), 54–61 (55).

[122] *The Spectator*, ed. Donald R. Bond, 5 vols. (Oxford, 1965), i. 124; Burridge, *Scourge*, 1.

[123] Villiers (Buckingham), *Rehearsal*, ed. Crane, 7.      [124] Ibid. 38.

'lines' which did not affect each other; comedies were often prepared over a shorter period than tragedies. Comic acting style is less documented than tragic style: Gildon has much to say about acting tragedy, nothing to say about acting comedy, perhaps because comedy was more 'realistic', less contrived. In George Etherege's *Man of Mode* (3.2) Harriet and young Bellair 'instruct' one another to create a dumbshow image of two lovers—'Shrug a little, draw up your Breasts, and let 'em fall | Again, gently, with a sigh'—exaggerated versions of very predictable gestures; Cibber tells how Nokes talking animatedly behind the scenes was taken for an actor rehearsing.[125] Tragedy seems to have demanded a more clearly stylized mode of behaviour: when, in 1663, Lord Digby spoke in Parliament against Chancellor Clarendon, Sir Carteret was full of contempt for the way he pointed 'like a stage-player' to parts of his own anatomy.[126] Certain exaggerated forms of action made (tragic) stage sense: directions are still given like '*Virgilius spyes Cicilia and falls in Love with her*'.[127] Sir Positive At-all, in Shadwell's *The Sullen Lovers*, gives a jokey example of the mannered way in which an emotion can be symbolized, when he equates hanging in a halter with 'the posture of a Pensive dejected Lover with his hands before him, and his head aside thus'.[128] Only Gildon in his *Betterton* articulates in detail rules for pronunciation and gesture, and many of his sources are French works on oratory, though, given the extent to which English theatre of the time was indebted to the French, the plagiarism need not discount the English relevance of the observations.[129] The book offers strict rules for determining gesture, but also recommends the study of 'History-Painting' as a means of teaching the actor beautiful ways 'to vary and change his Figure, which would make him not

---

[125] George Etherege, *Man of Mode* (1684), 31; Cibber, *Apology*, 82–3. The difference in acting style is perhaps traceable to the fact that 'comedy' was said to revolve around the 'humours' and tragedy around the 'passions'. See William Congreve, *Concerning Humour in Comedy* (1695; New York, 1964).

[126] *Pepys*, iv. 212.

[127] Killigrew's 1664 text of *The Princess*, quoted Albert Wertheim, 'Production Notes for Three Plays by Thomas Killigrew', *TS* 10 (1969), 105–13 (106).

[128] Shadwell, *Sullen*, 36.

[129] Wilbur Samuel Howell, *Eighteenth Century British Logic and Rhetoric* (Princeton, 1971), 189, observes that Curll in his *English Stage* (1741) accepted verbatim many of Gildon's precepts about gesture, which must therefore have had some continuing relevance.

always the same . . . in all Parts', thus offering instruction as to how to perform according to conventions, whilst at the same time being original.[130]

Action and pronunciation were still valued separately, though actors were only judged 'good' if they had equal skill in both: 'the best *Speaking* destitute of *Action* and *Gesture* (the Life of all Speaking) proves but heavy, dull, and dead Discourse'.[131] Though it is difficult to determine quite what theatrical speech was like, particular named ways of speaking give something of a clue—there was 'rant' (angry pronunciation), 'cant' (whining or loving pronunciation), and 'tone' (cadenced, musical pronunciation used for making declamations): these are parodied in comedies, and adhered to in tragedies.[132] Whatever form pronunciation took, it is generally described in musical terms, which perhaps explains why it needed to be taught, and could not necessarily be correctly guessed at by reading a text: few denied that 'there is a Musical Cadence in speaking; and that a Man may as well speak out of Tune, as sing out of Tune'; in Dryden's *Essay of Dramatic Poesy*, Neander advocates 'Variety of cadences' as 'the greatest help to the Actors'.[133] And, as with music, the audience might have very specific requirements about the way words were pronounced—Pepys, at *The Changes*, had 'never heard both men and women so ill pronounce their parts'—or might so enjoy the beauty of the sounds made by a fine-spoken actor, that they did not necessarily notice the substance of the speech themselves:

When these flowing Numbers came from the Mouth of a *Betterton*, the Multitude no more desired Sense to them, than our musical *Connoisseurs* think it essential in the celebrate Airs of an *Italian* Opera . . . there is very near as much Enchantment in the well-govern'd Voice of an Actor, as in the sweet pipe of an Eunuch[.][134]

---

[130] Gildon, *Betterton*, 63. The advice was literally followed. Nicolini is praised for the fact that 'there is scarce a Beautiful Posture in an old Statue which he does not plant himself in, as the different Circumstances of the Story give Occasion for it'—see Richard Steele, *The Tatler*, ed. Donald F. Bond, 3 vols. (Oxford, 1987), ii. 186.

[131] Curll, *English Stage*, 73.

[132] See John Harold Wilson, 'Rant, Cant and Tone on the Restoration Stage', *SP* 52 (1955), 592–8.

[133] Elkanah Settle, *The Fairy-Queen* (1692), A4ᵃ; John Dryden, *The Works*, ed. Samuel Holt Monk *et al.*, 20 vols. (Berkeley, 1956–89), xvii. 70.

[134] Cibber, *Apology*, 63.

Most preparation time was spent in establishing, memorizing, and then honing down pronunciation and gesture. The 'meaning' of a play resided in the way that the choreographed, individual parts were gathered together; the play itself was a collection of linear fragments as well as the whole production that they made.

## Actor-training and rehearsal

Several short-lived special schools seem to have existed in London for the training of actors. The best documented is George Jolly's Hatton Garden Nursery, which was cheaper than normal theatres, and put on performances only two or three times a week.[135] But by acting in public at all, Jolly was threatening the Duke's and King's Men's duopoly as well as breaking the law, and Davenant and Killigrew finally succeeded in driving him from London. The two legitimate London companies then set up a joint nursery of their own—the prologue to John Dover's *The Roman Generalls*, specifically mentions 'both the Houses *Nursery*'—while Jolly established a touring company centred in Norwich, a city that continued to be the training ground for actors until well into the eighteenth century.[136] Lady Davenant meanwhile set up a London nursery in 1671 that lasted into the 1680s; after that the nursery system of training seems to have disappeared in the capital.[137]

Long runs were crucial to nursery training: when Killigrew projected setting up his own nursery he decided to prepare only four operas a year, each to act for six weeks.[138] This stress on the educational value of repeated performance is telling, for the ensemble values of performance were not naturally offered very much in the preparation process; performance itself was seen as fulfilling the same role that frequent group rehearsal does today.

Admirable in principle, nurseries attracted small audiences ('They count Ten People There, an Audience'), their standard was low (as 'bad as could [be]', as Pepys uncharitably put it of a performance at Jolly's nursery), and even their poets were fledgling and unskilled: Stanford in Shadwell's *Sullen Lovers*

---

[135] Montague Summers, *The Restoration Theatre* (London, 1934), 36.
[136] See Freeburn, 'Charles II', 148; John Dover, *The Roman Generalls* (1667), A3a.
[137] *London Stage*, I, p. xxxviii.  [138] *Pepys*, v. 230 n.

speaks deprecatingly of the Bell-man who 'in a dismal Tone
repeats worse Rhimes | Then a Cast Poet of the Nursery can
make'.[139] The discontinuation of the nursery training system is
hardly surprising, for the concept of dividing novice performers
from established professionals was flawed: nursery productions
were always shoddy, for as soon as actors were trained to a level
of competence, they left to join professional theatres.[140] Most
importantly, as professional theatres also trained their actors—a
process they too described as 'nursing'—the existence of nurseries themselves in London was unnecessary.[141]

Inside the professional theatre, would-be players could still
become apprenticed to established actors. Davenant and his wife
kept several actresses in their house in the 1660s, who were thus
enabled to 'improve themselves daily'; Lady Davenant took
particular charge over Mrs Barry, and she, as well as Rochester,
was credited with that actress's stage success.[142] Mrs Bracegirdle
was similarly brought up, and trained by the Bettertons, as was
Mary Porter, who was so little when first put under Betterton's
tuition, that he used to threaten her, 'if she did not speak and act
as he would have her, to put her into a fruit-woman's basket and
cover her with a vine-leaf'.[143] One of the main objections to the
Cibber–Wilks–Doggett triumvirate early in the eighteenth century was that it 'took no Care to breed up young Actors': it had
ignored the rule of inherited teaching by apprenticeship, and
thus failed to do its duty in providing for the future of the

[139] John Dover, *The Roman Generalls* (1667), A3ᵃ; *Pepys*, ix. 89; Shadwell, *Sullen*,
4. For the threat that a bad play might end up in the nursery, see the prologue to
Thomas St Serfe's *Tarugo's Wiles*, in Danchin, I:i, 259: 'if your Masters | Play be not
provided with requisite Materials, both he and it will be condemned to the Nursery.'

[140] Some writers have become confused as to the extent of meaning 'nursery'
might have. It always designated a special training theatre; Robert Freeburn therefore
cannot be right when he describes Dublin's Theatre Royal as a 'nursery' to London
(it did indeed train young actors who eventually ended up on the London stage, but it
contained permanent, established actors as well as novices). The same is true of the
United Company, which Freeburn also calls a 'nursery' because of the evidence that
Betterton trained actors there. Training, of necessity, happened in all theatres in
which there were experienced and inexperienced actors; in nurseries, as the name
implies, entire companies of novices were 'nursed' to performance standard.

[141] See Duffet's 'Prologue in the Vacation'—'as old Nurse instructs young
smirking Maid . . . See by our penny how their shilling's made'—in Danchin, I:ii,
553.

[142] Gildon, *Betterton*, 7; Jaqueline Pearson, *The Prostituted Muse* (New York,
1988), 32.

[143] Curll, *English Stage*, 26; Davies, *Miscellanies*, iii. 276.

theatre.[144] Presumably the training of young actors involved passing on general acting skills (stage conventions as well as action and gesture) but the information that survives is about teaching apprentices their parts in plays, where, as ever, the training largely consists of imitation—in such instances, of a superior actor. Cibber records with guilt that his expectations of Anne Oldfield had originally been so low that 'I [concluded] that any Assistance I could give her, would be to little, or no purpose'.[145] Established actors seem to have instructed the performers of secondary roles, and certain actors built up a reputation for their teaching skills. On retiring, Mrs Betterton took to teaching and 'several good Actresses were the better for her Instruction'; William Wintershull is described as an 'Excellent, Judicious Actor; and the Best Instructor of others'.[146] Wilks, who 'in his leisure hours . . . would listen to Richards' recital of his parts and read to him the intervening speeches' was clearly helping the actor 'study' his lines, but was probably also instructing him (Vanbrugh was to pay Wilks £50 'For his care and Managemt of Rehearsalls' in 1706).[147]

New young players were given a three-month trial period within the company without salary while they were tested.[148] But they were also allowed the benefit of performance together as novice groups on Wednesdays and Fridays over Lent, again suggesting that ensemble production itself was educative.[149] 'Know, 'twas studied to be play'd in Lent' apologizes Motteux, in explanation, not just of the way his play was acted, but of the way it was written; Edward Ravenscroft's *The Careless Lovers* was also 'written at the Desire of the Young Men of the *Stage*, and given them for a *Lenten-Play*'.[150] By the beginning of the eighteenth century, the new members of the theatre had banded together to make up 'the Young Company' that performed over the summer months.[151] Making companies out of novices, and

---

[144] Cibber, *Apology*, 302.  [145] Ibid. 166.

[146] Ibid. 93; Villiers (Buckingham), *Rehearsal . . . with a Key*, p. xvii.

[147] *Farquhar*, i. p. xiii; Milhous and Hume, *Producible*, 59 n.

[148] Nicoll, *English Drama*, i. 324.

[149] See Philip H. Gray Jr., 'Lenten Casts and the Nursery', *PMLA* 53 (1938), 781–94.

[150] Peter Motteux, *Beauty in Distress* (1698), A4[a]; Edward Ravenscroft, *The Careless Lovers* (1673), A2[b].

[151] See Charles Johnson, *The Gentleman Cully*, (1702), A2[b].

encouraging groups of novices to perform together, again nar-
rows the gap between rehearsal and performance, but it also raises
questions about the perceived inadequacy of study alone.

Instruction was imitative in its nature, and many established
actors claimed to have based their best performances on patterns
laid down by other actors—generally the actors who had first
'instructed' them. Wilks 'form'd his manner of Acting, upon the
Model of *Monfort*', and Barton Booth his upon Betterton.[152]
Even established actors were burdened by the performances that
had preceded them. Betterton's fine Hamlet had been taught to
him in every particular by Davenant, as Downes explained; his
Alexander was haunted by a past production that he could not
quite remember:

[he] was at a loss to recover a particular emphasis of Hart, which gave a
force to some interesting situation of the Part; he applied, for information, to the players who stood near him. At last, one . . . repeated the
line exactly in Hart's key. Betterton . . . put a piece of money in his hand
as a reward for so acceptable a service.[153]

In the case of a new play, major actors were (ideally) to base
their performance on the part as taught by the author (or
whoever was seeing the play to the stage), and secondary
actors on the part as taught to them by major actors. Mrs
Barry, before her encounter with Rochester, had been rejected
by her actor-instructors as '[she had] little, or no Ear for Music,
which caused her to be thought dull when she was taught by the
Actors, because she could not readily catch the Manner of their
sounding Words'.[154] This followed almost inevitably from the
fact that the first rehearsal was a reading; the whole method of
instructing actors was a listen-and-learn routine. Actors, in their
training, were taught to imitate first their superior actors, later
authors, managers, or people who held a folk memory about the
way the part was originally (and therefore ought now to be)
played: asked to perform Falstaff for the first time, Betterton
consented only on the condition that his 'Noble Patrons' would
'give him all the Instructive Hints they possibly could' about
previous performances.[155]

Actors were never encouraged to seek freedom from the rules

[152] Cibber, *Apology*, 313.        [153] Davies, *Miscellanies*, iii. 161.
[154] Curll, *English Stage*, 16.       [155] Fitz-Crambo, *Tyranny*, 10.

and conventions that governed their performances, nor were they ever free of the notion that it was 'proper' to be, on some level, the imitation of a superior. When playing without an imposed pattern to dictate some aspect of their performance, actors are not described as 'fresh' or 'exciting' but as sloppy, under-prepared and over-bold, 'vainly' imagining themselves 'Masters' of the art of acting, when they clearly are not.[156] From the actor's point of view, the way parts were taught was bound, if precisely followed, to produce second-hand performances. Clearly it was wrong to accept an imitation absolutely, without varying it: Cibber describes the actor whose 'errors' show that his performance is 'but a Lesson given him, to be got by Heart, from some great Author, whose Sense is deeper than the Repeater's Understanding'.[157] But the basis of 'good' acting was not a new or original interpretation, but a subtle reworking of a given interpretation to make it personal.

*Composers, authors, and individual rehearsal*

When Thomas Clayton introduced what was, in effect, the first Italian-style opera into England (words translated by Motteux), he engaged the best singers he could find, and then used 'the utmost of my Diligence, in the instructing of them'.[158] Almost certainly he instructed through the medium of imitation, which was the way singing outside the theatre was taught: Roger North wrote disdainfully about the ladies who learnt their songs by rote from a master who would sing to them 'as to a parrot' until 'with infinite difficulty the tune is gott'.[159] It was in this manner that John Bannister seems to have instructed Mrs Knepp when he taught her 'a slight, silly, short ayre' that he had inserted into a play: the actress was not 'given' the song, slight as it was—she had to learn it from the composer.[160] Henry Purcell, too, provided his theatre singer with careful musical instruction, but added—'*he will grace it* [i.e. add 'ornament' to it] *more*

---

[156] Gildon, *Betterton*, 15.

[157] Cibber, *Apology*, 73–4. Davenant, in the prologue to his *Siege of Rhodes*, describes his fledgling actors as 'Infant-Players, scarce grown Puppets yet'—Danchin, I:i, 67.

[158] Thomas Clayton, preface to Peter Motteux's *Arsinoe* (1705), A2ᵃ.

[159] Roger North, *Roger North on Music*, ed. John Wilson (London, 1959), 21.

[160] *Pepys*, ix. 189.

*naturally than . . . I can teach him'.*[161] Instruction in the essentials, with decoration to be added by the individual, was what study sessions, musical and textual, ideally gave the performer. Usually the author instructed at least some of the actors. One actress is made to describe how she learnt her role in a prologue: the poet, 'busie at's Instructive part' corrected her pronunciation ('Hast thou the Accent found?'), and her gesture ('Stand streight, look brisk, and dart thy Eyes around').[162] Authors were particularly concerned about the way certain words were spoken: John Crowne printed the speeches for Bartoline phonetically 'in that manner of spelling, by which I taught it to Mr. *Lee'*, suggesting that the part can only 'properly' be acted (and, indeed, read) by being 'performed' in Lee's manner.[163] Clearly authors wrote not just words, but ways of performing those words: Joseph Haynes talks of the efforts taken by a new author 'to teach a Dull, Heavy Player the right accent of all his Witty Passages'.[164] The instructive method encouraged authors to see actors as 'pupils'. But actors became increasingly selective about the people by whom they were prepared to be mastered. Cibber is proud to be an imitator of actors in received parts (Sandford in *Richard III*, and Doggett in *The Old Batchelour*); he is ready enough to submit to professional writers like Sir John Vanbrugh for instruction in new parts; but he is also famous for his dismissive manner towards lesser-known authors. Actors learnt to be selective about the model they chose to fashion themselves around, and, though the idealized vision of the theatre of the past dictated that their model should be the author, fact shows that it often was not.

## GROUP REHEARSAL

Morning gatherings of some kind were normal. They are hailed as regular, and, at least during parts of the season, daily events: Haynes in Brown's *Life* came 'every morning to the Rehearsal'

[161] Anthony Aston, *Brief Supplement to the Life of Colley Cibber*, ed. Robert W. Lowe (1889; New York, 1966), ii. 312.

[162] Thomas Dilke, *The City Lady* (1697), A4[a].

[163] John Crowne, *City Politiques* (1683), A2[b].

[164] Thomas Brown, *The Reasons of Mr. Joseph Hains the Player's Conversion and Re-Conversion* (1690), 13.

(though he was 'idle' in vacation time); Cibber insisted that a 'menager' should attend 'two, or three Hours every Morning, at the Rehearsal of Plays'.[165] In *The Female Wits* morning rehearsal starts at ten o'clock, though this cannot necessarily be taken as a blanket rule: times of performance changed from three o'clock in the 1660s to six o'clock by the 1700s, and rehearsal time may also have changed as a result.[166]

*The London Stage* points out that both morning and evening rehearsals existed, but cannot really make any distinction between them: to the evening one it attributes 'conning lines and preparing scenes' as well as 'songs, dances, and other components of the performance'; morning rehearsals, it concludes, were simply a more 'formal' version of the same thing.[167] In fact, dialogue rehearsals took place in the morning before performance; music rehearsals—in which actors were taught songs and dances—tended to be held when the day's play was over. Mrs Knepp after a performance, for instance, invited Pepys to 'see the dancing preparatory to to-morrow for *The Goblins*'; even when she had to learn Bannister's song privately for a play to be performed the following day, she did so at home in the evening.[168] The stage was free after performance, and 'machines', perhaps already set up for the play that had just happened—or set up in advance for the play of the next day—could be used for practice, so that evening rehearsal could be a combination of a musical and technical run-through: ideal for rehearsing operas. Settle's Ned Stanmore in *The World in the Moon* has heard that 'after the Play's done, . . . the Actors [will] have a general Practice of the Musick and Machines of some part of their New Opera'.[169] Evening rehearsals were also less regular than morning ones: Pepys often goes directly home with Mrs Knepp after performance; and the 'Ladies of Quality' were given to taking Edward Kynaston out in their coaches straight from the theatre, still in costume.[170]

There seems to have been little of *The London Stage*'s

---

[165] Brown, *Life . . . Haynes*, 40, 35; Cibber, *Apology*, 291. In Richard Head and Francis Kirkman's *The English Rogue, Part 4* (1671), 189, the strolling players are joined in the morning by 'three or four Women, who with the rest rehearsed their parts in Actæon and Diana'. See also Downes, *Roscius*, 2.

[166] *Female Wits*, 1; *London Stage*, I, pp. lxix-lxx.

[167] *London Stage*, I, p. cliii.          [168] *Pepys*, viii. 27; ix. 189.

[169] Elkanah Settle, *The World in the Moon* (1697), 4.

[170] Cibber, *Apology*, 71.

'formality' attending morning rehearsals, which actors notoriously came to bad tempered, and badly dressed. Hillaria in Thomas Baker's *Tunbridge-Walks* insults Jenny Trapes, calling her 'trapish and dirty, like an Actress at a Morning Rehearsal'; Richard Burridge records seeing Betterton's company rehearse, and finding that 'some of 'em were . . . as bad Cloathed, as a Taffy'.[171] The status of preparation, and its nature (whether group or individual) determined where the rehearsal was held. While Burridge saw Betterton's men 'getting their . . . Parts . . . in the Sun-Shine',[172] more generally group rehearsals took place either, in the case of important rehearsals, on the stage, in the 'scene' or 'green' room, or in special 'practising rooms'. Charles Dieupart wrote to tell Christopher Rich that the singer Catherine Tofts should 'have the Roome called the Practicing Roome to Dress in'; the anonymous painting of a rehearsal of *Pyrrhus and Demetrius* (1709) shows a partial rehearsal (not all the players are there) in just such a room.[173]

Once more, the fact that several plays will have been prepared at the same time must be borne in mind; together with the fact that much important preparation happened in private study (though sometimes in group private study). Information about how many full and how many partial rehearsals were normal for a play is disappointingly sparse. John Crowne's *Calisto*, a play performed by the Royal Family (with the help of professional actors), was, Eleanor Boswell believes, probably the most elaborate production ever mounted at Whitehall.[174] It was carefully studied and rehearsed about twenty times (at the rate of three rehearsals a week): this is offered as an instance of extraordinary preparation, even for a court performance.[175]

---

[171] Baker, *Tunbridge*, 61; Burridge, *Scourge*, 1.         [172] Ibid. 1.

[173] Quoted in Nicoll, *History of English Drama*, ii. 290; Eric Walter White, 'The Rehearsal of an Opera', *TN* 14 (1959), 79–90 (89).

[174] Boswell, *Restoration*, 208.

[175] *Calisto* was rehearsed 'near Thirty times', according to Gerard Langbaine, *Account of the English Dramatick Poets*, facs. ed. Arthur Freeman (New York, 1973), 92, but this seems simply to be a paraphrase of Crowne's own introduction to the play—see John Crowne, *The Dramatic Works*, ed. James Maidment and W. H. Logan, 4 vols. (1874; New York, 1967), i. 238. 'I undertook the trouble . . . to give some refreshment to the audiences, who would have been weary of a better play at the second or third representation, and therefore must needs be weary of that at the 20th or 30th for near so often it had been rehearsed and acted.' See also Boswell, *Restoration*, 205.

Chappuzeau, writing about French rehearsal practice in 1673, offers no rules, but, as ever, puts the emphasis of production on private study, capped by upwards of three rehearsals; French strolling players put on plays after a single group rehearsal.[176] English theatre too has records of performances brought to the stage after one rehearsal, though by this time it is treated as unusual. Powell, during battles with the other house, had his actors learning parts in six hours; Cibber's own role 'was put into my Hands, between Eleven and Twelve' on the morning of performance and he was word-perfect 'when it came to my turn to rehearse' later that day.[177]

Buckingham's *Rehearsal* shows a 'last' rehearsal that also seems to be the first full company rehearsal:

2 PLAYER. I don't understand how [my part] is to be spoken
1 PLAYER. . . . the Author will be here presently, and he'l tell us all.[178]

And undoubtedly the final rehearsal was particularly important. When Crowne met Underhill the actor walking away from the playhouse 'upon the very last Day of Rehearsal', he reprimanded him for neglecting his part 'on a Day of so much consequence'; it seems also to have been a full dress rehearsal—'This morning is its last Rehearsal, in their habits, and all that'.[179]

For a revived play demanded at short notice there was sometimes a 'refresher' rehearsal, such as the one called for when Dryden's *Indian Emperor* was 'ordered on a sudden to be play'd'. Betterton chose to miss this rehearsal as he was feeling mildly ill (he was well enough to perform that evening)—an instance that illustrates the relative unimportance of the occasion.[180] There is no evidence for refresher rehearsals within a season, though players seem to have been expected to look over their parts

---

[176] Chappuzeau, *Le Théâtre français*, 61–2. French theatrical practice was, in many ways, reproduced in the English theatre, as discussed, though it is also true that the French had potentially more rehearsal time: when Chappuzeau was writing, only three performances were held a week (60); 'J.B.', *The Comical Romance*, 2 vols. (1665), i. 170 ('the next day the Comedians met together in one of those Chambers they had at the Inn, to reherse the Comedy they were to Act that afternoon'); 175 ('It was now high time, to reherse their parts, of a Play, which was to be Acted that same day in a Neighbouring Tennis-Court').

[177] Cibber, *Apology*, 115.

[178] Villiers (Buckingham), *Rehearsal*, ed. Crane, 7.

[179] John Dennis, quoted in the *London Stage*, I, 335; Villiers (Buckingham), *Rehearsal*, ed. Crane, 5.          [180] Chetwood, *History*, 164.

quietly the night before. One evening Pepys had been thinking of going out with Mrs Knepp 'but it was too late, and she to get her part against to-morrow, in *The Silent Woman*' (a play that had last been performed earlier that season).[181]

As before the Interregnum, the suggestion seems to be that there was a necessity for holding one final, 'general' group rehearsal (though examples above show that major actors did not necessarily attend it), and the possibility of holding more; partial rehearsal, in which small groups of actors are prepared together, seems, however, to have grown in importance.

### Authors and rehearsal

Authors often had a say in casting, though as they had written for a specific company and its crop of actors, their plays tended to cast themselves. Nevertheless, Nicholas Rowe 'gave the Part of *Artaban* [in *The Ambitious Stepmother*] to Mr Booth'; and William Congreve advised that Cibber be given Kynaston's part in *The Double Dealer*.[182] Playwrights might, however, be denied their casting choices. Nahum Tate, in the preface to *The Cuckold's Haven*, explains that he was 'disappointed of Mr. Nokes's Performance' and includes sorrowfully in the cast list 'Alderman *Touchstone*, intended for Mr. *Nokes*—By Mr. Percivall'. Betterton and Dryden clearly discussed casting together for *All for Love* and *The Conquest of Granada*, and Betterton accepted most, but not all, of Dryden's suggestions:[183] ultimately, managers could override the author.

After casting, the role of the author became nebulous. Novice authors who did not yet understand the ways of the theatre could cause disasters, as the ability to write a play by no means indicated an ability to teach or block it. John Oldmixon, famous as a politician, was allowed to take responsibility for much of the production of his *Amintas*. He confesses: 'The management of the representation, particularly that part on't which I undertook, was very ill contriv'd. The small acquaintance I have had with

---

[181] *Pepys*, ix. 310.
[182] Benjamin Victor, *Memoirs of the Life of Barton Booth, Esq* (1733), 7; Cibber, *Apology*, 104, see also Thomas Southerne's *Sir Anthony Love* (1691), A2ᵃ; and *The Fatal Marriage* (1694), A2ᵇ; Holland, *Ornament*, 70–86.
[183] Tate, *Cuckold's*, A1ᵃ, A4ᵇ; Dryden, *Letters*, 24.

such things did not qualify me to undertake what I did, and the success was answerable to the contrivance.'[184] Generally, no doubt as a result of similar occurrences, a process seems to have come about whereby authors could choose not to oversee their plays' production, but delegate the task to a more professional playwright. What pressure may or may not have been brought to bear on amateurs to force them to this is unrecorded. But the policy of giving over a production is well documented, and a play which was not to be put on by its own playwright was handed to a more experienced professional or semi-professional author.[185]

From the start of the Restoration, playwrights had 'theatricalized' each others' texts, for they had all been ambitious amateurs without play-writing experience, and it had then seemed sensible to submit plays to the scrutiny of whoever seemed most knowledgeable. Dryden acknowledges that his writing received daily amendments from Davenant 'and that's the reason why it is not so faulty'; he also received correction from the Earl of Rochester's 'noble hands'; and from the king himself, who modelled 'the most considerable event' in *Aureng-Zebe*.[186] It is telling, though, that when help is gratefully acknowledged, it has usually been given by the crowd of courtly theatrical enthusiasts: publicly announcing the name of the helper also identified the authors themselves as belonging to a certain set. Dryden and Howard corrected each other; Sir Charles Sedley gave Shadwell the benefit of his 'Correction and Alteration' in *A True Widow*; and Congreve's *The Old Batchelour* (1693) was shown to Dryden in rough draft—he 'putt it in the order it was playd' after consulting Thomas Southerne and Arthur Maynwaring.[187]

The above examples are for the most part from the 1670s and 1680s. Towards the end of the century the 'theatricalizers' of texts were much more frequently professional writers who were actors. Betterton had, for example, inherited from Davenant the idea that theatricalizing texts was part of his job as manager. But William Mountfort, the actor-writer, also received fulsome

---

[184] Oldmixon, *Amintas*, A2b.

[185] Plays were not handed to an actor as Milhous and Hume suggest in *Producible*, 60, unless the actor was also a writer.

[186] *Dryden*, x. 4; xi. 221; xii. 155.

[187] Maguire, *Regicide*, 119; Thomas Shadwell, *A True Widow* (1679), A2a; *London Stage*, I, 416.

praise for his additions: Settle was indebted to him for the whole last scene of *Distress'd Innocence*; and without irony Joseph Harris gratefully acknowledged 'my gratitude to Mr. *Montfort*, who in the fifth Act has not only corrected the tediousness by cutting out a whole Scene, but to make the Plot more clear, has put in one of his own, which heightens his own Character, and was very pleasing to the Audience'.[188]

As a body of professional writers emerged, it seems to have become more and more usual for plays to be actually staged by the people who had 'theatricalized' rather than written them. Playwrights were in effect 'ranked', so that in practice, specific authors held the stage and had control over their own and others' work. These professional authors tended to be contractually attached to certain companies, either by having a share in the company, or by being salaried to it; later they were to come from the ranks of the actor-writers; either way, they knew about the stage, and knew what audiences wanted to watch.[189] Dryden had a share together with a contract which made him responsible for seeing plays through production. In 1679, for instance, he 'brought five Plays upon the Stage . . . as he had six the Year before' (three of those plays will have been his, so eight must have belonged to other writers).[190] Alexander Davenant, writing in 1687, explains that Abraham Cowley, 'being an Ingenious Man And well skilled in Poetry', was given a half-share in the theatre for his skills in 'Writing [and] Correcting' other plays as well as creating his own 'Entertainments'.[191] Shadwell, meanwhile, saw to the stage William Cavendish, Duke of Newcastle's *Triumphant Widdow*, causing distress to Settle when he foisted 'a Scene of his own into the Play' in order to make 'a silly Heroick Poet in it, speak the very words he had heard me say'.[192] He also 'usher'd . . . to the Stage' *The Innocent Impostors*, the author of which was 'not one of the Laity' and preferred not to be known.[193]

---

[188] Elkanah Settle, *Distress'd Innocence* (1691), A3[a]; Joseph Harris, *The Mistakes* (1691), A2[b].

[189] For a list of known attached authors, see Milhous and Hume, *Producible*, 42–3.

[190] Mottley, *List*, 223.

[191] Hotson, *Commonwealth*, 221.

[192] Settle, *Ibrahim*, a2[a].

[193] *Gentlemen's Journal*, Mar. 1692, 9. These instances make me think that Shadwell was also 'attached', a suggestion also made by Milhous and Hume, *Producible*, 43.

A play was more likely to be accepted by a company if it was presented as being in the hands of a 'professional' writer. But, as the example of Shadwell and *The Triumphant Widdow* shows, professional writers often did not simply take plays to the stage: they improved, altered and moulded them to make them more stage-worthy—and more a product of their own. Various false attributions have been spawned because the writers who theatricalized and saw plays to the stage have become, understandably, confused with the authors of the plays themselves. Examples include 'Underhill's' *Win Her and Take Her*, 'Powell's' *The Cornish Comedy* and 'Pinkethman's' *Love without Interest*.[194] Shakespeare's plays were heavily adapted by writers who are then hailed as 'authors' on the title-pages—like Betterton's *Henry IV*, James Howard's *Romeo and Juliet*, and John Crowne's *Henry VI*, which he generously 'called . . . in the Prologue *Shakespear's* Play, though he has no Title to the *40th* part of it'.[195] Indeed, Alfred Harbage argues that a few 'lost' Elizabethan plays may well survive as the base texts behind some of the extant Restoration dramas, revised over and mounted by contemporary authors.[196]

New playwrights felt—or were encouraged to feel—that an active role in the production of their plays was socially unsuitable. Women in particular were told that being a visible authoress was unbecoming: 'A Poetess is so scandalous a Character' exclaims Hillaria in Baker's *The Tunbridge-Walks*, 'for when a Woman has the Face to appear at Rehearsals, and teach Actors their Parts, her Assurance will scruple nothing'; and *The Female Tatler* warns that 'no Woman ever yet turn'd *Poetess*, but lost her *Reputation* by appearing at *Rehearsals*, and *Conversing with Imoinda, Desdemona, and a Maidenhead Amintor*' (a reference to the corruptive nature of worldly-wise actresses—all the parts quoted in this reference were performed by Elizabeth Barry).[197]

As the century advanced, the fiction of authorial control, except in the cases of attached professionals, became harder to

---

[194] See Milhous and Hume, 'Attribution Problems', 5–39.

[195] John Crowne, *Henry VI* (1681), A3ᵇ. See also Michael Dobson, *The Making of the National Poet* (Oxford, 1992), 61.

[196] Alfred Harbage, 'Elizabethan-Restoration Palimpsest', *MLR* 35 (1940), 287–319.

[197] Baker, *Tunbridge*, 47; *The Female Tatler*, ed. Fidelis Morgan (London, 1992), 94.

maintain. When authors did attend rehearsal, the actors made clear that they knew better how to alter and stage the plays than amateur writers, as Higden explains: 'When I had given them leave to Act it, I was told it was theirs, and they would Cooke it according to their own humour . . . The Actors cut out what they pleased to shorten their parts according to their own humours, and I must stand by and see it mutilated and dismembered before my Face.'[198] Authors who were allowed to attend rehearsal learnt that their motives in holding rehearsals, and the actors' motives in attending them, were very different.

Playwrights received a benefit night for a salary, consisting of the gross takings for the third night's performance minus house charges;[199] they therefore wanted their plays to last for at least three days. That meant that they were interested in ensuring that the production was smooth-running, the scenery and props were in order, and the actors had learnt their lines: Marsilia in *The Female Wits* approves the scenery and sees to it that the property men have the false blood ready. They also needed to make sure that the aspects of the play that would win applause had been identified by the actors. Marsilia instances this as well: too bad a writer to have included a genuine rousing moment in her text (known as a 'clap-trap'), she tries to force the actors to bring about applause by ranting—'strain your Voice: I tell you, Mr. *Pinkethman*, this speaking Loud gets the Clap' (also a *double entendre*, of course).[200] Authors also needed to be on hand to make sure that actors felt positive about the play, for if they did not, they tended to give up in advance of performance. The anonymous *Comparison between the Two Stages* reports how John Bankes's *The Great Cyrus* was a play that 'the Players damn'd and wou'd not Act of a great while'; Wilks, at a rehearsal of *The Busie Body* overseen by the playwright Susanna Centlivre, threw his part 'into the Pitt for damn'd Stuff', and only 'mutteringly' took it up again after the author started to cry.[201] Most importantly, authors wanted to control—and with any luck, sanction—the actors' revisions that were imposed on the text during authorial rehearsals. For actors who had had difficulty with their parts in study

---

[198] Higden, *Wary Widdow*, A4ᵃ.

[199] By the late 17th c. he sometimes received the takings for the sixth night too—see Motteux, *Novelty*, A4ᵃ.

[200] *Female Wits*, 57.

[201] *Comparison*, 16; *Female Tatler*, 94.

sessions brought the offending lines for the author to 'correct' in rehearsal. Wilks complained about a 'crabbed Speech' in his part and asked the author 'to soften, or shorten it' (in fact it was simply cut out altogether); Cibber, on the other hand, is accused of being too 'solicitous' about shortening or cutting 'whatever Part fell to his Share'.[202] Additions too were made in rehearsal as necessary: when Mrs Barry complained to an author one morning that her exit at the end of the fourth act 'was too tame', he took 'two or three Turns cross the Stage' after which he came up with an agreeable six-line addition.[203] As these instances make clear, actors in group rehearsal—not all of whom had had the opportunity to speak to the author before—were still concerned with their own parts rather than with the group effect that alterations or changes would have on the play.

The revision process was seldom as smooth as the instances above. Edward Howard, whom Buckingham criticized at rehearsal, wrote a prologue in which the actors Joseph Haynes and Robert Shatterell complain because the poet did not allow 'his Wit to be cut, lin'd, and interlin'd at pleasure'—had he done so 'we might have perform'd his Play with some security'.[204] He is forcing the actors, within the semi-fiction of a prologue, to level a charge at him that almost certainly they had levelled in fact, thus showing the audience that he has triumphed over his performers. Particularly around the turn of the century, when plays had very short lives, there are instances of cuts made by actors that are damaging to the story of the play itself. Restoration promptbooks are lopped about in ways that, argues Edward Langhans, indicate that the playwright's intentions 'were of less concern to the players than meeting a reasonable running time'.[205] Many published texts, particularly defiant editions of failed plays, print the full, unaltered (pre-performance) copy of a play, arguing that the actors' clumsy cuts have destroyed the flow of the action and made it incomprehensible: 'The chief Parts [were] Acted by Women; and, for their Ease, and somewhat of decorum, as was pretended, whole scenes left out'; 'Had our Authour been alive she would have committed it to the Flames rather than suffer'd it

---

[202] Cibber, *Apology*, 134; *Laureat*, 45.
[203] Mottley, *List*, 287.
[204] Edward Howard, *The Man of Newmarket* (1678), A2[b].
[205] Langhans, *Restoration Promptbooks*, p. xxiii.

to have been Acted with such Omissions as was made'.[206] Authors, of course, wanted to observe—and ideally to approve—the changes actors made to their texts, though prefaces make clear how often they failed in this.

Playwrights were obviously more powerful in individual rehearsal; in group rehearsal even the most professional of them were under the sway of the actors. Author-baiting seems to have been normal, and actors teased authors in ways that were amusing but also threatening. Thomas Jevon purposefully misunderstood Settle's instructions to commit suicide by 'falling on his sword': 'he . . . laid it in the Scabbard at length upon the Ground and fell upon't, saying, now I am Dead; which put the Author into such a Fret, it made him speak Treble, instead of Double, Jevons answer was: did not you bid me fall upon my Sword.'[207] Another anecdote tells how the players mimicked Thomas Durfey's stutter. Furious at his actors' lack of punctuality at rehearsal, Durfey one morning 'ask'd, in a Passion, *Wh, wh, where wa, wa, was M, M, Mr,* Wi, Wilks? The Drole *Pinkethman* answered *H, h, he d, d, did n, n, not kn, kn, know.* But the choleric Poet broke his Head for his Joke.'[208] Prefaces try to be light-hearted in their depictions of an author losing control against a wilful actor, but the picture is clear enough—'I got those Actors I could to study and rehearse for me by the by'

---

[206] *Constant Nymph*, A2[b]; Behn, *Widdow*, A2[a]. Similar complaints are made by John Dennis, *Liberty Asserted* (1704), a1[b]: 'the last Scene of the Play . . . on the account of Length was left out in Acting'; Charles Goring, *Irene* (1708), π4[a]: 'IRENE appear'd to the greatest Disadvantage on the Stage, strip'd of Her Ornaments of Musick by a Superior Order'; Harris, *Mistakes*, A2[b]: 'severall Scenes . . . were entirely omitted in the Action, to modell it into the ordinary bulk of a Play'; Motteux, *Beauty*, A4[a]: 'several things were left out, to make the Play the shorter'; 'M.N.', *The Faithful General* (1706), A3[a]: 'It was expos'd upon the Stage, strip'd of . . . Ornaments . . . Whole Scenes were left out; the passions were weaken'd; some of the necessary Incidents Omitted'; and John Oldmixon, *The Grove* (1700), A3[a]: 'every thing wou'd have appear'd clear and natural, which, to shorten the Entertainment, had been before broken and disorder'd.' Langhans, in *Restoration Promptbooks*, p. xv, suggests that a playwright whose play had flopped would salvage what he could through publishing the prompt-book and puffing the piece 'as performed in the theatre'. At the same time, he bemoans the general lack of prompt-book traces in published texts. This is because failed plays were often printed to resemble pre-performance form, as can be seen from the preface to Charles Gildon's *Love's Victim* (1701), a3[b]: 'The Printer having a Copy, where the Names of *Guinoenda*, and *Morganius* were alter'd to *Alboina* and *Pelagins*, as us'd on the Stage, too much was printed off before I reflected on the Mistake, to alter it'.

[207] Downes, *Roscius*, 75.

[208] Mottley, *List*, 153.

writes Peter Motteux carefully.[209] For though actors needed
author figures to offer initial interpretative 'readings', to shorten
and alter plays, and to be icons for the old-fashioned ideals they
still claimed to be following, they also needed to make sure
authors knew who was in control.


## Managers and rehearsal

Because of the complex nature of the different companies in
existence during the Restoration, the role of managers is hard to
pin down: sometimes they were instructors, but sometimes, as in
the case of Christopher Rich and Thomas Skipwith, they were
simply in charge of finances, and left the running of their
companies to others. Sometimes they were, and sometimes
they were not the patentees, a job that, itself, was difficult to
define.[210] Both Davenant and Betterton (who in many ways took
on Davenant's mantle) in their times as manager had the task of
instructing players—not only as private 'instructors' but also
certainly more generally, when mounting productions of pre-
Restoration plays (in effect adopting the authorial role). For this
reason it is often claimed that the manager usually oversaw plays.
Yet Davenant and Betterton were both writers, and seem to have
taken charge of (older) plays in their capacities as revising
authorial figures rather than as managers. They both strongly
valued instruction as a means not just of teaching actors, but of
handing down the great acting of the past; Davenant remembered and 'passed on' (or claimed to pass on) performances that
had been initiated by Shakespeare, themselves then handed
down by Betterton, who also travelled to Stratford to research
the Great Poet's life.[211]

Other depictions of the manager's role are humdrum. One
constant was that the job included disciplining the actors: the
manager was supposed to look after rehearsals 'in ye nature of a
Monitor in a Schole' as Betterton's position was technically

---

[209] Motteux, *Novelty*, A4[b].

[210] In Vanbrugh's *Aesop* (part II), the patentees are described 'sometimes' as
'masters' and 'sometimes' as 'servants' depending on the whim of the actors—see
John Vanbrugh, *Works*, ed. W. C. Ward, 2 vols. (1893), i. 244.

[211] Downes more than once refers to Davenant's extraordinary care to have plays
from the past 'perfect and exactly perform'd' (*Roscius*, 56), see also 58; Nicholas
Rowe, *The Works of Mr William Shakespear*, 6 vols. (1709), i. p. xxxiv.

described.[212] Some kind of managerial figure was present at all group rehearsals held by authors, taking on the role of 'regulator'. Powell, Rich's deputy manager, attends Marsilia's rehearsal in *The Female Wits*, where his headmasterly corrections are directed towards the authoress herself—'Madam, if you won't let 'em proceed, we shan't do the first Act this Morning.'[213] Similarly Cibber suggests that managers should always go to rehearsals, not to teach the actors, but to control them, 'or else every Rehearsal would be but a rude Meeting of Mirth and Jollity'; and Betterton is praised because his rehearsals are held with 'Decorum' and 'Regularity'.[214] Naturally managers were also respected instructors: Betterton, like Heminges and Taylor years before him, was sent to the royal household to coach private productions—he helped Princesses Mary and Anne in Crowne's *Calisto*.[215]

Increasingly, the roles of manager and superior actor became intertwined. By 1695, those whom Cibber calls 'our merry menaging Actors' were managers of Lincoln's Inn, but even before then, designated managers had tended to arrange for certain actors to oversee rehearsals—Killigrew briefly delegated the practical direction of plays and rehearsals to Michael Mohun, Charles Hart, and John Lacy.[216] Harris, writing in 1691 explains how, after the death of Davenant, 'this Deponent and Mr Betterton were chose by all Parties interested in the said Theatre to manage the same: which was the first time any Person or Persons were chose or appointed to manage the said Theatre, the management . . . always before belonging to the Patentee.'[217] As it was, a stream of actor-managers came into being. Hart was keeping an eye on Drury Lane in late 1670s; Betterton and Harris ran the Duke's Company; after the 1695 succession, Betterton was in charge of those at Lincoln's Inn. At Drury Lane between 1695 and 1699, Rich employed Captain Philip Griffin as general manager and Powell as director of rehearsals;

---

[212] 'The Reply of the Patentees to the Petition of the Players', quoted in Milhous, *Betterton*, 241. The document is confusing, as it also says that Betterton has charge over rehearsal not as manager, but as 'Principall Actor' (241)—the division between manager, actor, and, indeed, author, was not always clear.
[213] *Female Wits*, 27.
[214] Cibber, *Apology*, 291; Fitz-Crambo, *Tyranny*, 9.
[215] Boswell, *Commonwealth*, 180.
[216] Cibber, *Apology*, 113; *London Stage*, I, p. lvii.
[217] Hotson, *Commonwealth*, 228.

after the turn of the century, Cibber was also given managerial and rehearsal duties.[218] The institution of the actor-manager led to a growth in the power of the authoritative actor over rehearsal—or perhaps symbolized it. Even when technically someone else was in charge, the actor-manager effectively was: Betterton under the patentees was given 'fifty Guineas for his generall care & pains in lookeing after Rehearsalls'.[219]

Whether Davenant revised texts in his charge as manager or as playwright is impossible to say: maybe he did not characterize his revising role under any of his other functions. Killigrew, who was supposed, as Master of the Revels, to revise texts to free them from 'profanities', may similarly not always have been able to separate the occasions when his revision was managerial, from the occasions when it was part of his official job. For one reason or another, managerial figures were responsible for textual change; significantly, they added to texts as well as cut away from them: Dryden claims that when Davenant helped writers, he 'sometimes added whole scenes together'.[220] Betterton, as manager, looked over new texts with a professional eye, and did what he could to 'theatricalize' them before they were shown to the actors: 'Above twelve hunder'd lines have been . . . so judiciously lopt by Mr. *Betterton*, . . . that the connexion of the story was not lost.'[221] At the same time he made himself responsible for alterations to the narrative told in the texts under his charge: 'I must own my obligation to Mr. *Betterton* in several hints he gave me in the Fable' records a grateful Charles Gildon, while Settle makes 'publick Acknowlegments to Mr. *Betterton* for his several extraordinary Hints to the heightening of my best Characters'.[222] Managers were reshaping the texts in their command, as they approved them for performance; by the time Cibber was writing, managerial revision was quite expected. When rehearsal began, the manager's revisions will already have been fixed in place and become components of

---

[218] Richard Hindry Barker, *Mr Cibber of Drury Lane* (New York, 1939), 57.

[219] 'The Reply of the Patentees to the Petition of the Players', quoted in Milhous, *Betterton*, 240–1.

[220] *Dryden*, x. 5.      [221] Ibid. xv. 66.

[222] Gildon, *Love's Victim*, a3$^b$; Settle, *Innocence*, A3$^a$. For Betterton's work as a reviser, see Judith Milhous, 'Thomas Betterton's Playwriting', *Bulletin of New York Public Library*, 77 (1974), 375–92.

the text. They were part of the fabric of the plays in a way that rehearsal-revisions often were not; for, as illustrated above, managerial revisions are usually heartily acknowledged.

The theatre had thus invented a figurehead for itself: a person who was not only in charge of behaviour, but also taught actors, and revised texts. As the next chapter will show, this left authors with little explicit role to play; over the eighteenth century, the involvement they had in their productions was to become less and less, as managers grew more and more powerful.

### Prompters and rehearsal

Downes, the prompter, describes his job as 'writing out all the Parts in each Play' as well as 'attending every Morning the Actors Rehearsals, and their Performances in Afternoons'.[223] He is mentioned holding the book during the rehearsal in *The Female Wits*, and seems to have generally provided yet another disciplinary back-up: the preface to *Wit Without Mony* (1707) praises the prompter for his vigilance in 'keeping the Order and Decorum of the Stage'.[224]

It is safe to assume that the prompter used group rehearsal for the technical benefits it offered: checking actors' familiarity with their lines, and establishing when to give calls for the entrances he was going to prompt. Langhans suggests that strange marks in the margin of the prompt-book for a Restoration production of John Fletcher's *Loyal Subject* may indicate entrances missed out in group rehearsal, and that an exclamation-mark after 'ring' in John Wilmot, Earl of Rochester's *Valentinian* may similarly have been the prompter's way of symbolizing a missed rehearsal bell-ring: if so, then the prompter is using the rehearsal primarily to ready the text for performance.[225] The prompter was also responsible for some of the minor casting, and provided substitutes when the original player was unable to perform: Chetwood describes how Downes gave Pizarro in Dryden's *Indian Emperor* to Thomas Griffith, and how Betterton, hearing an

---

[223] Downes, *Roscius*, 2. Downes was apparently general scribe for the company: Lewis Theobald in his *Double Falshood* (1728), A5ᵃ, claims to own a Restoration text of Shakespeare's *Cardenio* 'in the Hand-writing of Mr. *Downes*, the famous Old Prompter'.  [224] *Wit Without Mony* (1707), A1ᵇ.
[225] Langhans, *Restoration Promptbooks*, 5, 60.

unfamiliar voice on the stage as he prepared to enter, bellowed out *'Zounds*, Downs! *what sucking Scaramouch have you sent on there?'*[226] In these hesitant depictions prompters are shown performing (at a lower level) tasks of preparation, discipline, and casting also held by managers. As the next chapter makes clear, prompters came to take on even more of the managers' duties in the early eighteenth century.

### The Master of the Revels as reviser

The Master of the Revels continued to revise plays in his role as censor though the occasion no longer had the pretence of being a rehearsal. Nevertheless, the important though unpredictable role in the adaptation of plays held by the Master of the Revels merits attention, for it provides yet another occasion on which textual decisions were made that were out of an author's control. Until 1673 when Herbert died, fees for licensing plays seem—often, at least—to have been paid out, though the actual textual power Herbert had was severely curtailed towards the end of his life: Davenant and Killigrew were contractually allowed, as figure-heads for the Duke's and King's Companies, 'to peruse all playes that haue been formerly written, and to expunge all Prophanesse and Scurrility from the same, before they be represented', which made the Revels' job limited.[227] After Herbert, the revising role previously practised by the Master of the Revels alone was divided between him and his superior the Lord Chamberlain, though neither seems to have altered plays significantly except in times when it was expedient to do so: during the Popish Plot (1679–82); when careful political censorship was wise; and during the clamp-down on 'immorality' of the 1690s.[228] In 1688 when William and Mary took the throne, the censor was given greater power.[229] Killigrew, as Master of the Revels, was full of 'zealous Severity', but then again, he seems to have chosen his victims carefully—his famous, crude censorship of Cibber's *Richard III* (he 'expung'd the whole First Act, without sparing a

---

[226] Chetwood, *History*, 164. The young Cibber waited 'impatiently a long time for the prompter's notice' in order to make his way on the stage—see Davies, *Miscellanies*, iii. 249.  [227] Edmond, *Davenant*, 144.

[228] For plays censored over those years, see *London Stage*, I, p. lxiii.

[229] See *London Stage*, I, p. cxlix.

Line of it'[230]) was probably inspired largely by personal malice: Killigrew, as manager, would have been conscious of the literary damage his revision was doing. But Henry Higden, who simply suffered because of the hard line taken on obvious crudities in texts over the 1690s, shows how significant the Master of the Revels' revision could be: 'The Master of the Revells had expung'd what he pleas'd, least forsooth it should prove Bawdy or give offence, thereby making the sense imperfect which the Actours would not let me mend or supply.'[231] At what point the censorship took place is unclear. Though some plays are advertised as having been 'licensed by the Lord Chamberlain's secretary', others were not called in for revision until after performance (presumably because of audience complaints).[232] Evidence suggests that sometimes lines cut by the Master of the Revels were still spoken on stage—perhaps because actors chose to ignore the corrections, or perhaps because they had already learnt the original text. One final suggestion is made in *The Comparison* when Sullen declares that 'The four last Lines of this Scene [in Higgons' *The Generous Conqueror*] are notoriously Facetious', and that the Master of the Revels should not have passed them. Ramble replies that it may not be Killigrew who is to blame: 'ten to one he expung'd 'em, but the Author was so fond of 'em he wou'd have 'em spoke and printed.'[233] In this way, though textual revision by the Master of the Revels may sometimes have affected performances, it often did not affect the printed texts themselves.

## PERFORMANCE

### Actors and performance

A system that put so much stress on private study bred selfishness in the actor, which was then carried out onto the stage. When not speaking, a player felt no compunction to keep up the

---

[230] Cibber, *Apology*, 152. He adds in the published text (Colley Cibber, *The Tragical History of King Richard III* (1700), A3a), 'all the reason I could get for its being refus'd, was, that *Henry* the Sixth being a Character Unfortunate and Pitied, wou'd put the Audience in mind of the late *King James*'.

[231] Higden, *Wary Widdow*, A4ᵃ.      [232] *London Stage*, I, pp. cxlviii–cxlix.

[233] *Comparison*, 68.

theatrical illusion. Mrs Knepp winked at Pepys when she spotted him in the audience; Gildon's Betterton observed that: 'on the Stage, not only the Supernumeraries . . . or Attendants, mind nothing of the great Concern of the Scene, but even the Actors themselves, who are on the Stage, and not in the very principle Parts, shall be whispering to one another, or bowing to their Friends in the Pit, or gazing about.'[234] These distractions might be the result of thoughtlessness, or malice. Cibber implies the latter when he praises Mountfort for managing to 'fill' the stage without elbowing other actors or walking in front of them.[235] But the fact was that actors, trained to be successful in their parts, had often been encouraged only to be good in their roles, not to make the full play a success: the play as a unity and the actor as a player of parts were naturally opposed.

A general failure to consider how each separate part was an element of a fuller text contributed towards some of the absurd omissions that were allowed in performance. When Mrs Barry was taken ill in the fourth act of Crowne's *Darius, King of Persia*, the performers simply completed the play without her, though as a result the story no longer made sense: 'all her part in [the fifth] Act was wholly cut out and neither Spoke nor Read . . . the People went away without knowing the contexture of the Play, yet thought they knew all.'[236] Again, this shows actors' revisions and omissions happening, to an absurd degree, along linear lines (within separate actors' parts) rather than across the full play.

Another result of actors performing for themselves was that they had no compunction against giving up on a play during performance if it was not being well received; they had no interest in suffering an angry audience for a playwright's sake. Edward Howard records that the actors, finding his *Six Days Adventure* 'abusively treated, were apt enough to neglect that diligence required to their parts'.[237] Authors, of course, were concerned that their plays should be successful; actors were concerned to establish whether or not the play was successful or

---

[234] *Pepys*, ix. 435; Gildon, *Betterton*, 37. Later he discussed how impressed he was when Mrs Barry the actress continued to perform even though not speaking: 'I have frequently obser'd her change her Countenance several Times as the Discourse of others on the Stage have affected her in the Part she acted. This is being thoroughly concern'd, this is to know her Part' (p. 40).

[235] Cibber, *Apology*, 75.                    [236] *Crowne*, iii. 371.

[237] Edward Howard, *The Six Days Adventure* (1671), A3[a].

damnable, and then respond accordingly; by the time of performance, author and actor, too, could be in complete opposition.

## Actors and extemporization

*The Tatler* offers an ironic criticism of Cave Underhill, who 'has not the Merit of some ingenious Persons now on the Stage, of adding to his Authors'.[238] The problems created by actors' additions are enumerated some months later when the same paper addresses the actor who inserts 'Words of his own into the Part he is to act, so that it is impossible to see the Poet for the Player'.[239] That poet–player distinction was becoming muddied: who, by rights, owned the words in a player's part? Given that this was an age of short study, the ability to extemporize was essential. 'Norris was famous for it,' notes Sir John Hill.[240] But playwrights, unsurprisingly, found the skill objectionable: Curll reports with approval that in Congreve's *Love for Love* 'no one was guilty of the Affectation to insert Witticisms of his own'; Aphra Behn partly blames herself for having given her *Dutch Lover* to one who 'spoke but little of what I intended for him, but supply'd it with a deal of idle stuff . . . so that Jack-pudding ever us'd to do'.[241] On the other hand, fidelity to a text was scarcely possible in a theatre with such a quick-changing repertory; moreover, extemporization was often respected:[242] Booth is congratulated for his ability to 'soften or slide over . . . the Improprieties in a Part'.[243] Moreover, the way roles were learnt left actors with few ways of inserting themselves into their texts other than by changing the parts themselves. They therefore had a natural inclination to alter their lines and, again, it was the clown/fool figures, who were most likely to demand and

---

[238] *Tatler*, i. 176.   [239] Ibid. ii. 62–3.

[240] 'Sir' John Hill, *The Actor* (1755), 251.

[241] Curll, *English Stage*, 119; Behn, *Dutch*, a1[b].

[242] Mopus' part in John Wilson's *The Cheats*, ed. M. C. Nahm (Oxford, 1935), 195, is left 'open': 'here describe the person that Acts Bilbo'.

[243] Theophilus Cibber, *The Lives and Characters of the Most Eminent Actors and Actresses* (1753), 41. Conversely, the actor Bright was attacked for speaking (licensed) lines when performing Old Bellair in *The Man of Mode*—see J. W. Krutch, *Comedy and Conscience after the Restoration* (New York, 1924), 174–5—the suggestion being that he should personally have censored his part.

receive textual freedom. The flighty William Pinkethman decided, in a moment of whimsy, to play with the theatrical illusion. He refused to answer to the name of 'Thomas Apple-tree' (the role he was playing in George Farquhar's *The Recruit-ing Officer*) and when 'Captain Plume' (Wilks) asked what his name was, responded: 'Why, don't you know my name, Bob?' Wilks prompted 'Thomas Appletree' to him, but Pinkethman queried 'Thomas Appletree? Thomas Devil! My name is Will Pinkethman.'[244] Not the funniest of jokes, but Pinkethman was one of the 'stars' who was chiefly famous for playing himself, and the audience wanted (and expected) signs that he was standing up and asserting himself against the constraints of his text—something he was famous for. Pinkethman's roles are usually filled with references to the actor as actor:

> Was not my Part an odd one for the Stage—
> A Womans Taylor——and at *Pinkey's* Age?[245]

Other players famous for extemporization included John Lacy, who ad-libbed while acting the Country Gentleman in Edward Howard's *The Change of Crownes* and was imprisoned as a result of the insults he had inserted into his part levelled at Charles II; and Richard Estcourt who had 'the Vanity of imagining he could help the Author, and therefore often [added] to his Part, Things out of his own Head'.[246] Minor ad-libbing was always to be expected. During a clamp-down on stage blasphemy (the 'Collier crusade'), informers went to the theatre to note the oaths mouthed during performance, and comparisons between their findings and the texts themselves show that considerably more oaths were spoken on stage than were present in the scripts.[247]

In praising a particular performance, Edmund Curll mentions not only that the well-behaved actors did not add to their parts, but that they 'were careful of their Carriage'.[248] For actors could be involved in a different kind of extemporization: they might make physical additions to their parts as well as verbal ones.

---

[244] *Farquhar*, ii. 37.
[245] Thomas Betterton, *The Sequel of Henry the Fourth* (1721), A4ᵃ.
[246] *London Stage*, I, p. xcvi; Mottley, *List*, 228.
[247] See Krutch, *Comedy and Conscience*, 170–1.
[248] Curll, *English Stage*, 119.

Aphra Behn denies responsibility for the fact that Anthony Leigh
'*opens his Night Gown*' on his entrance into the bride's chamber
in *The Luckey Chance*: 'if he do, which is a Jest of his own
making, and which I never saw,' she observes testily, 'I hope he
has his Cloaths on underneath?'[249] More significantly, occasions
for manifesting 'passions' could be created, sometimes against
the grain of the text—these might take the form of unnecessary
rants, extra starts, heightened fear. Powell is accused of often
getting himself applause 'by adding Vehemence to Words where
there was no Passion, or inflaming a real Passion into Fustion'.[250]
Again, this was to be expected from actors casting about for
ways of asserting themselves within their roles—particularly
ways that would result in a plaudit not just for the text but for
themselves.

## Prompter and performance

'Our Stage at the best indeed is but a very cold Representation,
supported by loud prompting, to the eternal Disgust of the
Audience' complains Gildon's Betterton.[251] During performance, prompters, as ever, helped actors who were 'out', but
they had various other tasks. They stood where they could see
the actors but not be seen by the audience—probably to one side
or other of the stage, at the curtain-line—and from here they
could call actors and make backstage noises:[252] Downes claims in
1710 that he can still 'clash Swords when they represent a Battel'
and 'huzza' victories.[253] But the prompter also managed scene
and act changes, which were indicated with whistle and bell
respectively, as prompt-books testify: these sounds will have
been audible to the audience, making the prompter and the
prompter's devices elements of the production; for similar
reasons, argues Richard Southern, watching the scenes being

---

[249] Aphra Behn, *The Luckey Chance* (1687), A4ᵃ.

[250] *Spectator*, i. 171.                    [251] Gildon, *Betterton*, 38.

[252] Langhans, *Restoration Promptbooks*, p. xx, discusses where the prompter may
have been positioned. He considers the curtain-line, backstage, and in a box at the
front of the stage. The last is unlikely as the prompter was involved in making
behind-the-scene noises; the tiring house is questionable as the prompter needed to
see the action.

[253] Downe's quotation is from a letter in *Tatler*, iii. 44, which may well actually
have been written by Steele—however, Steele as a theatre man himself will have
understood the requirements of the prompter's job.

changed was part of the spectacle.[254] The audience seem to have
enjoyed the paraphernalia of prompting, as illustrated by what
are clearly metatheatrical 'jokes' in plays: at the close of Nahum
Tate's *Island Princess* (3.2), the Governor cries 'When I am
reveng'd, let the Gods whistle'[255]—heralding the little 'god' of
the theatre, who would immediately have whistled-in a change of
scene. Playhouse mechanism was part of the performance, and
was consciously foregrounded, just as the actors made much of
being actors. The end aimed at was a spectacular visual, and
auditory experience and a self-consciously theatrical event,
rather than one long, 'convincing' performance.

The existence of multiple texts to Edward Howard's *The
Change of Crownes* shows that a number of different people
had a prompting interest in performance—scene-shifters, musicians, and perhaps call-boys, all seem to have needed prompt-
books of their own.[256] It was with some backstage help, therefore, that prompters managed productions. Their tasks, though,
were extensions of what they had been in the preceding century.
As well as organizing act and scene breaks, prompting forgotten
lines, and producing sound-effects, prompters also cued
entrances and exits. Marsilia in *The Female Wits* snatches the
book from the prompter and takes on the job herself, assuring
the actor Powell 'I'll tell ye time enough for your Entrance'; and
Dennis explains that he has no intention of including entrances
and exits in the printed edition of *Liberty Asserted* as they 'are
nothing but Directions that are given to a Play House Prompter'.[257] So it remained the case that actors did not need to know
about entrances, exits, or scene-ends before taking to the stage;

---

[254] Langhans, *Restoration Promptbooks*, p. xxi; Richard Southern, *Changeable Scenery* (London, 1952), 17–25.

[255] Nahum Tate, *Island Princess* (1699), 26.

[256] See Langhans, *Restoration Promptbooks*, 26.

[257] *Female Wits*, 26; Dennis, *Liberty*, a3ᵃ. In prompt-books belonging to the King's Company, there are clear entrance-cue marks usually with a warning a page and a half in advance; and in books belonging to the Duke's Company there are none— Langhans in *Restoration Promptbooks*, p. xx, therefore wonders whether the Duke's prompter sat on the stage and signalled the actors from there while the King's prompter sat backstage and did not cue entrances. This seems unlikely. A play written for the King's Company, Thomas Betterton's *The Amorous Widow* (1710), has the remark (p. 17) 'give me but my Cue of Entrance'; perhaps there were separate prompt-books for the King's Company's call-boys, which have not survived.

they could all be prompted during performance. And given that both in the Renaissance and in the eighteenth century, prompters had charge of the pace of performance, they probably also had the same task during the Restoration. The emphasis of performance, then, remained at a remove from the workings of the text as a whole. All actors had to know in advance were their words, and how to manage certain given group 'moments' (songs, dances, fights), and technical matters (trap-doors, and use of props): they needed to know the minutiae of stage business but not the structure of the play itself.

## THE FIRST NIGHT

As before the Interregnum, first nights were treated in a different way from other performances. They still cost twice as much as usual,[258] and an especially judgemental and often cruel audience came to see them: Mottley refers to the spectators who chose to go to new plays in order 'to make Uproars', a process they called '*The Funn* [*sic*] *of the first Night*'.[259] In the early days of the Restoration theatre the nobility and literati flocked to first performances; at one opening performance Pepys saw a whole crowd of courtly theatrical judges, 'the Duke of Buckingham . . . with my Lord Buckhurst, and Sidly', as well as the author himself.[260] Indeed, sometimes the first 'Repetition' was held at court or in the house of a nobleman rather than at the theatre, in which case the distinction between 'performance' and 'rehearsal' is hazy: these rehearsals, like the private rehearsals for gentlemen, aimed at being impressively performance-like in order to please their observers. Dryden's *Albion*, was 'well performed at the repetition that has been made before his Majesty at the Duchess of Portsmouth's'; Durfey's *Don Quixote* (part 1) was 'rehearsed before Nobility and Gentry'.[261] Later, the body of people who made up the most critical section of the audience changed as the patronage of individuals was replaced by the patronage of

---

[258] *Pepys*, ii. 234.
[259] Mottley, *List*, 183.
[260] *Pepys*, ix. 54.
[261] Quoted, *London Stage*, I, p. cliv; David Roberts, *The Ladies: Female Patronage of Restoration Drama* (Oxford, 1989), 114–15.

groups.[262] But throughout the Restoration, audiences attended the first night in the hope of having a particular effect on the production. Even though the first night tended to be badly acted (Pepys decided not to attend 'the first time of acting' any more, as most of the actors were continually 'out'), a notoriously high standard of writing was demanded: 'You fail if you but Moderately excell'.[263] The audience would forgive a bad performance; they were attending primarily to criticize the play, not the acting.

The first-night audience would be responsible, not just for the retaining or damning of a play, but for textual changes made within the play between the first and the third ('benefit') night. This meant that playwrights had the first two nights to remould their plays to become what the audience liked, and there are many proofs of their doing just that, for, to ensure a full third night, anything the audience manifestly disliked would have to go. Probably for this reason, premières most often took place on a Saturday,[264] which left Sunday at least free for revisions by the author, and gave Sunday evening and Monday morning for relearning by the actors—witness Mrs Manley's dismay when Mrs Bracegirdle left the theatre just before *Almyna* was to have received its second performance 'with the Alterations annex'd'.[265] First-night prologues and epilogues plead with audiences, not for their approval, but for their third night's benediction.[266] One telling epilogue has a different final two lines 'spoken the third day, in the Room of the last thirteen lines' in which the author

---

[262] Roberts, 128.

[263] *Pepys*, iii. 39; Doggett, *Country-Wake*, A4[b]. Thomas Durfey writes of 'the indifferent performance the first day' of his *The Comical History of Don Quixote*, part 3 (1696), a1[a].

[264] *London Stage*, I, p. clvii.

[265] Mary de la Rivière Manley, *Almyna* (1707), A1[b].

[266] See e.g. the prologue to George Powell, *A Very Good Wife* (1693), A3[b]: 'I have but one thing more to say, | And that's in reference to our third day; | An odd request—may be you'll think it so; Pray come, whether you like the Play, or no'; George Powell, *Alphonso: King of Naples* (1691), A4[a]: 'Let Fancy . . . save my Play, | And then I'll laugh at Wits on my *Third Day*'. In Peter Motteux's, *The Island Princess* (1699), 47, Mrs Rogers, who speaks the epilogue, suggests that the audience tease the playwright by letting the play 'live' but then avoiding 'his third day'; William Mountfort in his *Injur'd Lovers* (1688), 71, is described as sitting in the scene room waiting to hear his censure: his 'Third [Day] . . . poor Soul's to come'. The assumption that the third-night audience will be roughly the same as the first is telling—presumably the audience that had prompted revision between first and second nights would be interested in seeing what the 'final' product was like.

thanks the goodness of his this days Friends,
You've fill'd the House, and he has gain'd his ends.[267]

After 'a third dayes Reign', as epilogues testify, many poets were 'stoutly unconcern'd at their Play's Fate', though obviously a long run was prestigious.[268]

The kind of textual change encouraged by the first-night audience varied in importance. Generally it merely involved altering the length of a piece which had not been shortened, or shortened enough, in rehearsal: 'tho' my *Play* might be too long, which is a general fault amongst us, and not to be remedy'd 'till the first day is over, and tho' some *Scenes* might seem Tedious 'till it was shorten'd, which is allways the Second Days work . . . I had the Confidence to think, that . . . I . . . might have oblig'd [the critics] to a *Civil Sufferance*, tho' not a liking.'[269] But it was also not unusual for an audience to get the actual particulars of the story altered to suit their fancy. Mrs Manley grits her teeth and allows the audience to dictate the fortune that their favourite Mrs Bracegirdle should have:

Mrs. *Bracegirdle* . . . so far Acted her self into the kind Wishes of the Town, that in Compliment to their better Opinion, the Author has thought fit to make her happy in her Lover. In the next Representation, the Ceremony in the first Act is design'd to be omitted, upon the dislike of that incomparable LADY, to whom this *Play* is inscrib'd.[270]

Similarly George Granville's *Heroick Love* received a different ending after the first night:

after the first Representation of this Play, the Conclusion was alter'd: *Agamemnon* is left to continue in a Swoon, and the Scene is clos'd with

[267] Powell, *Brothers*, I4[a]. Aaron Hill in *Elfrid: or, the Fair Inconstant* (1710?), A4[b], gives thanks to 'that generous Part of the Town, who remember'd, 'twas a *Third Night*, and made so favourable an Appearance in my Interest'.

[268] Elkanah Settle, *Cambyses, King of Persia* (1671), M4[a]. For third-night benefits, see Milhous and Hume, *Producible*, 46, who also show that, from 1690 or so, an additional sixth-night benefit performance was sometimes allowed.

[269] Thomas Durfey, *The Banditti* (1686), a3[b]. Thomas Durfey had a habit of presenting plays that needed cutting after the first night. See his *The Old Mode and the New* (1709), A2[b]: 'the faulty length, . . . and some ill Performance of under Parts, made that part of it tedious the first Day'; and his *The Marriage-Hater Match'd* (1692), A3[a]: 'the faulty length, which I will never be guilty of again, render'd it little Diversion the first day'. See also Peter Motteux, *The Novelty* (1697), A4[a]: 'You have the Farce as 'twas Acted the first day; the latter part being left out afterwards; some few of the Audience having been offended at it, but more at the length of that Act'.

[270] Manley, *Almyna*, A1[b].

these few lines spoken by *Ulysses* . . . Another Reason was Brevity, some having complain'd of the length of that Act. There was indeed such effectual Care taken not to seem tedious to the Audience, that the last Scene may be more properly said to have been Murder'd than Cut . . .[271]

Dennis, 'in complaisance to some Gentlemen whom I esteem' removed a satire from one of his scenes 'after the first Night'; Count Bellair disappeared from *The Beaux Stratagem* almost immediately ('perhaps after the first night') following the initial performance.[272] Other plays which appear to have had first-night alterations are Killigrew's *Pandora,* which was changed from a tragedy to a comedy to please the audience; and Farquhar's *The Constant Couple* (1699) in which scene 5.1 was rewritten.[273] Dryden, too famous to feel under a compunction to do what the audience wanted, taunts the ladies with the possibility of acceding to their wishes at some later date: ''Tis not . . . impossible' he suggests, 'but that I may alter the conclusion of my Play, to restore my self into the good Graces of my fair Criticks.'[274]

Prologues and epilogues were generally spoken only on the first three nights of an infant play: an established play usually went without. The purpose they served was vital, but impermanent: to plead the author's cause. Once the pleading had been successful, they were no longer necessary, and were generally then abandoned. 'Contrary to all other Epilogues, which are dropp'd after the third Representation of the Play, this [The Epilogue to Ambrose Philips' *The Distrest Mother*] has already been repeated nine times', relates *The Spectator* admiringly.[275] Downes finds it worth recording that not only did Betterton's

---

[271] Granville, *Heroick,* A2[a–b].

[272] Dennis, *Liberty,* a2[b]; Milhous and Hume, *Producible,* 44.

[273] Killigrew, *Pandora,* A8[b]; both Farquhar texts can be found in *Farquhar,* i. 141–4; 361–3.

[274] Dryden, xii. 157. Nicholas Rowe in *The Ambitious Stepmother* (1701), A2[b], refers to how 'Some people . . . have told me that they wisht I had given the latter part of the story quite another turn; that *Artaxerxes* and *Amestris* ought to have been preserv'd and made happy in the Conclusion of the Play'. Though he refused these suggestions, he did shorten the play after performance; as a result 'the Chain and Connexion, which ought to be in the Dialogue, was interrupted in many . . . places'. See also Cibber's admonishment to the audience in *She Would and She Would Not* (1703), reproduced in Colley Cibber, *Plays,* 2 vols. (1721), i. 3I[b]: 'From his Design no *Person* can be spar'd, | Or *Speeches* lopt, unless the whole be marr'd'.

[275] *Spectator,* iii. 266.

*Woman Made a Justice* act for 'fourteen Days together', but that
'The Prologue [was] spoke to it each Day'.[276]

In fact, as with Renaissance stage orations, many surviving
prologues and epilogues make specific reference to their new-
play/first-night status, meaning that they became outdated by the
third night. The Epilogue to Doggett's *The Country-Wake*
recognizes the theatrical potential of the first-night author
awaiting judgement and uses it: 'Yonder he stands in Sad and
Doleful Case | Waiting the Judgement you shall please to pass',
says Betterton indicating the forlorn author, 'I see he beckons to
me, to intreat | That you'd be Merciful as you are Great.'[277]
These addenda were thus badges that marked out a play's
minority—they told the audience that the play was still at the
judgemental stage—and still in a malleable form.[278]

First-night revision meant that there were two kinds of
pressure on authors. One was to save themselves and the
actors trouble, and give the audience the type of thing they
wanted in the first place:

> Our Author . . .
> Cools his Fancy to oblige your Taste:
> He underwrites to please, and frames his Wit,
> Exactly to the Level of the Pit.[279]

---

[276] Downes, *Roscius*, 65.

[277] Doggett, *The Country-Wake*, A4[b]. A standard prologue device—see also the
prologue to *The Country Wife* in Danchin, I:ii, 638. For playwrights waiting behind
the curtains to hear the result of their efforts, see Shadwell's reference in *Sullen*, A3[a],
to the miserable authors who 'peep through their loop-holes in the Theatre, to see
who looks grum [*sic*] upon their Plays'; Brown, *The Reasons*, 2: 'I am more impatient
. . . than a Poet is, to hear the success of his New Play behind the Curtain'; and
Thomas Durfey, *The Fool turn'd Critick* (1678), 28, where 'Tim' talks of the pleasure
it gives him 'to see the poor fellow the Poet, peep out between the Scenes, and shake
his empty head, to see his Ten Months labour so rewarded'.

[278] Other special epilogues, also spoken only on one night, were written for actors'
benefits—see *Prologues and Epilogues of the Eighteenth Century*, ed. Pierre Danchin, 2
vols. in 4 (Nancy, 1990– ), I:i, p. xvi. The impermanence of prologues and epilogues
explains the distant relationship they have to the play as a whole. In printed books, for
instance, they are usually placed before the numbered pages of the play begin, and
vary typographically from the rest of the text. Because they were often not kept with
the prompt-book, they were sometimes lost before printing: in Betterton, *Amorous*,
A4[a], the prologues and epilogues are missing, but 'their usual Leading and Bringing
up the Front and Rear of a Play being no Part of the Play it self, 'tis hop'd their Want
will be no Blemish to so excellent a Piece as this'. See also Behn, *Dutch*, a2[a]: 'The
Prologue is by misfortune lost'.

[279] Charles Gildon, *The Roman Brides Revenge* (1697), A2[b]. See also Tate, *Island*,
A4[a]; Killigrew, *Pandora* (1664), E2[a].

Another was to provide a fairly unfinished text for the first night—one that could be painlessly reshaped when the audience had made its opinion apparent. Thomas Baker writes his thanks to the town for accepting what he calls 'this Rough Draft', and Crauford in *Courtship A-la-Mode* hopes to win his audience around by tailoring his epilogue to their responses—'if they Hiss' one set of lines is to be spoken, 'if they don't Hiss', another.[280] Other works initially existed in both tragic and comic form: *Romeo and Juliet* played alternate tragic and comic endings, as did Sir Robert Howard's *Vestal Virgins*, and Sir John Suckling's *Aglaura*.[281] It was common for more experienced, workaday playwrights neither to claim to be writing good plays, nor to expect every word they wrote to be sacred. On the contrary, they were often ready enough to do down their own works in the very act of publishing them, denying the reader the critical rights of the audience, both by censuring themselves, and by nonchalantly implying that the play was well received anyway: 'this triffle [*sic*] of a Comedy, was only a slight piece of Scribble'; 'in a thing written in five weeks, as this was, there must be many Errours'.[282]

The first performance, with the opportunities it offered for radically reshaping a play, was thus an extraordinary event. Because of the changes the first-night audience were going to encourage, the text, in the form in which it was acted on that first day, was quite possibly never going to be played that way again. This also explains why rehearsal could not be too detailed, for a text might be damned on its first night, and could change between first and third night. Only after a third night was it necessary to consider seriously working on one's part, and by that time, group rehearsal sessions were over (unless the play was to be revived the following year). Once again, the onus was on the actor (particularly an actor with a revised text) to do whatever further work was necessary in individual study sessions.

---

[280] Thomas Baker, *The Humour of the Age* (1701), A3ᵃ; Crauford, *Courtship*, H2ᵇ.

[281] *London Stage*, I, p. cxl; H. J. Oliver, *Sir Robert Howard* (Durham, NC, 1963), 80.

[282] George Powell, *The Imposture Defeated* (1698), A3ᵃ; Thomas Shadwell, *Psyche* (1675), a4ᵇ.

CONCLUSION

The nature of rehearsal bred tensions that were responsible for various kinds of theatrical revision. But rehearsal itself often involved different levels of textual change, for the term rehearsal continued to extend its meaning out into the first night. Rehearsal subtly flipped between the actors practising a part, and the text practising itself: 'rehearsal' stretched out beyond acting ability into the very status and stability of a play itself; so that, in talking of rehearsal, it is necessary to talk first of the process of mounting a play and the way actors, prompters, managers, and authors mould that play; then of the process of textual change.

The text faced the possibility of revision at various stages during its theatrical life. Firstly it was overseen by friends; then by the theatre manager or professional 'theatricalizer'—in both instances the revision usually had the author's approval, and will almost certainly have been firmly entrenched before performance. 'Purging', generally consisting of minor changes, might take place later at the hands of the Master of the Revels. By the actors the text was shortened and sometimes altered, sometimes with, but often without, the author's consent; performance changes might also be made by the actors: these were out of the author's control, though they might become part of a new, post-performance, text. First-night revisions demanded by the audience but scripted by the playwright or playwright's substitute were often made. These might involve textual cuts or more substantial changes—one of the main kinds of *authorial* revision, therefore, was the frantic, scatty, undigested rewrites that took place between first and third night. Revision might then happen again if the play survived another season, when changes within the theatre companies brought about different textual requirements. If a professional had taken over the text in rehearsal, then he or she would have been responsible for these major revisions.

Sometimes texts and performances were left underprepared and fluid for the first night, and were fixed by subsequent performances. Comic actors, particularly, might add to their script; a text could change more drastically within one part than equally throughout a play. A 'lasting' text reached its fixed form for the season on about the third night of playing; a 'damned' text was often perceived, by the author, to have had its fixed form somewhere way back within the preparation process.[283] As a kind of half-way house, there are the texts printed with italic sections to indicate the parts that were cut in performance, giving an amalgam of a reading and a performance experience. The only significant way in which the routine varied was when, as in Shadwell's *Psyche* (which, being an opera, was carefully rehearsed, and much more fixed in format), the text was published before performance, as an advertisement.[284] To print a play 'as it is acted', is not simply a puff about the theatrical acceptability of a text, but a statement that playhouse amendments have been approved. A play as performed, a play as rehearsed, and a play as written were different, as a result of rehearsals that took textual control away from authors and gave it to the actors.

[283] All the complaints about shortened texts quoted above accompany full, uncut plays; for editions that include playhouse changes ('as it is acted'), see Holland, *Ornament*, 106–14.

[284] See Judith Milhous and Robert D. Hume, 'Dating Play Premières from Publication Data', *HLB* 22 (1974), 374–405 (383).

# 5

# Rehearsal in Cibber's Theatre

## INTRODUCTION

'All the World's a Stage, and ev'ry Man, and Woman, [*sic*] merely Actors': so wrote William Chetwood, prompter for Drury Lane, on the title-page to his history of the stage. He was recalling more than simply the second-rate 'corrected' versions of *As You Like It* in performance at the time. The reputed motto of Shakespeare's Globe, 'Totus mundus agit histrionem', hung above the stage at the Drury Lane Theatre, as *The Spectator* (5 May 1712) makes clear.[1] Subsequently, and significantly, the motto was changed—probably when the theatre was redecorated in 1715.[2] The new motto was 'Vivitur Ingenio', 'let it live by wit'.[3] No longer do the stage and the world link hands; now the actors manage a world of their own.

Play prefaces between 1710 and 1740 (the span of this chapter) are, for the most part, not the telling, chatty introductions they were in the Restoration, nor are they as loquacious as they came to be in the time of David Garrick. Drury Lane and Lincoln's Inn were under different kinds of management, and questions as to whether actors, managers, managers who were actors, or disinterested patentees should run the theatre— and what kind of control they should have over individual plays—were constantly raised. Theatrical information about this specific period, therefore, has to be gleaned from angry

---

[1] Joseph Addison and Richard Steele, *The Spectator*, ed. Donald R. Bond, 5 vols. (Oxford, 1965), iii. 393.

[2] See *London Stage*, part III: *1729–1747*, ed. Arthur H. Scouten (Carbondale, Ill., 1961), 414.

[3] See William Rufus Chetwood, *A General History of the Stage* (1749), 26; *The Female Tatler*, ed. Fidelis Morgan (London, 1992), 17 (for 25–7 July 1710); and *Wit without Mony* (1707), A3ᵃ. Depictions of the Drury Lane stage often show the second motto—see the frontispiece to Chetwood, *General History*; the frontispiece to *Harlequin-Horace* (1735); Hogarth's *Just View of the British Stage* (1725).

prefaces written by disappointed playwrights, idealistic theorizers (as ever, taking many of their ideas from France, with its strong tradition of theatrical rule-books), and from the shaky memories of old men, writing retrospectively from the latter end of the eighteenth century.

As the theatre during this period followed the whim of certain powerful individuals, establishing the 'laws' by which the stage was managed is very difficult, especially as, from 1705 onwards, 'London witnessed an almost yearly reorganization of theatrical companies'.[4] In this chapter, rather than looking for established, solid 'rules' to define, for instance, what the job of prompter should ultimately entail, I will ask first what *generally* were a prompter's tasks, and secondly, what William Chetwood, prompter to Drury Lane, did. Naturally this brings into question whether it is possible to discover general facts about rehearsal over the period. Yet there were some basic laws, and a few obvious goals which the promoters or detractors of rehearsal seem to have worked to—or worked towards. Actors and writers, over the short period in which there was a proliferation of small theatres, readily and easily flitted from company to company, venue to venue, illustrating the compatibility of one theatre's system with another. Aaron Hill (largely in theory) and Henry Fielding (largely in practice) posited and explored ideals of group rehearsal; at best these same ideals were manifested in the Drury Lane Company under Colley Cibber, Robert Wilks, and Barton Booth.

There is a problem, however, in that similar jobs in the various theatres could be divided up differently: the prompter's tasks in Drury Lane might be the responsibility of the under manager at Lincoln's Inn Fields. Even amongst the three Drury Lane managers duties were shared, so that each manager had a different professional emphasis—instruction, textual revision, finance. This produces difficulties, particularly when trying to balance Drury Lane, a theatre run by actor-managers, with Lincoln's Inn, a theatre with an 'untheatrical' patentee who gave over the job of managing, under a number of different terms, to others.

In order to find a pathway through the diverse theatrical

[4] *London Stage*, part II: *1700–1729*, ed. Emmett L. Avery (Carbondale, Ill., 1960), p. lxxxi.

material of the early eighteenth century, Colley Cibber, actor and manager of Drury Lane, has been made the focus of this chapter, with instances from other theatres brought in where necessary. Partly this decision was based on necessity: Cibber angered and pleased enough people in his time to be frequently written about; he also produced his own *Apology*, a rich source of information for the eighteenth-century theatre historian: there is simply more material about Cibber than other actors in the early eighteenth century. But by using as wide a variety of sources as possible, about as many different stages as possible, an attempt is made to find facts that are generally true for all early eighteenth-century theatres.

## BACKGROUND

Between 1710 and 1714 there was a single theatrical company playing in the capital. After this, London returned to the system of having two major theatrical companies, one at the new Lincoln's Inn Fields (under Christopher Rich and, later, under his son John), one at Drury Lane; while the Haymarket Theatre was set aside for the performances of operas. However, the next few years saw the creation and rise of several experimental little theatres, notably Odell's Theatre in Goodman's Fields and the New (or Little) Haymarket. After 1728 more and more small theatres were established: long runs of John Gay's *Beggar's Opera*, and Colley Cibber–Sir John Vanbrugh's *Provoked Husband*, had demonstrated that there was a large potential audience if it could only be successfully harnessed.[5] This exciting theatrical expansion was stopped in its tracks by the establishment of the Licensing Act in 1737: the act decreed that there were to be only two houses with patents for dramatic performances—Lincoln's Inn Fields and Drury Lane. Between 1737 and 1747 various smaller theatres struggled along, finding ways to side-step the strict licensing rules, but by 1747 much of the 'illegitimate' theatrical activity had been halted.

Within the same time period, Drury Lane was having particular problems. In 1710 the daily running of the theatre had been

[5] *London Stage*, III, p. cxxxix.

put in the hands of three actor-managers, Colley Cibber, Robert
Wilks, and Thomas Doggett (the last was replaced by Barton
Booth after a quarrel in 1714). William Collier, who had legally
owned the theatre, had been content merely to collect his money
and leave well alone; however, when the Drury Lane licence
terminated with the death of Queen Anne, the three actor-
managers decided to find a different kind of titular head for
their company. They chose Sir Richard Steele, a playwright
who, they believed, could offer practical help as well as use his
influence with the court to their advantage. And, in the early
stages, when Steele had helped to establish a new patent for the
theatre in his name, all had gone well. But between 1720 and
1723, the actor-managers became restless, feeling that Steele was
drawing a handsome salary, but not actually contributing very
much to the theatre itself. When, in 1729, Steele died, the
management of the theatre was therefore thrown into question.
A new patent was granted in 1732 directly to the managers,
Wilks, Cibber, and Booth, but over the next year, Booth sold half
his share to John Highmore, Cibber gave over the job of manager
to his son Theophilus, and Wilks died. The following year saw
the patent divided and subdivided as owners of shares died or
sold on their portions; as a result, the muddled actors lost their
respect for their managers and, in 1733, with Theophilus Cibber
at their head, walked out of the theatre. They returned the
following year, amidst a sea of newspaper articles exploring
and attempting to define the nature of 'proper' theatrical
management. Fleetwood, who had bought out Highmore, now
owned the patent—he kept it for the next ten years with Charles
Macklin as his stage manager.

### PUBLIC THEATRE REHEARSAL

The standard of rehearsal during the early eighteenth century
varied enormously. There are play prefaces larded with grateful
praise for carefully prepared performances ('The Author . . .
thinks himself obliged to every Actor for the Care taken'[6]); and

---

[6] William Popple, *The Lady's Revenge* (1734), a1[a]. Henry Fielding in *Love in
Several Masques* (1728), A4[a–b], declares that he 'cannot rest' until he has 'been in
some measure grateful to the Performers'. Singling out Wilks and Cibber for praise,

others bitterly resentful over 'the want . . . of regular *rehearsals to mellow and perfect the action*'.[7] Theatre historians have reached a consensus that there was regular and regulated rehearsal at Drury Lane between 1710 and 1720, and at smaller theatres more-or-less throughout, but that at other times and in other places rehearsal was scanty.[8] This argument, though broadly true, ignores the internal theatrical conditions that affect the quality of rehearsal. Generally, for instance, many rehearsals are needed for a completely new play, few for a stock one. More 'refresher' rehearsals are necessary at the beginning of a season when a repertory is being built up than later on, while during an established 'run' time can be taken out from rehearsal. Facts like these are important, because Drury Lane between 1710 and 1720 made itself into the kind of company that had few rehearsal requirements. The three actor-managers, with their instinctive distrust of new writing (Booth 'often declared in public company, that he and his partners lost money by new plays; and that, if he were not obliged to it, he would seldom give his consent to perform one of them') mounted as few new plays as possible, and were therefore under less obligation to rehearse; on the other hand, when they *did* decide to make an effort, they had the time for serious preparation.[9] Conversely, young or inexperienced companies trained actors by means of rehearsal, like the group (too hastily thrown together and disbanded to be called a 'company', Hume argues) at the New Haymarket under the meticulous Fielding in the 1730s.[10] Fielding's troupe mounted many new plays when doing so was theatrically unusual; they naturally had greater rehearsal requirements as a result.

The surge in theatrical activity at the main theatres prompted by the establishment of smaller theatres offering rival productions,

he also refers to 'How advantagiously both they and the other Personages set off their respective Parts at that Time'. Lewis Theobald, *Double Falshood* (1728), A5[b], concurs: 'As to the Performance of the respective *Actors* concern'd in this Play, my applauding It here would be altogether superfluous.'

[7] Fettiplace Bellers, *Injur'd Innocence* (1732), A3[b].

[8] See *London Stage*, III, p. cxxvi.

[9] Thomas Davies, *Memoirs of the Life of David Garrick*, 2 vols, 2nd edn. (1780), i. 208. For numbers of new plays produced per season at Drury Lane, see John Loftis, *Steele at Drury Lane* (Berkeley, 1952), 84.

[10] Robert D. Hume, *Henry Fielding and the London Theatre, 1728–37* (Oxford, 1988), 203.

manifested itself in the production of a number of new after-pieces, so that entertainments consisting of old, stock plays with new afterpieces (rather than full new productions) were normal.[11] Mini-rehearsals were presumably held for afterpieces, though they are not recorded; fewer rehearsals were obviously needed for stock plays.

## *Rehearsal plays and rehearsal*

Buckingham's *The Rehearsal* retained its popularity, and as ever, was adapted to embrace modern subjects of criticism. Cibber inserted into his part of Bayes satirical lines aimed at John Gay's *Three Hours after Marriage*, to the extreme irritation of its author; at other times he directed his parody specifically at the play-wright Thomas Durfey.[12] But Charles Gildon in his 1714 play *A New Rehearsal* illustrates how *The Rehearsal*, in its continued popularity, had failed to achieve its original purpose: he depicts an author who is so impressed with the way Bayes amuses his audience that he chooses to learn how to write plays from him;[13] a criticism that finds its reality in Henry Fielding, who decided to parody heroic drama (in the manner of *The Rehearsal*) in his *Tragedy of Tragedies*, though the form had not been particularly popular, even in revivals, for the last thirty years.[14] Rehearsal plays were clearly second-hand: Phoebe Clinket in Gay's *Three Hours* is described by Parker as 'a very silly Imitation of *Bays* in the *Rehearsal*'; that *Three Hours* should then itself be burlesqued by Cibber in *The Rehearsal* is an irony to which its authors were

[11] For the rise in the importance of the afterpiece, see Kevin Pry, 'Theatrical Competition and the Rise of the Afterpiece Tradition, 1700–24', *TN* 36 (1982), 21–7; Hume, *Fielding*, 15. For the general reliance on the stock play, see Shirley Strum Kenny, 'Perennial Favorites: Congreve, Vanbrugh, Cibber, Farquhar, and Steele', *MP* 73 (1976), S4–S11.

[12] Thomas Davies, *Dramatic Miscellanies*, 3 vols. (Dublin, 1784), iii. 178–9; Barker, *Mr Cibber of Drury Lane*, 106. Estcourt and Cibber were the most popular performers of Bayes during this period—see Emmet L. Avery, 'The Stage Popularity of The Rehearsal 1671–1777', *Research Studies of the State College of Washington*, 7 (1939), 201–4.

[13] Charles Gildon, *A New Rehearsal* (1714), 84–5.

[14] Indeed, many of Fielding's targets were so outmoded that his jests could only be understood when read in conjunction with the explanatory notes that accompanied the text. *Tragedy of Tragedies* thus functioned in exactly the same way as Villiers' (Buckingham's) 1709 *Rehearsal . . . with a Key,* a version of the rehearsal parody that had a specific kind of textual life different from its performance life.

keenly sensitive.[15] Other burlesques inherited the serious and educational intentions behind the original *Rehearsal*, sometimes at the expense of the humour: Fielding's *Pasquin*, recently described as 'shrill and preachy', aimed at satirizing the new fashion for pantomime.[16]

In the early eighteenth century, the word 'rehearsal' became imbued with a number of new meanings which affected the way people viewed it, and the way they wrote rehearsal plays. For instance, it became opera house policy (and, very occasionally, theatre policy), to have a 'public rehearsal' before the first performance of a piece: in effect, a public preview. The large audiences that these performances appealed to were, as before, composed of the literati, so that the special first nights referred to in the previous chapter as kinds of rehearsal, were, in opera, actually given the designation 'public rehearsals'. Lady Henrietta Wentworth writes that her husband tried to persuade her to hear 'the famous Etallion sing att the rehersall of the Operer'; Viscount Percival, First Earl of Egmont, goes 'to the practice of the revived opera Tamerlan'; *The Daily Journal* records the 'prodigious Concourse of Nobility' to see the rehearsal of the opera *King Richard I*.[17] It is this kind of event that Thomas Arne the composer is referring to when he offers to show the opera of *Rosamond* as a 'private rehearsal to such as will pay for it':[18] financially, too, these opera 'rehearsals' were no different from performances. Public rehearsal, then, functioned to ensure that the section of the audience who mattered most had positive impressions in advance of the first performance. In such rehearsals, as before, the opera itself was being put on trial, 'rehearsed'—not the actors.

Confusingly, though, this depiction of performance-like dress-rehearsal for operas coincides with the traditional (but hitherto semi-fictional) representation of rehearsal in rehearsal plays: rehearsal plays suddenly became similar to a particular kind of

---

[15] Edward Parker, *A complete Key to the new farce, call'd Three hours after marriage* (1717), 5. By calling what is in fact a criticism of the farce a 'key', Parker heightens links between Gay's play and Villiers' (Buckingham's) *The Rehearsal* (famously published with a 'key' in 1709), perhaps suggesting that Gay is something of a 'Bayes' himself.

[16] Hume, *Fielding*, 213.

[17] See *London Stage*, II, 180; III, p. clxxx; *Daily Journal*, 9 Nov. 1727.

[18] *London Stage*, III, 273.

'rehearsal', but not, it must be stressed, to regular theatrical rehearsal. Perhaps it is for this reason, and following on the success of Gay's *Beggar's Opera*, that there was a sudden flourishing of rehearsal plays specifically about operas: *Bays's Opera*, *Harlequin's Opera*, *Musical Folly*.

The admixture of theatrical fact and fiction, however, remains a feature of burlesque rehearsal plays. So, for instance, though casual clothes were worn to genuine rehearsals ('A rehearsal should . . . be a play compleatly acted, so as to want only dresses, and spectators'), rehearsal plays continue to take place in full costume, a phenomenon they have to explain: in Edward Phillips's *Stage-Mutineers*, 'Mr. *Crambo* the author, has persuaded the Managers to Order the Actors to be in their proper Habits'.[19]

A different kind of 'open' private rehearsal also started to take place that was clearly a version of the 'rehearsal for gentlemen' of the previous chapter. In tandem with the establishment of powerful London newspapers came the institution of pre-performance 'rehearsals' for journalists, which were as much about softening the potential critic as about acting: *The Universal Spectator*'s visitor to rehearsal was made much of by the playwright, and was consequently disposed to respond favourably towards the play—'We were no sooner arriv'd . . . but the Author came and made his Compliments . . . The Company then . . . went thro' with the Play . . . I was highly pleas'd with it.'[20] Naturally the use of newspapers to publicize forthcoming productions had the knock-on effect of giving additional publicity to the whole idea of rehearsal: saying a play was 'in rehearsal' was a way of whetting the town's appetite, and advertisements naming the play to come became frequent— 'We hear that the Grubstreet Opera . . . will . . . be perform'd within a Fortnight, being now in Rehearsal.'[21] Rehearsal, and the state of rehearsal, was thus no longer a private issue: it had entered the public domain.

The proliferation of performance-type rehearsals seems to

[19] Aaron Hill, *The Prompter*, ed. William A. Appleton and Kalman A. Burnim (New York, 1966), 67; Edward Phillips, *The Stage-Mutineers* (1733), 1.

[20] *Universal Spectator*, 13 Feb. 1731.

[21] *Daily Post*, May 1731, quoted in Hume, *Fielding*, 96. See also John Hill, *Orpheus* (1740), B1[b]: 'Mr. Rich . . . has . . . been carrying on his Preparation for [the play], and making the Town almost every Month expect it, but in vain.'

have led to a subtle change within the theatre. Theatrical practice had always favoured 'private study' above group rehearsal; now, however, the stage itself seemed to be offering an ideal of group rehearsal full of ensemble values. The question of the right way to prepare a play for performance was beginning to be raised. Some of the early theatrical theorists, notably Aaron Hill, realizing that the goals and aims of rehearsal were unclear, began trying to establish what rehearsal was and what purpose it should serve, stressing the importance of group preparation. At the same time, the small companies, quickly formed and as quickly disbanded in the illegitimate theatres, taught their trade in group rehearsal for they lacked the time and the professional trainers for much individual study. The balance of private to group preparation was beginning to be questioned.

### Number of days to produce a play

The amount of rehearsal a play received was dictated by the nature of the theatrical season. Companies tended to begin performing in September with a range of stock plays acted on alternate days, and the first new play was often not introduced until November, after the stock repertory had been built up.[22] Rehearsal was concentrated at the early and middle stages of the season, while a new work that was introduced into the season late received short shrift: Charles Johnson's *Gentleman Cully* 'stole into the Theatre in the very Heat of late Summer . . . was study'd in a Hurry, and play'd . . . under these Disadvantages'.[23]

There is no real evidence for Arthur Scouten's assertion that it was usual to give two weeks over to rehearsal before performance.[24] In general, the Restoration 'hierarchy' of plays seems to have continued to be recognized, with the suggestion that, where possible, about five weeks should be spent on a tragedy, about two weeks on a farce, and something in between on a comedy. Henry Brooke's tragedy *Gustavus Vasa* 'was about five weeks in Rehearsal'; John Dennis's *The Invader of His Country* (based on *Coriolanus*) similarly had 'about five Weeks Rehearsal'; Susanna Centlivre's comedy *The Artifice* was first rehearsed on 20

---

[22] See *London Stage*, II, p. cxii; III, p. xliii.
[23] Johnson, *Gentleman Cully*, A2[b].
[24] *London Stage*, III, p. clxxix.

September, and performed on 2 October 1722; while Cibber's *The Refusal*, also a comedy, began rehearsals on 23 January, and first played on 14 February 1721.[25] As there was no actual rule that governed rehearsal time, so there are instances of plays mounted over considerably shorter periods; the many references to insufficient rehearsals indicate in a roundabout way how much time was considered to be acceptable (or unacceptable) for preparing a play (they also show that a play generally thought to be underrehearsed was often still put on): examples include farces mounted in under a week ('It was read for the first Time to the Performers, *Tuesday* the *15th*, and acted *Monday* the *21st*', 'I ... finish'd it on the *Saturday* ... and it was acted the *Tuesday* after'[26]); comedies in ten days ('THIS Play was written in Five Days, and by the Actors got up in Ten more'[27]); tragedies put on in two weeks or less ('the Play was got up with indefatigable Application, in Twelve Days time from the first Reading, which is less than ever any Tragedy was known to be got ready in', 'the Play was but a fortnight in Rehearsal').[28] Flexible preparation was allowed for by a system in which a manifestly unready play could be changed or cancelled on the very day of performance: the company at Lincoln's Inn preparing Lewis Theobald's *Richard II* for what was supposed to be its première on 10 December 1719, were 'oblig'd to lie still' that day 'for a Practice of the Tragedy'; while on 30 May 1729 the Drury Lane Company actually refused to perform because they were getting up their revivals once again—'The company being employ'd in reviving several Plays, &c. are oblig'd to defer Acting till farther Notice'[29]—the first proof that revivals themselves were re-rehearsed.

Rehearsals could take place in the morning or the evening. Fielding in *The Historical Register* refers to being 'early at the Rehearsal this Morning'; in *Pasquin* he makes his Player com-

---

[25] Henry Brooke, *Gustavas Vasa* (1739), a3ᵃ (the play was not actually performed because the Lord Chamberlain objected to it); John Dennis, *The Invader of His Country* (1720), A3ᵇ; *London Stage*, II, p. cliv.

[26] John Hewitt, *A Tutor for the Beaus* (1737), A3ᵃ; Christopher Bullock, *The Cobler of Preston* (1723), p. ix.

[27] Charles Shadwell, *The Sham Prince* in *Five New Plays* (1720), F8ᵇ.

[28] Lewis Theobald, *The Perfidious Brother* (1715), A3ᵇ; Benjamin Martyn, *Timoleon* (1730), A4ᵃ.

[29] Quoted in *London Stage*, II, p. cliv, 1036.

plain that the author is not there 'and it's past Ten o'Clock'.[30] That ten o'clock was Fielding's general rehearsal time is confirmed by his announcement in the *Daily Advertiser* that he will 'Rehearse his Play . . . at his own house . . . at Ten this Morning'; Fielding may well have borrowed the practice from Drury Lane where his first plays were performed, for Swift describes a Drury Lane rehearsal as beginning at ten.[31] Emmett Avery uses the records for expenditure on food in Drury Lane between 1712 and 1716 to conjecture that rehearsals lasted until lunch time, concluding both that practices could last longer than three hours, and that they always took place in the morning. In fact Cibber, describing Drury Lane morning rehearsals under the three managers, suggests that they usually lasted 'two, or three Hours';[32] and records for food may well betoken evening rehearsals: in 1717 Sir Thomas Moore, preparing his *Mangora, King of the Timbusians* for performance, gave the actors 'many good Dinners and Suppers during the Rehearsals of this Play'.[33] So, as in the Restoration, both morning and evening rehearsals took place, though they were not always for the play to be performed that day: *Cato* was rehearsed on the morning that *Julius Caesar* was acted.[34] 'Public rehearsals' were held at noon ('Mr Handel opens Tomorrow . . . with the Opera of Pastor Fide . . . and we hear there was a Rehearsal this Day at Twelve o'Clock'[35]): noon may have distinguished 'public rehearsal' from a performance as well as allowing time for a normal rehearsal of the play before or afterwards.

## Actor training

The system of giving full plays over to young actors at certain times of the year selectively continued: novices performed in the

[30] Henry Fielding, *The Historical Register for 1736* [1737], i; Henry Fielding, *Pasquin* (1736), i.

[31] *London Stage*, III, 407; Jonathan Swift, *Journal to Stella*, ed. Harold Williams, 2 vols. (Oxford, 1948), ii. 654. Giffard also conducted rehearsals at Goodman's Fields in 1735 from 10 a.m. to 1 p.m.—see *London Stage*, III, p. clxxix.

[32] Cibber, *Apology*, 291.

[33] Benjamin Victor, *The History of the Theatres of London and Dublin, from the year 1730 to the Present Time*, 2 vols. (1761), ii. 143.

[34] *London Stage*, II, 299.

[35] *The Bee*, 9 Nov. 1734, quoted in *London Stage*, III, 430.

summer[36] and sometimes over Easter.[37] Once again, they tended
to be allowed only second-rate plays to put on: plays that could
not make it onto the seasonal stage. New actors therefore
became associated with second-rate texts, and still had no
experience of playing in the good ones. But training did at
least involve full performances, in which ensemble values
naturally featured. Aaron Hill, who promoted group rehearsal
in his theatrical periodical *The Prompter*, tried to gather his own
troupe of actors together to perform at the Little Haymarket
Theatre in 1722, and took great pains 'to form and instruct'
them.[38] Indeed, hard-working managers of the smaller theatres—like Henry Giffard, Henry Fielding, and William
Hallam—generally trained their actors well: they had neither
the time nor the money to give much individual instruction, so
they taught collectively through the means of regular, group
rehearsal.[39] Yet it is not the case, as has sometimes been claimed,
that novices at Drury Lane under John Highmore, John Ellys,
and Charles Fleetwood, or at Covent Garden when it was run by
Rich, were not properly trained because non-actor managers ran
the big theatres.[40] The confusion arises from the assumption that
if a manager is not highly involved in rehearsal, then no one is. In
fact at Drury Lane over the summer novice actors put on plays
'under the Direction of Mr. *Mills*, sen.', learning their trade, as
they had historically, from an actor.[41] But the strong and
prescriptive educational value that was being placed on group
rehearsal by periodicals and newspapers, and the fact that
novices in training theatres and professional theatres alike were
given special group rehearsals, turned individual or private

[36] Henry Carey, *The Honest Yorkshireman* (1736), A1[a–b]: 'the Young Actors
having, as usual, formed themselves into a Summer Company . . . the late Managers
always indulging the young Company with the House during the Summer Season.'
See also Victor, *Theatres from 1730*, ii. 97: 'The Managers of the Theatre-Royal in
*Drury-Lane* constantly permitted the younger Part of their Company to perform
Plays three Nights a Week all the Summer.'

[37] *London Stage*, III, p. xlvii.                    [38] Mottley, *List*, 248.

[39] For Giffard as a trainer of actors—including Garrick—see *London Stage*, III,
pp. lxxxi–lxxxv. Before idealizing the training that went on in little theatres it is worth
bearing in mind this depiction of preparation by Pinkethman's company of
Richmond Wells: 'as for [Mrs Morgan] I am a Stranger to her Merit, not having
had her at any *Rehearsal*, nor ever seen her till about two Hours before she appear'd
publickly in her Character'—John Williams, *Richmond Wells* (1723), A3[a].

[40] As is claimed in *London Stage*, III, p. cxxvi.

[41] Victor, *Theatres from 1730*, ii. 97.

rehearsal into a status symbol: established actors learnt to look down on group rehearsal, and those who were associated with it, in a way that reduced its power to teach them anything.

READING

At Drury Lane, in the time of the three managers, the representative authority-figure who judged plays was Colley Cibber— 'I try, acquit, or condemn,' a parody makes him say, 'and there's nought to be represented but what is stamped by my approbation.'[42] Cibber became notorious for his willingness to reject plays out of hand, a process that, as Davies records, he liked to call '*the choaking of singing birds*'.[43] He himself maintained that he seldom found one new play in twenty 'which upon hearing, proves to be fit for [the stage]'.[44] Cibber's reasons for discarding so many new plays were various, but there was undoubtedly a glut of fresh material being offered that he simply did not need— stock plays were safer and required less maintenance. As a result, initial playreadings were often treated in a consciously negative fashion, with every effort made to put off the enthusiastic young author. James Miller's *The Coffee-House* is about just such a reading: the audition takes place in a coffee house filled with Cibber's friends, so that while the author struggles to get a line read, Cibber is totally preoccupied by town business and gossip: 'Dear Mr. *Cibber*,' pleads the author, ' . . . hear me read but one Speech, and I'll be satisfy'd.'[45] Much the same story is told in the anonymous pamphlet, *The Laureat*, which relates how Cibber, having read only two lines of a new play, thrust it back at its yearning author 'with these Words, *Sir, it will not do*'.[46]

The purpose of the judgemental reading was to decide whether a play would take at all, and if so, how greatly it

[42] *Visits from the Shades* (1704), 24.

[43] Davies, *Garrick*, i. 246–8.

[44] Cibber, *Apology*, 291.

[45] James Miller, *The Coffee-House* (1737), 15.

[46] *The Laureat: or the Right Side of Colly Cibber* (1640), 66–7. In Fielding's *Pasquin*, 40, these words are used when the master of the playhouse 'tells you [the play] won't do, and returns it you again'. Theophilus Cibber obviously inherited the phrase: Robert Drury in his *The Rival Milliners* (1737), p. vi, talks of visiting the younger Cibber to discuss his play, and of how 'the Discourse terminated with, It will not do'.

would need to be revised—and who should do the revision. Steele's rational criticism of Joseph Addison's *The Drummer* (and naturally Addison came in for better treatment than a struggling unknown author) is typical: 'My Brother-Sharers were of Opinion at the first reading of it, that it was like a Picture in which the Strokes were not strong enough to appear with Advantage at a Distance.'[47] 'Theatricalizing' was always deemed to be necessary to ensure a play's success, and the revisers and adapters (in a theatre that put on too few new plays to need 'attached' authors[48]) were the managers themselves— particularly Colley Cibber, and later, his son Theophilus. Both Cibbers were accused of textual brutality. Fielding attacks them in his 1734 revised version of *The Author's Farce*, making Mar-play Junior (his Theophilus-character) claim: 'We are the persons, Sir, who lick [plays] into form, what mould them into shape. The poet make the play indeed! . . . my father and I, Sir, are a couple of poetical tailors: when a play is brought to us we consider it as a tailor does his coat; we cut it, Sir'.[49] That is not to say that the playwright always objected to what the manager did. Richard Savage thanked Theophilus Cibber for his alterations, acknowledging that 'Tho' an *Author* knows the meaning of his Scenes, he may be unacquainted with a *Theatrical* Method of setting 'em in the most advantageous Appearance'.[50] Hence my choice of the term 'theatricalizing': managers savaged texts in (often) theatrically appropriate ways.

Having made it through the judgemental reading, and replete

---

[47] Joseph Addison, *The Drummer* (1716), A3[b]. See also Barton Booth's response to Charles Shadwell's *The Fair Quaker of Deal* (1710), b1[a], 'that with a little Alteration 'twould please the Town'.

[48] Hume, *Fielding*, 52.

[49] Henry Fielding, *The Author's Farce*, quoted in D. Smith, *Plays about the Theatre in England*, 143. In *Register*, 26, Fielding characterizes Cibber as Ground-Ivy and makes him declare 'it was a Maxim of mine, when I was at the Head of Theatrical affairs, that no Play, tho' ever so good, would do without Alteration'. Dennis in *Invader*, A3[b], relates how his play suffered under Cibber: it had two scenes 'maim'd . . . to that Degree, that I could hardly know them'. Theophilus Cibber's input into *Harlequin Shepherd* distressed its author, who declared that no one would have pitied the protagonist if he 'had been . . . as silly a Rogue . . . as the ingenious and witty Managers have made him'—see *Weekly Journal or Saturday's Post*, 5 Dec. 1724.

[50] Richard Savage, *Tragedy of Sir Thomas Overbury* (1724), p. x. Susanna Centlivre in *The Man's Bewitch'd* (n.d. 1710?), A4[b], claims that she 'willingly submitted to Mr. *Cibber*'s Superiour Judgment in shortning the Scene of the Ghost in the last Act, and believed him perfectly in the right', but that she had problems with Estcourt who 'slic'd most of it out'.

with appropriate revisions, a play was 'read for the first Time to
the Performers'.[51] Generally this reading was given by authors
themselves, and, generally, this was their best (and sometimes
only) opportunity to offer a personal interpretation of their play.
The actors continued to conceive of their reading as another test
of the play, however, and once again, the author found himself
up against people seemingly anxious to criticize and discard his
work. The *Tatler* tells the story of a playwright whose comedies
have been 'rejected by the Players' on so many occasions that he
is reduced to making a friend masquerade as the author—in the
hope that a new face will get the play through the critical
reading.[52] There is even a suggestion that actors formalized
the judgemental side of the process to the extent of choosing
one of their number to be resident critic: 'let me propose an
objection or two to you concerning your performance,' says
Player to Author in the anonymous *Humours of the Court*, 'You
must know I act in quality of a critic to this company of
Comedians.'[53]

Player and author naturally approached plays from a very
different standpoint: 'the *Player* . . . fixes his whole Attention on
the mechanical Part of a Play and, if there is Hurry, Perplexity,
and Intrigue, sufficient to keep him in a Flutter thro' the Whole,
he is satisfied . . . On the other Hand, if the Tale is simple,
natural, and uniform, it clashes with [the actors'] sickly Tastes.'[54]
Already author and actor were at loggerheads; their battle would
continue through the rehearsal period, but with one vital
difference: the managers, often actors themselves, would weigh
in heavily on the actors' side.

As the previous chapter emphasized, giving a bad reading was
dangerous. Anxious to show how second-rate John Hill's
*Orpheus* was, and how different (and how much better) was
his own play on that theme, Christopher Rich made an actor
read Hill's play out loud 'without a Stop or Accent, in a cant
Tone, as if it had been a Sheet of Law *French* . . . Mr. *Rich* then
read his own himself, with his best Grace and Diction, and not
without some Flourishes of Action'.[55] Rich, it is claimed,

[51] Hewitt, *Tutor*, A3ᵃ.      [52] *Tatler*, ii. 72.
[53] *Humours of the Court* (1732), B1ᵃ.
[54] *A Proposal for the Better Regulation of the Stage* (1732), 8.
[55] Hill, *Orpheus*, B2ᵃ.

influenced the listeners through the medium of a favourable reading. Playwrights, conscious of the powerful negative effect of a bad recital, would sometimes sacrifice their right to read to the players (even though by so doing they risked losing complete control of the play), simply in the hope that a more slick performance might enhance their play's standing. Addison gave his reading over to the young Colley Cibber, but linked this renunciation with an authoritative judgement about casting:

When Mr. Addison carried this admirable Tragedy to the Green-Room, he of course, as the Author, read it first to the Players: but being a man of uncommon bashfulness and diffidence, after this, he desired Cibber would supply his place, who read it so much to the satisfaction of the Author that he requested him to play the part of *Cato*.[56]

Although, as Benjamin Victor claimed, for a new play 'the first three Readings fell to the Share of the Author', the author's reading might well be suffered rather than relished by the actors, and the author's then tentative suggestions about casting could often be ignored.[57] Addison's judgement, for instance, was superseded, and 'Cato' was given to Booth 'by two of his Masters, who were Acting Managers'.[58] The actress Laetitia Cross complains that she was specifically asked to attend 'the first publicke Reading' of Ambrose Philips's *The Distrest Mother*, because the playwright, as he told her, had 'design'd the part of *Andromache* for me' but again, the playwright was not given his (and Mrs Cross's) wishes following the reading, and the role was given to Anne Oldfield.[59] John Hughes was too ill to attend the reading of his *Siege of Damascus*, but instead wrote to Wilks making the casting suggestions he hoped for, almost none of which were taken up.[60] Though *The London Stage* suspects that authors cast their own plays and managers cast revivals,[61] it is clear that casting was ultimately in the hands of the managers at

---

[56] William Cooke, *Memoirs of Charles Macklin* (1804), 359. Cibber is described by *The Laureat*, 95, as pressing to take over readings.

[57] Victor, *Theatres from 1730*, ii. 4–5.

[58] Benjamin Victor, *Memoirs of the Life of Barton Booth, Esq* (1733), 7. Davies in *Garrick*, i. 21, claims, however, that it was Addison who cast Ryan as Marcus.

[59] Milhous and Hume, 'Theatrical Politics at Drury Lane', *Bulletin of Research in the Humanities*, 85 (1982), 412–29 (416).

[60] *Letters by Several Eminent Persons Deceased*, 2 vols. (1772), i. 170. See also *London Stage*, III, p. cli.          [61] *London Stage*, II, p. cli.

any stage of a play's life. Francis Hawling's *Impertinent Lovers* simply had its 'Parts Cast by those in the Management'; the *Daily Journal* explained the position more accurately when it described casting as being in the hands of 'the Manager (or Author over-persuaded by the Manager)'.[62] Clearly the manager nodded to the author concerned, but clearly too, the manager was in the forefront and the playwright was of secondary concern: 'The Manager may . . . cast . . . Players, with the consent of the Author . . . in such a manner as to provide for them.'[63] In the 'Rules & Regulations for the management of the Theatres' the managers agree 'That no new play be receiv'd, that is not | approv'd by all the Menagers, nor any Play Reviv'd | or the Parts of it cast without the approbation of | all the Three'.[64] At the moment of the reading itself, authors often lost authority to the actors, immediately following which they lost control to the managers.

## Casts and parts

The verb 'to cast', meaning to allot parts to an actor in the theatre, is first recorded in 1711 (*OED* sig. 48), but in the eighteenth century the noun 'cast' when applied to an actor had the same meaning that an actor's 'line' had had the century before; so that to 'cast' a play was simply to give out parts to the appropriate stereotypes. 'I have play'd *Jane Shore*, *Cleopatra*, and *Lady Townly* . . . in short, Sir, I have play'd none but characters of that Cast' says the Lady in Charlotte Charke's *The Art of Management*.[65] Theophilus Keene is described as an actor whom no actor could excel 'in the Part of *Gloster* . . . and others of that Cast'.[66] Without 'attached' playwrights, parts were not written so specifically for only one actor or actress, but for a specific kind of stereotype, a system that may have led authors to write to a lower standard, and certainly demanded that actors perform to one: actors were less parodies of themselves—which at least involved

---

[62] Francis Hawling, *Impertinent Lovers* (1723), p. iv; *Daily Journal*, 17 Jan. 1737.
[63] *Daily Journal*, 22 Dec. 1736.
[64] Allardyce Nicoll, *A History of English Drama*, 3 vols. (1923, Cambridge, 1952), ii. 281.
[65] Charlotte Charke, *The Art of Management* (1735), 25.
[66] Chetwood, *General History*, 177.

working up their individual traits—than parodies of a type. A respected actor, maintains the correspondent for the *Daily Journal*, has a '*peculiar Right*' not only to his own roles, but to any other '*Species*' of similar character subsequently written:[67] an actor's 'cast' became more important even as plays were less specifically designated. Stereotyping meant that actors were encouraged to carry with them a particular and consistent method of playing any role—each performance therefore made reference to each other performance, and actors had, in effect, a single across-play character. *The Tatler* complained that, irrespective of the actual part Wilks was playing, 'the vulgar Spectators turn their Thoughts upon Sir *Harry Wildair*'.[68] There was, therefore, every incentive for actors not to branch out or explore other ways of acting.

Cued parts were distributed and learnt as before, advertisements using a 'now in parts' formula as a way of indicating that plays were in preparation but were not as far advanced as plays 'now in rehearsal': 'We hear the following new Pieces are writ into Parts and are to be play'd . . . with all convenient Expedition.'[69] Because of the ownership of parts—one actor would 'possess' a scripted role—there could be no understudies. So when particular actors were unable to perform, theatres ran into enormous difficulties. Mrs Charke was at one point 'stock-reader . . . in case of Disaster', meaning that she would go on with part in hand and read the relevant text;[70] on other occasions plays would have to be cancelled altogether when the appropriate performer could not perform: 'A New Tragedy' had to be deferred because of 'Mrs Bullock's hourly Expectation of being brought to Bed, she having the Principal Part in the Play'.[71] So actor and part remained inextricably bound together, sometimes at the expense of the play.

Inherited roles were taught as the original actor had performed

---

[67] *Daily Journal*, 17 Jan. 1737.

[68] *Tatler*, iii. 75.

[69] *Daily Post*, 17 Nov. 1732.

[70] Charke, *Art of Management*, 59. Laetitia Cross sent her part in to the theatre when she was unable to perform so that someone else could read it: see Milhous and Hume, 'Theatrical Politics', 426. Theophilus Cibber explains that when Booth was very ill, he lent his new part to Charles Williams 'to study, as doubting the certainty of his being able to appear in it himself'—*The Lives and Characters of the Most Eminent Actors and Actresses* (1753), 82.     [71] *London Stage*, II, 611.

them: Mary Porter, for instance, was trained up by Elizabeth Barry, and finally succeeded to her parts. Mrs Barry gave a reason for desiring to do this: '*Dear Porter*', she is said to have gushed, '*I will never die whilst you live*'—if, as a major actor, you train your pupil carefully enough, then 'your' performance will last for ever.[72] Knowledge of the prototype performance was so necessary that if the original actor was no longer available, someone else who knew how to perform the part 'properly' had to be found, as when Rich offered to train Charles Dibdin into all of Richard Leveridge's parts (Dibdin had not himself seen Leveridge perform) by teaching him exactly 'where to lay the *emphasy*—for which last purpose he had marked the part of Juba for me in his own hand'.[73] Again, imitators did not always know when to stop. Hallam mimicked Wilks so 'diligently' as Aumerle in *Richard II* that he copied his 'peculiar custom' of pulling down his ruffles and rolling his stockings.[74] And over time more and more objections were made to actors who followed the originals *too* exactly: 'a Copy has neither the free Spirit nor easy Grace of an Original' explains Dennis in his *Invader*; *The Censor* directs its criticism at the 'Under-*Players*' who mimic 'the chief Actors, with a servile Imitation' and 'run rather into the Imperfections of the Originals than their Excellencies'.[75] The tenor of such censoring is slightly different from the century before: conscious of the absurdity of imitation at its extreme, new criticism was starting to betray a restlessness with the whole idea of inherited performances. A middle ground was sought, and was found. Chetwood records a conversation overheard between two theatrical gentlemen about 'the Propriety' of a particular speech. One disputant rejected an imitative interpretation with '*that was the old way of Acting!* A truly great Actor, that stood by, reply'd, *learn the old Way first, and when you are perfect, then begin a new one, if you can find it out*'.[76] The old manner

[72] Patrick Fitz-Crambo, *Tyranny Triumphant* (1743), 13.

[73] Charles Dibdin, *The Professional Life of Mr. Dibdin*, 4 vols. (1803), i. 25.

[74] Davies, *Miscellanies*, i. 100.

[75] Dennis, *Invader*, A5ᵃ; *The Censor*, 2nd edn., 4 vols. (1717), i. 65. See also Lewis Theobald, *The Tragedy of King Richard II* (1720), 2B2ᵇ: 'Had it not been for the Division of the Companies, the Town might never have seen Mr. *RYAN* in the beautiful Lights, in which it has since admir'd Him [.] they lik'd him in the First Characters of *Old* Plays, and so were prepar'd to receive him better in any good *New* One: where He could have no Pattern before his Eye to act by Imitation.'

[76] Chetwood, *General History*, 32.

becomes the basis for a new interpretation. Not, at first sight, a very radical suggestion, but slight rereadings of parts in revivals were beginning to be not only acknowledged, but expected.[77]

## *Study*

In 1738 'rehearsal' is described as the process by which actors are made '*more* ready and perfect in their parts',[78] thus maintaining the idea that actors should be well advanced in their preparation before they come to rehearsal. Certainly when the managers promised that Francis Hawling's *Impertinent Lovers* would be 'got up with the best Study and Care', and Abraham Langford praised the application with which the actors 'studied' his play, they were, as ever, referring to the diligence of actors in learning their lines alone; lack of study might still be blamed as the main reason for poor performances.[79] Nevertheless, the balance between 'rehearsal' and 'study' did slightly change during the early eighteenth century. Victor described the full rehearsal process under the triumvirate, during which, he explained, a few part-in-hand read-throughs were followed by private study, after which a bout of more collective rehearsals was held when the actor was 'quite perfect in the Words and Cues'.[80] As this makes clear, rehearsal and study were (ideally) more intermingled than before—so, for instance, Booth is described both as 'studying the Part of *Julio*' and as having 'rehearsed it several times'; while Robert Drury explains how his play was 'wrote out in Parts and delivered to the Actors and rehearsed for several Days'.[81]

Because there were fewer new plays performed in the major theatres, added to the fact that many stock plays were available in

[77] See, for instance, Booth's careful distinction in Davies, *Miscellanies*, ii. 180. He would 'read a scene in a part, acted by Betterton, in that great actor's manner . . . but, when asked why he would not so represent a character throughout, his constant answer was, that it was too much for him. He stole what he could from his great exemplar, and fitted it to his own powers'.

[78] Ephraim Chambers, *Cyclopaedia* (1738), my italics.

[79] Hawling, *Impertinent*, pp. iv–v; Abraham Langford, *The Lover his Own Rival* (1736), A2ᵃ. Charles Molloy in *The Half-Pay Officers* (1720), A2ᵇ, relates how 'some of the Comedians, who are allow'd to be Excellent in their Way, had not time to make themselves Masters of their Parts'.

[80] Victor, *Theatres from 1730*, ii. 4.

[81] Theophilus Cibber, *Lives*, 82; Drury, *Rival Milliners*, p. ix.

full, printed copies, novice actors trying to get on might well study a part 'in hope of sometime playing it', like the young player in Fielding's *Pasquin*; or like Charlotte Charke, who presented herself at the theatre claiming to be 'universally studied'.[82] A dichotomy existed: full play texts for most stock plays were readily available; ensemble rehearsal was heralded as important in pamphlets about the theatre—yet study still taught actors not to value more than their own lines. Known actors continued to receive instruction, which emphasized the importance of private study to their performance: part-based rather than full-play knowledge was thus a sign of positive acting superiority.

In the time of Cibber, the same formalized principles of action and pronunciation, gestures and emphases were maintained (one of the players in Fielding's *Historical Register* is called 'Mr Emphasis'). Just how set vocal routines might be can be seen in *The Young Ladies Miscellany*, an acting guide for schoolgirls, which claims to take its rules from the theatre of the day:

as all the PASSIONS have their proper Variations, so there are distinct and peculiar Tones to all the Tropes and Figures of Speech . . . all Personal Names . . . and all Epithets, Adjectives, or Qualities, by which Substantives, Beings, or Things are . . . distinguish'd, as, Black, White, Good, Bad . . . and the like, should always be read or spoken with a clear, open, and distinct Voice, as they are for the most part very emphatical and the Beauty of Expression depends much upon them.[83]

Similarly gesture was defined, again largely by codes: *The Censor* discusses 'Motions of the Arms and Body, peculiar to the expression of the respective passions'.[84] With the rise of interest in scientific study of all kinds, came a number of quite technical attempts to define and formalize what the passions were in real life—as well as how they could be manifested on the stage. Le Brun, who had first identified the meanings that could be conveyed through the face in 1698, was used as an actor's reference guide throughout the eighteenth century; Aaron Hill identified ten primary passions and offered a limited range of

[82] Fielding, *Pasquin*, 9; Charke, *Art of Management*, 103.
[83] D. Bellamy, *The Young Ladies Miscellany* (1723), pp. vi, ix.
[84] *Censor*, iii. 205.

ways to portray them.[85] But as important parts still had to be taught, it is clear that something further was aimed at in a good performance, beyond set rules. *The Censor* explains that the actor must mingle what he has 'borrowed from Nature and Genius', with 'Instruction and Artificial Improvements': 'A Man may in some Measure be born an Actor, and struck out for a Degree of Imitation; but his Excellence must depend on an acquir'd Talent, his Gestures and Motions must be regulated from Circumstances of the Stage, and a Knowledge of the Character which he is to support.'[86] The 'circumstances' of the stage here demand that a different set of laws be followed— acting was far from being a representation of any kind of 'reality'. The ultimate way in which a good performance was made was through 'knowledge of the character', which still seems to have meant knowledge of the passions. Barton Booth was a great actor, writes Aaron Hill, because he had the talent for 'discovering the Passions, where they lay hid', and Victor gives a marked-up fragment of *Othello* to illustrate just how Booth did this:

*a long pause, the eye kept looking after Iago . . .*
This fellow's of exceeding honesty                    *Spoken in a low*
And knows all qualities with a learned spirit    *tone of voice.*
Of human dealings.

                                                                    *Pause, the look starting*
                                                                    *into anger.*[87]

Instruction in individual rehearsal was still entirely dictatorial. When Mrs Clinket, the mad poetess of John Gay's *Three Hours after Marriage*, talks to the player, she tells him to 'read me the last Lines I writ upon the Deluge, and take care to pronounce them as I taught you',[88] another throwback to Hamlet's 'speak the speech'. Aaron Hill trained Mrs Cibber, Theophilus' wife, to play the lead role in *Zara*, by interlining a part for her, on which he marked every single accent and inflection—in effect he gave her a verbal score.[89] Later in life she was particularly singled out

[85] See McKenzie, 'Countenance', 758–73; Hill, *Essay on the Art of Acting* (c.1746) in *The Works of the Late Aaron Hill*, 4 vols. (1753), iv. 384.

[86] *Censor*, iii. 204.

[87] Quoted in Alan S. Downer, 'Nature to Advantage Dressed', *PMLA* 58 (1943), 1002–37 (1007).

[88] John Gay, *Three Hours after Marriage* (1717), 5.          [89] Barker, *Cibber*, 181.

as an actress who shows her 'natural Genious' by 'never . . .
varying in either Tone or voice or Action from the Way she was
taught'.[90] As before, the instructors of individual rehearsal
could be the author, a manager, another player, or a friend,
so that the interpretation produced might directly contradict
that of the playwright, who had only selective access to this part
of the rehearsal procedure—there is even something mildly
furtive about the way Steele and Addison felt obliged to
remove Lacy Ryan from the other actors and managers 'to a
tavern some time before [Addison's *Cato*] was acted, and
[instruct] him in his part'.[91]

Minor actors did not receive much instruction, and might be
put under the charge of anyone available—usually a second-rate
teacher, who gave them little chance to improve. Steele, a
theatrical theorizer rather than a practitioner, found himself
supposed, amongst a list of other tasks, 'to Instruct the Younger
Actors' (he denied that he had undertaken to do this).[92] As
having had proper 'instruction' reflected actors' positions in the
theatrical hierarchy, there was an onus on players taught by an
impressive figure to let the 'originator' show through their
performances, so broadcasting their famous 'ancestor'. Naturally, this created hand-me-down performances that were not
actually very impressive: Cibber's Sir John Brute was described
as 'copied from Betterton, as far as a weak pipe and an
inexpressive meagre countenance would bear any resemblance
to the vigorous original'; Wilks was advised to forget the pattern
given him by Betterton 'for that he failed in no Part of *Othello*,
but where he had him in View'.[93] Actors of intelligence both
acknowledged the status they held by being given serious
instruction, and, at the same time, felt stifled by the instruction
process—they continued to find ways of accepting instruction
while challenging the procedure, through the way they dealt with
their texts.

[90] *Daily Journal*, 27 Jan. 1736. Similarly when Cibber was asked his opinion on a
part by the first Mrs Macklin, the elderly actor simply read out the lines 'appro-
priately' to her—Cooke, *Macklin*, 396.

[91] Davies, *Garrick*, i. 21.

[92] PRO CII/2416/49, quoted in Loftis, *Steele*, 36.

[93] Davies, *Miscellanies*, iii. 254; *Tatler*, iii. 75.

GROUP REHEARSAL

*Nature of rehearsal*

Music and acting rehearsals remained separate events. The 'Regulations for y$^e$ Directors of y$^e$ Playhouse', set down in 1710, stipulated that actors should be 'taught to dance | & sing three times a week' aside from normal rehearsals.[94] The number of group rehearsals held for a production altogether is, however, still unclear: they occupied more of the preparation process than they had before, but it is hard to separate the fact from the suggestion, the reality from the ideal.

Aaron Hill argued in favour of rehearsals full of ensemble qualities, rehearsals that would familiarize actors with the story in which they were taking part, and teach them to consider 'their' characters in relation to those performed by other people. So he vigorously supported the idea of full and well-attended collective practices, claiming that ideally 'a rehearsal' should be 'a play completely acted . . . The words of a part should be perfect on the memory *before*, and the purpose of rehearsing serve . . . to show how every actor's character relates to and should be influenced by another's.'[95] This is an early example of the suggestion that group rehearsals can offer the chance to develop a character using information not present in the part. But that Hill had to present this as a novel idea is testimony to the fact that it was not generally happening at the time. Indeed, a few days earlier he had depicted contemporary practice (that is, the practice of 1735), as singularly lacking in 'order and propriety', where the actors knew their studied parts but could not be bothered to grapple with the 'business' that rehearsal might otherwise teach them:

If an actor does not know precisely the minute circumstances that relate to his role, as to entrances, exits, the part of the stage he is to fill up, and the action he is to be in when he has nothing to say, he may be very perfect in the sense and meaning of the author and yet commit most egregious blunders in the representation. This is what actors generally trust to their memory, instead of performing at rehearsals . . .[96]

Benjamin Victor claimed that 'the time of Booth, Cibber and Wilks' (just five years before Hill was writing), had been

---

[94] Nicoll, *A History of English Drama*, ii. 279–80.
[95] Hill, *Prompter*, 67.     [96] Ibid. 59.

precisely when such procedures were followed. Then, he maintained, a new play received three readings, succeeded by part-in-hand rehearsals, succeeded by 'study'; the process would conclude with collective rehearsals in which the actor could 'be instructed, and practise his proper Entrances, Emphasis, Attitudes, and Exits'.[97] Interestingly, those very effects that Betterton had claimed could not possibly be learnt in rehearsal—study, voice, looks, and gesture—had become (ideally) specifically the business of rehearsal: the rules that governed rehearsal were being reshaped. At the same time, these depictions of ideal rehearsals under the triumvirate cannot be taken fully at face-value. Victor's account is given in a text that lavishes praise and affection onto his 'Dear Friend' Colley Cibber, and it is telling to compare his adulatory account with Swift's description of an actual Drury Lane rehearsal during the time of the three managers. Swift watched Addison rehearse his *Cato* in a collective rehearsal held in 1713, and saw 'the actors prompted every moment and the poet directing them and the drab [Mrs Oldfield] that acts Cato's daughter out in the midst of a passionate part and then calling out, "What's next?"'[98] Here the author is depicted trying to manage a group of actors who clearly have not learnt their parts 'without book', as Victor claims they did before 'instructive' rehearsals. Nevertheless, versions of the ideal do seem to have happened, like the part-in-hand read-through ('come,' says Player in the anonymous *Humours of the Court*, 'I'll go in and give out the Parts, and then we shall see how it will do on a Rehearsal').[99] But when, at Covent Garden, Thomas Walker gave up his role of Young Courtlove in William Popple's *Double Deceit* just before performance because 'he had study'd his Part, but could not make himself Master of it' ('The Part is about Eight Lengths', sneers the *Daily Journal*, 'and was above eight Weeks in Mr Walker's Hands'), it is clear that no one up to this time had known that the actor was struggling—in other words, that no without-book ensemble rehearsal had taken place in which the actor's difficulties might be revealed.[100]

Moreover, Victor's ideal rehearsal in Cibber's time carefully

[97] Victor, *Theatres from 1730*, ii. 4.
[98] Swift, *Stella*, ii. 654.
[99] *Humours of the Court*, p. vii.
[100] *London Stage*, III, 484; *Daily Journal*, 29 Apr. 1735.

ignores the way major and insignificant actors were divided from each other during rehearsal and even performance, and the effect this had on the group presentation of a play. Players of small rank and low salary could not, for instance, use the green room, but had a different room for themselves, necessarily leading to separate, partial rehearsals: the first player in Fielding's *Pasquin* 'dare not go into the *Green-Room*; my Salary is not high enough'.[101] Actors of standing had a tendency to reduce all rehearsal to partial rehearsal—they would merely mutter over their lines, claims Aaron Hill, and then retreat to the green room again, from where the prompter's boy would fetch them when they were waited for in the scene: 'Then in rush they, one after another, mumbling their parts as they run . . . hurrying with a ridiculous impatience till they have catched and beat back the cues, and then, immediately, forsaking the stage as if they had nothing to do in the play but to parrot a sound without consequence.'[102] Moreover, private study continued to take place within the shared space of green room and stage, though it was usually denominated 'rehearsal'. In Smock Alley, every actor in rehearsal is described as having his or her 'different Employments':

Here stands a *Tragedy* Hero . . . settling *Attitudes* before a Glass; . . . In one Corner you may see *Hermione,* clinching her Fists and frowning at the Wainscot . . . At one end of the room is a *Dancer* cutting Capers; at another, *Musick* melting in Piano . . . There are two practising a Love-Scene in dumb Show . . . there stalks *Banquo* adjusting the Deportment of a Ghost. Here stands *Macbeth* with her Eyes fix'd in her head, rubbing out a *damned spot*, and trying how she can walk in her sleep.[103]

Sometimes attendance at rehearsal was grudging and unproductive. Cibber himself refers to 'a Stale Actress at a Rehearsal'.[104] Moreover, there was a problem in getting respected actors to attend at all after they had studied a part: they had a tendency to

---

[101] W. J. Macqueen Pope, *Theatre Royal Drury Lane* (London, 1945), 36; Fielding, *Pasquin,* 12–13.

[102] Hill, *Prompter,* 67.

[103] George Stayley, *The Rival Theatres* (1737), 24. See also Phillips, *Stage-Mutineers,* 16, where Miss Crotchet talks of the 'confus'd miscellaneous Noise of the Green Room, where stern *Cato* is pouring out Oaths and *Roxana* scraps of Tragedy; . . . where *Caesar* is disputing with Captain *Mackheath,* and *Cleopatra* with *Jenny Diver*'.

[104] Colley Cibber, *Love's Last Shift* (1696), 20.

'excuse themselves from Rehearsals' as Chetwood, the Drury Lane prompter, put it.[105] Francis Hawling similarly complains that 'the Company had not Regularly attended the Rehearsals' for his play:[106] although the kind of rehearsal described by Victor and promoted by others existed in part, and as a notional ideal, it can hardly be described as the norm, even under the three managers, because it was undercut by the actors' natural urge not to work more than they needed to.

Each person involved in group rehearsal had a different reason for being there; they were not always in accordance. The theatre management set up the events largely for technical reasons (and well might they do so: Leigh, 'a young Lad belonging to . . . Drury-Lane', broke his arm while trying out the mechanism for a flying machine in rehearsal[107]). The property man and the prompter attended to make or approve specific property decisions: at practices of Brooke's *Gustavus Vasa*, claims Thomas Earl, the property man made pleas in favour of economic props when the author and prompter became too fanciful.[108] Author and prompter, of course, each had their own agendas.

## Prompters and rehearsal

Langhans has found prompt-book markings which seem to show prompters reminding themselves to follow closely the speeches an actor had had problems with in rehearsal—prompters here are using rehearsal to anticipate, and presumably to try to forestall, the prompting needs of performance.[109] But prompters also needed rehearsal to see what the property requirements of the play would be, to plan the sheets for the call-boys, and to sort out the timing—too long a play would have to be cut. Despite the claim made in *The Biographical Dictionary* that Chetwood went over to Smock Alley in 1741 'not as a prompter but as a technical consultant', in fact the role of prompter also included technical advising.[110] So Fielding in

---

[105] Chetwood, *General History*, 35.    [106] Hawling, *Impertinent*, p. vi.
[107] *Universal Spectator*, 16 Nov. 1729.
[108] Thomas Earl, *The Country Correspondent* (1739), 21.
[109] Edward A. Langhans, 'Three Early Eighteenth Century Manuscript Prompt-Books', *MP* 65 (1967), 114–29 (116).
[110] Philip Highfill, Fr., Kalman Burnim, Edward Langhans, *A Biographical Dictionary*, 12 vols. (Carbondale, Ill., 1973–93), iii. 193.

*Pasquin* has his playwright Fustian ensuring that the prompter
is in full command of the technical requirements of his play
('Mr. *Prompter*, observe, the Moment the first Ghost descends,
the second is to rise'); while Thomas Earl sneeringly explains
how Brooke and his prompter at a rehearsal of *Gustavus Vasa*
decided that the actor playing Gustavus should be 'allowed a
sufficient Quantity of burnt Cork, or Snuffs of Candles' for his
chin in order to create the unshaven look.[111] The prompter
seems also sometimes to have been involved in the casting
process: in Fielding's *Historical Register* the prompter casts in
full the internal play 'Apollo', as does the prompter in his
*Tumble-Down Dick* (1736).

Chetwood, Drury Lane's main prompter (off and on) between
1715 and 1741, wrote a history of the stage. Being also a
bookseller, he printed the edition himself, which suggests that
its illustrations have authorial sanction. The edition opens on
two engravings: one of Chetwood himself; and one of a scene
happening on the stage of the Drury Lane Theatre. Chetwood is
flanked by symbolic theatrical paraphernalia—a mask, a lyre, a
dagger, a wreath of bay—each representing a different form of
drama, all of which he has seen to the stage. Some of these
varying dramatic forms are illustrated on the opposite page: on
the stage of the theatre is a harlequin, a tragedy queen, dagger
and handkerchief in hand, and a comedy actress, with a comic
mask in the skirts of her dress. What is not represented is
Chetwood's bell and whistle—the actual accoutrements of his
trade. Chetwood, a backstage man, is presenting himself at the
forefront of theatrical production.

Chetwood clearly did not view his performance duties as the
main part of what he did. He had important backstage duties
and an increasing responsibility for the plays under his charge.
The prompter's tasks, defined by Arthur Scouten as '[drafting]
the playbills ... [conducting] routine rehearsals ... [informing] the
manager whether a last minute change in casting was necessary', in
fact also involved teaching actors and revising texts.[112] And some
of the rehearsals Chetwood was asked to overlook were hardly

---

[111] Fielding, *Pasquin*, 48; Earl, *Correspondent*, 15 see also 21. The prompter also
invented a way to deal with the line 'Get on the Bank, Gustavus' by proposing to give
the player a joint-stool covered with painted cloth to look like a bank, 29.

[112] *London Stage*, III, p. xcviii.

'routine': Spranger Barry 'received the first Rudiments' of acting
at the prompter's hands as did Charles Macklin; Mademoiselle
Chateauneuf received private instruction from him for one of the
most coveted roles of the time, that of Polly in John Gay's *Beggar's
Opera*.[113] This is high-level personal tuition, not standard rehearsal.

Chetwood was also asked to cut and correct plays—in other
words, to have a literary role in the production. So respected was
his judgement, that his name frequently features in play prefaces:
James Ayres, for instance, records how he was directed to
Chetwood 'as a proper Person to shorten' *Sancho at Court*.[114]
One manuscript that contains Chetwood's own reworkings,
shows the prompter's feelings of possession towards plays he
had had a hand in producing: writing to the Lord Chamberlain
for permission to have Edward Phillips's *Britons, Strike Home*
performed, he refers pointedly to *his* intentions and *his* theatre:
'*Sir*, I intend to have perform'd this Farce at my Theatre if
approved of and Licensed.'[115] Moreover, printed texts marketed
as 'corrected from the prompt-book' started to be published:
readers trusted 'Chetwood' plays, so that editions might even try
to claim prompter's sanction when they actually did not have it.
R. Walker's 1733 *Dramatick Works of William Shakespeare* was
publicly rubbished by Chetwood, who wrote an address to the
people who 'industriously report, that the said Plays are printed
from copies made use of at the Theatres', declaring 'That no
Person ever had directly or indirectly from me, any such Copy or
Copies'.[116]

Were these tasks given specifically to Chetwood because he
was so literate, or has the general importance of the prompter in
the revising process been underestimated? The all-purpose
prompter figure in Fielding's *Tumble-Down Dick* also cuts
plays during rehearsal, though admittedly he shows no sense
or judgement in what he does:

---

[113] Chetwood, *General History,* 129; Davies, *Miscellanies,* iii. 262.

[114] James Ayres, *Sancho at Court* (1742), A2[b]. See also Hawling, *Impertinent,* p. iv:
'the following Play . . . was given to Mr. *Chetwood*; (who I must acknowledge hath
ever seem'd sensibly to resent its Ill usage).'

[115] *Britons Strike Home*, Huntington Library Larpent MS, l.a.16 (1739). All future
references to 'Larpent' plays are to manuscript texts in the Huntington.

[116] William Shakespeare, *Works of Shakespeare*, ed. Jacob Tonson, 7 vols. (1734), i.
A2[a].

MR MACHINE. . . . Mr. Prompter, I must insist that you cut out a great
  deal of *Othello*, if my Pantomime is perform'd with it . . .
PROMPTER. We'll cut the Fifth Act, Sir, if you please.[117]

Though undoubtedly Chetwood was particularly involved in the
production process, prompters in the early eighteenth century
were being given more responsibility in general, and were taking
on managerial duties: for while the manager attended rehearsals
only on special occasions, the prompter attended most rehearsals. When Aaron Hill decided to call his critical periodical *The
Prompter*, he named it after Chetwood because although that
'useful officer . . . seemed not to command' (and note the
prudent use of the word 'seemed'), yet 'in the modest character
of an adviser he had the whole management and direction of that
little commonwealth'.[118]

### *Authors and rehearsal*

Rehearsal plays of the period, which continue to offer the
picture of a dictatorial and intrusive author in rehearsal, have
inherited the 'rehearsal-format', and are formulaic in outline; in
their contemporary in-jokes and passing references to the
minutiae of performance they are more realistic. The plays of
Fielding display a particularly confusing mixture of the formulaic and the 'true'. For instance, Fielding's meddlesome
author Trapwit teaches gesture in group rehearsal in much
the same way as Bayes had done: 'seem a little more affected, I
beseech you; . . . make a low Bow, lay your Hand upon your
Heart, fetch a deep Sigh, and pull out your Handkerchief.'[119]
How close this was to real rehearsal is complicated by the fact
that Fielding famously put on plays by new young authors,
whom he encouraged to attend rehearsals regularly: George
Lillo was present for much of the preparation of his *Fatal
Curiosity*, and was 'invited to give his opinion how a particular
sentiment should be uttered by the actor',[120] but the word
'invited' speaks for itself—there was no assumption that an
author's opinion mattered most. Fielding was later to define 'an

---

[117] Henry Fielding, *Tumble-Down Dick* (1736), 2.
[118] Hill, *Prompter*, 1.                          [119] Fielding, *Pasquin*, 4.
[120] George Lillo, *Lillo's Dramatic Works*, ed. Thomas Davies, 2 vols. (1810), i. 11.

author' as 'a laughing Stock. It means likewise a poor Fellow, and in general an Object of Contempt.'[121]

In fact, after the reading, the author's role was unclear. To participate actively in rehearsal was not always possible or socially appropriate, in which case the play was seen to the stage by another author. For women, the position of visible authoress was still badly thought of: Mrs Clinket, the mad playwright in Gay's *Three Hours*, gives her play to Plotwell, observing that 'your personating the Author will infallibly introduce my Play on the Stage'; 'THIS Tragedy was writ by a young Lady, and entrusted to my Management,' reads the preface to *The Fatal Legacy*, 'I introduced it into the Play-house for her Interest.'[122] Various authors tried to see to it that their names were not associated with their texts. The writer of *The Female Fop* freely acknowledges that the play is faulty, declaring he or she had neither time nor inclination to correct it '[not] intending to subscribe my Name to the Play'.[123] Stand-in authors might also take responsibility for plays whose actual authors were dead ('I am to meet some Players to Night about finishing a Play left imperfect by a Man of great Genius'[124]), or were too ill to see the production through themselves ('Mr Southerne', writes the playwright John Hughes to Wilks, ' . . . will deliver *The Siege of Damascus* to you . . . and will, whenever it may be necessary, attend the rehearsals'[125]). But a combination of managers, prompters, and actors, rather than playwrights real

---

[121] Henry Fielding, *Covent Garden Journal*, 14 Jan. 1752.

[122] Gay, *Three Hours*, 17; J. Robe, *The Fatal Legacy* (1723), A3ᵃ.

[123] [Sandford?], *Female Fop* (1724), p. iv. See also [John Mottley?], *The Widow Bewitch'd* (1730), A2ᵃ: 'there are some Reasons why the Author of this Comedy desires to be conceal'd'; *The Younger Brother* (1719), A3ᵃ⁻ᵇ: 'a certain Nobleman has concern'd himself in the promoting of this Play, therefore some make him the Author, and say he was at several Rehearsals, &c. . . . This might be easily set right, if the Person conceal'd thought fit to appear'; Parker's *Key to . . . Three Hours*, 4, reveals 'MR. *Gay's* two Friends, who (*he says*), *will not allow him the Honour of having their Names join'd with His*, are, Mr. *Pope*, and Dr. *Arbuthnott*', claiming to know this because the two 'constantly attended the Rehearsal of this *Surprizing* Performance'.

[124] Gildon, *New Rehearsal*, 86; see also Eliza Haywood, *The Fair Captive* (1721), a2ᵃ: 'This Tragedy was originally writ by Capt. *Hurst*, . . . but . . . the Author [being] oblig'd to leave the Kingdom, Mr. *Rich* became the Purchaser of it . . . last January he . . . made me some Proposals concerning the new modelling it'.

[125] *Letters, by . . . Persons Deceased*, i. 169. But see Davies, *Garrick*, i. 209, which describes how, in the event, it was Cibber who 'obliged Mr. Hughes to alter the most material circumstance in his Siege of Damascus, and thereby rendered feeble, and almost ineffectual, the author's scene between Phocyas and Eudocia'.

or substitute, were responsible for much of the 'correction' and revision of texts.

Playwrights present at rehearsal were given to know that they were not in charge; their reasons for attending were anyway not so much to control the action as to stop the actors from damning the play in advance.[126] And it was relatively clear that authors who wanted to be accepted had to do with their texts what the actors decreed. *A Proposal* explains how, in the war between the poets and the players, 'the actual Sovereignty' is in the player's hands, the poets having 'only the Title', and goes on to berate the players for 'that Haughtiness, that Contempt, that Insolence which Poets are now-a-days treated with'.[127] Fielding makes his author Fustian explain how actors who object to their parts 'are continually plaguing you with Alterations'.[128] Plays are full of references to authors flailing around trying to keep their text whole against the actors' demands. The Reverend James Miller's *The Universal Passion* versifies the actress's response to the words that she is given to recite: 'Lard! Sir, said I, why this will never do | They'll pelt me off the Stage, and hoot at you.'[129] In Fielding's *Pasquin* the Harlequin takes objection to a sentence and exclaims 'I wish, Sir, you would cut out that Line, or alter it if you please.'[130] *The Tatler*, in its story about the playwright whose 'friend' pretends to be the author, has the chief actor insisting on removing, amongst other more weighty matters, the word 'and', though it stands at the end of a couplet as the rhyme to 'stand'. The phoney poet consents to give up 'and' rather than dispute over a monosyllable. 'For a Monosyllable, says the real Author! . . . I tell you, Sir, *and* is the Connexion of the Matter in that Place.'[131] In extreme cases actors might take exception to the length of their whole role: '[The part] was . . . given to Mrs *Hamilton*, who on Saturday about one in the Afternoon, declared she could not do it unless it was cut.'[132] These revisions are still ultimately part-related; when Fielding, in jest, makes the First Player concern himself with another part, it is only

---

[126] Authors who failed in this attempt include Bellers, *Injur'd Innocence*, A3[b]: '[the actors] did their utmost, by themselves and their emissaries, to decry it in all places where their judgments would pass'.

[127] *Proposal for . . . Regulation*, 5.                    [128] Fielding, *Pasquin*, 41.

[129] Reverend James Miller, *The Universal Passion* (1737), 76.

[130] Fielding, *Pasquin*, 62.                              [131] *Tatler*, ii. 72–3.

[132] Hewitt, *Tutor*, A3[b]. Admittedly this actress was asked to perform at very short notice.

to advise the author to 'cut the Ghost out, Sir; for I am terribly afraid he'll be damn'd, if you don't.'[133]

Sometimes the author's opinion was not sought at all. Complaints in prefaces frequently refer to the absence of the author altogether from important revision sessions—Osborne Sydney Wandesford complains of being surprised in performance by the 'Omission of some Speeches, and Alteration of others'[134]— and often give a sense of general authorial helplessness ('many Speeches were *cut* to gratify the prevailing Custom of the Actors'[135]).

## Managers and rehearsal

Managers at the two main theatres tended either to be actors, or to have their plays mounted by actors. So John Rich assigned the management of Lincoln's Inn in 1717 and 1718 to the players Theophilus Keene and Christopher Bullock; in 1724–5 Lacy Ryan received an additional 3s. 4d. nightly for helping with the rehearsals and training of performers; later he was replaced by Macklin.[136] Rich himself also took some interest in the training of actors, assuring Charles Dibdin that 'if I would let him *larn* me, my fortune was made'.[137]

Drury Lane between 1720 and 1730 was under strict regulation. With a choice of three managers it could potentially offer careful rehearsals, full revision, and the infusion of smart theatrical know-how into a cranky play. Between 1710 and 1714 the actor-managers reorganized Drury Lane with tremendous effect, sorting out the financial system by which the company was run, and instituting a comprehensive routine for the production of new plays and revivals.[138] 'Regulations for y^e

---

[133] Fielding, *Pasquin*, 2.

[134] Osborne Sydney Wandesford, *Fatal Love* (1730), p. iv. See also *The Faithful General* (1706), A3^a, which 'was . . . strip'd of all those Ornaments I endeavour'd to give it. Whole Scenes were left out; . . . some of the necessary Incidents Omitted'; Williams, *Richmond*, A2^b, from which 'whole SPEECHES were cut out' and 'Acts left unfinished'. Timothy Scrubb, of Rag-Fair, Esq, in *The Fall of Bob* (1736), A4^b, 'would willingly ward against the Charge of ill Nature, in making *Worm*, hang himself, but I assure the Reader, I did not hear that a Distiller had really been so rash, till the Piece was out of my Hands and Power of altering'.

[135] William Hatchett, *The Fall of Mortimer* (1731), A1^b.

[136] *London Stage*, II, 461; p. cxxii.      [137] Dibdin, *Professional Life*, i. 24.

[138] Barker, *Cibber*, 99.

Directors of y$^c$ Playhouse' had been established by the Lord
Chamberlain for managing Drury Lane in 1710, and these
included directives that, for instance, 'One of y$^c$ directors w$^{th}$
salarys [is] to be present at all Rehear/-salls.'[139] Cibber claims in
*The Apology*, that during the time of the three managers, Drury
Lane practised this 'ideal' management. He describes how

> Every Menager, is oblig'd, in his turn, to attend two, or three Hours
> every Morning, at the Rehearsal of Plays . . . or else every Rehearsal
> would be but a rude Meeting of Mirth and Jollity . . . A Menager ought
> to be at the Reading of every new Play, when it is first offer'd to the
> Stage . . . to order all new Cloaths, . . . to limit the Expence, . . . to direct
> and oversee the Painters, Machinists, Musicians, Singers, and Dan-
> cers.[140]

But the place in *The Apology* at which this explanation is offered
must be taken into account: Cibber is defending his decision to
give himself and the other two managers an additional salary of
£1 13s. 4d. each acting day, and his description of the managerial job is an idealized and perhaps exaggerated justification of
this decision. That the 'principles' of management had to be
redefined in 1733 when the managerial system at Drury Lane
broke down suggests that the comprehensive definition established in 1710 had failed or become superseded.

Nevertheless, there are plenty of play prefaces that do praise
'The Care the Managers took in getting up the Play'.[141] Even
Theophilus Cibber, characterized as 'The Great Mogul' for his
Oriental despotism (Fielding, as a joke, took on this name for his
company at the Haymarket), is thanked for his careful management of rehearsal: '[he] endeavour'd to instruct every one
concern'd in the Play; a Mechanism, which my Inexperience,
as an *Actor*, made me incapable of'.[142] There was a distinct
worsening of the system of managerial control when the three
actor-managers disbanded in 1720, and at various points over

---

[139] Nicoll, *A History of English Drama*, ii. 279–80.

[140] Cibber, *Apology*, 291–2.

[141] Charles Shadwell, *The Humours of the Army* (1713), A3$^b$.

[142] Savage, *Overbury*, pp. ix–x. Drury, in *Rival Milliners*, pp. v–vii, calls Theophilus Cibber 'the Great Imperator', accuses him of 'Vanity' in his criticism, and
wonders whether his 'Prescience is the result of a never Erring Judgment, or proceeds
from a Spirit of Divination'. *Apology For . . . T—— C——, Comedian* (1740), 108,
mentions Theophilus' fury when he found his 'Power Clip'd in Relation of presiding
over Rehearsals'.

the next decade, as the theatre's fortunes fluctuated. And angry prefaces to plays illustrate how the absence of managerial help was thought debilitating. Hawling describes how the managers attended the rehearsal of his *Impertinent Lovers*—or at least claimed to have done so—but have been unable to rally the actors to do likewise; when the author turned up to see his play rehearsed, 'I had a formal Excuse made me, That the Company had not Regularly attended the Rehearsals, and they began to be fearful they should not be capable of Playing it'.[143] In a strongly critical anonymous play entitled *The Author's Triumph,* the lackadaisical Manager is made to say that he will attend the company for the evening's performance, but that he's sure 'You won't want me at the Rehearsal'.[144] Benjamin Martyn relates about Drury Lane in 1730 that his *Timoleon* 'was but a Fortnight in Rehearsal, and . . . no Assistance was given by either of the Managers in attending any one of the Rehearsals'.[145] Intrusive as managers were, they controlled actors and helped insecure playwrights; when they exercised their authority, playwrights felt manipulated; when they ceased to have authority, playwrights felt stranded.

Managers, particularly when they had already revised a play during the acceptance procedure, had feelings of ownership for the text; when they attended rehearsals they became like the 'attached' playwrights of the previous century. *A Proposal for the Better Regulation of the Stage* (1732) is a prolonged whine about the power managers and actors wield over authors. To an outsider's eye, the text argues, the stage of former times and the stage now may appear to be run along the same lines, but, explains the writer 'the Managers were not then so great, neither were Authors so little'.[146] And this is indeed the case—under Betterton, managers were only part of the process of preparing a play for the stage, and 'theatricalizers', who often were not managers, took many of the important decisions. Under Cibber, of course, the roles of theatricalizer and manager had become linked, leaving the author no means of redress if he did not like what the manager was doing. An interesting example of

[143] Hawling, *Impertinent*, p. vi.
[144] 'Lover of the Muses', *The Author's Triumph* (1737), 24.
[145] Martyn, *Timoleon*, A4ᵃ.
[146] *Proposal for . . . Regulation*, 28.

the overinvolvement of managers is offered by Steele, who himself held the patent to the theatre, and was technically an authority over Cibber. Unsurprisingly, in the *Conscious Lovers* he gratefully thanks Cibber for his 'Care and Application in instructing the Actors, and altering the Disposition of the Scenes'; more telling, however, is his later retraction of the acknowledgement: on second thoughts he decided that the changes Cibber had made to the play were ham-fisted and injurious.[147] When Fleetwood finally acquired the Drury Lane patent, Aaron Hill was delighted, primarily because he hoped that this would at last put an end 'to that mean submission that . . . had been exacted by the proud manager [Cibber] who . . . has treated [poets] with the contempt more justly due to himself'.[148] One problem was that managers' textual changes tended to be made for reasons of theatrical rather than literary expedience—their alterations were therefore generally unpopular with writers, and generally popular with the actors. The author of *The Author's Triumph*, 'Lover of the Muses' (whose muse has been considerably curtailed), prints in italics 'the Passages excepted against by the managing Player'. Ironically, the very lines in *Author's Triumph* in which the fictional playwright boasts his authorial power over the actors have been unceremoniously lopped: '*you* [actors] *are not upon the Par with an Author*', reads a censored section, '*What is a Player, pray, . . . but the Factors of the Poet's Wit*'. As the play is left, the section hops from the Manager's 'My Lord, Authors are a Pack of Scoundrels' to Maecenas' 'Ho'now, Impertinent!', giving the text a very different reading.[149] For actors, managerial revision was much better than authorial revision; managers were not possessive over every word in the text, and were willing to make changes. In Edward Phillips's *Stage-Mutineers*, the actress Madam Haughty actually refuses a part because the author will not permit Mr Pistol the manager to rework it.[150]

Finally, managers might take upon themselves the creation of the prototype for the characters that the play was to consist of—

---

[147] Richard Steele, *The Conscious Lovers* (1723), Z2[b]; See Loftis, *Steele*, 192.

[148] Hill, *Prompter*, 35.

[149] 'Lover of the Muses', *Author's Triumph*, A3[b]-A4[a].

[150] Phillips, *Stage-Mutineers*, 6. 'Pistol' is a reference to Theophilus Cibber, famous for playing that role.

something else that, a few years earlier, had been partly the playwrights' prerogative. In the (managerially censored) *Stage-Mutineers* 'the managers' are allowed to claim that the actors are 'but our Vassals, and we are to consider 'em in no other Light than as they are useful to us'.[151] Indeed, the more experimental managers, Giffard at Goodman's Fields, Aaron Hill briefly at Drury Lane, Fielding at the New Haymarket, were always heartily, and perhaps overly involved in the preparation of plays, taking upon themselves the instruction of the actors to an intrusive degree. Fielding 'was not merely content to revise The Fatal Curiosity', he also '[instructed] the actors how to do justice to their parts'.[152] He himself depicts a frank manager-and-actor tussle at rehearsal, with each trying to dictate to the other the way a part should be played: 'the Manager comes out [of Covent Garden Playhouse door]; the *Tragedy King* repeats a Speech out of a Play; the Manager and he quarrel about an Emphasis'.[153] On the other hand, Lillo was grateful for Fielding's help, for authors expected to have a talented superior in charge. The problem was that authors and managers did not share clear ideas about what form managerial support should take.

## Actors and rehearsal

Acting continued to be very much part-based, even to the point of absurdity: Addison writes of operas in which the main singer, imported from Italy, performed his part in Italian, while the subsidiary singers performed in English, so that the opera remained a loose collection of separate parts even in performance.[154] The same criticisms are raised as before: that actors perform only while actually speaking; and that their performances show that they do not know the story of the play they are acting in—or care about it:

They relax themselves as soon as any speech in their own part is over, into an absent unattentiveness to whatever is replied by another, looking round and examining the company of spectators with an ear only watchful of the cue, at which, like soldiers upon the word of command, they start suddenly back to their postures[155]

---

[151] Ibid. 22.  [152] *Lillo's . . . Works*, i. 12.
[153] Direction in Fielding, *Tumble*, 17.  [154] *Spectator*, i. 80.
[155] Hill, *Prompter*, 78.

Actorial additions, therefore, continued to be largely part-based
or circumstantial (having no reference either to the part or the
play). Parts were still 'a kind of *Property, not to be taken away
without Injustice*',[156] and extemporization remained the major
way of asserting oneself against the constraints of a taught part,
allowing actors the freedom of changing their roles to suit
themselves. Comedy lent itself readily to extemporization: ''Tis
what the top-Players often do' explains Plotwell.[157] Indeed, the
comedy actor Henry Norris was purposely called upon to
supply an extempore epilogue when the original was having
licensing problems—so that, absurdly, unlicensed extempore
was allowed to replace unlicensed text.[158] Another actor
famous for his skill at extemporization was William Pinkethman, who 'could not forsake' chatting to the galleries on a
regular basis. He was 'content' to receive three strokes from
Wilks's cane whenever he had held too much converse with the
gods, but Wilks himself is accredited with the old joke of
rebuking a member of the audience who had thrown an
orange at him with 'this is not a *civil* Orange'.[159] As has
often been pointed out, the early eighteenth century was the
age of the actor rather than of the author, but the antagonism
between the two is less frequently referred to. Major actors had
regular yearly benefits—and sometimes twice-yearly benefits—
from March onwards, at the most congenial time of the year.
Authors took their benefits when actors allowed their plays to
be staged, generally between November and February.[160]
Actors altered authors' plays: there is a special kind of irony
in the intention expressed by the players in the anonymous
*Author's Triumph* that they will drive out authors and write
texts themselves—they are claiming not just to despise writers,
but to be more capable of writing than them.[161] At the same
time, actors' performances were rescuing the texts in their
charge; whatever they did to enliven the often stilted poetry
and wooden dialogues died with them; few plays of the period

---

[156] *Daily Journal*, 17 Jan. 1737.                    [157] Gay, *Three Hours*, 16.
[158] Susanna Centlivre, *The Perplex'd Lovers* (1712), A3[a–b].
[159] Davies, *Miscellanies*, iii. 51; George Stayley, *The Life and Opinions of an Actor*, 2
vols. (1762), ii. 57.
[160] *London Stage*, II, pp. xcvi, clvi.
[161] 'Lover of the Muses', *Author's Triumph*, 15.

survive a modern reading. Often, and hardly surprisingly, there are examples of actors clearly using their texts simply as vehicles for their own set-pieces—set-pieces that may be at a total remove from the script itself. But when the set-pieces become political rants, actors start to run into danger with the government:

At the performance of Love Runs all Dangers . . . one of the Comedians took the liberty to throw out some Reflections upon the Prime Minister and the Excise, which were not designed by the Author; Lord Walpole, being in the House, went behind the Scenes, and demanded of the Prompter, whether such Words were in the Play, and he answering they were not, his Lordship immediately corrected the Comedian with his own hands very severely.[162]

Occasions such as this, as much as specific 'party plays', were behind the Licensing Act of 1737.

Physical extemporization continued—sometimes criticized for being obviously extraneous, not to say uncouth, as when Pinkethman 'shuffled down his Breeches' while doing a dance.[163] Other, more subtle freedoms of physical extemporization also persisted and often did good things for bad texts: actors' superiority is manifest in claims that, for instance, a sophisticated performance might elevate a mediocre play—'strong Applauses have follow'd from a just and fine Posture, without being indebted to the Poet's Thought or Expression.'[164]

---

[162] *London Stage*, III, p. clxvii. Killigrew complains that 'one should not blame him for . . . what the actors can add on their own when playing their roles, because his power does not go so far as to force actors to present the plays precisely as he had corrected them'—see Judith Milhous and Robert Hume, 'Charles Killigrew's Petition about the Master of the Revel's Power as Censor (1715)', *TN* 41 (1987), 74–9 (76). After the Licensing Act of 1737, such freedom was no longer allowed: 'I have myself often seen a thin pale man looking over the Prompter's book at the stage-door almost during the performance of a whole play; . . . he was the Deputy Licencer, and . . . he stood there to see if any words were spoke on the stage which were not in the book,' Thomas Cooke, *The Mournful Nuptials* (1739), p. viii.

[163] *Weekly Journal or Saturday's Post*, 20 Jan. 1722, quoted in *London Stage*, II, p. cxxv.

[164] *Censor*, iii. 205. See also *Spectator*, iv. 453–4.

PERFORMANCE

*The prompter and performance*

The prompter owned the prompt-book—often the only full copy
of a play in existence, generally the only full copy in the
playhouse. Actors had separate parts, so the play in its com-
pleteness was a sacred rarity that not only unified but created
performance: when Cibber took the book of *King John* away,
performance could no longer happen.[165] The prompter's complete text united the disparate parts, and, for the actors, the
prompter, like the book, was a linchpin holding the whole
production together.

While a play was happening, the prompter was in control. He
co-ordinated props, music, the curtain, and entrances (Chetwood's marked-up prompt-book of *The Old Batchelor* indicates
whether entrances are to be 'prompt side' (P.S.) or 'opposite
prompt' (O.P.)[166]); he confined running-time and provided
relevant sound effects. Like a conductor, he paced the production, prompting not just words, but timing, so that actors did not
dare 'to crack a joke till [he] gave them the cue, and the most
despairing of lovers [refrained] from sighs and tears till they had
his permission to be miserable'.[167] *The Prompter*, a theatrical bi-
weekly periodical, refers to the continued use of the prompter's
bell and whistle—the bell to indicate an act break, the whistle to
herald a change of scene.[168] These mechanical devices intruded
audibly into plays and were part of the theatrical event: '[*a Bell
rings*,]' reads a stage direction in the anonymous *Wanton Jesuit*,
to which the Player responds 'I perceive the Actors are dressed,
and it is time to entertain the Audience'; James Miller's *An
Hospital for Fools* has an actor demanding 'Mr. *Chetwood*, ring
for the Overture'.[169] To the audience, the prompter, with his
devices for directing a play from the stage, was somehow part of
that play itself: so that to both actors and audience the prompter

---

[165] Barker, *Cibber*, 182.

[166] Leo Hughes and A. H. Scouten, 'Congreve at Drury Lane: Two Eighteenth
Century Prompt Books', *MP* 79 (1981), 146–56.

[167] Hill, *Prompter*, 1. See also Davies' suggestion that *2 Henry IV*, 4.1, was 'dull'
owing to 'the frittering of the scene by the prompter', *Miscellanies*, i. 173.

[168] Hill, *Prompter*, 1–2; *The Wanton Jesuit* (1731), B2ᵇ.

[169] *The Wanton Jesuit*, B2ᵇ; James Miller, *An Hospital for Fools* (1739), B2ᵇ.

was at the heart of the play, skilfully timing its progress and bringing the disparate parts together; the prompter, negotiating between unified text and disparate actors, scenes and music, was, though half-hidden, a kind of focus for the performance itself.

## CONCLUSION

### *The first-night audience*

As before, the first performance was the test of a text, and was therefore part of the revision stage: the text on its opening night had not yet been 'fixed', which throws some light on the attitude actors of the time had to rehearsal. It continued to be usual for a play to be premièred on a Saturday, leaving Sunday free for corrections before the second performance; authors still received benefits on third and sixth nights.[170] Play prefaces are full of references to authorial changes made after first performance, as a direct response to audience criticism: 'The Second Night the particular Things objected to, being taken out, the Play was acted from Beginning to End, without one single Mark of Displeasure in the Audience' writes William Popple of *The Lady's Revenge*.[171] Robert Dodsley adds a couplet to his *Sir John Cockle at Court*:

> Small Faults, we hope, with Candour you'll excuse,
> Nor harshly treat a self-convicted Muse . . .

He footnotes the couplet, explaining:

These two Lines were added after the first Night's Performance, occasioned by some Things which the Audience very justly found Fault with; and which, the second Time, were left out or alter'd as much as possible: And the Author takes this Opportunity of thanking the Town for so judiciously and favourably correcting him.[172]

It seems to have been relatively normal for a play to be too long at the first performance—audience approval and disapproval

---

[170] *London Stage*, II, p. clvi.
[171] Popple, *Lady's Revenge*, A4ª.
[172] Robert Dodsley, *Sir John Cockle at Court* (1738), A3ᵇ.

would then hone down the text for subsequent performances.[173] This did not always work, of course: Gabriel Odingsells mangled his play to suit the audience, but 'When the Town thought fit to pass Sentence on this trifling Piece, corrected by their Judgment, I determin'd to finish the Execution, and bury it in Oblivion'.[174]

The audience, watching a series of parts brought together, tended themselves to think in part terms rather than in terms of the play as a unity. There are several examples of this: one shows the audience taking exception to a single part—that of the Nonconforming Pastor—in Charles Coffey's *Devil to Pay*, so that the play was subsequently revised with 'that Part left out'; the other shows an (admittedly country) audience becoming bored with Mrs Charke's part of Pyrrhus in Ambrose Philips's *The Distrest Mother*, and asking her to intermingle it with the part of Scrub, 'assuring me, it would give much more Satisfaction to the Spectators'.[175] Despite the new ideas about collective rehearsal and ensemble production being hesitantly explored in the theatres, audiences, trained in the old ways, still tended to watch plays from a part-based standpoint.

### The author and the text

Strangely, given their general objection to theatre people changing their texts, playwrights continued to solicit pre-performance alterations by the literati as a sign of approval. Authors of the period readily pander to the nobility by adopting their words and thoughts into the text. When thanking people for their useful help, the rank and reputation of the helper is usually made abundantly clear—the text subsumes into itself the reputation of its corrector: 'I must now do my

[173] See Vanbrugh, *The Provok'd Husband*, completed by Cibber (1728), a1[a]: 'the Reader will . . . find here a Scene or two of the Lower Humour, that were left out after the first Day's Presentation'; Theophilus Cibber, *The Lover* (1730), A4[a]: 'The Reader will find several Speeches printed in this Play, which were omitted in the Performance, after the First Night, to avoid an improper Length.'

[174] Gabriel Odingsells, *Bays Opera* (1730), A2[a]. For examples of other theatrical issues being submitted to the audience, see *London Stage*, III, pp. clxvi–clxvii.

[175] Mottley, *List*, 199; Charke, *Art of Management*, 208. At the performance of *Caelia: Or the Perjur'd Lover* (1733), the author Charles Johnson 'Had the Mortification to . . . hear the Characters of Mother *Lupine* and her Women disapprov'd by several of the Audience' (1733, A4a).

self the pleasure to address those Gentlemen of known Judgement and great Candour, whose Corrections (tho' in so short a
time for making them) have done me Honour, and given
Reputation to the Piece.'[176] 'Correction' by the literati or
nobility was such a status symbol that William Grodall actually
complains when no one will change his text for him: a rich
person, he gripes, 'shall have an hundred Perusals, and a
thousand Amendments, and not one of them his own', but
'there's a great Difference between a Person of Fortune, who
writes at his Leisure, and has his Purse to correct his Works,
and a Person who has neither Time, Money, nor Learning'.[177]
In other words, rich writers could buy not only reputation but
stageability: poor writers had to rely on their own talents.

Revision by the Lord Chamberlain was, before 1737, somewhat unpredictable. He was often not given the play until just
before performance, with the result that his corrections may well
have been ignored on stage (as censorship does not extend to
printed texts, corrections are not necessarily included in published plays[178]). In extreme cases the Lord Chamberlain's only
redress for a play that needed substantial alteration was to ban it:
Henry Brooke's *Gustavus Vasa* 'was forbid to be acted, by an
Order from the Lord Chamberlain, when it had been rehearsed
at the Theatre Royal in *Drury-Lane*, and the Actors all ready in
their Parts'; John Gay's *Polly* was stopped by 'a Message . . .
from the Lord *Chamberlain*, that *it was not allowed to be acted*'
just when 'every Thing was ready for a Rehearsal of it'.[179] After
1737, however, the new, stricter laws required the Lord Chamberlain to be given a complete copy of the play two weeks before
performance, which, technically, meant that actors and managers could no longer continue to alter the play either over the
fortnight preceding performance, or as a result of the first night
itself; but there is no sign that these rules were rigidly observed
after the first few years.[180]

---

[176] William Havard, *King Charles the First* (1737), A3[b]. Boswell explains that
Cibber had a similar reason for giving *The Careless Husband* to Anne Mason to
revise—Boswell, *Life of Johnson*, i. 174 n.
[177] *The False Guardians Outwitted* from William Goodall, *True Englishman's
Miscellany* (1740), A2[a].
[178] See L. W. Conolly, *The Censorship of English Drama 1737–1824* (San Marino,
Calif., 1976), 5.
[179] Mottley, *List*, 182, 239.           [180] Conolly, *Censorship*, 15.

Plays were strongly re-authored during the rehearsal process, by actors, but also by managers and prompters, and given that the correcting manager (Cibber) and the correcting prompter (Chetwood) held their respective positions for such a number of years, most plays produced at Drury Lane during the early eighteenth century will, in some way, have born their insignia. Revision after the first night was still practised; revision for a revival might be very severe indeed: it was not unusual for a moderately successful play after its initial production to be pruned to its most popular section and reintroduced as an afterpiece, like Coffey's *The Devil to Pay* which was 'cut shorter, and so reduced to one Act'.[181] Confident authors wrote texts that were flexible and left room for development in the theatre. Fielding catered for actor intrusion by allowing small regulated moments of freedom into a text: sometimes he simply leaves suggestions for actors to extemporize around, as in *Tumble Down Dick* where, in a long stage direction, 'the *Tragedy King* repeats a Speech out of a Play; the Manager and he quarrel'.[182] Similarly in Henry Carey's *Hanging and Marriage* (1722) Mother Stubble cries 'Aw law! . . . what shall I do, &c' and the stage direction suggests she add 'a great deal more of this stuff'.[183] The nature of correction in the theatre left the actor more of these freedoms: when Congreves's *The Double Dealer* was censored for eighteenth-century performance, the prompter removed terms likely to upset the delicate sensibilities of the audience (like 'bepiss') but did not replace the missing word in the text, leaving it 'to be supplied, one supposes, by the actor'.[184] Sensible writers were learning to leave bits of their text open, possessive writers were having revision imposed on them. Even authors' choice of which version of the play to send to the printers reflected this dichotomy: disappointed authors often publish from a version of the pre-performance text (and sometimes from the pre-rehearsal text); successful authors either had very little interest in the state of the printed text

---

[181] Mottley, *List*, 199. See also Ayres, *Sancho*, A2$^b$: '[the manager] was of Opinion, that if it was judiciously cut, or shorten'd, it would make an excellent Entertainment, but thought it would not furnish a whole Night'.

[182] Fielding, *Tumble*, 17.

[183] Quoted in Nicoll, *A History of English Drama*, ii. 42.

[184] Hughes, 'Congreve at Drury Lane', 154.

or its provenance, or chose a post-performance text.[185] Later in the eighteenth century, with Garrick's carefully managed rehearsals, there was even less room for playwrights who would not give way over—or give up—their textual ownership.

[185] The embittered prefaces I have quoted front pre-performance texts (sometimes indicating theatrical cuts with italics); for the attitude of successful playwrights, see Shirley Strum Kenny, 'The Publication of Plays', in Robert D. Hume (ed.), *The London Theatre World, 1660–1800* (Carbondale, Ill., 1980), 318. Kenny also draws attention to successful playwrights who published separately their post-performance texts (p. 327).

# 6

# Rehearsal in Garrick's Theatre— and Later

John Rich remained in charge of Covent Garden until his death in 1761; he was replaced by John Beard, actor, singer, and son-in-law to Rich. In Drury Lane, Charles Fleetwood, who was technically manager from 1734 to 1745, delegated rehearsals and other managerial duties to Charles Macklin. During the early 1740s, Fleetwood's actors became increasingly unhappy at their unstable salaries and insolent treatment; with Macklin and the young David Garrick at the helm, they finally organized a rebellion. That December, many, including Garrick, returned and signed a new agreement with Fleetwood. Macklin felt let down, and Fleetwood felt, ultimately, unable to cope: he put the patent up for sale, and two businessmen bought it. They were quickly succeeded by the actor James Lacy, who joined with Garrick to purchase the patent in 1747. Garrick was manager of Drury Lane from then until 1776, when he retired; his share in the theatre, and managerial duties, were both taken up by Richard Brinsley Sheridan. In 1779, Garrick died.

Garrick is famous for revolutionizing acting itself in the eighteenth century, introducing a new form of 'naturalism', and casting aside the old inherited parts, some of them now third- or fourth- hand. He is often praised for his dedication to carefully rehearsed productions, and this chapter will discuss exactly what comprised that rehearsal. It will show that 'new acting' did not lead to new preparation, or new ways of thinking about the text, but was imposed within the old preparation and performance framework.

REHEARSAL PLAYS

*The Critic* had not been fully written when it was put into rehearsal, and the actors had to lock its author Richard Sheridan into the green room to make him complete it.[1] *Pizarro* (1779), also by Sheridan, was still unfinished as its first performance started; the last act was delivered to the actors during the production, and learnt between scene-breaks. Young Primmer, a parody of Sheridan in *The Critick Anticipated*, is late to a rehearsal of his own play;[2] 'of all authors', declared the *Morning Chronicle*, Sheridan was 'the least anxious about having his own works well produced'.[3] Sheridan's famous rehearsal play *The Critic*, on the other hand, shows, as ever, a careful dress-rehearsal overlooked by a hysterically anxious author: it follows the format established by Buckingham's seventeenth-century play *The Rehearsal*, and has nothing to do with actual rehearsal as practised by Sheridan.

Buckingham's *Rehearsal* continued to provide a useful formula for parodies, for it allowed a satire to be accompanied by a commentary. So popular had the form become, that 'rehearsal' in a play was a shorthand way of indicating that the scenes to follow were to be burlesques; Samuel Foote's otherwise unnecessary 'rehearsal' introduction to *The Minor* serves just this purpose. Naturally, rehearsal plays were at a remove from the business of rehearsal itself, with which they were not, after all, concerned. This is often indicated in their titles which stress a connection, not to real rehearsal, but to Buckingham's prototype—*The New Rehearsal, or Bayes the Younger; Bayes in Chromatics; The Rehearsal, or Bayes in Petticoats*.[4] Such plays take up not just Buckingham's framework, but his depiction of rehearsal itself, sharing recognizable generic qualities with each other but not with eighteenth-century practice. So, though only 'in cases where much was expected of the performance' were plays actually given dress-rehearsals,[5] rehearsal plays continued

---

[1] Smith, *Plays . . . from 1671*, 141.

[2] 'R.B.S. Esq', *The Critick Anticipated* (1779).

[3] Quoted in Richard Brinsley Sheridan, *The Dramatic Works*, ed. Cecil Price, 2 vols. (Oxford, 1973), i. 298.

[4] See Dane Farnsworth Smith and M. L. Lawhon, *Plays about the Theatre in England, 1737–1800* (New Jersey, 1979), 14.

[5] Thomas Shepherd Munden, *Memoirs of Joseph Shepherd Munden, comedian: by his son* (1844), 307.

to take place in stage costume, a fact that then had to be explained away:

PROMPTER. 'Tis a very extraordinary thing, indeed, to rehearse only one act of a performance, and with dress and decorations as if it were really before an audience.

PATENT. It is a novelty indeed . . . We shan't often repeat the same experiment   (*A Peep Behind the Curtain*).[6]

Similarly, though in reality visitors were generally discouraged from turning up at rehearsals (Garrick wrote to a member of the nobility explaining that when 'noble and learned gentlemen [intrude]' on his practice, 'annoyance exceeds honour'[7]), in rehearsal plays where the 'gentlemen' were a necessary critical presence, visitors continued to be warmly invited to attend. Such plays, despite their fictional rehearsal, gave the appearance of being up to date, because they were in other respects 'contemporary'. They were performed, often *in propria persona*, by actors and even prompters: 'Hopkins', the Drury Lane prompter, was a walk-on in *A Peep Behind the Curtain*; Kitty Clive performed the title role in her own *Bayes in Petticoats*, where she complained about the bad attitude of such actresses as 'Mrs. Clive'.[8] But Mrs Clive's 'Bayes' contained another level of theatrical reference, for the actress had earlier cross-dressed to play the *Rehearsal* Bayes in breeches, which 'she did . . . most wretchedly':[9] her new Bayes was directed towards the critics who had aimed at her acting, showing that she was fully capable of playing the part—on her own terms. Fiction met reality and commented on it in eighteenth-century rehearsal plays, which provided a forum for 'modern' theatrical observations, within a mythical and pseudo-historical framework.

Garrick kept *The Rehearsal* itself in vogue, though it was so

---

[6] David Garrick, *The Plays*, ed. Harry William Pedicord and Fredrick Louis Bergman, 7 vols. (Carbondale, Ill., 1982), ii. 76. Though Smith and Lawhon, *Plays . . . 1737–1800*, 14 claim that, for instance, *A Peep Behind* is 'decidedly contemporary', they are contradicted by reviews of the time which criticize its attempt to take on 'the design of The Old Rehearsal'—see the *Theatrical Monitor*, quoted in *Plays of Garrick*, ii. 330.

[7] 'David Garrick at Rehearsal', p. 80 of *Behind the Curtain*, n.d. attached to vol. ii of an extra-illustrated *Life of Garrick* by Davies (1780), Folger Library, Bd.W.W.b.473–6.

[8] Catherine [Kitty] Clive, *The Rehearsal, or Bayes in Petticoats* (1753), 14.

[9] Quoted in *London Stage*, III, 1055.

outdated that no one really understood the brunt of its criticism—its popularity rested, claimed 'Theatricus' in 1776, on
Garrick's performance.[10] What Garrick actually did was to use
the medium of Bayes to criticize contemporary acting, changing
the play's thrust from the 'bombast poets of a former day', to 'the
absurd stile of acting' that he was struggling to update.[11] 'Bayes'
was a biting parody of the mannered performances of the now
elderly generation, and was directed towards proponents of
'rant' and 'tone', particularly the aged Colley Cibber, whose
heart, Arthur Murphy claimed, was broken by the viciousness of
Garrick's attack.[12] Other actors caricatured by Garrick's Bayes
over the years included Dennis Delane, Roger Bridgwater,
William Mills, Sacheverel Hale, and even Henry Giffard, Garrick's mentor.[13] Yet, as Garrick played him, Bayes was patheti-
cally unaware of 'all the ridicule of the part', and ignorant of the
jokes that were being made at his expense:[14] though Garrick was
using the anti-hero to attack other performers, he also fashionably sentimentalized the character, making him more likeable
than before, an effect he often had on the parts he undertook.
Against the tired inherited roles that audiences were used to
seeing, Garrick offered fresh interpretations, in which familiar
*dramatis personae* were not only revitalized but made more
sympathetic.[15] Garrick reinvented established characterizations,
turning them into thoroughly eighteenth-century products; as a
result, he lost the 'archetypical' performances that had survived
(in mutilated form) in inherited roles.

This new Bayes did, however, have to remain superficially 'old-
fashioned' to exploit the authority that historical distancing had
given to *The Rehearsal* (Thomas Davies seriously compares
Buckingham's burlesque to *Don Quixote* and the comedies of
the Greeks[16]). In revisions, Garrick left the dated 'ayes' and
'egads' in *The Rehearsal,* though his extemporizations were
decidedly up to date, thereby also keeping in view Bayes'
'modern' application. Richard Cross, the prompter, records

---

[10] Quoted in James J. Lynch, *Box, Pit, and Gallery* (1953; Berkeley, 1971), 146.

[11] Arthur Murphy, *The Life of David Garrick Esq.*, 2 vols. (1801), i. 51.

[12] *The Theatrical Review: Volume 2* (1772), 152; Arthur Murphy, *The Spouter* (1756), 24.   [13] *Plays of Garrick*, v. 312.

[14] Thomas Davies, *Dramatic Miscellanies*, 3 vols. (Dublin, 1784), iii. 180.

[15] See Leigh Woods, *Garrick Claims the Stage* (Westport, Conn., 1984), 35.

[16] Davies, *Miscellanies*, iii. 170, 172.

that when the actor Edward (Ned) Shuter took a place in the Covent Garden Company 'Garrick in Bayes said you are a good Actor & I am sorry you have left me'.[17] Bayes now carefully straddled the old and new: 'old' enough for his criticism to have the authority of a past age; 'new' enough to be a direct comment on the modern theatre.

Garrick also widened the thrust of Bayes, writing new plays for him, and encouraging others to do likewise. In his various incarnations, Bayes was obsessed with the composition of operas, the teaching of acting, the managing of theatres: the only constant was that whatever Bayes thought he could do, he patently could not. In this way, the critical range aimed at in the character of Bayes extended over every aspect of the modern theatre. At the same time, Bayes also kept his ennobling link with his seventeenth-century model in most modern dramas: in *Meeting of the Company*, Bayes tells the contemporary Drury Lane acting troupe that 'you and your players used me and my play very ill', as though the events of Buckingham's *Rehearsal* had just taken place with them.[18] Garrick was also careful to keep secondary Bayes figures slightly apart from the Bayes of *The Rehearsal*, making sure that the power of the latter was never seriously undercut by a second-rate or mistimed modern production. Garrick himself, for instance, would perform the *Rehearsal* Bayes and no others; the lasting, historical Bayes was linked to but separated from the imitations.

The audience, who had long enjoyed rehearsal plays, readily accepted the performance-like rehearsals that such plays offered. But there were specific kinds of performance with strong 'rehearsal' elements that gave additional credence to such plays. First nights continued to be 'rehearsals' (this will be discussed below), but so, at one stage, were all 'illegitimate' performances. The 1737 Licensing Act, which permitted only two companies to act professionally, forced other troupes wishing to perform to find 'formulas' to signify that they were putting on a play. One offered an expensive 'dish of tea' for which a 'rehearsal' was thrown in free; another offered 'a

---

[17] Richard Cross and William Hopkins, *Diary 1747–1776: Drury Lane*, 13 vols., Folger Library MS, W.a.104, 21 May 1753. Some other Garrick ad libs made while in the character of Bayes are listed in *Plays of Garrick*, v. 313.

[18] *Plays of Garrick*, ii. 241.

Concert' including 'Gratis a Rehearsal'.[19] Some performances therefore were, in form, 'rehearsals', similar in nature to rehearsal plays, but not similar to any other kind of rehearsal. This chapter will explore the way productions were mounted in the eighteenth century, against a background of rehearsal plays. It will cover the period from the first performance of Garrick in 1741 to shortly after his death in 1779, for Garrick was a perfectionist, who knew more about actual eighteenth-century rehearsal than most, yet who maintained and even promoted the *Rehearsal* myth in his writing.

## PUBLIC THEATRE REHEARSAL

### *Number of rehearsals*

The theatrical season began in September with three performances a week, increasing to six performances by mid-October. Just before the start of the season, and in the early stages of the season itself, more rehearsal time was available, but the total number of new plays mounted was remarkably small in comparison with earlier years, which meant that there was more time in general for preparation. After the 1737 Licensing Act, only the two legitimate theatres were allowed to put on plays, and though others struggled on for a time, and the Haymarket eventually obtained permission to function as a summer theatre,[20] there were, during the season itself, usually only two theatres in operation. They occasionally sparred, but on the whole had an equitable relationship: Rich, at Covent Garden, showed a marked preference for light-hearted pantomimes, and was largely uninterested in the trouble of getting up new plays; Garrick, in Drury Lane, put on fine performances of the staple stock productions, and mounted about four new plays a year.[21] The programme for the evening in both theatres continued to be varied, consisting of a mainpiece, interspersed

---

[19] Cecil Price, *Theatre in the Age of Garrick* (Oxford, 1973), 4; *Daily Advertiser*, 25 Aug. 1744, quoted in *London Stage*, III, p. lv.

[20] See Lynch, *Box*, 122.

[21] See ibid. 124–6; *London Stage*, IV: *1747–1776*, ed. George Winchester Stone, Jr. (Carbondale, Ill., 1962), pp. clxii–clxvi.

with 'entertainments', and an afterpiece; new afterpieces were also regular features of both theatres.[22]

Garrick was strict, and plays were carefully prepared under him, so that 'rehearsals were held frequently both of new plays and revivals'.[23] So many accounts exist that praise Garrick's care in rehearsing, that modern critics sometimes imagine that the one month given, as ever, to normal production, was spent in constant practice.[24] Records do not suggest this. Garrick did rehearse more carefully than his predecessors, but his care consisted in more 'study', known sometimes, confusingly, as 'individual rehearsal' (and 'rehearsal' for short), and in more 'partial' rehearsals, which, together, did not amount to more than a few hours of rehearsal in all. George Anne Bellamy makes clear what 'frequent' rehearsal might mean. She records the 'indefatigable pains' that were undergone over *The Orphan of China*: 'We rehearsed three times a day, and . . . got the piece ready for representation in less than a week',[25] a total of fifteen to eighteen rehearsals at most. This does emerge as being extraordinary against other records. Robert Jephson's *Count of Narbonne* was given two full rehearsals, and Horace Walpole, who was overseeing the production, complained because he was obliged to spend 'three hours each time, on two several days, in a cold theatre with the gout on me'.[26] Slightly later, for the well-documented year of 1794, Charles Beecher Hogan has found examples of four full and six partial rehearsals for a new play

---

[22] *London Stage*, IV, pp. clxvi–clxix.

[23] Munden, *Memoirs*, 307.

[24] For records of a month in production see Hume, *London Theatre World*, 176; and Kalman A. Burnim, *David Garrick: Director* (Carbondale, Ill., 1961), 46. Burnim also believes that this time was often spent in constant rehearsal: see 46–7. Reviewing Clinton-Baddeley's *All Right on the Night*, *PQ* 34 (1955), 256, Arthur Scouten rightly criticizes the idea that rehearsals were not taken seriously under Garrick. But there is a difference between being serious and rehearsing intensively. Scouten argues that during 1767 Sylas Neville attended a theatre 'on one night out of three', often read the play before the performance began, and always noted altered stage business: Neville, he claims, would have recorded the fact that a play was underrehearsed—if it had been. In fact *The Diary of Sylas Neville*, ed. Basil Cozens-Hardy (London, 1950), reveals that Neville only went to the theatre a total of nine times during the season in question, and only once bought a copy of the play he was to see in advance or made any reference at all to stage business.

[25] George Anne Bellamy, *An Apology for the life of George Anne Bellamy*, 5 vols., 3rd edn. (1785), iii. 181.

[26] Horace Walpole, *The Letters*, ed. Mrs Paget Toynbee, 16 vols. (Oxford, 1903–5), xii. 98.

(Richard Cumberland's *The Jew*) and two rehearsals for the
revival of a stock play (*Measure for Measure*, last performed nine
years previously).[27] As ever, rehearsals were in fact held not up
to a certain number, but until a play was ready: Richard Cross,
the prompter, notes that 'Harlequins Invasion is now ready
whenever the Managers will please to give it out.'[28]

Mrs Bellamy's fifteen odd rehearsals, if like other rehearsal
sessions of the time, would have consisted of a reading, many
private rehearsals, some partial rehearsals, a 'rough rehearsal',
and one or more general rehearsals. Partial rehearsals occupied
most of the group rehearsal period: Edward Cape Everard, as an
actor of small roles and figure dances, would be summoned 'At
ten o'clock, if you please, to As You Like It . . . At eleven, in the
Green Room, to the reading of the New Play . . . At twelve, to
Much ado' and so on.[29] In the Drury Lane of 1794, the
'business' was run through at eleven in the morning, and 'the
dialogue, and music at 12': business, dialogue and music, still
remained separate units of performance.[30] These partial rehearsals were held daily, usually in the morning,[31] though evening
rehearsals occasionally took place;[32] they lasted two hours at the
most—in George Colman's *True State of the Differences . . .
between the Proprietors of Covent Garden Theatre* rehearsals are
called for 'Mahamet at 10; Musical Lady at 12'.[33] The 'rough'
rehearsal that capped this process involved most of the company
and was attended by the manager and, sometimes, the author. It
illustrated the state the play had reached, and so determined how
much more preparation was necessary; it was therefore almost
certainly a rehearsal of the whole play. Thomas Harris told
Walpole that 'he had had a rough rehearsal yesterday morning'
and had been pleased enough to order 'a regular rehearsal on
Saturday'; Garrick told Joseph Reed to rehearse his play until it

---

[27] Hogan, 'An Eighteenth Century Prompter's Notes', 39.

[28] Cross–Hopkins, 1 Nov. 1763; on 12 Dec. 1763, note is made that '*The Company*
[is] *ready* to play the *Stratagem*'.

[29] Everard, *Memoirs*, 40. For other references to partial rehearsal see Joseph Reed,
*Theatrical Duplicity* (n.d., watermarked 1833), Folger Library MS, T.a.112, 82; Mrs
Inchbald, *Diaries*, Folger Library MS, M.a.152. *passim*; *Walpole*, xii. 95.

[30] See Hogan, 'Prompter's Notes', 39.

[31] George Colman the Younger, *New Hay at the Old Market* (1795), 31.

[32] See Bellamy, *Apology*, ii. 24.

[33] George Colman, *A True State of the Differences . . . between the Proprietors of
Covent Garden Theatre* (1768), 32.

was 'rough hew'd', after which he would supply the finishing touches.[34] But a letter sent by Garrick to Susannah Cibber is telling. He suggests that Arthur Murphy's new play *The Way to Keep Him* will 'require four or five regular Rehearsals at least . . . and tho *You* may be able to appear with two, Yet I am afraid the rest of the Dramatis Personae will be . . . disjointed if they have not the advantage of your Character to Rehearse with them'.[35] 'Capital' actors, it is clear, did their best not to frequent even final group rehearsals, partly because they were too proud, partly, as Garrick indicates, because their presence, though useful to others, would not greatly alter their own final performances. When the prompter in the anonymous *Theatrical Manager* writes to ask the player of Richard III to attend 'tomorrow Morning at the Rehearsal' because the tragedy is to be performed that same evening, he finds the actor unwilling to do even this.[36] Garrick himself was relatively helpless against major actors who were content to rehearse privately, but made it constantly clear that they were above group rehearsal. Mrs Cibber expected to be paid a higher wage simply for having shown up: 'I am Surprised' wrote Garrick, 'that She Should Urge an attendance upon Rehearsals as a Sufficient plea for her Sallary', especially as it was 'far from being the Case' that she had attended all the practices; Kitty Clive, in 1765, grudgingly consented to attend rehearsal 'if you could not do without me'.[37] The system of fines hardly indicates (as some have argued) that actors attended rehearsal more regularly. Mrs Clive simply complained when she was docked money 'for not coming to rehearse two parts that I could repeat in my sleep'; and Cross the prompter includes on his record of actors who did not attend a 'D.G.' (Garrick) rehearsal, the reason why they are to be let off: 'absent at Rehearsal of the Midsummer Night's dream . . . M$^r$ Obrien excus'd on acc$^t$ of playing'.[38]

---

[34] *Walpole*, xii. 85.; Reed, *Theatrical Duplicity*, 50.

[35] David Garrick, *The Letters*, ed. David M. Little and George M. Kahrl, 3 vols. (Oxford, 1963), i. 321.

[36] *The Theatrical Manager* (1751), 1–2.

[37] *Letters of Garrick*, i. 313; David Garrick, *The Private Correspondence*, ed. James Boaden, 2 vols. (1831–2), i. 204.

[38] *Correspondence of Garrick*, i. 203 (see also i. 374); 'Papers connected with the production of a version of A Midsummer Night's Dream', Folger Library MS, W.b.469. William O'Brien is clearly not performing at the time (Garrick is at

Capital actors were sometimes allowed to choose when they wanted their rehearsals, but this did not stop them from cancelling at the last minute. William Hopkins, Drury Lane's prompter, notes how 'A Rehearsal of *as you like It* was call'd by M^rs Barrys desire. At Ten she sent word to have the Rehearsal put off for half an hour the performers staid for her till past Eleven but she not coming they went away.'[39] The scenario was not abnormal. James Quin, approaching the part of Lear for the first time, had called twenty-two rehearsals, but actually attended only two of them, 'being at that time young and dissipated'.[40] The Prompter in the anonymous *Hodge Podge* explains to a new actor who is surprised to find himself alone at rehearsal, that 'the Theatre is Devoted to the Necessary Rehearsals—but nobody will attend them';[41] calling group rehearsals and having them were different matters. Under the pseudonym 'The Prompter before the Curtain' Garrick finally attacked his own actors in the *Morning Post*, claiming that 'Garrick' had overindulged them and was now the victim of their 'whims', for contemporary actors seemed to find it acceptable to miss not just rehearsals, but performances themselves.[42] Secondary actors on the other hand, were not always given the time necessary even for basic preparation. George Stayley, a minor actor, complained that while capital players might be allowed 'almost a Dozen Rehearsals', he himself had had to perform parts 'twice the Length of *Macbeth*' at two days' notice and with no rehearsal.[43] Likewise Mary Porter, in a letter to the Lord Chamberlain, boasts of occasions

rehearsal rather than on the stage): he must be unwilling to rehearse because he is playing that evening and has a part to prepare. More examples of fines are listed in *London Stage*, IV, p. liv. Stone also illustrates 'specific critical items which would seem to negate the Garrick accomplishment of producing excellent ensemble acting' (p. xciv), but argues that these are special instances. Compare this with V. C. Clinton-Baddeley's claim, in *All Right on the Night* (London, 1954), 84, that 'there was no team work in the Georgian Theatre'.

[39] Hopkins, 'A Memorandum Book', MS in R. J. Smith, *A Collection of Material,* viii. British Library, 11826. R.S.

[40] Davies, *Miscellanies*, ii. 179; see also George Stayley, *The Rival Theatres* (1737), 24, where the prompter, seeing how few people have turned up, is made to observe that 'I don't see we are likely to have any Rehearsal this morning'.

[41] *The Hodge Podge* (1781), Larpent MS, l.a.569.

[42] Charles Harold Gray, *Theatrical Criticism in London* (1931, New York, 1964), 233.

[43] George Stayley, *The Life and Opinions of an Actor*, 2 vols. (1762), i. 60.

when she studied principal parts 'at a night's notice' and played them perfectly the following day.[44]

Various factors affected the amount of group rehearsal a play would be given. For instance, actors' 'benefits'—when individual actors would be given the revenue for a particular night's performance—were held towards the end of the season. Benefits always caused huge tension, not least because players were sometimes positively unwilling to rehearse for each other's 'night', as the Prompter explains in *The Hodge Podge*, meaning that plays rehearsed after March (when actors' benefits began) were often less well prepared.[45] Kalman A. Burnim argues that stock plays were always put on with diligence, but the fact is that, as ever, circumstance determined whether a play would be afforded much time or not. When the king was to attend the theatre, 'I will order a Rehearsal of Macbeth immediatly [*sic*] . . . No Time shall be lost in getting the Play up'; similarly nineteen days were spent in rehearsals for a royal performance of *Cymbeline* at Covent Garden, 1767.[46] But Thomas Davies boasts of 'the frequent rehearsal' of Jonson's *Every Man in His Humour*, as a way of proving 'Garrick's great anxiety for its public approbation':[47] not all plays, new or old, were so treated. In fact, stock plays regularly performed were not usually rehearsed within the season: when Everard was to take over a part in a stock play, he was individually practised six times, twice by Garrick, twice by an actress, and 'twice on the stage', but was never actually given a group rehearsal—this preparation Garrick declared to be 'quite sufficient'.[48]

## Reading

New plays were significantly revised, even during the judgemental reading. Horace Walpole complained that Garrick only ever put on his own plays or those of 'creatures still duller, who suffer him to alter their pieces as he pleases'; the *Theatrical*

---

[44] Quoted in Highfill, *Biographical Dictionary*, xii. 92.

[45] *London Stage*, IV, p. cii.

[46] *Letters of Garrick*, ii. 629; Colman, *A True State of the Differences*, 33–4. See also *London Stage*, III, 1030, where performance is deferred while the company gets up revivals.

[47] Davies, *Miscellanies*, ii. 43.

[48] Everard, *Memoirs*, 82.

*Examiner* advises a potential playwright to let Garrick 'cut out this scene, and alter that act', otherwise, in that well-worn phrase, '*it can never do*'.[49] Almost no play seems to have passed through Garrick's hands without serious revision, and the potential for 'amendment' was clearly one of the factors that determined a play's acceptance. In letters sent to Garrick accompanying submissions, authors fall over themselves to explain how flexible their texts are: the Reverend Charles Jenner will 'esteem those parts you shall please to correct, the most valuable part of the work'; while John Cleland's 'rough draught' is 'susceptible of every addition or alteration that should appear requisite'.[50] Elizabeth Griffith begs Garrick to 'use your judicious *style*, and strike out all the languid parts' on one occasion; on another she denotes her play a '*sketch*', explaining, 'I consider it as *such*, till it has received . . . approbation from greater names than mine.'[51]

Accepted and altered, a new play was read to the company, sometimes by the author, though by this stage the tradition seemed rather pointless: 'here I cannot help remarking on a ridiculous custom of *authors* reading their pieces to the performers, this is giving [them] a false consequence'.[52] At its worst, an author's reading was thought to be potentially destructive, for the 'instructed' might 'catch up the *peculiarities* instead of the *beauties* of the *instructors*: it may be advanced that an author best knows his own ideas, I grant it intellectually, but expressively makes a wide difference'.[53] Arguments like this explain why Garrick not only read out revived plays, and plays whose authors did not want to be involved with the production;[54] he also, when possible, created situations where authors who had intended to read their plays themselves resigned the task to him. Murphy was ill when he suddenly learnt that his play was to go into rehearsal. He was surprised, arguing that this was 'rather premature', especially as he would be unable to attend 'If the play is read this morning'—as it was.[55]

[49] *Walpole*, vii. 181; *Theatrical Examiner* (1757), 22.
[50] *Correspondence of Garrick*, i. 383; i. 544. See also i. 364.
[51] Ibid. ii. 316; i. 539. See also George Colman, *The Jealous Wife* (1761), A4ᵃ.
[52] Francis Gentleman, *The Modish Wife . . . to Which is Prefixed a Summary View of the Stage* (1775), 22.
[53] Gentleman, *Modish Wife*, 22.
[54] *Letters of Garrick*, ii. 630.        [55] *Correspondence of Garrick*, i. 283.

Garrick's close involvement with a production from its inception was prudent, for he was largely responsible for mounting plays. In addition, he would '[season] the dry part of the lecture with acute remarks, shrewd applications to the company present',[56] conveying the new ideas he had not only about the production but also about acting itself.[57] In many ways it made sense simply to leave the reading to Garrick, but authors knew that this meant sacrificing what little chance they had to offer their own advice. Conscious that their role in rehearsal was likely to be minimal, playwrights might jealously insist on reading, against the wishes of manager and actors alike:

The amiable author read his Boadicea to the actors. But surely his manner of conveying the meaning of his poem was very unhappy; his voice was harsh, and his elocution disagreeable. Mr. Garrick was vexed to see him mangle his own work, and politely offered to relieve him by reading an act or two; but the author imagining that he was the only person fit to unfold his intention to the players, persisted to read the play to the end.[58]

There were several reasons why writers might choose (or try to choose) to give their own readings. One was that Garrick tended to make all readings extensions of the judgemental one, and continued to alter (or even reject) plays accordingly. At each company reading of Beaumont and Fletcher's *A King and No King*, Garrick's pleasure had 'suffered a visible diminution' as a result of which he decided not to continue with the production.[59] Moreover, actors would still sometimes use the reading to have their lines altered before they received their parts, and authors might hope at least to be involved in the revision process. Mrs Bellamy relates how she took objection to a sentence she was to be given, which seemed to her inappropriate for a lady to speak. The playwright was upset, not least because 'he thought it the most forcible line in the piece', but Mrs Bellamy kept her ground until 'He . . . struck out the line'.[60] As this shows, however, even authors who were present were relatively powerless, and, indeed,

[56] Davies, *Miscellanies*, ii. 43.
[57] Gentleman, *Modish Wife*, 22.
[58] Thomas Davies, *Memoirs of the Life of David Garrick*, 2 vols., 2nd edn. (1780), i. 173. Thomson, more sensibly, gave over his reading to Garrick as soon as the actors started laughing at his Scottish accent—'Do you, sir, take my play, and go on with it; for, though I can write a tragedy, I find I cannot read one' (Davies, *Miscellanies*, iii., 278 n).
[59] Ibid. ii. 27.          [60] Bellamy, *Apology*, ii. 118–20.

throughout the rehearsal period, authors in attendance had few rights over their texts. Often they simply left everything to the man who was so clearly in charge: Garrick.

## Parts

Actors' 'parts' were often known as 'lengths',[61] and calculations about the time it would take to mount a new play were frequently 'length'-based. John Brownsmith even printed a catalogue of several hundred parts in different plays 'with the Number of *Lengths* noted that each Part contains' so that managers could see how long each play would take to prepare (and performers could decide whether they had been given reasonable time for study).[62] The connection between length of time and length of part is telling, for it emphasizes the fact that complexity was not a consideration when determining how long it would take to commit a part to memory. This becomes particularly clear when actors try to advertise themselves by their ability to learn by heart stated lengths within given times: Thomas Holcroft, for instance, assured Sheridan that 'I can repeat any part under four lengths at six hours' study'.[63] Authors, when writing, had to consider carefully the appearance of each actor's 'length', making sure it would neither look insultingly short, nor dauntingly long. Murphy warns Garrick that his role contains many half-lines, so that although the part will have 'great bulk in appearance, . . . in fact there is not much more, sometimes, than half for the actor to speak'.[64] In other words, playwrights were bound to make themselves conscious of 'parts' as separate physical entities, Mrs Cibber even going so far as to tell the author Reed to make Garrick's part of 'Oneas' clearly longer than those of Dido, 'Narbab', and 'Achales', if he wanted his play accepted.[65]

'Parts' themselves continued to be the units in which plays were learnt, as evidenced by the frequent jokes made about performers who know nothing about the story in which they are

---

[61] 'Take half a sheet of foolscap paper and divide it, the two sides are called a length by the players; and in this form their parts are always written out by the Prompter or his clerk'—*Correspondence of Garrick*, i. 120 n.

[62] John Brownsmith, *The Theatrical Alphabet* (1767), title-page.

[63] See Clinton-Baddeley, *All Right on the Night*, 187.

[64] *Correspondence of Garrick*, i. 70.     [65] Reed, *Theatrical Duplicity*, 14.

acting outside their lines. 'Marianne' in Frederick Reynolds's
*The Dramatist* is vague when she claims that she 'once acted at a
private theatre' but 'can't tell' in which play; in Charles Macklin's *Covent Garden Theatre*, the actor who practises his part of
Harlequin 'three Hours every Morning' goes on to ask what the
farce is about.[66] The actual author of the latter himself encouraged part-only knowledge from actors. He was so fearful that his
comedy might be pirated that, having given the performers their
individual parts, he locked up the full-play manuscript so that no
one could steal it—which also meant, of course, that no one
could read it.[67] Even actors who had easy access to whole plays
were not trained to think of reading beyond their parts. John
O'Keeffe tells a story of a minor actor in *Macbeth* who had learnt
no more than that his name, 'Seyton', was his cue in the last act,
and who consequently dived onto the stage at rehearsals whenever he heard it.[68] Even more extraordinary is the claim made by
both Samuel Johnson and Thomas Davies, that Hannah Pritchard (famous for her Lady Macbeth) 'had never read the tragedy
of *Macbeth* all through. She no more thought of the play out of
which her part was taken, than a shoemaker thinks of the skin,
out of which . . . he is making a pair of shoes, is cut.'[69]

Actors who could perform a completed, perfected chunk of a
play anywhere, were always popular: Everard, on his travels, met
a gentleman 'distressed . . . for a person to play *Justice
Woodchurch*', and went back with him immediately to perform
the role; in James Powell's *Private Theatricals*, Buskin brings 'one
of the best private Romeos' to Alderman Grubb.[70] Between the
two London theatres it had been agreed that an actor who
'possessed' a part in Covent Garden could perform it in Drury
Lane if the actor who owned it there was ill, and vice versa (the
part system continued to make it impossible to have understudies for roles).[71] But getting the opportunity to own a part

[66] Frederick Reynolds, *The Dramatist* (1790), 19; Charles Macklin, *The Covent Garden Theatre*, Larpent MS, l.a.96 (1752), transcribed with introd. by Jean B. Kern (Los Angeles, 1965).

[67] Kern, in Macklin, *Covent Garden*, p. ii.

[68] John O'Keeffe, *Recollections of the Life of John O'Keeffe*, 2 vols. (1826), i. 156.

[69] James Boswell, *Life of Johnson*, ed. R. W. Chapman (1953; Oxford, 1979), 616; Davies, *Garrick*, i. 117 n.

[70] Everard, *Memoirs*, 84; James Powell, *The Narcotic and Private Theatricals* (1787), 3.          [71] Reed, *Theatrical Duplicity*, 10.

was hard for a young actor, and many, for this reason, went to Dublin, which offered more opportunities for playing capital roles. They would then return to England boasting a useful stock repertory: 'send me a fresh list of y$^c$ Parts You have play'd', Garrick writes to Elizabeth Younge, 'mark them as You Yourself feel Y$^r$ Merit in them, your favourites Num$^r$ 1, y$^c$ next 2, & so on'.[72] A performance created in one place could be lifted and put into a play elsewhere, and productions do not seem to have been consciously changed to embrace a new or different performance: John Gross considers the 'strangely incoherent' effect Macklin's revolutionary new Shylock would have had, when flanked by Kitty Clive's comic Portia.[73]

The emphasis on parts meant that study was still valued over group rehearsal. Stayley claims that 'first Rate Actors' could have up to four months to study a new character and, though this is likely to be an exaggeration, the actor Alexander Pope certainly annoyed his brother-actors by agreeing to prepare a part in three weeks when custom had determined four weeks as normal.[74] Indeed, actors set such great store by study that they would sometimes only accept new characters if they could be guaranteed months for their preparation: Barry refused to appear in Reed's *Dido* unless it was put on in the following season so that he could work on it over the theatrical vacation.[75] One reason why study was more highly valued than ever was that actors were actually learning new skills during the process, for, under Garrick, acting itself was being altered. Study became the forum for creating and manifesting 'new' performances; study was therefore sharply differentiated from the process of simply learning lines. Victor writes disparagingly of players who claim to have '*studied* a Part of great Length in a few Hours', when all they have done is to become 'perfect in the Words'.[76] Similarly, when young John Palmer offered to take on the part of Harcourt in Garrick's *The Country Girl*, the author snappily put him down: '"*To read it*," said GARRICK; "*for I am sure you cannot*

---

[72] *Letters of Garrick*, ii. 746.

[73] John Gross, *Shylock* (London, 1994), 96.

[74] Stayley, *Life*, i. 60; Hume, *London Theatre World*, 176.

[75] Reed, *Theatrical Duplicity*, 73.

[76] Benjamin Victor, *The History of the Theatres of London from the year 1760 to the Present Time*, 3 vols. (1771), ii. 38.

*study it*".[77] Study determined, as before, 'not the words . . . but the character itself', but this now required an element of thought; London players, complained Stayley, would always perform better than Irish ones because of the time they had to 'consider . . . thoroughly' every role.[78] The theatre, with its 'new' performances, was regarded in a fresh light by audiences, themselves discovering 'new' ways of criticizing literature. Theatrical study, now known to be, on some level, intellectual, could be compared to literary study, and even, on occasion, substituted for it, as 'The bulk of mankind' did not have the time to think about plays themselves.[79] Garrick's performances were said to provide commentaries on the plays: his acting elucidated hard texts, it was claimed, and even improved them (his Iago 'supplied the deficiencies of the Author where the part did not convey enough, by the silent eloquence of gestures, looks, and pauses'); Garrick became Shakespeare's greatest 'living editor'; plans were in fact made for him to edit his own Complete Shakespeare.[80] Thomas Davies' *Dramatic Miscellanies* with its mixed subject-matter, part explanatory commentary on plays, and part anecdotes about the people who performed them, is illustrative of the way good acting was an acknowledged kind of literary criticism. Of course, the whole suggestion that actors were producing a 'reading' or 'interpretation' had only become possible with the institution of 'new' acting which gave audiences fresh instead of inherited performances; hence the audience's enthusiasm, their feeling that texts were being opened up by what they were seeing.

Study at its best involved entering into 'the spirit of the Sentiment and Expression' required by the part,[81] but there were still rules to determine how each sentiment should be displayed. Indeed, when examining the evidence, the innovations of the latter half of the eighteenth century seem surprisingly tame. The 'new' ways of acting, proclaimed to be less stylized than the 'old' ways, were still very stylized indeed. Garrick's

---

[77] Joseph Haslewood, *The Secret History of the Green Rooms*, 2 vols. (1790), i. 48.
[78] Edward Cape Everard, *Memoirs of an Unfortunate Son of Thespis* (1818), 81; Stayley, *Life*, 31.
[79] James Boaden, *Memoirs of Mrs. Siddons*, 2 vols. (1827), ii. 177–8.
[80] *Correspondence of Garrick*, i. 523; *Theatrical Review* (1779), 9, quoted in Lynch, *Box*, 62.
[81] Theophilus Cibber, *Two Dissertations on the Theatre* (1756), 57.

speech, praised for its naturalism, was tonal enough to be taken down in musical notation; his mechanical wig, which had hairs that actually 'stood up' for moments of surprise in *Hamlet*, hardly meets claims that his performance was 'realistic'.[82] The differences between the 'old' and the 'new' methods of acting prepared in study, were largely matters of degree.

The aged Colley Cibber was a prototype of 'old' acting, and continued to be a niggling presence in the theatre until his death. He 'was continually advising Mrs. Pritchard . . . to *tone* her words', trying to ensure the survival of the mannered, heavily cadenced enunciation that he favoured.[83] He instructed his granddaughter in the part of Alicia in *Jane Shore* for Garrick, who declared that her potential ability had now been 'eclips'd by the Manner of Speaking yᵉ Laureat has taught her'.[84] For Garrick and Macklin had subdued the rant—Macklin would 'check all the cant and cadence of tragedy'[85]—and reformed not only the style in which words were spoken but also the way they were actually pronounced. A story is told about players performing as centurions who, when James Quin told them to lower their fasces, 'bowed their heads [faces] together'. The joke rests on the fact that '*Mr. Quin*'s pronunciation was of the old school', to which Garrick had recently 'made an alteration. The one pronounced the letter *a* open; the other sounded it like an *e*.'[86] Garrick had branded his way of pronouncing, making it obviously different from other ways of speaking: he was creating recognizable hallmarks, and Garrick-trained actors were instantly distinguishable from other performers.

Similarly, acting styles were changed and modified, though, again, differences between the two seemed more marked to

[82] Burnim, *David Garrick*, 160.

[83] Davies, *Miscellanies*, i. 23.

[84] *Letters of Garrick*, i. 158.

[85] 'Sir' John Hill, *The Actor* (1750), 239. See also Cooke, *Macklin*, 148: 'We have seen [Macklin] . . . more than once, instructing pupils in the art of acting; and the principal part of his method seemed to be, in restraining them from those *artificial* habits of speaking'.

[86] Bellamy, *Apology*, ii. 24. John Walker, preparing his dictionary, went to Garrick to settle questions about the pronunciation of words like 'transition' and 'mourn', showing that Garrick's new way of speaking quickly became the standard—see Esther K. Sheldon, 'Walker's Influence on the Pronunciation of English', *PMLA* 62 (1947), 130–46 (142). Noah Webster, who was to become America's first great lexicographer, bemoaned the 'innumerable corruptions in pronunciation [that] have been introduced by Garrick'—see his *Dissertations on the English Language* (1789), 30.

contemporaries than they appear now. Garrick promoted 'starts' followed by pauses during which an attitude was held; the pauses, indicating (and encouraging) reflection about the part performed, were elements of the new 'intellectual' acting: 'Each start, is Nature; and each pause, is Thought' writes Charles Churchill on Garrick's manner of playing.[87] Performances were thus punctured with telling vignettes of the kind recorded in paintings or prints of Garrick on the stage: his famous 'astonishment' as he starts up in Richard III from his nightmare, his 'terror' when, as Hamlet, he sees the ghost of his father.[88] Another way of seeing 'new acting' was as a series of applaudable *tableaux*, or high-class clap-traps, and so Garrick's detractors emphasized:

[Garrick, as Romeo,] is now going to the Tomb . . . Yet, on the opening of the Scene,—the Actor . . . advances about 3 or 4 Steps,—then jumps, and starts into an Attitude of Surprize:—At what?—why, at the Sight of a Monument he went to look for:—And there he stands, 'till a Clap from the Audience relieves him from his Post.[89]

Parts were thus divided into a series of 'moments' that were both key to the characterization and separate from it, in that, like Garrick's party-trick of performing each passion in turn, they were detachable.[90] Such 'moments' were then separated from the rest of the action, both by the actor who paused, and by the audience who applauded; actor and audience alike showed more interest in a series of defining emotional statements, than in gradual character development.[91] Good performances in many ways were traceable to playing rather than to plays, which explains the slight disrespect given to texts themselves, a disrespect which even authors accepted: the Reverend Jenner in his *Man of Family* concedes that 'We may . . . perhaps find, that by

[87] Charles Churchill, *The Rosciad* (1761), 32. For other depictions of Garrick's 'starts', see Woods, *Garrick*, 18–19.

[88] Reproduced in Christopher Lennox-Boyd *et al.*, *Theatre: The Age of Garrick* (London, 1994). For a discussion of these pictures as exemplars of particular 'passions', see Alan Hughes, 'Art and Eighteenth Century Acting Style, Part III: Passions', *TN* 41 (1987), 128–39 (132).

[89] Theophilus Cibber, *Two Dissertations*, 69. See 'Garrick at Rehearsal', 82, for Garrick's own description of how his 'ghastliness of aspect', occasioned actually by slipping on the stage in new shoes, 'brought forth one round of admiration from all'.

[90] Burnim, *David Garrick*, 1. See also *Correspondence of Garrick*, i. 375.

[91] See George Taylor, 'The Just Delineation of the Passions', ch. 3 of Kenneth Richards and Peter Thomson (eds.), *Essays on The Eighteenth-Century English Stage* (London, 1972).

the . . . excellent pantomime of the actor, the audience will be allured from a critical enquiry into the merits of the piece'; Murphy concurs in *Zenobia* with 'where-ever my inaccuracy has left imperfections, they are so happily varnished over by your skill, that either they are not seen, or you extort forgiveness for them'.[92] The much-praised 'attitudes' held had, however, been determined in very much the old way—by mimicking 'the best *Paintings, Statues* and *Prints*':[93] as with most late eighteenth-century changes to acting style, the surface was made to seem different, but the substance remained the same.

The basis of a tragic part was still its 'passions' and their manifestation, but recent scientific writing had suggested that the seat of the passions was not the 'animal spirits' but the muscles.[94] Newer, more subtle, muscular requirements were therefore made, further proscribing and restricting an actor's physical range on the stage. David Ross was criticized because he was 'too plump-faced' to show the motion of his muscles 'in exhibiting the passions'; but Peg Woffington also came under censure for distorting her mouth in the expression of cunning and shyness 'into little better than deformity'.[95] On top of these, versions of the old rules still applied. Roger Pickering's *Reflections upon Theatrical Expression in Tragedy* (1755) speaks for itself in its title—it explains how to manage the hands and feet in astonishment, surprise, terror, etc., as well as offering suggestions about where to put the tragic handkerchief when wearing a toga. Such laws are shown in operation when Charles Dignum, a fat actor, observed that he found it troublesome reaching over his right hand to touch his heart and 'wished to know if his left would not do as well'. His worried friends were able to correct him before he could commit so gross an error on the public stage.[96]

---

[92] [Charles Jenner], *The Man of Family* (1771), A5[a]; Arthur Murphy, *Zenobia* (1768), A3[b].

[93] Roger Pickering, *Reflections upon Theatrical Expression in Tragedy* (1755), 20. Theophilus Cibber in *Two Dissertations*, 49 mocks a Garrick pose with 'Oh! But it's a pretty Attitude forsooth, he caught it perhaps, from a *French* Print, where a Gentleman leans against the high Base of a Pillar, in a Garden'. For more on this topic see Alan Downer, 'Nature to Advantage Dressed', *PMLA* 58 (1943), 1002–37; and McKenzie, 'Countenance', 758–73.

[94] Shearer West, *The Image of the Actor* (London, 1991), 93. Similarly, the basis of a comic part was still the 'humours' (p. 91).

[95] *Theatrical Review for the years 1757 and beginning of 1758* (1758), 32, 38.

[96] Haslewood, *Secret History*, i. 87–8. For descriptions, with illustrations, of some

Parts were learnt and studied in the same way, though manifested differently. Words might be mastered in preliminary sessions alone: 'you may learn y$^e$ Songs with [the music master], & the dialogue part by Y$^r$self' writes Garrick to Jane Pope; Mrs Woffington, whose husband (rightly) suspected her of unfaithfulness when he found a man's wig in her bedroom, was given the explanation that 'I am going to play a breeches part; and that . . . is the very individual wig I was practising in.'[97] Gesture, especially when pertaining to important 'moments', might also be rehearsed in private: 'I studied all my Attitudes and used to practise for Hours together before the Glass'.[98] But in general Garrick recommended 'Rehearsals before y$^e$ Person You may think capable of instructing You', probably a self-conscious reference to the rules for study laid down by Betterton.[99] However, with several observably different styles of acting manifested on the eighteenth-century stage, the nature and personality of the private instructor made a very obvious difference, for the instructors themselves would be clearly evident in the performances of their pupils. Thomas Sheridan was furious that Garrick had 'stolen' one of his players and taught him, but, as Garrick explained to Richard Sheridan, 'I meant not to interfere . . . I imagin'd (foolishly indeed) that my attending Bannister's rehearsal of the part I once play'd, & w$^{ch}$ y$^r$ Father never saw, might have assisted y$^e$ Cause.'[100] Instruction had become such an issue in theatre politics that actors could even use it to promote themselves, as when Thomas Chapman 'flattered the manager's vanity by submitting to be taught by him'.[101] Nor could instruction always be honestly offered or taken. Authors, especially when dealing with such strong-minded managers as Garrick, might give most of their instruction in secret: in 1759 Murphy, anticipating Mrs Cibber's 'illness', secretly taught Mary Yates for a part in his *Orphan of*

---

of these 'rules', see Dene Barnett, 'The Performance and Practice of Acting': 'Ensemble Acting', *TRI* 2 (1977), 157–85; 'The Hands', *TRI* 3 (1977), 1–19; 'The Arms', *TRI* 3 (1978), 79–93; 'The Eyes, the Face, and the Head', *TRI* 5 (1979–80), 1–13.

[97] *Letters of Garrick*, i. 339; Cooke, *Macklin*, 118.

[98] Charles Bonnor, *The Manager an Actor in Spite of Himself*, Larpent MS, l.a.664 (1784).

[99] *Letters of Garrick*, ii. 559.          [100] Ibid. iii. 1251.

[101] Davies, *Miscellanies*, i. 93. The manager referred to is Rich.

*China.*[102] But then, authorial instruction was not always desired by the actors. Mrs Clive tellingly makes her authoress Mrs Hazard declare, 'Mrs. Clive . . . [is] so conceited and insolent that she won't let me teach . . . her'; when actors did condescend to submit to authorial instruction they were secure enough in their superior knowledge to argue that the instructive process should, at least, be mutual:

The great advantage of playing an original character, is derived from the instructions of the author. From him the learning of the part must be communicated to his instrument, the player: if he is a master in his profession, he will, in his turn, impart useful hints to the poet, which will contribute to the improvement of the scene.[103]

Technically it was still possible for anyone to offer instruction, and, occasionally, respected members of the public with fixed ideas about pronunciation and gesture found opportunities to offer their own advice. Dr Johnson, for instance, was a guest at a final dress-rehearsal, and took it upon himself to instruct the unwilling Mrs Bellamy in how to stress 'Thou shalt not murder':

*Doctor Johnson* caught me by the arm . . . somewhat *too briskly*, saying, . . . 'It is a commandment, and must be spoken, "Thou shalt *not* murder."' As I had not then the honour of knowing personally that great genius, I was not a little displeased at his *inforcing* his instructions with so much vehemence.[104]

But the most pervasive instruction offered over the period included not simply advice on how to perform a particular part, but advice about how to perform in the 'new' way; and leading proponents of this instruction were, of course, the leading proponents of new acting, Garrick and Macklin. Their teaching was to change the nature of eighteenth-century performance.

### Garrick, Macklin, and instruction

Garrick was famous for his 'originality', a new term of praise in the theatre. He took two months to rehearse Benedick privately in order to model his action 'to his own idea of the part'; he

---

[102] Davies, *Garrick*, i. 220.
[103] Catherine [Kitty] Clive, *The Rehearsal, or Bayes in Petticoats* (1753), 14; Davies, *Miscellanies*, iii. 160–1.    [104] Bellamy, *Apology*, iii. 77–8.

'scorned to lacky after any actor whatever; he . . . was completely an original performer'.[105] But Garrick's novelty did not mean that he allowed freer or more flexible interpretations of parts in general. His 'new' performances were carefully crafted into immutable 'fixed' entities: he was, for instance, furious when Barry took to the other theatre 'his' method of playing Romeo.[106] Although Garrick broke with the old imitative tradition, he very seldom encouraged others to do likewise. Instead, he created new interpretations for his players, which he then taught in much the same way as parts had always been taught—by imitation. 'Now, sir, say *this* after me', was Garrick's manner of training the young Everard who duly 'repeated it, catching the emphasis, his tone and manner, as nearly as possible', and so got himself a part.[107] Similarly Garrick taught Thomas King to play Lord Ogleby in his *Clandestine Marriage* by acting the part to him in private, 'hoping that King would . . . catch from him the manner of executing it'.[108] In Thomas Lowndes's *The Theatrical Manager*, Patricide, the Garrick-figure, states his preference for an actor incapable of reading, whom he can instruct in every particular; and a hint of the range of vocal change and gesture covered by Garrick's instructions can be seen from the advice he offered a vicar about speaking the common prayer, subsequently noted down for the use of other clergymen:

*wherefore—*
Here Mr. Garrick made a most significant pause, with the voice as if suddenly broken off, and suspended in such a manner, as to keep the expectation still alive for what is to follow.
*let us beseech him*
In speaking the last words, give a *respectful* look *upward*.[109]

Garrick's attempts to prescribe in minute detail every particular of a performance did not stop even with the most elevated actors, from whom 'he expected an implicit submission', causing

---

[105] John Genest, *Some Account of the English Stage, from the Restoration . . . to 1830*, 10 vols. (1832), v. 593; Murphy, *Garrick*, i. 22.

[106] Davies, *Garrick*, i. 125.

[107] Everard, *Memoirs*, 17.

[108] Murphy, *Garrick*, ii. 30.

[109] Thomas Lowndes, *The Theatrical Manager* (1751), 44; J. W. Anderson, *The manner pointed out in which the Common Prayer was read in private by . . . Mr. Garrick* (1797), 16.

some of the bad feeling which perhaps made capital players unwilling to attend group rehearsal.[110] But overbearing instruction was responsible for more immediate theatrical problems, in that, as much as Garrick was completely original, so his actors were completely unoriginal: they were, almost all of them, pale imitations of their mentor. 'While [John Savigny] attempts to tread in Mr Garrick's shoes, he will forever go slipshod' complained the *Theatrical Review*; even Mrs Yates's 'Agnes' was obviously 'Mr. Garrick in petticoats'.[111] Garrick had over-taught, and left his actors little room to develop their own methods; the result was that Garrick was like 'Childers' the famous horse, 'the best racer in England *himself*, but could never *get a colt*';[112] for what worked so excellently in the great actor seemed second-hand in others. Moreover, Garrick's players were naturally held up against Garrick himself, and found to be inferior. Holland was both praised for being 'the best Copyer of Excellence . . . on the stage', and criticized for his part as 'a mere copy of the original'; the (brief) new darling of the stage, William Powell, suffered when the audience 'compared him with his great original' for then they 'instantly saw the difference'.[113]

In one sense, this was what Garrick had intended: he had stamped his mannerisms on his actors, in such a way that he was always a presence on the stage irrespective of whether he was actually performing.[114] This ensured both that his personal novelty-value extended throughout his company (which made good marketing sense), and, in the long term, that his performances would live in the theatre for years to come. The actual result was that Garrick's innovations simply replaced the old prototypes with new ones: he did not change the way actors thought about or dealt with inherited parts. Characterizations created by Garrick were to be learnt and handed down in rote fashion as before: Mrs Clive, who had most of her roles fresh from Garrick, then passed them on as received both to Mrs Pope, who was eventually 'considered a sort of reflection of

[110] Davies, *Miscellanies*, ii. 43.
[111] *Theatrical Review* (1772), ii. 86; *Correspondence of Garrick*, i. 335.
[112] Samuel Foote, *Wit for the Ton!* (1778), 26.
[113] Victor, *Theatres from 1760*, iii. 158; Murphy, *Garrick*, ii. 8; Cooke, *Macklin*, 391. [114] Davies, *Garrick*, i. 177.

Clive's character and talent', and Elizabeth Vincent, whom she visited several times to 'teach . . . the part of Polly'.[115]

New-moulding characterizations and stamping a particular brand of acting onto each performer, involved Garrick in an extraordinary quantity of teaching. He tried to rehearse almost all his actors on some level, even going so far as to teach stock role replacements—a task that, in another theatre, would have been given to the prompter.[116] Mrs Clive intends to flatter Garrick with her observation that the audience who think his actors are performing well '[do] not see you pull the wires'. Her feeling that Garrick's instruction masked the mediocre abilities of some of the actors was backed by Garrick's own prompter: after a new actor's good performance he reminds himself 'N.B. Mr. D. Garrick instructed him in this Part—when I see him in another, shall be able to judge better of his Capabilities.'[117] Garrick further increased his teaching load by his deep-seated fear of the corruptive instruction of others; he even warned Everard against George Garrick (his devoted brother): 'let him keep his advice and instructions to himself; . . . you'll have my help when I can.'[118] There seems to have been no aspect of preparation that Garrick was altogether happy to leave to other people, instructing not just his province—acting—but also the physical arts: Catherine Galindo accused Sarah Siddons of flirting with Garrick by taking her fencing lessons from him when no one else was by.[119]

There were two obvious occasions during which Garrick could undertake the bulk of his teaching. One provided the forum for the rehearsal of secondary actors: group rehearsal. Here Garrick could 'instruct' several actors at the same time, and it seems to have been this, rather than the ensemble potentialities of the event, that made him so particular about collective practice. The other provided the forum for intensive individual instruction: exclusive rehearsal at Garrick's Hampton residence.

---

[115] Percy Hetherington Fitzgerald, *The Life of Mrs. Catherine Clive* (1888), 88; *Correspondence of Garrick*, i. 204. For more about stock characterizations, see Lynch, *Box*, 158; Clinton-Baddeley, *All Right on the Night*, 32.

[116] See *Letters of Garrick*, ii. 593.

[117] *Correspondence of Garrick*, ii. 128; Dougald MacMillan, *Drury Lane Calendar 1747–1776* (Oxford, 1938), 98.

[118] Everard, *Memoirs*, 81.

[119] Catherine Galindo, *Letter to Mrs. Siddons* (1809), 6.

Here Garrick would spend the summer, and help chosen actors 'create' their roles: 'young Palmer', for instance, was rewarded for his surprisingly good performance by being 'invited to the Manager's house at Hampton to rehearse parts with him'.[120] The parts that were carefully developed under Garrick in his summer retreat were, of course, prepared well outside the period of production, and out of context from the rest of the play in which they occurred. By selecting certain actors for this favour, Garrick always had at least one thoroughly Garrick-like performer in each play; naturally this outweighed any influence on the production a playwright might try to have, particularly as playwrights were not similarly invited to Garrick's house.

Macklin, another 'innovator', taught in much the same way as Garrick. Again, actors who followed his pattern did well, but could not always manage without him, like the man who was much praised for the performance of Montano that Macklin had taught him, but who, 'left to himself, . . . lost the reputation he had acquired'.[121] Instruction with Macklin is vividly depicted by Samuel Foote, whose *Diversions of the Morning* shows Puzzle (Macklin) teaching an actor the part of Othello:

PUZZLE. . . . bring it from the bottom of your stomach with a grind—as to—r—rr—

BOUNCE. Torr—rture me— . . . Never pray more; abandon all remorse—

PUZZLE. Now out with your arm, and shew your chest.—There's a figure!

BOUNCE. On horror's head—

PUZZLE. Now out with your voice.

BOUNCE. Horrors accumulate—

PUZZLE. Now tender.

BOUNCE. Do deeds to make heav'n weep—

PUZZLE. Now, terror.

BOUNCE. All earth amaz'd—For no thing canst thou to damna—

PUZZLE. Grind na—na, na, na, tion—

BOUNCE. Na, na, na, tion add greater than that.[122]

---

[120] Haslewood, *Secret History*, i. 49.

[121] William Cooke, *Memoirs of Samuel Foote* (1805), i. 40 n.

[122] Samuel Foote, *Diversions of the Morning* (1758), a new second act added to *Taste*, reproduced in Tate Wilkinson, *The Wandering Patentee*, 4 vols. (1795), iv. 237–50 (246). Davies, *Miscellanies*, iii. 262, records that 'it is to Macklin we chiefly owe the many admirable strokes of passion with which Barry surprised us in Othello'.

This illustrates clearly the tendency in 'new' acting, here greatly exaggerated, to divide parts into 'moments' of strained emotional pitch, each of which were supposed to win applause from the audience. It also, of course, illustrates how Macklin, who for a time ran an acting school, was inclined to treat his players as vehicles for his own performances: the 'new' acting was at least as prescriptive as the 'old'.

### The content of rehearsal

William Cooke quotes Benjamin Victor (see previous chapter) on the subject of rehearsal—to the detriment of contemporary (1804) practice. In Macklin's day, Cooke asserts, 'players were not permitted to "mouth over their parts," and hurry from one passage to another, without attending to the enunciation, or exhibition of the character' in rehearsal, indicating that this was what they now did.[123] Actual reports about Macklin's rehearsals suggest that his method was similar to that practised in Cooke's day. Particularly when preparing a 'new' characterization, Macklin would rehearse 'under his voice and general powers, . . . reserving his fire till the night of representation' (similarly Cooke would 'give no intimation of the manner he [intended] to act').[124] In other words, the 'real' performance to come was hidden in group rehearsal rather than exercised or primed there. Women, particularly, would often keep rehearsal secrets, providing second-rate clothes for the dress-rehearsal, to frustrate their fellow actresses by their true finery on stage in the evening. Managers too might keep vital elements of the play from the group. At Smock Alley, all the parts for Isaac Bickerstaff's *The Maid of the Mill* were distributed except that of Lord Aimsworth. Naturally this aroused curiosity as to who would be cast for the part, but 'The secret was . . . kept back till within a few days of the performance'—meaning, of course, that there was little time to rehearse with that character.[125] Though the value of ensemble rehearsal was constantly stated, no one, not even the managers, actually had an ensemble mentality. 'Modern rehearsals' were thus still actually a gathering of parts, and were, throughout the

---

[123]  Cooke, *Macklin*, 401.
[124]  Ibid. 91; William Dunlap, *Memoirs of George Fred Cooke esq*, 2 vols. (1813), i. 112.                                                    [125]  Cooke, *Macklin*, 259.

eighteenth century, to remain 'little better than a *theatrical muster*'.[126] With all Garrick's attempts at boosting the importance of rehearsal ('Punctuality in attendance at rehearsals was exacted and complied with'[127]), he himself was largely responsible for the dishonesty of the event, for he was so dictatorial that actors feared to contradict his suggestions publicly. Henry Woodward 'seemed very attentive to Garrick's ideas of Bobadil' while Garrick led a rehearsal of Jonson's *Every Man in his Humour*, but was caught secretly elaborating on his own interpretation when he thought the manager was absent.[128]

Major actors' unwillingness to attend rehearsals has already been mentioned. Frequently actors point out that they personally can gain nothing from rehearsal, and suggest that their presence may be dispensable. Ann Dancer attempted to be excused rehearsal 'lest it should prevent her preparing parts of more consequence to you': she preferred to use the time for private study.[129] There was often less than a full complement of actors at group rehearsal—Sarah Gardner's *The Advertisement* (1770) 'was called to rehearsal every day, but it might almost as well have been left alone; for so few performers attended, and those who did attend . . . paid so little attention to their parts'.[130] Actors came up with a great number of excuses to get out of rehearsals. The ladies were famous for their 'headaches' and 'fatigue', the men for a variety of illnesses, real and feigned, including, in the case of Samuel Reddish, insanity.[131] One jest, illustrative of the trivial excuses offered by actors, relates how John Moody refused to attend rehearsals of *Henry VIII* because he had failed to grasp the play's subtitle ('one of Shakespeare's hist. plays') 'mistaking the abbreviation of the word historical, for a fixed mark of popular censure'.[132] The more famous actors were, the harder it was to persuade them to rehearse with their subordinates. Mrs

---

[126] William Cooke, *The Elements of Dramatic Criticism* (1775), 195.

[127] Davies, *Garrick*, i. 111.

[128] Davies, *Miscellanies*, ii. 43. Thomas King was one of the few who dared to stand up to the manager. Garrick praised him for following his own conception and '[striking] out a manner that becomes you better than if you had imitated me'—see Murphy, *Garrick*, ii. 30.

[129] *Correspondence of Garrick*, i. 121. See also Clive, *Rehearsal*, 24.

[130] Preface to Sarah Gardner's *The Advertisement*, quoted in F. Grice and A. Clarke, 'Mrs Sarah Gardner', *TN* 7 (1953), 76–81 (78).

[131] Cross–Hopkins, 1 Apr. 1775. See also Stayley, *Rival Theatres*, 22.

[132] *The Theatrical Jester* (1795), 10.

Bellamy records that her fellow performers had so little faith in her when she first arrived at Covent Garden, that 'the two gentlemen who were to play my lovers' at first did not appear at her rehearsal at all, and then when 'persuaded' by heavy fining, tried to ambush her chances—'Mr. Hall *mumbled over* Castalio, and Mr. Ryan *whistled* Polydore.'[133] A famous actor, such as Quin, tried to avoid even getting to know his fellow actors, let alone sharing preparation with them. He 'never condescended to enter the Green-room, or to mix with other performers' (entrance into the green room itself was still confined to actors of a certain standing and salary).[134] When forced to attend against their wills, usually by fining, but sometimes by the threat of removing parts, or less favourable casting in subsequent productions, actors displayed their displeasure in a variety of ways. They were frequently late—a staple in contemporary plays about the theatre is *The Hodge Podge*'s 'You are the first, and you are above an hour after the time, Sir.'[135] They would also reserve their attention for their own 'parts': Munden writes of rehearsals in which 'it was as if [the actors] had never seen each other before, each intent upon his particular part only', the result being an absence of 'perfect grouping', and 'harmony of action'.[136] They would even quit the stage when not required to speak, which left them still largely ignorant about the play they were in, and negated all practical benefit they might have gained from rehearsal.[137] Brownsmith the prompter maintained that this was not only to be expected, but was appropriate: no actor, he argued, should be allowed on the stage who was not actually rehearsing the scene in question; instead, a vigilant call-boy should be in constant attendance, because performers would be unsettled if 'obliged every minute to attend to the scene in action'.[138]

At other times, actors misbehaved to irritate each other or amuse themselves:

Lee Lewis . . . jumped over a table which was set on stage—Lewis interrupted the performance to show one of the actors a paragraph in the

---

[133] Bellamy, *Apology*, i. 51–2.
[134] Ibid. i. 49; Clinton-Baddeley, *All Right on the Night*, 173.
[135] *The Hodge Podge* (1781), Larpent MS, l.a.569.
[136] Munden, *Memoirs*, 308.
[137] Genest, *Some Account of the English Stage*, vi. 396.
[138] John Brownsmith, *The Contrast* (1776), 15–17.

newspaper—Mrs. Mattocks requested the Prompter to take good care of her, as she was very imperfect—and Miss Younge did not attend at all [of a rehearsal of Christopher Bullock's *Woman's a Riddle*, 1780].[139]

When actors did display any interest in the play, they jostled with fellow actors, attempting to force interpretations onto each other, so, as ever, treating rehearsal like an extension of private instruction. Mrs Cibber, for instance, tried to 'prevail on Winstone to make Austria appear as odious to an audience as he ought';[140] again, this resulted in their largely ignoring the ensemble potentialities of the event. Nevertheless, there was more rehearsal than there had been in previous years, and some fine performances were traced to it: 'This tragedy [Arthur Murphy's *The Grecian Daughter*] . . . is very carefully got up & well perform'd, & receiv'd uncommon applause.'[141]

Partial rehearsals followed one after another; the notion of a complete play as a single unity was thus seldom paramount before 'final' rehearsals. Mrs Pritchard, for instance, 'rehearsed almost at the same time the part of a furious queen [Elvira] in the green room and that of a coquette [Millamant] on the stage, and passed several times from one to the other with the utmost ease and happiness.'[142] But ensemble rehearsals were not supposed to accomplish very much in terms of action. Macklin was criticized for overstepping the bounds, even of manager, when he tried to arrange blocking in rehearsal, rather than leaving it to the actors and prompter in performance—he would 'grow tedious in arranging the *etiquette* of the scene, in respect to sitting or standing; crossing the Stage, or remaining still; and many other little peculiarities, that in great measure must be left to the discretion of the performer'.[143] As such criticism makes clear, even the potential range of group rehearsal was limited, particularly as major actors had their own ideas about how to rehearse, which might, on occasion, include keeping the secondary actors second-rate, for lesser actors had either to be very carefully rehearsed, or

[139] Genest, *Some Account of the English Stage*, vi. 396.
[140] Davies, *Miscellanies*, i. 22.
[141] Cross–Hopkins, 26 Feb. 1772.
[142] Edward Gibbon, *Journal*, ed. D. M. Low (London, 1929), 186.
[143] Cooke, *Macklin*, 403. This, of course is why Burnim, *David Garrick*, 54, found so little indication of 'the arrangement of the characters on the stage during the playing of the scene'.

not properly rehearsed at all: no one would come out well from a mediocre or merely competent performance. Against the tales of Garrick's careful rehearsals, are tales of extraordinary rehearsal negligence. Some parts, such as walk-ons and small roles, often performed by non-professionals taken on at the last moment, were not rehearsed at all: a famous legend tells how one of the murderers in a performance of *Macbeth* was so startled by Garrick's 'There's blood upon thy face' that he responded 'Is there by God!'[144] Referring to the 'incomparable badness' of the players in Aaron Hill's *Zara*, George Steevens denigrates the 'stuff' flanking Lusignan, asking 'can you be so mistaken as to suppose you need these wretched foils to shew you off?'[145] When Walpole too accuses Garrick of surrounding himself with 'the worst performers of his troop' in order to 'give greater brilliancy to his own setting',[146] he indicates an essential truth about performance in the late eighteenth century: no one, even at the highest level, wanted it to be of a uniformly adequate standard. Naturally this took its toll on the way rehearsal was managed.

## *Authors and rehearsal*

Playwrights were divided in the late eighteenth century between two extremes: the one-off writers, and the constant writers (over half the new plays acted were written by just seven authors[147]). Naturally a number of novices expected or, indeed, hoped not to be involved in their productions, such as, for instance, the gentleman playwright Richard Bentley who 'died at the thought of being known for an author even by his own acquaintance'.[148] By the middle of the eighteenth century, it was, anyway, unusual for playwrights to attend rehearsals, for they followed the system of priorities that existed at the time, wanting, primarily, good privately rehearsed major actors, without worrying unduly about minor actors or harmonious ensembles. 'I'll leave the conduct of the rehearsal of some scenes to you, Sir' says the playwright 'Young Psalter' in *The Critick Anticipated* (1779); Thomas Arne delegated the attendance of general rehearsals of his music to the

[144] Burnim, *David Garrick*, 33.
[145] Quoted in Price, *Theatre in the Age of Garrick*, 28.
[146] *Walpole*, ix. 420.          [147] Lynch, *Box*, 26.
[148] *Walpole*, v. 92.

young Charles Burney.[149] Garrick often took charge of plays from scratch: *The Choleric Man* was left 'with Mr. Garrick for representation' and he rehearsed it while its author, Cumberland, was at Bath. Similarly Murphy was happy enough to put his *Grecian Daughter* straight into Garrick's hands, explaining 'were the play to be got up at another playhouse, I should think it absolutely necessary to attend the rehearsals, but when you are willing to undertake that trouble, the anxiety of an author . . . is superfluous'.[150] Occasionally authors were specifically asked to attend for revision purposes, but even then they might prove inadequate and have to be replaced. James Love was invited to correct his pantomime *The Rites of Hecate* during rehearsals, but was judged 'not to have the least Genius in contriving anything of that Kind' and was dropped in favour of Colman.[151] Frequently Garrick, to save time, simply made his own revisions to plays, as illustrated below.

Lack of general authorial control took its toll, particularly on plays about which the actors were unsure. Tales abound of actors purposefully damning productions by refusing to rehearse properly. In the anonymous *Author on the Wheel*, one actor is so 'convinc'd the audience would never hear [the play] out' that he does not even learn the last act of his part.[152] That this happened in reality is attested to by Sarah Gardner, whose actors at performance were still unfamiliar with their parts, 'and one had not even bothered to study his lines'; and by Fanny Burney, whose second most important character 'had but two lines of his part by heart!'[153] But most telling is a fragment of Reed's rant, aimed directly at Garrick. There he explains that the actors are so swayed by Garrick's judgement that they will damn where he damns and praise where he praises, irrespective of the merits of the play itself.[154] Play and author, in other words, were continually judged by Garrick, and continually subject to his

---

[149] 'R.B.S. Esq.', *The Critick Anticipated*, 13; Roger Lonsdale, *Dr. Charles Burney* (Oxford, 1965), 10.

[150] Richard Cumberland, *Memoirs* (1806), 277; *Correspondence of Garrick*, i. 503. At other theatres, the presence of authors was still actually useful: Stayley records, at about the same time in Ireland, that a play was called off as the author did not, as was expected, come over to supervise rehearsals—see Stayley's *Alexander's Feast*, attached to his *Life*, ii. 23. [151] MacMillan, *Calendar*, 102.

[152] *Author on the Wheel*, Larpent MS, l.a.144 (1785).

[153] Sarah Gardner's *Advertisement*, 79; Fanny Burney, *Diary and Letters of Madame D'Arblay*, 7 vols. (1846), vi. 34. [154] Reed, *Theatrical Duplicity*, 43.

changing emotions—the 'judgemental stage' therefore extended not just throughout the reading period, but through the whole of rehearsal and even into early performance, with Garrick ultimately in charge of all textual change: a text mounted by Garrick therefore became fixed at a very late date.

## Managers and rehearsal

As manager, Garrick was totally in charge of most productions mounted at Drury Lane, making all the important decisions affecting a play. He cast it, as Cumberland illustrates when he refers to casting 'discussions' with Garrick in which 'I took no part . . . for I was entitled to no opinion'.[155] Then he attended rehearsals, almost always present at least from 'rough' rehearsals onwards. His irritation with authors who insisted on seeing through their productions manifested itself in the high-handed way in which he treated them. Murphy wrote Garrick an acid letter to complain that he had 'imagined when a piece is carried into the Green Room, it is to put it into rehearsal, and not to treat the author as if he was going to school'.[156] But generally, as shown before, authors now expected managerial control of important rehearsals, to the extent of resenting its absence. *Dido* was prepared in a 'slovenly' fashion, claimed Reed, because Garrick did not attend practices.[157] Surprisingly few authors resented the fact that Garrick then heavily cut and altered, as it would seem, most of the plays in his charge; for alteration itself was now, formally, the manager's job rather than the author's. The ominous 'cutting session' took place without Puff's presence in Sheridan's *Critic*; 'my task' records Charles Dibdin, 'has been as troublesome as that of a manager in the shortening of an overgrown play'.[158] Moreover, signs that Garrick's hand was in a

---

[155] Cumberland, *Memoirs*, 217. See also Burnim, *David Garrick*, 27–33.

[156] *Correspondence of Garrick*, i. 71. For other examples of author-directors, see Burnim, *David Garrick*, 40.

[157] Reed, *Theatrical Duplicity*, 50.

[158] Charles Dibdin, *A Complete History of the English Stage*, 5 vols. (1797–1800), i. p. iv. At Drury Lane 1747–76, nineteen plays are known to have been altered by Garrick; four by Colman the Elder; two each by Isaac Bickerstaffe, Francis Gentleman, and John Hawkesworth; others by their authors but almost certainly with managerial help—see Harry William Pedicord, *The Theatrical Public in the Time of Garrick* (New York, 1954), 64.

play testified, first, that he had approved it, secondly that he had worked it into the kind of play the audience liked, so that prefaces often broadcast the fact that they front 'Garrick texts': Samuel Crisp thanks 'Mr. GARRICK . . . for his friendly Advice, by which the Play is . . . rendered much more Dramatick'; Philip Francis gives '*Garrick* . . . my sincerest Gratitude, for . . . his Assistance in a thousand alterations'; conversely, Reed was furious because Garrick was not prepared seriously to revise his play, and had suggested only three alterations in all, one of those being to change 'fie' to 'hold'.[159] So powerful was the lure of Garrick's revision that one text even boasts that Garrick 'revis'd the following Farce' although he then 'refus'd' the play.[160] Generally, managerial revisions were made to add theatricality, which, by this stage, meant reducing static moments in favour of the bursts of emotion that 'new acting' required. Self-conscious 'literary' features were often the first to go: Garrick had to be 'restrained' from paring any more from Murphy's *Orphan of China* by William Whitehead who questioned: 'If you cut out so many beauties from this play, what must be the fates of future poor authors?'[161] Yet his ability to hack a play about to increase its theatrical potential was partly what made Garrick a shrewd manager: 'by the touches of his pen, [he] gave new life and spirit to the dialogue' of John Burgoyne's *Maid of the Oaks*; 'no manager', enthuses Davies, 'was better qualified to serve an author in the correcting, pruning, or enlarging of a dramatick piece, than Mr. Garrick. His acute judgement and great experience had rendered him a consummate judge of stage effect; and many authors now living . . . will own their obligations to his taste and sagacity'.[162] That Garrick was manager did not override the

---

[159] Samuel Crisp, *Virginia* (1754), A3ᵃ; Philip Francis, *Eugenia* (1752), A1ᵇ; Reed, *Theatrical Duplicity*, 50. See Leo Hughes, 'Redating Two Eighteenth Century Theatrical Documents', *MP* 80 (1982), 54–6, for a list of the alterations made on a regular basis to *Harlequin's Invasion*. For other examples of plays boasting Garrick's revisions, see [Dorothea Celisia], *Almida* (1771), A4ᵃ: 'The judicious and friendly hand of Mr. Garrick made a few additions and alterations'; Richard Cumberland, *The Fashionable Lover* (1772), A1ᵃ: 'I am . . . materially indebted to [Garrick's] judgment, and owe the good effect of many incidents in both to his suggestions and advice'; Hugh Kelly, *False Delicacy* (1768), A1ᵃ: '[the play's] success has been greatly owing to [Garrick's] judicious advice'.

[160] *Angelica* (1758), A2ᵃ.

[161] Jessé Foot, *The Life of Arthur Murphy, esq* (1811), 154.

[162] Murphy, *Garrick*, ii. 106; Davies, *Garrick*, i. 212.

fact that he was also an actor. Theophilus Cibber felt that Garrick revised plays to make his own parts more impressive, and though this smacks of bitterness, Garrick certainly sometimes pressed for revisions that would heighten his character, as when he told Cumberland to hype the entrance of the West Indian in the play of that name: 'Never let me see a hero step upon the stage without his trumpeters'.[163] In other ways Garrick's preferences as actor seriously affected the repertory he offered: it was said that Roman plays, including *Julius Caesar*, ceased to be performed after Garrick realized that togas did not suit him.[164]

### Prompters and rehearsal

Despite Garrick's marked effect on the plays in his charge, the day-to-day preparatory and partial rehearsals were still in the hands of the prompter, who also had a constant (but under-acknowledged) effect on text and production. Often eclipsed by powerful managers whom Sheridan described as 'required for *state days* and *holidays*', a steady prompter was 'the *cornerstone* of the building'.[165] In fact, a dictionary definition of the time describes 'Prompt' not just as 'to help at a loss' but also 'To assist by private instruction':[166] one of the prompter's defining tasks was now his individual teaching—showing to what extent his importance had grown. The prompter had a hand in almost every aspect of rehearsal: a stage direction in Stayley's *The Rival Theatres* presents the overworked prompter individually rehearsing an actor while writing a part—'*Prompter discovered writing; his Man waiting; an Actor walking about reading his Part, &c, as at a Rehearsal.*'[167] In the main, the prompter copied and distributed the actors' parts, arranged the daily rehearsals, and supervised line run-throughs:[168] he 'regulated' the stage. Particularly, he was in charge of regular partial rehearsals, in which a medley of scenes and dances from a number of different plays took place in succession: Thomas Dibdin, as prompter, records how he has 'been on Drury Lane Stage, with one play-book after another in

[163] Cumberland, *Memoirs*, 216.       [164] Lynch, *Box*, 153.
[165] *Reminiscences of Michael Kelly* [compiled by Theodore Hook], 2 vols. (1826), ii. 41.
[166] William Kenrick, *A New Dictionary of the English Language* (1783).
[167] Stayley, *Rival Theatres*, 19.
[168] Colman, *A True State of the Differences*, 31.

my benumbed fingers'.[169] These rehearsals were useful for determining the prompting needs of performance, but the prompter tended also to be actively, theatrically involved in them. He would not simply watch and prompt, but read for absent performers *'without respect to persons'*, as a result of which he was the obvious stand-in in time of sickness: witness Cross's casual 'Cibber sick, i did Bayes'.[170] Prompters were involved in plays from the inside and the outside, and their lives too were often intertwined with the theatre—Cross records the death of one of his children in the margin of a theatre notebook. Plays seemed to 'belong' ultimately to the prompter, who, after all, had charge of the prompt-book from which the play was acted. Indeed, in the late eighteenth century, a fashion grew for publishing 'prompt-book' texts, indicated by the formula 'regulated from the prompt-book by [name of prompter]', or, even more telling, 'printed conformable to the representation at [name of theatre] under the inspection of [name of prompter]'. 'Inspection' is a key word. Plays were almost all lightly revised by prompters, who were still responsible for purifying texts for the Lord Chamberlain (now a greater task than before, as the new 'sensibility' of the audience sanctioned few impurities);[171] a prompt-book text came with the assurance that it had been thoroughly purged. Yet given that censored passages *could* be printed, it is extraordinary how popular prompter's texts were. Prompter's authority actually sold plays, for readers often wanted the texts given them to be bolstered by a variety of trusted theatrical names; 'original' and 'unaltered' texts were not actually particularly desirable. A preference for the acted text also indicates the way the audience not only watched plays, but took to checking players for accuracy against the theatre text (with a copy of Bell's *Shakespeare*, 'those who take books to the THEATRE, will not be so apt to condemn the performers for being imperfect'[172]); audiences were not only looking up to the prompter but taking on his admonitory role.

[169] Thomas Dibdin, *The Reminiscences*, 2 vols. (1827), ii. 11.

[170] Brownsmith, *Contrast*, 15; Harry William Pedicord, 'Rylands English MS.IIII: An Early Diary of Richard Cross', *John Rylands Library Bulletin*, 37 (1954), 503–27 (505).

[171] See *London Stage*, IV, p. xxii. For the extent of Lord Chamberlain's revisions on Larpent texts, see Conolly, *Censorship*.

[172] Quoted in Michael Dobson, *The Making of the National Poet: Shakespearian Adaptation and Authorship, 1660–1769* (Oxford, 1992), 210.

## PERFORMANCE

*Actors in performance*

Actors were still prepared only up to a certain point before
performance, and continued to be directed on stage by the
prompter, who co-ordinated both the words (bad actors suffered the 'absurdity of being *prompted in the passions*'[173]), and
elementary blocking (with the help of a call-boy). The central
importance of the prompter to the staging is shown by the fact
that an actor's position had come, in stage directions, to be
always described in relation to that of the prompter: 'O.P.'—
opposite prompt; 'P.S.'—prompt side. The co-ordinating
nature of the prompter, and the very separate nature of each
part, still seem to have been clear both to theatrical people and
to their audience. Despite the increased number of group
rehearsals held, productions were not obviously more ensemble
as a result, and the old criticisms about cue-script actors were
frequently made. 'Sir' John Hill, in 1755, offered a warning
against 'the young actor's practice of knowing when he is to
speak by the words of his cues'; this was repeated twenty years
later by Cooke:[174] little had obviously changed in the interim.
Cooke's full demands on the actor were not even particularly
rigorous: he encouraged performers to 'remember the *substance*
of every other persons part, (particularly those in the same
scenes with himself) as well as the *words* of his own', but
acknowledged that this 'may seem like laying too heavy a
burden on an actor'.[175] Actors still seem often to have taken a
sense of 'part' onto the stage with them; bad first nights are
attributed to the lack of '*mutual play of action*'.[176] Pickering
claimed that actors were so focused on their own speeches that
they were incapable of reacting even to lines spoken directly to
them: unscripted 'silent' moments seemed

to be considered by the Generality of Actors, as intended merely for the
*Recovery of their Breath*; and are commonly employed in surveying the
Number and quality of the *Audience*. We shall find, among some, a
Speech calculated to *excite* a *latent Passion* . . . received with perfect

---

[173] Cooke, *Elements*, 204.     [174] Hill, *Actor*, 254.
[175] Cooke, *Elements*, 205.     [176] Ibid. 196.

*Apathy* and *Indifference*; and the Answer, all at once, preposterously
returned in the *Rage* of *Passion*, or *Theatrical Throws of Distress*.[177]

There were often specific reasons behind actors' failure to
respond to each other's performances. 'Sir' John Hill writes
that lesser players, outraged by the smallness of the audience,
would give up on the play and 'take snuff, or talk of their beer-
engagements in the most interesting scenes'; Sarah Ward, during
'one of the most pathetic scenes of *The Fair Penitent*' dedicated
herself to adjusting the knot on her glove to upstage a fellow
performer; Stayley tells of an actor who keeps himself in the
limelight by reprimanding the music, frowning at the prompter,
and crossing the stage 'from Side to Side when another was
speaking, to scold some Body behind the Scenes'.[178] But even
without disruptive intent, the casual markings on the manuscript
part of Gomez in Dryden's *The Spanish Friar* show an actor
whose concern is to know how long he has to wait before he can
speak again, rather than to think of theatrical responses he can
have in the interim: 'apart for 20 lines' he notes; 'for 13'; 'for
15'.[179] Players were still not actively involved in the story in
which they performed, because they had been taught only to
offer the audience a series of prepared set-pieces when required
to do so: their 'silences' had not been instructed, and they had no
rules to determine how to respond to them.

The audience was involved more in 'dramatic collusion' than
dramatic illusion, for they not only countenanced actors who
side-stepped or queried the plays they were in, but, in several
respects, required them to do so. The system of immediate
audience approval or condemnation expressed with claps and
hisses demanded direct response. It was at least expected that a
player 'as the servant and creature of the public, ought not to
refuse repeating any line or sentence ... when demanded by the
spectators'.[180] At other times audiences took part in productions,
as when a mob from the pit 'rescued' Harlequin when he was to
be hanged on the stage in Richard Bentley's *The Wishes*.[181] Not

---

[177] Ibid.; Pickering, *Reflections*, 52. See also Gentleman, *Modish Wife*, 26–7.

[178] Hill, *Actor*, 178; Bellamy, *Apology*, ii. 114; Stayley, *Life*, ii. 100. For other,
similar, examples, see Lynch, *Box*, 140; Clinton-Baddeley, *All Right on the Night*, 21–
2; *Correspondence of Garrick*, i. 165.

[179] Edward Langhans, *Eighteenth Century British and Irish Promptbooks* (New York,
1987), 45.                          [180] Davies, *Miscellanies*, ii. 141.

[181] Smith and Lawhon, *Plays . . . 1737–1800*, 187.

only were audiences responding to the theatrical experience, they were involved in it, moulding and remoulding it with their comments and reactions. Naturally enough, actors tended to address the audience rather than one another, even though this too threatened the believability of the spectacle. Richard Yates, a famous and respected actor, is described as directing his dialogue so particularly to the pit that he leaned his whole upper body out over the orchestra, which looked 'unpardonably absurd, when there [was] any body on the stage whom he might address'.[182]

An inimical relationship, but a relationship nevertheless, was built up between individual actors and the people variously described as 'The Town'[183] and 'Mr Town'. The latter actually existed: there was a key member of the pit, 'ludicrously denominated Mr. Town', who was spokesman for the more intellectual spectators, so that 'the audience' really did have a face and a name.[184] This may have encouraged the intimate banter and regular dialogue between actor and audience that manifested itself even while plays were performing, or may have brought it about. Mrs Bellamy, as Juliet, heard a laugh just when she was about to drink her poison. She left the stage in a huff, refusing to continue until the perpetrator of the laugh had confessed and apologized.[185] Quin, on the other hand, found his concentration broken by the applause he was receiving in the character of Volpone in Jonson's *Volpone*; he 'stopped short in the middle of a Speech', exhorting the audience with 'For Heaven's Sake, Gentlemen . . . let me go on with my Part! You do not know how you distress me.'[186] Audiences similarly would demand apologies from actors who had displeased them. When Samuel Reddish forgot to turn up to the theatre to play his role one evening, he was forced to go before the spectators and explain his absence; he swore that 'he had entirely forgot that it was a play night . . .[and] his looks were so truly pitiable, the Audience

---

[182] *Theatrical Review* (1758), 11.

[183] For example Cross–Hopkins, 1 Feb. 1773: 'as the Author was kept a secret The Town fancy'd that is [*sic*] one of Mr Bickerstaffs and call'd out to know who was the Author.'

[184] Bellamy, *Apology*, i. 54. She identifies a Mr Chitty as being Drury Lane's Mr Town; in *Covent Garden Theatre*, Larpent MS, l.a.96 (1752), 15, Mr Town is also called 'Jack Hydra', a single, evil collective.

[185] Bellamy, *Apology*, iii. 71.                    [186] Stayley, *Life*, ii. 56.

had Compassion and excus'd him'.[187] Unsurprisingly, plays which referred outside themselves to the circumstances that brought them about, or brought the audience to the theatre, or the actors to the stage, were popular, for the circumstances surrounding a play were clearly a substantial part of the evening's entertainment. A play itself was only one of a number of theatrical spectacles that the audience had come to watch and participate in, and this naturally influenced the way plays were performed and revised.

*Actors and extemporization*

Comment is frequently made in contemporary accounts to the effect that Garrick 'steadily discouraged' extemporization, so that it all but disappeared from the English stage.[188] At the same time, anecdotes are still full of actor–audience exchanges, as well as extra-theatrical textual references. Small fragments of word-play, and short interlocutions with the audience, seem not to have counted as extemporization: the notion of fidelity to a text was looser than it is today. Garrick himself was a perpetrator of 'additional' jokes. Reference has already been made to Garrick's extemporizations when performing Bayes, but in other plays too he stepped outside character to address the audience in his own person. In Ben Jonson's *Alchemist* one evening, when 'Face' asked 'Drugger' (Garrick) whether he had any interest with the players 'M$^r$ G answer'd I believe I had once—but dont know if I have now or not—It had a good Effect—his hav$^g$ Just Sold his Share of the Patent.'[189] The great actor exploited the audience's interest in theatrical gossip and in the actor as actor. Woodward did much the same when he was addressing Mrs Clive as Lady Froth, and decided to alter his lines from 'your coachman having a red face' to 'your Ladyship having a red face' (which was true) to amuse the spectators.[190] In both instances, the actor colludes with the audience on points of fact outside the play, and the audience is prepared to sacrifice the credibility of the production for the thrill of sharing a joke with the actor. This introduces a point often made, that 'it is not the play, but the player; not the

---

[187] Cross–Hopkins, 9 Mar. 1772/3.   [188] Davies, *Garrick*, i. 112.
[189] Cross–Hopkins, 18 Jan. 1776.   [190] Davies, *Miscellanies*, iii. 192.

exploits of a Richard or a Tamerlane, but the fame of their representative that the people come to see'.[191] Indeed, that the audience was frequently watching the actor first and the play second is illustrated by the regularity with which applause for a famous actor was continued 'till the curtain fell, without suffering the [play] to be regularly finished'. It was even taken as a mark of respect to leave the theatre when the character played by a capital actor died, irrespective of whether or not the play itself was over at that point.[192] One German visitor to London recalled how a tragic actress was so moved by her own part that she fainted away, and most of the audience, unable themselves to 'endure the strain' of the play, departed, leaving behind only the most 'hard-boiled' amongst them:[193] the play was so affecting as to demand its own incompletion, for the spectators willing to see the story through are criticized for their lack of sensibility. Plays seem to have been written with this potential response in mind, so that major characters often do not die until the final scene; or, alternatively, the 'plot' is explained at some point before the end of the play itself, for, explains a knowing playwright, 'the beginnings and ends of plays were never wrote to be heard'.[194] Plays were thus shaped not only by the way actors learnt their lines, but by anticipation of the way the audience might respond; a good author needed such a detailed knowledge of each aspect of the theatre, that, unsurprisingly, most successful playwrights in this period were actors themselves.

Minor textual jokes of the kind illustrated above indicate that the spectators had a strong familiarity with stock plays, for part of the humour of stepping outside a text in this way depended on the audience knowing the lines that should have been spoken. Similarly they responded to theatrical references that might be no more than physical 'moments' lifted from other plays, as when the actors in Isaac Jackman's *All the World's a Stage*, imitate 'the scene in the Beggar's Opera, where Peachum drags his daughter from Macheath'.[195] The audience needed to be able to overlay the play as they were seeing it with the play

[191] Wilkinson, *Wandering Patentee*, 292.

[192] Cooke, *Foote*, 86; O'Keeffe, *Recollections*, i. 288; Clinton-Baddeley, *All Right on the Night*, 43.

[193] Pedicord, *Theatrical Public*, 62.

[194] Richard Bentley, *The Wishes*, Larpent MS, l.a.199 (1761).

[195] Isaac Jackman, *All the World's a Stage* (1777), 31.

in its ideal form: they were trained to applaud what should have been as well as what was, so they responded favourably to the aged Colley Cibber's Cardinal Pandolph (*King John*), even when they 'could only be entertained with his Attitudes and Conduct' as he had lost all his teeth and had become inaudible.[196] The process of watching successful plays was cumulative, involving building up a complex knowledge of the ways of text, action, and actors over successive performances. A new play thus emerges as a completely different entity from an old play, to be watched from a different perspective.

### First performance

In 1760 George Colman articulated something that I have argued is clear about first performances from the Restoration onwards. 'The first night's representation', he writes, of *Polly Honeycombe*, ' . . . like most other first nights, was nothing more than a Publick Rehearsal.'[197] After this 'rehearsal' Colman willingly received suggestions about revisions he should make, many proposed by his mother: the rehearsal was textual. He is joined by Sheridan, who tactfully claims to view 'a First Night's Audience, as a candid and judicious friend attending, in behalf of the Public, at his last Rehearsal'.[198]

Examples of audience-based revisions extend from the usual shortening of scenes after first performance,[199] to the elimination of overtly tragic moments on stage. Late eighteenth-century audiences were angrily sensitive; they forced Johnson's Irene to leave the stage alive by their hisses, rather than suffer her to be strangled in front of them with a bowstring.[200] The text was then rewritten as a result, so that Irene died off-stage, and the coy removal to 'other rooms' of most tragic occurrences shows other plays revised in advance to take account of audience sensibility.[201]

---

[196] Victor, *Theatres from 1760*, ii. 163.  [197] Colman, *Polly*, p. vi.
[198] Richard Brinsley Sheridan, *The Rivals* (1775), p. ix.
[199] See, for instance, Thomas Hull, *The Perplexities* (1767), A2[b]: 'Since the copy was delivered to the press, some few passages have been shortened in representation'; Arthur Murphy, *School for Guardians* (1767), A2[b]: 'N.B. An entire scene in the second act . . . has been omitted since the first representation'.
[200] Lynch, *Box*, 229.
[201] Examples are Gloucester in *Lear*, who loses his eyes 'in an adjoining room', and Gertrude in *Hamlet*, who is 'led from her seat' off-stage, where she is reported to be

At the end of a new play, the audience would learn which revisions were to be made in response to their wishes. The diaries kept by successive prompters Richard Cross and William Hopkins depict Garrick explaining to the audience that 'as we find the new scene, tho' it pleases some offends others & as we wou'd please all, we shall omit it after this night'; and William Havard telling spectators that the passages of Frances Sheridan's new play which had given 'offence', would be 'omitted the next Night'.[202] On the same occasion, audiences would also be allowed the opportunity to decide whether or not to damn the play entirely: the manager would ask if 'under the sanction of your kind approbation' the play could be performed again, and cries of 'aye' and 'no' would give him the answer.[203] Alterations as the result of the first night were so normal (Elizabeth Inchbald casually mentions that she is 'pleased to find the farce of the positive man changed' since last performance[204]) that there was a routine for dealing with them. When Foote's play *Taste* was objected to, the tired prompter simply placed an advertisement in the paper, 'to signifie the author had withdrawn it to alter &c &c'.[205] An obvious question arises as to whether audience-censored texts were resubmitted to the Lord Chamberlain. L. W. Conolly's research shows that almost certainly they were not, which means that the audience's opinion was somehow beyond censoring; indeed it formed the basis of many popular 'prompter-texts'.[206]

Prologues and epilogues continued to signify the particular novice status of a play; 'new' plays were separated from 'old' plays by additional theatrical paraphernalia. Indeed, when Mrs Clive was, unusually, made by the audience to speak her epilogue every evening, the prompter still saw that it was 'left

---

insane, rather than poisoned in front of the audience. See Davies, *Miscellanies*, ii. 197; iii. 87.

[202] Cross–Hopkins, 13 Dec. 1752; 10 Dec. 1763. It was still absolutely normal to shorten a play after its first performance: Cross–Hopkins, 11 Jan. 1752 related how 'No alterations were made in the farce, but cutting out a little'.

[203] Dibdin, *Reminiscences*, i. 7. If a play for which dissatisfaction had been expressed were rerun without revision, audiences might well insist on its being changed—see Cross–Hopkins, 2 Dec. 1772: 'it was hiss'd from the beginning & [the audience] w$^d$ not suffer it to be given out again therefore M$^r$ King went & told them it should not be perform'd again until it be alter'd.'

[204] Mrs Inchbald, *Diary*, 10 Feb. 1788.

[205] Cross–Hopkins, 11 Jan. 1572.        [206] Conolly, *Censorship*, 21.

out of y$^c$ bills after y$^c$ 6$^{th}$ Night', presumably because a billed epilogue would give out a wrong message about the play itself.[207] The only exception to this was when new actors were taking to the stage. Then, even if they were to perform in an old play, a supplicatory prologue or epilogue would be written to introduce them and to beg the audience for mercy.[208] Prologues and epilogues were thus always defensive, and were connected not only with novelty but also with unproved (and therefore questionable) ability.

Naturally a play was not completely rehearsed until 'approved'. Garrick grudgingly let Reed's *Dido* have one performance, but to his surprise, the play took. He then suggested mounting the play, for 'as it has undergone the fiery Trial there will be no danger of getting it through its "rights"';[209] the play was, however, to be put on the following season with a completely different set of actors, which gives an indication of the extent to which the first night was a rehearsal of the play rather than the performers. Generally after a first night, the semi-rehearsed actors then solidified their performance: 'It is a saying almost in every body's mouth on the first night of a new, or revived play, if there should appear any little lapses of memory, or inaccuracies in acting, "that when the performers are more *practised* they will do better" '.[210] Garrick would take up a position behind the scenes on the first night to evaluate his actors' performances and offer further criticism.[211] As a young man, he had himself sought help from Macklin in the role of Lear, asking him to 'sit in judgement . . . the first night' and offer a commentary afterwards. This Macklin duly did, Garrick noting down afterwards the 'improvements' suggested.[212] This approach rendered the final ensemble rehearsal before performance less important: an actor did not have to be perfect on the first night, so the idea of creating a finished product by rehearsing was less crucial. Even the newspapers seemed to find the notion of starting off on the wrong foot and then correcting one's mistakes almost acceptable: the 'Critic' of the

---

[207] Cross–Hopkins, 25 Oct. 1750.      [208] *Walpole*, ix. 42.

[209] Reed, *Theatrical Duplicity*, 68.

[210] Cooke, *Elements*, 195.      [211] Everard, *Memoirs*, 24.

[212] Cooke, *Macklin*, 104. For another 'long meditated character', Abel Drugger in Ben Jonson's *The Alchemist*, he 'had several private rehearsals . . . before Macklin and other friends', see p. 110.

*Oxford Magazine* noted a few 'trifling improprieties' on the first night of Murphy's *Grecian Daughter*, but was sure that 'they . . . will undergo a critical and managerial Castigation, during the run of the piece: Which has generally been the case with most modern productions of the Stage.'[213]

The time between first and second night was spent in frantic revisions, mostly made by the author.[214] *The Author on the Wheel* (1785), shows how sometimes only a day would be allowed for revisions—and how, even then, the author was not necessarily invited to be present. The first scene is a depiction of an 'alteration' session for a very bad play that the audience greatly disliked. 'I wonder he [Vainwit, the author] can be so obstinate in persisting to have it plai'd again' muses Drama, the manager, who has invited all his actors together so that they can 'mutually consult' about what to do with the play. He himself doubts the audience will agree to see the piece again at all, but suggests that, if they do, 'such parts as appear'd exceptionable to [them], should be expung'd'.[215] Not all the actors bother to attend this alteration session; one who has 'a cold' sends in her part so that revisions can be marked on it, desiring that 'you'll let her have it as soon as possible that she may have time to be perfect at night'. As depicted in this play, parts on which alterations are marked have not always been revised in the presence of the actors concerned. *Author on the Wheel* also illustrates the way actors received and learnt their revised parts, and, again, suggests that revisions were not always rehearsed.

### Part-based revision

Tate Wilkinson's servant would not go to watch the young John Philip Kemble perform Hamlet as 'it is Mr. Cummin's part'.[216] Actors and their roles continued to be connected in the minds of the audience, which naturally led to a part-based interest in plays. This can be seen in the way that Sylas Neville prepared to see Mrs Yates perform Medea in 1769: he 'Read her part before the play began'.[217] Indeed, the theatre encouraged plays to be

---

[213] Quoted in Burnim, *David Garrick*, 46.
[214] *The Schemers* (1775), A3ᵃ, met with such applause that the 'Public' can hope 'Mr. *Garrick* will, at his Leisure, make . . . further Alterations'.
[215] *Author* (Larpent MS).
[216] Wilkinson, *Wandering Patentee*, ii. 11.        [217] *London Stage*, IV, p. clxxix.

watched unequally, teaching the audience to pay more fervent attention to some parts than to others: '*hush* men' kept spectators quiet whenever Garrick played, but did not stop chatter during any other actor's performance.[218] The result was that when, for instance, Quin became unpopular in 1750–1, he was hissed 'even in his best parts': the performer, but also his part, and a section therefore of any play he was in, was sacrificed to the audience's displeasure.[219] The reverse was also true: popular players might be well received even when consciously performing in an inappropriate way. Mrs Clive, who inserted parodies of known lawyers into the trial scene when playing Portia, was clearly ruining the '*solemn, pathetic,* and *affecting*' portrayal Shakespeare had intended but was, after all, 'greatly Comic'.[220] The audience was left with a fragmentary knowledge of sections and moments from great plays, and this, in turn, was reflected in the way they formed their amateur acting groups. A fashion grew up for 'Spouter Clubs' in which the would-be actors could meet together 'to rehearse Parts and Speeches of Plays' rather than to mount full performances.[221] Literary and theatrical criticism of the time is, unsurprisingly, often dedicated to discussions of single actors and single roles—indeed, the whole idea of examining Shakespeare in terms of close character-analysis, which originated during this period, seems to have arisen from the focused way the audience watched and thought about their drama.[222]

Part-based thinking led to part-based revisions of two kinds. As roles were still 'as much the *property* of performers, as their weekly salary',[223] they were revised internally by the actors who owned them: textual change continued to happen at different rates within single plays. Actors' ownership of their roles was, moreover, accepted on a more profound level: though the anonymous *Guide to the Stage* complains that 'the actors of the last class claim a right to alter or expunge whatever they disapprove of in their respective parts',[224] in fact, acting text-books of the time

---

[218] Boaden, *Siddons*, ii. 377.
[219] Lynch, *Box*, 209.
[220] Victor, *Theatres from 1760*, iii, 144.
[221] Henry Dell, *The Spouter* (1756), 13.
[222] Gray, *Theatrical Criticism*, 154.
[223] Bellamy, *Apology*, i. 100.
[224] *A Guide to the Stage* (1751), 15.

specifically tell actors to 'mend' what they have been given. Cooke advises the aspiring player to make sure he has 'a knowledge of grammar', so that he can 'detect the lapses of authors' and correct them; 'Sir' John Hill is circumspect:

> as the actor may sometimes add a word, there are also passages he may drop: . . . Mr. Mills used to boast, that he spoke perfectly a very dull soliloquy, which Wilks never was able to remember. He was told, and justly, that there was more merit in Mr. Wilks's forgetting that, than in all he ever remembered.[225]

No wonder, therefore, the casual notes to the effect that, for instance, 'Mrs. Clive . . . made additions to the last scene on this occasion.'[226] This freedom had come about as another result of the way audiences watched and judged performers. Actors were accepted as having responsibility for the nature of what they spoke—hence the stories of actresses refusing saucy songs or racy lines for fear their reputations would suffer—they were supposed to 'protect' the audience by making responsible revisions to their speeches. Such revision was, as ever, to the exclusion of the author; indeed, actors' alterations could reflect any negative feelings they had towards their parts. Theophilus Cibber tells an anecdote about a comedian who 'whenever he had a Part, where the Redundancy of the Author run into too great a Length in the Scenes, . . . had recourse to a whimsical Expedient for the shortning of 'em: He had the whole Part wrote out, and then, gave it his Cat to play with: ——What Puss claw'd off, the Actor left out; yet he generally found enough remain'd to satisfy the Audience'[227] An audience might, as a result of actor's revision, never see a play as written at all.

On another level, part-revision was reflected in what authors and theatricalizers did, not to whole plays, but to elements of them. David Mallet was prepared to alter his *Alfred* twice, the first time to make 'the great part . . . that of the Hermit', because it was to be played by his friend Quin, the second time to make Alfred 'the most striking part', as it was to be played by Garrick.[228] Mallet's play was specifically altered to meet the

---

[225] Cooke, *Elements*, 183; Hill, *Actor*, 265.
[226] Genest, *Some Account of the English Stage*, iv. 326.
[227] Theophilus Cibber, *Two Dissertations*, 34–5.
[228] Bellamy, *Apology*, ii. 138.

requirements of the actors who were to perform it. Similarly Garrick's *Lethe* was revised along one part that became outdated: the 'Fine Gentleman', directed towards the men who stood behind the scenes at playhouses, was, when that particular custom was abolished, replaced with an 'entirely new written' part: that of Fribble.[229] Even the Lord Chamberlain revised parts, taking exception to 'the Bawd' and 'the whole character of Lady *Wrinkle*' in *Dido*, so that Reed had to revise away the ladies and substitute a new female character.[230] The Reed complaints are instructive, because most of them are connected to the fates of 'parts' rather than to the fate of his whole plays: when he wrote 'Mrs Doggerel', a single part insertion, to be added into *The Register Office* for his benefit, he did so intending later 'to remove [her] . . . into another piece'.[231] To his chagrin, however, Garrick 'stole' Mrs Doggerel and put her into a production of *Zenobia* before Reed could recover her.[232] Parts could, as this makes clear, have an external existence outside the play they were written for—another result of their being closely connected to the actor who played them rather than to the play in which they occurred.

## CONCLUSION

One of the greatest theatrical events of the late eighteenth century, Garrick's famous Stratford Jubilee (1767), did not include a single production of a Shakespeare play.[233] The event itself was theatrical without being closely identified with a text, and the same might be said for many late eighteenth-century productions. The theatre's obsession with 'theatricality', was not contradicted by a loose concern for the integrity of plays themselves. As actors rather than plays were the focus of late eighteenth-century theatre—actors' quarrels were simply another aspect of 'the Entertainment of Mr. and Mrs. Town'[234]—many alterations were actor- and part-related, rather than play-related. The very kind of acting that Garrick promoted, which involved creating

---

[229] *Theatrical Review* (1772), 22.   [230] Reed, *Theatrical Duplicity*, 5–6.
[231] Ibid. 79.   [232] Ibid. 88.
[233] See Dobson, *Making of the National Poet*, 214.
[234] Thomas Holcroft, *The Rival Queens*, Larpent MS, l.a.1039 (1794), 17.

new interpretations for old roles, was clearly moving away from concepts of authorial intention; Garrick revised plays, old and new, to fit them to his conception, rather than trying to fit his conception to the plays. The audience accepted this, for their interest in actively judging performances demanded flexibility from the actors which required potential flexibility of text: the playwright's intentions were not of great importance.

As plays had a relatively low value as commodities, it is hardly surprising that they were cavalierly treated throughout the period. With Garrick as manager, plays were mercilessly lopped not only as a response to audience criticism, but also in anticipation of it. Several plays seem, as a result, to have gone through two or three very different manifestations, over which the author had little or no control, so that 'what is head' of a play one night '[is] tail another'.[235] Thus in its final form, a five-act play might have become a one-act farce. In a new prologue to Henry Fielding's *The Miser*, a Poet enters carrying a farce in his hand. His words are 'CONFUSION! how th'have farcified my Play, | Oh! what a deal of wit th'have clip'd away'.[236] Even theatrical fictions were starting to accept that the author did not 'own' his play in the way that the theatre did. This prologue is met by tales, that, for example, Murphy one day arrived at Covent Garden to see his opera *Robin Hood*, and found it 'performed as an afterpiece, having been, without his knowledge, cut down into two acts'; or, to instance a similar event described in positive form, that Colman was able to save a damned version of *A Midsummer Night's Dream*, when 'he luckily thought of turning it into a Farce, which Alteration he made in one Night'.[237] Explaining his preference for 'a few well-chosen scenes from a good Comedy', Brownlow Forde explains how 'custom has long adopted the method of turning Plays into Farces; witness the Wanton Wife, the Ghost, Friendship a la mode . . .'.[238]

Group rehearsal failed to make the actors aware of the play as a whole or of their common goal in performing it together, because that was not the emphasis of acting. The possession of

---

[235] Gentleman, *Modish Wife*, 12.
[236] *Theatrical Review* (1763), 130.
[237] O'Keeffe, *Recollections*, i. 44; MacMillan, *Calendar*, 100.
[238] Brownlow Forde, *The Miraculous Cure* (1771), A2ᵃ.

parts, the stress on private instruction, even the benefit system itself, which made certain nights more financially lucrative for one actor than for another, promoted the idea of the individual against the group; this was reflected in the way that plays were written and revised. With such mental barriers against a full, 'whole' production, it is unsurprising that the playwright received such short shrift: the 'rehearsal' in which an overall conception governing a play could be discussed with the actors only existed notionally (though it flourished in rehearsal plays). Almost all capital actors made it clear that they only attended general rehearsals at all on sufferance, and did not expect to get anything out of the process themselves. Group rehearsals were called, partly for the prompter, who wanted to test line-knowledge, and work out entrances and exits, partly for the manager, who could 'individually rehearse' several actors at once during the occasion, partly for minor actors, to ensure that they produced a reasonable framework in which the major actors could perform. They were useful, too, for the practice of specific group activities like fights and dances, but were seen as, at best, a continuation of private rehearsal, not a kind of rehearsal in their own right.

Thus by the time of Garrick, the theatre was, in many ways, an extreme version of what it had been throughout the sixteenth, seventeenth, and eighteenth centuries—and this was frequently acknowledged. Shakespeare's theatre when it was addressed, was described as a primitive version of the eighteenth-century theatre, for the two shared fundamental ideas of what acting was about, Shakespeare requiring a mastery of 'action and passion' totally understandable to early theatre historians.[239] Davies thus had no difficulty explaining theatrical terms in Shakespearian plays, for they were still current. He glossed Malcolm's 'one that had been studied in his death' (*Macbeth*) as 'a phrase borrowed from the theatre: to be studied in a part is to have . . . made yourself a master of it'; and King John's 'mark'd, Quoted and sign'd to do a deed of shame' as 'a playhouse word. The characters who are to be called by the prompter's boy to be ready for the scene, are quoted by him in the margin of the play.'[240] Theatrical preparation did not

[239] Davies, *Miscellanies*, i. 19.     [240] Ibid. ii. 76; i. 62.

fundamentally alter between the sixteenth and eighteenth centuries, though its emphases changed. What seems to have remained fairly constant is the way 'rehearsal' bred tensions that led to a wealth of different kinds of textual revision, especially as 'rehearsal' spread its meaning into the first night, so that, in writing about rehearsal, it has been necessary to write about the relationship of actors to plays, and plays to actors, and the relationship of the audience to both. Rehearsal extends beyond the way in which plays are prepared for performance into the process of textual change itself.

The story of detailed individual rehearsal and cursory group rehearsal continues along the same lines until well into the nineteenth century: Edmund Kean, arriving at the Croydon theatre to act *The Merchant of Venice* and Colman's *The Iron Chest* for the first time, told the stage manager that 'I will not require rehearsals for my plays'.[241] At the very end of the eighteenth century, a few years after the death of Garrick, even a superficial interest in group rehearsal could not be depended upon. In 1796 Colman the Younger bitterly depicted a Drury Lane rehearsal as '*lucus* a non *lucendo*. They yclep it rehearsal, I conjecture, because *they do* NOT *rehearse*'.[242] Without Garrick, there were few proponents of group rehearsal around in the theatre except for unheeded playwrights. To the writers of the time, group rehearsal, like *The Rehearsal* (discarded in the 1780s and replaced by Sheridan's *The Critic*), seemed to be history.

---

[241] Quoted in Norman Marshall, *The Producer and the Play*, 3rd edn. (1957, London, 1975), 12.

[242] Colman, *Iron Chest*, p. iv.

# Select Bibliography

Using the Readex Microprint series, *Three Centuries of English and American Plays 1500–1830* (New York: Readex Microprints, 1963), every play published between 1550 and 1780 has been consulted. This bibliography contains only the plays and secondary literature cited in footnotes.

PRIMARY SOURCES

*Manuscripts*

[ANON.], *Author on the Wheel*, Huntington Library, Larpent MS, l.a.144 (1785)

[ANON.], *Britons Strike Home*, Huntington Library, Larpent MS, l.a.16 (1739)

[ANON.], *The Hodge Podge*, Huntington Library, Larpent MS, l.a.569 (1781)

[ANON.], *Music Alamode, or, Bays in Chromatics*, Huntington Library, Larpent MS, l.a.237 (1764)

[ANON.], *Theatrical Miscellany*, Folger Library MS, T.b.1

BENTLEY, RICHARD, *The Wishes*, Huntington Library, Larpent MS, l.a.199 (1761)

BONNER, CHARLES, *The Manager an Actor in Spite of Himself*, Huntington Library, Larpent MS, l.a.664 (1784)

COLMAN, GEORGE [THE YOUNGER], *Poor Old Haymarket*, Huntington Library, Larpent MS, l.a.951 (1792)

Corporation of London Records Office, Repertories of the Court of Aldermen, Rep. 29, fol. 233$^r$

CROSS, RICHARD, and HOPKINS WILLIAM, *Diary 1747–1776: Drury Lane*, 13 vols., Folger Library MS, W.a.104

HOLCROFT, THOMAS, *The Rival Queens*, Huntington Library, Larpent MS, l.a.1039 (1794)

HOPKINS, WILLIAM, 'A Memorandum Book', MS in R. J. Smith, *A Collection of Material*, vol. viii, British Library, 11826. R. S.

INCHBALD, ELIZABETH, *Diaries*, Folger Library MS, M.a.152.

Papers connected with the production of a version of A Midsummer Night's Dream', Folger Library MS, W.b.469.

REED, JOSEPH, *Theatrical Duplicity* (n.d., watermarked 1833), Folger Library MS, T.a.112

*Newspapers and periodicals*

ADDISON, JOSEPH and STEELE, RICHARD, *The Spectator*, ed. Donald R. Bond, 5 vols. (Oxford: Clarendon Press, 1965)
*The Censor*, 2nd edn. 4 vols. (1717)
*Daily Courant* (1702–35)
*Daily Journal* (London, 1720–7)
*Daily Post* (1719–47)
*The Female Tatler*, ed. Fidelis Morgan (London: Dent, 1992)
MOTTEUX, PETER, *The Gentlemen's Journal* (London, 1691–5)
*Grubb St. Journal* (1730–7)
*Theatrical Examiner* (1757)
*Theatrical Review for the years 1757 and beginning of 1758* (1758)
*The Theatrical Review: Volume 2* (1772)
*The Theatrical Review* (1779)
*The Theatrical Manager* (1751)
STEELE, RICHARD, *The Tatler*, ed. Donald F. Bond, 3 vols. (Oxford: Clarendon Press, 1987)
STONECASTLE, HENRY, *The Universal Spectator*, 4 vols. (1747)
WARD, EDWARD, *The London Spy* (1698–1700)
*Weekly Journal or Saturday's Post* (1720–5)

*Electronic Sources*

CHADWYCK-HEALEY, *English Verse Drama*, CD-ROM © 1995
—— *The English Poetry Full-Text Database*, CD-ROM © 1995

*Printed Sources*

[ANON.], *Angelica; or Quixote in Petticoats* (1758)
—— *Apology For . . . T— C—, Comedian* (1740)
—— *The Constant Nymph, or, The Rambling Shepheard* (1678)
—— *A Dialogue in the Green Room upon a Disturbance in the Pit* (1783)
—— *The Female Wits*, facs. for The Augustan Reprint Society, ed. Lucyle Hook (Los Angeles: Univ. of California, 1967)
—— *A Guide to the Stage* (1751)
—— *The History of the Tryall of Cheualry* (1605)
—— *Humours of the Court* (1732)
—— *Lady Alimony* (1659)
—— *The Laureat: or the Right Side of Colly Cibber* (1740)

—— *Letters by Several Eminent Persons Deceased*, 2 vols. (1772)

—— *Narcissus: A Twelfe Night Merriment*, ed. Margaret C. Lee (1893)

—— *A Proposal for the Better Regulation of the Stage* (1732)

—— *Ratseis Ghost* (1605)

—— *The Schemers* (1775)

—— *The Theatrical Jester: or Green-room Witticisms* (1795)

—— *The Theatrical Review* (1763)

—— *The Three Parnassus Plays*, ed. J. B. Leishman (London: Ivor Nicholson and Watson Ltd, 1949)

—— *The Two Merry Milke-Maids* (1620)

—— *Visits from the Shades* (1704)

—— *The Wanton Jesuit* (1731)

—— *Wily Beguilde* (1606)

—— *Wit for the Ton!* (1778)

—— [——], *Wit Without Mony* (1707)

—— *The Younger Brother* (1719)

—— 'Muses, Lover of the', *The Author's Triumph* (1737)

ADDISON, JOSEPH, *The Drummer* (1716)

*An Alvearie or Quadruple Dictionarie* (1580)

ANDERSON, J. W., *The manner pointed out in which the Common Prayer was read in private by . . . Mr. Garrick: for the instruction of a young Clergyman: from whose MS. notes this pamphlet is composed* (1797)

ARMIN, ROBERT, *Collected Works*, ed. J. P. Feather, 2 vols. (New York: Johnson Reprint Corporation, 1972)

—— *A Nest of Ninnies*, ed. P. M. Zall (Lincoln, Nebr.: Univ. of Nebraska Press, 1970).

ASTON, ANTHONY, *Brief Supplement to the Life of Colley Cibber*, ed. Robert W. Lowe (1889; New York: AMS, 1966)

AUBREY, JOHN, *Brief Lives*, ed. Oliver Lawson Dick (1949; London: Penguin, 1962)

AYRES, JAMES, *Sancho at Court* (1742)

BAILLIE, WILLIAM M., (ed.), *A Choice Ternary of English Plays* (Binghamton, NY: State Univ. of New York, 1984)

BAKER, RICHARD, *Theatrum Redivivum* (1662)

BAKER, THOMAS, *The Humour of the Age* (1701)

—— *The Tunbridge-Walks* (1703)

BALDWIN, WILLIAM, *Beware the Cat*, ed. William A. Ringler Jr. and Michael Flachman (San Marino, Calif.: Huntington Library, 1988)

BALE, JOHN, *The Complete Plays of John Bale*, ed. Peter Happé, 2 vols. (Cambridge: D. S. Brewer, 1985)

BAWCUTT, N. W., *Malone Society Collections: XV* (Oxford: Malone Society, 1993)

BEAUMONT, FRANCIS, *Knight of the Burning Pestle* (1613)

BEAUMONT, FRANCIS, *Poems by Francis Beaumont* (1653)

——and JOHN FLETCHER, *Comedies and Tragedies written by Francis Beaumont and John Fletcher* (1647)

—— —— *The Dramatic Works in the Beaumont and Fletcher Canon*, ed. Fredson Bowers, 9 vols. (Cambridge: CUP, 1966–94)

—— ——*Philaster* (3rd impression, 1628)

—— —— *The Woman-Hater* (1607)

*Behind the Curtain*, nineteenth-century pamphlet, n.d., attached to vol. ii of an extra-illustrated *Life of Garrick* by Davies (1780), Folger Library, Bd.W.W.b.473–76

BEHN, APHRA, *The Dutch Lover* (1673)

—— *The False Count* (1682)

—— *The Luckey Chance* (1687)

—— *The Widdow Ranter* (1690)

BELLAMY, D., *The Young Ladies Miscellany . . . To which is Prefixed, a Short Essay on the Art of Pronunciation . . .* (1723)

BELLAMY, GEORGE ANNE, *An Apology for the life of George Anne Bellamy*, 5 vols., 3rd edn. (1785)

BELLERS, FETTIPLACE, *Injur'd Innocence* (1732)

BETTERTON, THOMAS, *The Sequel of Henry the Fourth* (1721)

—— and BEHN, APHRA, *The Amorous Widow* (1706)

BOADEN, JAMES, *Memoirs of Mrs. Siddons*, 2 vols. (1827)

BOSWELL, JAMES, *Life of Johnson*, ed. R. W. Chapman (Oxford: OUP, 1953, rev. edn. 1979)

BRINSLEY, JOHN, *Ludus Literarius: Or The Grammar School* (1612)

BROME, RICHARD, *The Dramatic Works of Richard Brome*, ed. R. H. Shepherd, 3 vols. (1873; New York: AMS Press, Inc., 1966)

—— *The English Moore* ed. Sara Jayne Steen (Columbia, Mo.: Univ. of Missouri Press, 1983)

BROOKE, HENRY, *Gustavas Vasa* (1739)

BROWN, THOMAS [PSEUD. TOBIAS THOMAS], *The Life of the Famous Comedian Jo Haynes* (1701)

—— *The Reasons of Mr. Joseph Hains the Player's Conversion and Re-Conversion* (1690)

—— *The Works*, 4 vols. (1778–9)

BROWNSMITH, JOHN, *The Contrast* (1776)

—— *The Theatrical Alphabet* (1767)

BULLOCK, CHRISTOPHER, *The Cobler of Preston* (1723)

BULWER, JOHN, *Chirologia and Chironomia* (1644)

[BURNELL, HENRY], *Landgartha* (1641)

BURNEY, FANNY, *Diary and Letters of Madame D'Arblay*, 7 vols. (1846)

BURRIDGE, RICHARD, *A Scourge for the Play-Houses* (1702)

CAREW, RICHARD, *The Survey of Cornwall* (1602)

CAREY, HENRY, *The Honest Yorkshireman* (1736)
—— *Margery* (1738)
CARLELL, LODOWICK, *Two New Playes* (1657)
CARRINGTON, S., *The History of the Life and Death of His Most Serene Highness, Oliver, Late Lord Protector* (1659)
[CELISIA, DOROTHEA], *Almida* (1771)
CENTLIVRE, SUSANNA, *The Man's Bewitch'd* (n.d. 1710?)
—— *The Perplex'd Lovers* (1712)
CHAMBERS, EPHRAIM, *Cyclopaedia* (1738)
CHAPMAN, GEORGE, *The Plays of George Chapman: The Comedies*, ed. Allan Holaday and Michael Kiernan *et al.* (Urbana, Ill.: Univ. of Illinois Press, 1970)
CHAPPUZEAU, SAMUEL, *Le Théâtre français* (1867)
CHARKE, CHARLOTTE, *The Art of Management* (1735)
CHETWOOD, WILLIAM RUFUS, *A General History of The Stage* (1749)
CHURCHILL, CHARLES, *The Rosciad* (1761)
CIBBER, COLLEY, *An Apology for the Life of Mr Colley Cibber, written by himself*, ed. B. R. S. Fone (Ann Arbor: Univ. of Michigan Press, 1968)
—— *Plays written by Mr. Cibber*, 2 vols. (1721)
—— *Love's Last Shift* (1696)
—— *The Tragical History of King Richard III* (1700)
CIBBER, THEOPHILUS, *The Lives and Characters of the Most Eminent Actors and Actresses* (1753)
—— *The Lover* (1730)
—— *Two Dissertations on the Theatre* (1756)
CLAVELL, JOHN, *The So[l]ddered Citizen*, ed. John Henry Pyle Pafford and W. W. Greg (Oxford: Malone Society, 1936)
CLIVE, CATHERINE [KITTY], *The Rehearsal, or Bayes in Petticoats* (1753)
COHEN, GUSTAVE, *Le Livre de conduite du régisseur . . . pour le mystère de la Passion* (Paris: Librairie Ancienne Honoré Champion, 1925)
COHN, ALBERT, *Shakespeare in Germany in the Sixteenth and the Seventeenth Centuries* (1865)
COLERIDGE, SAMUEL TAYLOR, *Biographia Literaria*, ed. George Watson (1817; London: Dent, 1975)
COLMAN, GEORGE [THE ELDER], *The Jealous Wife* (1761)
—— *Man and Wife* in *Dramatic Works*, 4 vols. (1777)
—— *Musical Lady* (1762)
—— *New Brooms!* (1776)
—— *The Oxonian* (1769)
—— *Polly Honeycombe* (1760)
—— *A True State of the Differences . . . between the Proprietors of Covent Garden Theatre* (1768)

COLMAN, GEORGE [THE YOUNGER], *Memoirs of Samuel Foote* (1805)

—— *New Hay at the Old Market* (1795)

—— *Poor Old Haymarket* (1792)

CONGREVE, WILLIAM, *Concerning Humour in Comedy* (1695; New York: Russell and Russell, 1964)

COOK, DAVID, and WILSON, F. P., *Collections VI: Chamber Accounts, Payments to Players, etc.* (Oxford: Malone Society, 1962)

COOKE, JOHN, *Greenes Tu Quoque* (1614)

COOKE, THOMAS, *The Mournful Nuptials* (1739)

COOKE, WILLIAM, *The Elements of Dramatic Criticism* (1775)

—— *Memoirs of Charles Macklin, comedian* (1804)

—— *Memoirs of Samuel Foote, esq*, 3 vols. (1805)

COTGRAVE, RANDLE, *A Dictionarie of the French and English Tongues* (1611)

COWLEY, ABRAHAM, *The Complete Works in Verse and Prose of Abraham Cowley* (1656)

—— *Love's Riddle* (1638)

CRAUFORD, DAVID, *Courtship A-la-mode* (1700)

CRISP, SAMUEL, *Virginia* (1754)

CROWNE, JOHN, *City Politiques* (1683)

—— *The Dramatic Works of Crowne*, ed. James Maidment and W. H. Logan, 4 vols. (1874; New York: Benjamin Blom, 1967)

—— *Henry VI* (1681)

CUMBERLAND, RICHARD, *The Fashionable Lover* (1772)

—— *Memoirs of Richard Cumberland* (1806)

CUNLIFFE, JOHN W. (ed.), *Early English Classical Tragedies* (Oxford: Clarendon Press, 1912)

CURLL, EDMUND, *Memoirs of the Life of Robert Wilks* (1732)

—— [pseud. Thomas Betterton], *The History of the English Stage* (1741)

DANCHIN, PIERRE (ed.), *Prologues and Epilogues of the Eighteenth Century*, 2 vols. in 4 (Nancy: Presse Universitaires de Nancy, 1990– )

—— *Prologues and Epilogues of the Restoration, 1660–1672*, 1 vol. in 2 (Nancy: Presse Universitaires de Nancy, 1981)

DANIEL, SAMUEL, *The Whole Works of Samuel Daniel Esq* (1623)

DAVENANT, WILLIAM, *The Works of Sir William Davenant*, 3 vols. in 1 (1673)

DAVIES, JOHN, *The Complete Works of John Davies of Hereford*, ed. A. B. Grosart, 2 vols. (1878)

—— *Microcosmos* (1603)

DAVIES, THOMAS, *Dramatic Miscellanies*, 3 vols. (Dublin, 1784)

—— *Memoirs of the Life of David Garrick*, 2 vols., 2nd edn. (1780)

DAWSON, GILES E. (ed.), *Malone Society Collections: VII. Records of*

*Plays and Players in Kent, 1450–1642* (Oxford: Malone Society, 1965)

DAY, JOHN, *Works of John Day*, ed. A. H. Bullen, 2nd edn., rev. Robin Jeffs (London: Holland Press, 1963)

DEKKER, THOMAS, *The Dramatic Works of Thomas Dekker*, ed. Fredson Bowers, 4 vols. (Cambridge: CUP, 1953–61)

—— *Guls Horne-Booke* (1609)

—— *The Non-Dramatic Works of Thomas Dekker*, ed. Alexander B. Grosart, 5 vols. (New York: Russell & Russell, 1963)

—— *The Roaring Girl* (1611)

DELL, HENRY, *The Spouter* (1756)

DENHAM, SIR JOHN, *The Sophy* (1642)

DENNIS, JOHN, *Gibraltar* (1705)

—— *The Invader of His Country* (1720)

—— *Liberty Asserted* (1704)

DIBDIN, CHARLES, *The Professional Life of Mr. Dibdin*, 4 vols. (1803)

—— *A Complete History of the English Stage*, 5 vols. (1797–1800)

DIBDIN, THOMAS, *The Reminiscences of Thomas Dibdin*, 2 vols. (1827)

DILKE, THOMAS, *The City Lady* (1697)

DODSLEY, ROBERT (ed.), *A Select Collection of Old English Plays*, 2nd edn. rev. W. Carew Hazlitt, 15 vols. (1874–6)

—— *Sir John Cockle at Court* (1738)

DOGGETT, THOMAS, *The Country-Wake* (1696)

DOVER, JOHN, *The Roman Generalls* (1667)

DOWNES, JOHN, *Roscius Anglicanus*, ed. J. Milhous and R. D. Hume (London: Society for Theatre Research, 1987)

DRURY, ROBERT, *The Rival Milliners* (1737)

DRYDEN, JOHN, *The Letters of John Dryden*, ed. Charles E. Ward (1942; New York: AMS Press Inc., 1965)

—— *Of Dramatic Poesy*, ed. George Watson, 2 vols. (London: Dent, 1962)

—— *The Works of John Dryden*, ed. Samuel Holt Monk *et al.*, 20 vols. (Berkeley: Univ. of California Press, 1956–89)

DUNLAP, WILLIAM, *Memoirs of George Fred Cooke, esq.*, 2 vols. (1813)

DURFEY, THOMAS, *The Banditti* (1686)

—— *The Comical History of Don Quixote*, part 3 (1696)

—— *The Fool turn'd Critick* (1678)

—— *The Marriage-Hater Match'd* (1692)

—— *Old Mode and the New* (1703)

EARL, THOMAS, *The Country Correspondent, or the Stage Monitor, IV* (1739)

ELIOT, THOMAS, *The Dictionary* (1538)

ETHEREGE, GEORGE, *Man of Mode* (1684)

EVELYN, JOHN, *Diary of John Evelyn*, ed. E. S. de Beer, 6 vols. (Oxford: Clarendon Press, 1955)

EVERARD, EDWARD CAPE, *Memoirs of an Unfortunate Son of Thespis* (1818)

FAIRFAX, BRIAN, *A Catalogue of the Curious Collection of Pictures of George Villiers, Duke of Buckingham* . . . (1758)

FARQUHAR, GEORGE, *The Complete Works of George Farquhar*, ed. Charles Stonehill, 2 vols. (Bloomsbury: Nonsuch Press, 1930)

—— *The Recruiting Officer*, ed. John Ross (London: A & C Black, 1991)

—— *The Works of the Late Ingenious Mr Farquhar* (1660)

FENNOR, WILLIAM, *Fennors Descriptions* (1616)

FIELD, NATHAN, *Amends for Ladies* (1618)

FIELDING, HENRY, *The Covent Garden Journal*, 14 January 1752

—— *The Historical Register for 1736* [1737]

—— *Love in Several Masques* (1728)

—— *Pasquin* (1736)

—— *Tumble-Down Dick* (1736)

FITZ-CRAMBO, PATRICK, *Tyranny Triumphant* (1743)

FITZGERALD, PERCY, HETHERINGTON, *The Life of Mrs. Catherine Clive* (1888)

FLECKNOE, RICHARD, *Love's Kingdom* . . . *with a short Treatise of the English Stage* (1664)

FLETCHER, JOHN, *The Faithfull Shepheardesse* [1609]

—— *Monsieur Thomas* (1639)

FOAKES, R. A., and RICKERT, R. T. (eds.), *Henslowe's Diary* (Cambridge: CUP, 1961)

FOOT, JESSÉ, *The Life of Arthur Murphy, esq,* (1811)

FOOTE, SAMUEL, *Diversions of the Morning* (1758)

—— *A Treatise on the Passions* (1747)

—— *Wit for the Ton!* (1778)

FORD, JOHN, *The Broken Heart* (1633)

—— *The Ladies Triall* (1639)

—— *The Lovers Melancholy* (1629)

FORDE, BROWNLOW, *The Miraculous Cure* (1771)

FRANCIS, PHILIP, *Eugenia* (1752)

FRAUNCE, ABRAHAM, *The Arcadian Rhetorike* (1588), facs. in Scolar Press Facsimile ed. R. C. Alston (Menston: Scolar Press, 1969)

GALINDO, CATHERINE, *Letter to Mrs. Siddons* (1809)

GARRICK, DAVID, *The Letters of David Garrick*, ed. David M. Little and George M. Kahrl, 3 vols. (Oxford: OUP, 1963)

—— *The Private Correspondence of David Garrick with the Most Celebrated Persons of his Time*, ed. James Boaden, 2 vols. (1831–2)

—— *The Plays of David Garrick*, ed. Harry William Pedicord and

Fredrick Louis Bergman, 7 vols. (Carbondale and Edwardsville, Ill.: Southern Illinois Univ. Press, 1982)

GAY, JOHN, *Dramatic Works*, ed. by John Fuller, 2 vols. (Oxford: Clarendon Press, 1983)

—— *Three Hours after Marriage* (1717)

GAYTON, EDMUND, *Pleasant Notes upon Don Quixote* (1654)

GEE, JOHN, *New Shreds of the Old Snare* (1624)

GENEST, JOHN, *Some Account of the English Stage, from the Restoration . . . to 1830*, 10 vols. (1832)

GENTLEMAN, FRANCIS, *The Modish Wife . . . to Which is Prefixed a Summary View of the Stage* (1775)

GIBBON, EDWARD, *Gibbon's Journal to January 28th 1763*, ed. D. M. Low (London: Chatto and Windus, 1929)

GILDON, CHARLES, *The Lives and Characters of the English Dramatick Poets* (1699)

—— *Life of Mr. Thomas Betterton* (1710)

—— *Love's Victim* (1701)

—— *A New Rehearsal* (1714)

—— *The Roman Brides Revenge* (1697)

GLAPTHORNE, HENRY, *The Plays and Poems of Henry Glapthorne*, 2 vols. (1874)

—— *Ladies Privilege* (1640)

[GOFFE, THOMAS], *The Careles Shepherdess* (1656)

GORDALL, WILLIAM, *True Englishman's Miscellany* (1740)

GORING, CHARLES, *Irene* (1708)

GOSSON, STEPHEN, *The Ephemerides of Phialo* (1579)

GOULDMAN, FRANCIS, *A Copious Dictionary in Three Parts* (1664)

GRANVILLE, GEORGE, Baron Lansdowne, *Heroick Love* (1698)

GREENE, ROBERT, *The Life and Complete Works*, ed. Alexander Grosart, 15 vols. (1881–6; New York: Russell and Russell, 1964)

[GREENE, R.? and CHETTLE, H.?], *John of Bordeaux*, ed. William Lindsay Renwick (Oxford: Malone Society, 1936)

GREG, W. W. (ed.), *Henslowe Papers*, 3 vols. (London: A. H. Bullen, 1907)

—— (ed.), *Malone Society Collections: I.ii* (1908; Oxford: Malone Society, 1964)

—— (ed.), *Malone Society Collections: II.iii* (Oxford: Malone Society, 1931)

HALL, JOSEPH, *The Poems of Joseph Hall*, ed. Arnold Davenport (Liverpool: Liverpool Univ. Press, 1969)

HAMILTON, ANTHONY, *Memoirs of the Comte de Gramont*, trans. Peter Quennell (London: Routledge, 1930)

[HARDING, SAMUEL], *Sicily and Naples* (1640)

HARRIS, JOSEPH, *The Mistakes* (1691)

HASLEWOOD, JOSEPH, *The Secret History of the Green Rooms*, 2 vols. (1790)

[HATCHETT, WILLIAM], *The Fall of Mortimer* (1731)

HAVARD, WILLIAM, *King Charles the First* (1737)

HAWLING, FRANCIS, *Impertinent Lovers* (1723)

HAYWOOD, ELIZA, *The Fair Captive* (1721)

HEAD, RICHARD and KIRKMAN, FRANCIS, *The English Rogue, Part 4* (1671)

HERRICK, ROBERT, *The Poetical Works*, (ed.) L. C. Martin (Oxford: Clarendon Press, 1956)

HEWITT, JOHN, *A Tutor for the Beaus* (1737)

HEXHAM, HENRY, *Copious English and Netherduytch Dictionarie* (1648)

HEYWOOD, THOMAS, *Apology for Actors* (1612)

—— *The Foure Prentises of London* (1615)

—— *The Golden Age* (1611)

—— *How a Man May Chuse a Good Wife from a Bad* (1602)

—— *Rape of Lucrece* (1608)

—— *The Royall King, and the Loyall Subject* (1637)

—— *The Second Part of King Edward the Fourth* (1599)

HIGDEN, HENRY, *The Wary Widdow* (1693)

HILL, AARON, *The Prompter*, ed. William A. Appleton and Kalman A. Burnim (New York: B. Blom, 1966)

—— *Elfrid: or, the Fair Inconstant* [1710]

—— *The Works of the Late Aaron Hill*, 4 vols. (1753)

HILL, JOHN, *The Actor* (1750)

—— *Orpheus* (1740)

HOSKINS, JOHN, *Sermons Preached at Pauls Crosse and Else-where . . . Part 3: . . . the Conclusion of the Rehearsall Sermon at Pauls Crosse 1614* (1615)

HOUGH, JOHN, *Second Thought is Best* (1788)

HOWARD, EDWARD, *The Man of Newmarket* (1678)

—— *The Six Days Adventure* (1671)

—— *The Womens Conquest* (1671)

HOWARD, SIR ROBERT, and VILLIERS, GEORGE, DUKE OF BUCKINGHAM, *The Country Gentleman*, (ed.) Arthur H. Scouten and Robert D. Hume (London: J. M. Dent & Sons, 1976)

[HULL, THOMAS], *The Perplexities* (1767)

JACKMAN, ISAAC, *All the World's a Stage* (1777)

J.B. *The Comical Romance*, 2 vols. (1665)

[JENNER, CHARLES], *The Man of Family* (Dublin, 1771)

JOHNSON, CHARLES, *The Gentleman Cully* (1702)

—— *Caelia: Or the Perjur'd Lover* (1733)

JONSON, BEN, *The comicall satyre of Every Man out of his humor* (1600)
—— *Sejanus His Fall* (1605)
—— *The Works of Benjamin Jonson*, ed. C. H. Herford and P. and E. Simpson, 11 vols. (Oxford: Clarendon Press, 1925–52)
JORDAN, THOMAS, *Money is an Asse* (1668)
KELLY, HUGH, *False Delicacy* (1768)
KELLY, MICHAEL, *Reminiscences of Michael Kelly* [compiled by Theodore Hook], 2 vols. (1826)
KEMPE, WILLIAM, *The Education of Children in Learning* (1588)
KENRICK, WILLIAM, *A New Dictionary of the English Language* (1773)
KILLIGREW, THOMAS, *Pallantus and Eudora* (1653)
KILLIGREW, WILLIAM, *Pandora* (1664)
[KIRKE, JOHN], *The Seven Champions of Christendome* (1638)
KYD, THOMAS, *The Spanish Tragedy* (1592)
LANGBAINE, GERARD, *Account of the English Dramatick Poets*, facs. ed. Arthur Freeman (New York and London: Garland Publishing, Inc., 1973)
LANGFORD, ABRAHAM, *The Lover his Own Rival* (1736)
LEANERD, JOHN, *The Country Innocence* (1677)
LILLO, GEORGE, *Lillo's Dramatic Works*, (ed.) Thomas Davies, 2 vols. (1810)
—— *Silvia* (1731)
LLOYD, ROBERT, *The Actor* (1760)
LOWNDES, THOMAS, *The Theatrical Manager* (1751)
MACHIN, LEWIS, *Every Woman in her Humour*, ed. Archie Mervin Tyson (London: Garland, 1980)
MACKLIN, CHARLES, *The Covent Garden Theatre*, ed. Jean B. Kern (Los Angeles: Univ. of California Press, 1965)
MALONE, EDMOND, *Supplement to the Edition of Shakspeare's Plays Published in 1778 by Samuel Johnson and George Steevens*, 2 vols. (1780)
MANLEY, MARY DE LA RIVIÈRE, *Almyna* (1707)
MANUCHE, COSMO, *The Just General* (1652)
MARLOWE, CHRISTOPHER, *The Complete Works of Christopher Marlowe* (ed.) Fredson Bowers, 2 vols. (Cambridge: CUP, 1973)
MARSTON, JOHN, *Antonio and Mellida*, ed. W. Reavley Gair (Manchester and New York: Manchester Univ. Press, 1991)
—— *The Plays of John Marston*, ed. H. Harvey Wood, 3 vols. (London: Oliver and Boyd, 1934)
MARTYN, BENJAMIN, *Timoleon* (1730)
MASSINGER, PHILIP, *The Plays and Poems of Philip Massinger*, ed. Philip Edwards and Colin Gibson, 5 vols. (Oxford: Clarendon Press, 1976)
MAYNE, JASPER, *The Citye Match* (1639)

MIDDLETON, THOMAS, *The Mayor of Quinborough* (1661)
—— *The Spanish Gipsie* (1653)
—— *Your Five Gallants* [1608]
—— [and SHIRLEY, JAMES?], *No Wit/Help like a Womans* (1657)
—— and WILLIAM ROWLEY, *The Changeling* (1653)
—— and DEKKER, THOMAS, *The Roaring Girl* (1611)
MILLER, JAMES, *The Coffee-House* (1737)
—— *An Hospital for Fools* (1739)
—— *The Universal Passion* (1737)
M.N., *The Faithful General* (1706)
MOLLOY, CHARLES, *The Half-Pay Officers* (1720)
MORRIS, EDWARD, *False Colours* (1793)
MOTTEUX, PETER, *Arsinoe* (1705)
—— *Beauty in Distress* (1698)
—— *The Island Princess* (1699)
—— *The Loves of Mars and Venus* (1696)
—— *et al.*, *The Novelty* (1697)
MOTTLEY, JOHN, *A List of all the English Dramatic Poets*, appended to
    Thomas Whincop's *Scanderbeg* (1747)
[——] *The Widow Bewitch'd* (1730)
MOUNTFORT, WALTER, *The Launching of the Mary*, ed. John Henry
    Walter (Oxford: Malone Society, 1933)
MOUNTFORT, WILLIAM, *The Injur'd Lovers* (1688)
MUNDAY, ANTHONY, *John a Kent and John a Cumber*, facs. ed. Muriel
    St. Clare Byrne (Oxford: Malone Society, 1923)
—— and CHETTLE, HENRY, *The Downfall of Robert, Earl of Huntington*,
    facs. ed. John C. Meagher (Oxford: Malone Society, 1965)
MUNDEN, THOMAS SHEPHERD, *Memoirs of Joseph Shepherd Munden*,
    *comedian: by his Son* (1844)
MURPHY, ARTHUR, *The Apprentice* (1756)
—— *The Life of David Garrick Esq.*, 2 vols. (1801)
—— *School for Guardians* (1767)
—— *The Spouter* (1756)
—— *The Works*, 7 vols. (1786)
—— *Zenobia* (1768)
NABBES, THOMAS, *The Bride* (1640)
—— *Hannibal and Scipio* (1637)
—— *Totenham Court* (1638)
NEVILLE, SYLAS, *The Diary of Sylas Neville*, (ed.) Basil Cozens-Hardy
    (London: OUP, 1950)
NEWMAN, THOMAS, *The Two First Comedies of Terence called Andria,*
    *and the Eunuch newly Englished* (1627)

NORTH, ROGER, *Roger North on Music,* ed. John Wilson (London: Novello and Company, 1959)

NORTHBROOKE, JOHN, *Spiritus est vicarius Christi in [terra]: A Treatise wherein Dicing, Dauncing, Vaine playes or Enterluds . . . are reproved by the Authority of the word of God and auntient writers* (1577)

ODINGSELLS, GABRIEL, *Bay's Opera* (1730)

O'KEEFFE, JOHN, *Recollections of the Life of John O'Keeffe,* 2 vols. (1826)

OLDFIELD, ANNE, *Theatrical Correspondence in Death* (1743)

OLDMIXON, JOHN, *Apollo Turn'd Stroller* (1787)

——*Amintas* (1698)

—— *The Grove* (1700)

OULTON, WALLEY CHAMBERLAIN, *Precious Relics* (1796)

OVERBURY, THOMAS, *The Overburian Characters to which is added A Wife by Sir Thomas Overbury,* ed. W. J. Paylor (Oxford: Basil Blackwell, 1936)

PARKER, EDWARD, *A complete Key to the new Farce, call'd Three Hours after Marriage* (1717)

PEPYS, SAMUEL, *The Diary of Samuel Pepys,* (ed.) Robert Latham and William Matthews, 11 vols. (London: G. Bell and Sons Ltd., 1970–83)

PHILLIPS, EDWARD, *Britons,* Strike Home (1739)

—— *The Stage-Mutineers* (1733)

PICKERING, ROGER, *Reflections upon Theatrical Expression in Tragedy* (1755)

PIX, MARY, *The Innocent Mistress* (1697)

POPE, W. J. MACQUEEN, *Theatre Royal Drury Lane* (London: W. H. Allen, 1945)

POPPLE, WILLIAM, *The Lady's Revenge* (1734)

PORTER, THOMAS, *The Carnival* (1664)

POWELL, GEORGE, *Alphonso: King of Naples* (1691)

—— *Bonduca* (1696)

—— *The Imposture Defeated* (1698)

—— *The Treacherous Brothers* (1690)

——*A Very Good Wife* (1693)

POWELL, JAMES, *The Narcotic and Private Theatricals: Two Dramatic Pieces* (1787)

PRATT, SAMUEL JACKSON, *Garrick's Looking-Glass* (1776)

PRIOR, MATTHEW, *The Literary Works of Matthew Prior,* ed. H. Bunker Wright and Monroe K. Speares, 2 vols. (Oxford: Clarendon Press, 1959)

RAVENSCROFT, EDWARD, *The Careless Lovers* (1673)

—— *The Italian Husband* (1698)

RAWLINS, THOMAS, the elder *The Rebellion* (1640)

R.B.S. Esq [pseud.], *The Critick Anticipated* (1779)

REYNOLDS, FREDERICK, *The Dramatist* (1790)

—— *Fortune's Fool* (1796)

—— *The Management* (1799)

—— *The Rage* (1795)

RIDER, JOHN, *Bibliotheca Scholastica* (1589)

ROACH, JOHN, *Roach's New and Complete History of the Stage . . .* (1796)

ROLT, R., *A Poetical Epistle* (1752)

ROWE, NICHOLAS, *The Ambitious Stepmother* (1701)

ROWLANDS, SAMUEL, *The Letting of Humours Blood in the Vaine* (1600)

RUGGLE, GEORGE, *Ignoramus*, (ed.) John Hawkins (1777)

SAINT-ÉVREMOND, CHARLES, *Mixt Essays . . . written originally in French* (1685)

—— *Sir Politick Would-Be*, (ed.) Robert Finch and Eugène Joliat (Geneva: Librairie Droz S. A., 1978)

—— *The Works of Monsieur de St. Evremond, made English from the French Original*, 3 vols. (1714)

[SANDFORD?], *Female Fop* (1724)

SAVAGE, RICHARD, *Tragedy of Sir Thomas Overbury* (1724)

SCRUBB, TIMOTHY, OF RAG-FAIR, ESQ., *The Fall of Bob* (1736)

SETTLE, ELKANAH, *Cambyses, King of Persia* (1671)

—— *Distress'd Innocence* (1691)

—— *The Empress of Morocco* (1673)

—— *The Fairy-Queen* (1692)

—— *Ibrahim, the Illustrious Bassa* (1677)

—— *The World in the Moon* (1697)

SHADWELL, CHARLES, *The Fair Quaker of Deal* (1710)

—— *Five New Plays* (1720)

—— *The Complete Works of Thomas Shadwell*, (ed.) Montague Summers, 5 vols. (1927; New York: Benjamin Blom, 1968)

—— *The History of Timon of Athens* (1678)

—— *The Humourists* (1671)

—— *The Humours of the Army* (1713)

—— *Psyche* (1675)

—— *The Sullen Lovers* (1668)

—— *A True Widow* (1679)

SHAKESPEARE, WILLIAM, *The Cronicle History of Henry the fift* (1600)

—— *The Complete Works of William Shakespeare: Compact Edition*, ed. Stanley Wells and Gary Taylor (Oxford: Clarendon Press, 1988)

—— *The Famous Historie of Troylus and Cresseid* (1609)

—— *The First Folio*, facs. ed. Charlton Hinman (New York: W. W. Norton & Company, 1968)

——*Hamlet*, (ed.) Harold Jenkins (London and New York: Methuen, 1982)

——*Hamlet*, (ed.) G. R. Hibbard (Oxford: Oxford University Press, 1987)

——*Henry V*, ed. Gary Taylor (Oxford: Clarendon Press, 1982)

——*Historie of the life and death of King Lear* (1608)

——*A Midsummer Night's Dream*, ed. Peter Holland (Oxford: OUP, 1995)

——*M$^r$. William Shakespear's Comedies, Histories, and Tragedies . . . The third Impression* (1664)

——*A New Variorum Edition of Shakespeare: Othello*, ed. Horace Howard Furness (1886)

——*The Plays and Poems of William Shakespeare*, (ed.) J. Boswell, 21 vols. (1821)

——*Romeo and Juliet* (1597)

——*The Shakespeare's Globe Acting Editions*, (ed.) Patrick Tucker and Michael Holden (London: MH Publications, 1990– )

——*Shakespeare's Plays in Quarto*, facs. ed. Michael J. B. Allen and Kenneth Muir (Berkeley: Univ. of California, 1981)

——*The Tragicall Historie of Hamlet* (1603)

——*The Works of Mr William Shakespear*, (ed.) Nicholas Rowe, 6 vols. (1709)

——*Works of Shakespeare*, (ed.) Jacob Tonson, 7 vols. (1734)

——*The Works of William Shakespeare*, (ed.) Alexander Pope, 6 vols. (1723)

SHARPE, LEWIS, *The Noble Stranger* (1640)

SHARPHAM, EDWARD, *Cupids Whirligig* (1607)

SHAW, BERNARD, *The Art of Rehearsal* (London: Samuel French, 1928)

——*Collected Plays with their Prefaces* revised 1930, 7 vols. (1930; London: Bodley Head, 1970)

SHERIDAN, RICHARD BRINSLEY, *The Dramatic Works of Richard Brinsley Sheridan*, (ed.) Cecil Price, 2 vols. (Oxford: Clarendon Press, 1973)

——*The Rivals* (1775)

SHIRLEY, JAMES, *The Bird in a Cage* (1633)

——*The Cardinal* (1652)

——*The Court Secret, never Acted but prepared for the Scene at Black-Friers* (1653)

——*The Dukes Mistris* (1638)

——*Hide Parke* (1637)

——*The Humorous Courtier*, (ed.) Marvin Morrillo (New York and London: Garland, 1979)

——*The Humorous Courtier* (1640)

——*The Sisters* (1652)

SHIRLEY, JAMES, *The Wedding* (1629)

'SIMON, SMOKE'EM', *The Campaign* (1775)

SMITH, CAPTAIN ALEXANDER, *The History of the Lives of the Most Noted Highway-men*, 2 vols. (1714)

SMITH, WENTWORTH, *The Hector of Germany* (1615)

SOUTHERNE, THOMAS, *The Fatal Marriage* (1694)

—— *Sir Anthony Love* (1691)

SPENCE, JOSEPH, *Observations, Anecdotes, and Characters of Books and Men*, (ed.) J. M. Osborn, 2 vols. (Oxford: Clarendon Press, 1966)

STAYLEY, GEORGE, *The Life and Opinions of an Actor*, 2 vols. (1762)

—— *The Rival Theatres* (1737)

STEELE, RICHARD, *The Conscious Lovers* (1723)

—— *The Funeral* (1702)

STEPHENS, JOHN, *Cinthia's Revenge: or Maenander's Extasie* (1613)

—— *Satyrical Essayes, Characters and Others* (1615)

STEVENS, GEORGE ALEXANDER, *The Court of Alexander* (1770)

—— *Distress Upon Distress* (1752)

STOPPARD, TOM, *Jumpers* (London: Faber, 1972)

STREITBERGER, W. R. (ed.), *Collections: XIII: Jacobean and Caroline Revels Accounts, 1603–1642* (Oxford: Malone Society, 1986)

SUCKLING, JOHN, *The Works of Sir John Suckling*, ed. L. A. Beaurline (Oxford: Clarendon Press, 1971)

SWIFT, JONATHAN, *Journal to Stella*, (ed.) Harold Williams, 2 vols. (Oxford: Clarendon Press, 1948)

TATE, NAHUM, *The Cuckolds Haven* (1685)

—— *The Island Princess* (1669)

TATHAM, JOHN, *The Fancies Theater* (1649)

—— *Ostella* (1650)

TAYLOR, JOHN, *Works*, 3 vols. (1630)

THEOBALD, LEWIS, *Double Falshood* (1728)

—— *The Perfidious Brother* (1715)

—— *The Tragedy of King Richard II* (1720)

THOMAS, THOMAS, *Dictionarium Linguae Latinae et Anglicanae* (1587)

TOMKIS, THOMAS, *Lingua* (1602)

VANBRUGH, JOHN, *Sir John Vanbrugh*, (ed.) W. C. Ward, 2 vols. (1893)

—— and CIBBER, COLLEY, *The Provok'd Husband* (1728)

VICTOR, BENJAMIN, *The History of the Theatres of London and Dublin, from the year 1730 to the Present Time*, 2 vols. (1761)

—— *The History of the Theatres of London from 1760 to the Present Time* (1771)

—— *Memoirs of the Life of Barton Booth, Esq* (1733)

VILLIERS, GEORGE, DUKE OF BUCKINGHAM, *The Rehearsal: a comedy.*

*Written by his Grace, George late Duke of Buckingham. To expose some Plays then in Vogue, & their Authors. With a Key and Remarks* (1709)

—— *The Rehearsal,* ed. Montague Summers (Stratford-upon-Avon: The Shakespeare Head Press, 1914)

—— *The Rehearsal,* (ed.) D. E. L. Crane (Durham: Univ. of Durham, 1976)

—— *The Rehearsal,* in *The Rehearsal and The Critic* ed. by A. G. Barnes (London: Methuen and Co., 1927)

[WALKER, WILLIAM], *Marry, or do Worse* (1704)

WALPOLE, HORACE, *The Letters of Horace Walpole,* (ed.) Mrs Paget Toynbee, 16 vols. (Oxford: Clarendon Press, 1903–5)

WANDESFORD, OSBORNE SYDNEY, *Fatal Love* (1730)

WASE, CHRISTOPHER, *Dictionarium Minus* (1662)

WEBSTER, JOHN, *The Works of John Webster,* ed. David Gunby *et al.,* 2 vols. (Cambridge: CUP, 1995)

WEBSTER, NOAH, *Dissertations on the English Language* (1789)

WELLS, STARING B. (ed.), *The Comparison between the Two Stages* (Princeton: Princeton Univ. Press, 1942)

WHINCOP, THOMAS, *Scanderbeg* (1747)

WILKINSON, TATE, *The Wandering Patentee,* 4 vols. (1795)

WILLIAMS, JOHN, *Richmond Wells* (1723)

WILLIS, R., *Mount Tabor, Or Private Exercises of a Penitent Sinner . . . Also Certain Occasional Observations* (1639)

WILSON, JOHN, *The Cheats,* (ed.) M. C. Nahm (Oxford: Blackwell, 1935)

WOODES, NATHANIEL, *The Conflict of Conscience* (1581)

WRIGHT, JAMES, *Historia Histrionica* (1699)

WRIGHT, JOHN, *Thyestes* and *Mock Thyestes* (1674)

WRIGHT, THOMAS, *The Passions of the Mind in General* (1604)

ZOUCHE, RICHARD, *The Sophister* (1639)

SECONDARY SOURCES

*Articles*

AERCKE, KRISTIAAN P., 'An Orange Stuff'd with Cloves: Bayesian Baroque Rehearsed', *ELN* 25 (1988), 33–45

ARMSTRONG, WILLIAM A., 'Actors and Theatres', *SSu* 17 (1964), 191–204

—— 'Shakespeare and the Acting of Edward Alleyn', *SSu* 7 (1954), 82–9

AVERY, EMMETT L., 'The Restoration Audience', *PQ* 45 (1966), 54–61

—— 'The Stage Popularity of The Rehearsal 1671–1777', *Research Studies of the State College of Washington,* 7 (1939), 201–04

BARNETT, DENE, 'The Performance and Practice of Acting: Ensemble Acting', *TRI* 2 (1977), 157–85

—— 'The Performance and Practice of Acting: The Hands', *TRI* 3 (1977), 1–19

—— 'The Performance and Practice of Acting: The Arms', *TRI* 3 (1978), 79–93

—— 'The Performance and Practice of Acting: The Eyes, the Face, and the Head', *TRI* 5 (1979–80), 1–13

BATESON, F. W., 'Notes on the Texts of two Sheridan Plays', *RES* 16 (1940), 312–17

BECKERMAN, BERNARD, 'Theatre Plots and Elizabethan Stage Practice', in W. R. Elton and William B. Long (eds.), *Shakespeare and Dramatic Tradition: Essays in Honor of S.F. Johnson*, (Newark, Del.: Univ. of Delaware Press, 1989), 109–24

BERRY, HERBERT, 'The Player's Apprentice', *Essays in Theatre*, 1 (1983), 73–80

BODY, G. W., *Players of Interludes in North Yorkshire in the Early Seventeenth Century, North Yorkshire County Record Office Publications*, 3 (1976), 95–130

BROWN, JOHN RUSSELL, 'The Nature of Speech in Shakespeare's Plays', in Marvin and Ruth Thompson (eds.), *Shakespeare and the Sense of Performance* (Newark, Del.: Univ. of Delaware Press, 1989), 48–59

BUTTERWORTH, PHILIP, 'Book-Carriers: Medieval and Tudor Staging Conventions, *TN* 46 (1992), 15–30

CARNEGIE, DAVID, 'Actors' Parts and the "Play of Poore"', *HLB* 30 (1982), 5–24

CARSON, NEIL, 'Collaborative Playwriting: The Chettle, Dekker, Heywood Syndicate', *TRI* 14 (1989), 13–23

CHAMBERS, E. K., 'Elizabethan Stage Gleanings', *RES* 1 (1925), 182–96

COLDEWEY, JOHN C., 'That Enterprising Property Player: Semi-professional Drama in Sixteenth Century England', *TN* 31 (1977), pp. 5–12

DAVIDSON, CLIFFORD, 'What hempen home-spuns have we swagg'ring here?': Amateur Actors in *A Midsummer Night's Dream* and the Coventry Civic Plays and Pageants', *ShakS* 19 (1987), 87–99

DOWNER, ALAN, 'Nature to Advantage Dressed', *PMLA* 58 (1943), 1002–37

ECCLES, MARK, 'Martin Peerson and the Blackfriars', *SSu* 11 (1958), 100–6

FREEBURN, ROBERT D., 'Charles II, the Theatre Patentees and the Actors' Nursery', *TN* 48 (1994), 148–56

FRUSHELL, R. C., 'Kitty Clive as Dramatist', *DUJ* 63 (1970–1), 125–32

GRAVES, THORNTON S., 'Some References to Elizabethan Theatres', *SP* 19 (1922), 317–27

GRAY, PHILIP B., 'Lenten Casts and the Nursery', *PMLA* 53 (1938), 781–94

GRICE, F., and CLARKE, A. 'Mrs Sarah Gardner', *TN* 7 (1953), 76–81

HARBAGE, ALFRED, 'Elizabethan-Restoration Palimpsest', *MLR* 35 (1940), 287–319

HART, ALFRED, 'Did Shakespeare Produce His Own Plays?', *MLR* 36 (1941), 173–83

HOGAN, CHARLES BEECHER, 'An Eighteenth Century Prompter's Notes', *TN* 10 (1955), 37–44

HOLMES, MARTIN, 'A New Theory about the Swan Drawing', *TN* 10 (1955), 80–3

HUGHES, ALAN, 'Art and Eighteenth Century Acting Style, PART III: PASSIONS', *TN* 41 (1987), 128–39

HUGHES, LEO, 'Redating Two Eighteenth Century Theatrical Documents', *MP* 80 (1982), 54–6

—— and SCOUTEN, A. H., 'Congreve at Drury Lane: Two Eighteenth Century Prompt-Books', *MP* 79 (1981), 146–56

HUME, ROBERT D., 'Securing a Repertory: Plays on the London Stage 1660–5', in Antony Coleman and Antony Hammond (eds.), *Poetry and Drama 1570–1700: Essays in Honour of Harold F. Brooks* (London: Methuen, 1981), 156–72

HUNTER, G. K., 'Flatcaps and Bluecoats', *Essays and Studies,* 30 (1980), 16–47

INGRAM, WILLIAM, 'The Early Career of James Burbage', in C. E. McGee (ed.), *The Elizabethan Theatre X* (Waterloo: P. D. Meany in collaboration with Univ. of Waterloo, 1983), 18–36

KENNY, SHIRLEY STRUM, 'Perennial Favorites: Congreve, Vanbrugh, Cibber, Farquhar, and Steele', *MP* 73 (1976), S4–S11

—— 'Theatrical Warfare, 1695–1710' *TN* 27 (1973), 130–75

KING, T. J., 'The King's Men on Stage: Actors and their Parts 1611–32', in G. R. Hibbard (ed.), *The Elizabethan Theatre IX* (Waterloo: P. D. Meany in collaboration with Univ. of Waterloo, 1981), 21–40

KLEIN, DAVID, 'Did Shakespeare Produce His Own Plays?', *MLR* 57 (1962), 556–60

KNUTSON, ROSLYN L., '*Henslowe's Diary* and the Economics of Play Revision for Revival, 1592–1603', *TRI* 10 (1985), 1–18

LANGHANS, EDWARD A., 'Three Early Eighteenth Century Manuscript Prompt-Books', *MP* 65 (1967), 114–29

—— 'A Restoration Actor's Part', *HLB* 23 (1975), 180–5

LEVIN, RICHARD, 'Performance-Critics verses Close Readers in the Study of English Renaissance Drama', *MLR* 81 (1986), 545–9

LEWIS, P., 'The Rehearsal: A Study of its Satirical Methods', *DUJ* 62 (1969–70), 96–113

LONG, WILLIAM B., 'John a Kent and John a Cumber: An Elizabethan Playbook and its Implications', in W. R. Elton and William B. Long (eds.), *Shakespeare and Dramatic Tradition: Essays in Honor of S.F. Johnson*, (Newark, Del.: Univ. of Delaware Press, 1989), 125–43

——'The Versatility of Shakespeare's Actors', in W. R. Elton and William B. Long (eds.), *Shakespeare and Dramatic Tradition: Essays in Honor of S.F. Johnson*, (Newark, Del.: Univ. of Delaware Press, 1989), 144–50

LOVE, HARROLD, 'Who were the Restoration Audience?', *YES* 10 (1980), 21–44

LYON, ELEANOR, 'Stages of Theatrical Rehearsal', *Journal of Popular Culture*, 16 (1982), 75–89

MCFADDEN, GEORGE, 'Political Satire in The Rehearsal', *YES* 4 (1974), 120–8

MILHOUS, JUDITH, 'Thomas Betterton's Playwriting', *Bulletin of New York Public Library*, 77 (1974), 375–92

—— and HUME, ROBERT D. 'Attribution Problems in English Drama', *HLB* 31 (1983), 5–39

—— ——'Charles Killigrew's Petition about the Master of the Revel's Power as Censor (1715)', *TN* 41 (1987), 74–9

—— ——'Dating Play Premières from Publication Data', *HLB* 22 (1974), 374–405

—— ——'Theatrical Politics at Drury Lane', *Bulletin of Research in the Humanities*, 85 (1982), 412–29

MONTROSE, LOUIS A., 'A Kingdom of Shadows', in David L. Smith, Richard Strier and David Bevington (eds.), *The Theatrical City: Culture, Theatre and Politics in London, 1576–1649*, (Cambridge: CUP, 1995), 68–86

ORGEL, STEPHEN, 'The Authentic Shakespeare', *Representations*, 21 (1988), 1–27

ORRELL, JOHN, 'A New Witness of the Restoration Stage, 1660–1669', *TRI* 2 (1976), 16–28

PEDICORD, HARRY WILLIAM, 'Garrick Produces King John', *Theatre Journal*, 34 (1982), 441–9

——'Rylands English MS.III: An Early Diary of Richard Cross', *John Rylands Library Bulletin*, 37 (1954), 503–27

PHIALAS, P. G., 'Middleton's Early Contact with the Law', *SP* 52 (1955), 186–94

PRICE, CECIL, 'An Eighteenth Century Agreement', *TN* 2 (1948), 31–4

PRY, KEVIN, 'Theatrical Competition and the Rise of the Afterpeice Tradition, 1700–24', *TN* 36 (1982), 21–7

RASMUSSEN, ERIC, 'The Revision of Scripts', in John D. Cox and David Scott Kastan (eds.), *A New History of Early English Drama* (New York: Columbia University Press, 1997), 441–60

ROACH, JOSEPH R., 'Garrick, the Ghost and the Machine', *Theatre Journal*, 34 (1982), 431–40

ROSENBURG, MARVIN, 'Elizabethan Actors: Men or Marionettes?', *PMLA* 69 (1954), 915–27

ROSENFELD, SYBIL MARION, *Foreign Theatrical Companies in Great Britain in the Seventeenth and Eighteenth Centuries*, Society for Theatre Research Pamphlet, 4 (1955)

—— 'The Restoration Stage in Newspapers and Journals', *MLR* 30 (1935), 445–59

SCHAAL, DAVID G., 'The English Background of American Rehearsal-Direction Practices in the Eighteenth Century', *Educational Theatre Journal*, 12 (1962), 262–69

SCOUTEN, ARTHUR, Review of Clinton-Baddeley's *All Right on the Night*, *PQ* 34 (1955), 256

—— and HUME, ROBERT D. 'Restoration Comedy and its Audiences, 1660–1776', *YES* 10 (1980), 45–69

SHELDON, ESTHER K., 'Walker's Influence on the Pronunciation of English', *PMLA* 62 (1947), 130–46

SIEVERS, DAVID W., 'The Play Rehearsal Schedule and its Psychology', *Quarterly Journal of Speech*, 30 (1944), 80–4

SPRAGUE, ARTHUR COLBY, 'Did Betterton Chant?', *TN* 1 (1946), 54–5

STERN, TIFFANY, 'Was Totus Mundus Agit Histrionem ever the Motto of the Globe Theatre?', *TN* (1997), 122–7

STONE, GEORGE WINCHESTER, 'Garrick's Handling of Macbeth', *SP* 38 (1941), 609–28

—— 'Garrick's Presentation of Anthony and Cleopatra', *RES* 13 (1937), 20–38

—— 'A Midsummer Night's Dream in the Hands of Garrick and Colman', *PMLA* 54 (1939), 476–82

TAYLOR, GEORGE, 'The Just Delineation of the Passions', chapter 3 of Kenneth Richards and Peter Thomson (eds.), *Essays on The Eighteenth-Century English Stage* (London: Methuen, 1972), 52–72

TRIBBY, WILLIAM L., 'The Medieval Prompter', *Theatre Survey*, 5 (1964), 71–8

TROUSDALE, MARION, 'A Second Look at Critical Bibliography and the Acting of Plays', *SQ* 41 (1990), 87–96

WERTHEIM, ALBERT, 'Production Notes for Three Plays by Thomas Killigrew', *TS* 10 (1969), 105–13

WHITE, ERIC WALTER, 'The Rehearsal of an Opera', *TN* 14 (1959), 79–90

WILLIAMS, PENRY, 'Shakespeare's Midsummer Night's Dream: Social Tensions Contained', in David L. Smith, Richard Strier and David Bevington (eds.), *The Theatrical City: Culture, Theatre and Politics in London, 1576–1649* (Cambridge: CUP, 1995), 55–67

WILSON, JOHN HAROLD, 'Rant, Cant and Tone on the Restoration Stage', *SP* 52 (1955), 592–98

WORTHEM, W. B., 'Deeper Meanings and Theatrical Technique', *SQ* 40 (1989), 441–55

*Studies*

ALBRIGHT, EVELYN MAY, *Dramatic Publication in England, 1580–1640* (New York and London: OUP, 1927)

ANDREWS, RICHARD, *Scripts and Scenarios: The Performance of Comedy in Renaissance Italy* (Cambridge: CUP, 1993)

ANDERSON, J. J. (ed.), *REED: Newcastle Upon Tyne* (Manchester: Manchester Univ. Press, 1982)

ASTON, ELAINE, *Theatre as a Sign System* (London and New York: Routledge, 1991)

BALDWIN, T. W., *The Organization and Personnel of the Shakespearean Company* (Princeton: Princeton Univ. Press, 1927)

BALUKHATY, S. D. (ed.), *The Seagull Produced by Stanislavsky*, trans. David Magarshack (London: Dennis Dobson, 1952)

BARKER, RICHARD HINDRY, *Mr Cibber of Drury Lane* (New York: Columbia Univ. Press, 1939)

BARTON, JOHN, *Playing Shakespeare* (London and New York: Methuen, 1984)

BARROLL, J. LEEDS, *Politics, Plague, and Shakespeare's Theater* (Ithaca, NY, and London: Cornell Univ. Press, 1991)

BATE, JONATHAN, *The Genius of Shakespeare* (London: Picador, 1997)

—— (ed.), *William Shakespeare: Titus Andronicus* (London and New York: Routledge, 1995)

BAWCUTT, N. W., *The Control and Censorship of Caroline Drama: The Records of Sir Henry Herbert, Master of the Revels* (Oxford: Clarendon Press, 1996)

BEARE, W., *The Roman Stage* (London: Methuen, 1950)

BECKERMAN, BERNARD, *Shakespeare at the Globe 1599–1609* (New York: Macmillan, 1962)

BENTLEY, GERARD EADES, *The Jacobean and Caroline Stage*, 7 vols. (Oxford: Clarendon Press, 1941–68)

—— *The Profession of Dramatist in Shakespeare's Time, 1590–1642* (Princeton: Princeton Univ. Press, 1986)

—— *The Profession of Player in Shakespeare's Time, 1590–1642* (Princeton: Princeton Univ. Press, 1984)

BERRY, HERBERT (ed.), *The First Public Playhouse: The Theatre in Shoreditch, 1576–1598* (Montreal: McGill-Queen's Univ. Press, 1979)

BERRY, RALPH, *Changing Styles in Shakespeare* (London: George Allen and Unwin, 1981)

—— *On Directing Shakespeare* (New York: Barnes and Noble Books, 1977)

BEVINGTON, DAVID, *From 'Mankind' to Marlowe: Growth of Structure in the Popular Drama of Elizabethan England* (Cambridge, Mass.: Harvard Univ. Press, 1962)

BEVIS, RICHARD W., *English Drama: Restoration and Eighteenth Century, 1660–1759* (London and New York: Longman, 1988)

—— *The Laughing Tradition* (Athens, G.A: Univ. of Georgia Press, 1980)

BOAS, F. S., *University Drama in the Tudor Age* (Oxford: Clarendon Press, 1914)

BOLTE, JOHANNES, *Das Danziger Theater in 16. und 17. Jahrhunderd* (Hamburg and Leipzig: Leopold Voss, 1895)

BOSWELL, ELEANOR, *The Restoration Court Stage* (1932, New York: Barnes and Noble, 1966)

BOTICA, ALLAN RICHARD, 'Audience, Playhouse and Play in Restoration Theatre, 1660–1700' (unpublished doctoral thesis, Univ. of Oxford, 1985)

BOWERS, FREDSON, *On Editing Shakespeare and the Elizabethan Dramatists* (Philadelphia: Univ. of Pennsylvania Library, 1955)

BRADBROOK, MURIEL, *The Rise of the Common Player* (London: Chatto and Windus, 1962)

BRADBY, DAVID, and WILLIAMS, DAVID, *Director's Theatre* (London: Macmillan, 1988)

BRADLEY, DAVID, *From Text to Performance in the Elizabethan Theatre: Preparing the Play for the Stage* (Cambridge: CUP, 1992)

BRANDT, GEORGE W. (ed.), *German and Dutch Theatre 1640–1848* (Cambridge: CUP, 1993)

BRAUNMULLER, A. R. and HATTAWAY, MICHAEL (eds.), *The Cambridge Companion to English Renaissance Drama* (Cambridge: CUP, 1990)

BRAUNMULLER, A. R. *A Seventeenth-Century Letter-Book: A Facsimile Edition of Folger MS.V.a.321.* (Newark, Del.: Univ. of Delaware Press, 1983)

BURNIM, KALMAN A., *David Garrick: Director* (Carbondale and Edwardsville, Ill.: Southern Illinois Univ. Press, 1961)

BUTLER, MARTIN, *Theatre and Crisis 1632–1642* (Cambridge: CUP, 1984)

CAPUTI, ANTHONY, *John Marston, Satirist* (New York: Cornell Univ. Press, 1961)

CARSON, NEIL, *Companion to Henslowe's Diary* (Cambridge: CUP, 1988)

CHAMBERS, E. K., *The Elizabethan Stage*, 4 vols. (Oxford: Clarendon Press, 1923)

—— *Medieval Stage*, 2 vols. (Oxford: OUP, 1903)

—— *William Shakespeare*, 2 vols. (Oxford: Clarendon Press, 1930)

CLINTON-BADDELEY, V. C., *All Right on the Night* (London: Putnam, 1954)

—— *The Burlesque Tradition in the English Theatre after 1660* (London: Methuen, 1952)

CLOPPER, LAWRENCE M. (ed.), *REED: Chester* (Manchester: Manchester Univ. Press, 1979)

COLE, SUSAN LETZLER, *Directors in Rehearsal* (New York and London: Routledge, 1992)

COLLIER, J. PAYNE, *Memoirs of the Principal Actors in the Plays of Shakespeare* (London: Shakespeare Society, 1846)

COLEMAN, ANTONY, and HAMMOND, ANTONY (eds.), *Poetry and Drama 1570–1700: Essays in Honour of Harold F. Brooks* (London: Methuen, 1981)

CONOLLY, L. W., *The Censorship of English Drama 1737–1824* (San Marino, Calif.: Huntington Library, 1976)

COX, JOHN D. and KASTAN, DAVID SCOTT (eds.), *A New History of Early English Drama* (New York: Columbia University Press, 1997)

CREIZENACH, W., *Die Schauspiele der englischen Komödianten* (1889)

CUNLIFFE, JOHN W. (ed.), *Early English Classical Tragedies* (Oxford: Clarendon Press, 1912)

DAY, DORIS M., *How to Produce a Play* (London: W. H. Allen and Co., 1990)

DESSEN, ALAN C., *Elizabethan Stage Conventions and Modern Interpreters* (Cambridge: CUP, 1984)

DOBSON, MICHAEL, *The Making of the National Poet: Shakespearean Adaptation, and Authorship, 1660–1769* (Oxford: Clarendon Press, 1992)

DOUGLAS, ANDREY C., and GREENFIELD, PETER (eds.), *REED: Cumberland / Westmoreland / Gloucester* (Manchester: Manchester Univ. Press, 1986)

DUTTON, RICHARD, *Mastering the Revels* (London: Macmillan, 1991)

EDMOND, MARY, *Rare Sir William Davenant* (Manchester: Manchester Univ. Press, 1987)

ELTON, W. R., and LONG, WILLIAM B. (eds.), *Shakespeare and Dramatic Tradition: Essays in Honor of S.F. Johnson* (Newark, Del.: Univ. of Delaware Press, 1989)

FEUILLERAT, ALBERT, *Documents Relating to the Office of the Revels in the Time of Queen Elizabeth* (Louvain: A. Uystpruyst, 1908)

FISKE, ROGER, *English Theatre Music in the Eighteenth Century* (Oxford: OUP, 1986)

FOAKES, R. A., *Illustrations of the English Stage 1580–1642* (London: Scholar Press, 1985)

GAIR, REAVLEY, *The Children of Paul's: The Story of a Theatre Company, 1553–1608* (Cambridge: CUP, 1982)

GALLOWAY, DAVID (ed.), *REED: Norwich* (Manchester: Manchester Univ. Press, 1984)

—— *The Elizabethan Theatre II* (Waterloo: Univ of Waterloo, 1970)

GASKELL, PHILIP, *From Writer to Reader* (Oxford: OUP, 1978)

GEORGE, DAVID (ed.), *REED: Lancashire* (Manchester: Manchester Univ. Press, 1991)

GILLET, J. E., *Molière en Angleterre, 1660–1700* (Paris: Honoré Champion, 1913)

GODFREY, WALTER H., and ROBERTS, SIR HOWARD (eds.), *The Survey of London: Bankside Volume*, 22 (London: County Council, 1950)

GRAY, CHARLES HAROLD, *Theatrical Criticism in London* (1931; New York: B. Blom, 1964)

GREG, W. W., *Dramatic Documents from the Elizabethan Playhouse* (Oxford: OUP, 1969)

—— *The Shakespeare First Folio: Its Bibliographical and Textual History* (Oxford: OUP, 1955)

—— *Two Elizabethan Stage Abridgements: 'The Battle of Alcazar' and 'Orlando Furioso'* (Oxford: Malone Society, 1922)

GROSS, JOHN, *Shylock* (London: Vintage, 1994)

GURR, ANDREW, *Playgoing in Shakespeare's London*, 2nd edn. (Cambridge: CUP, 1996)

—— *The Shakespearian Playing Companies* (Oxford: Clarendon Press, 1996)

—— *The Shakespearean Stage 1574–1642*, 3rd edn. (Cambridge: CUP, 1992)

HALL, PETER, *Peter Hall's Diaries*, (ed.) John Goodwin (London: Hamish Hamilton, 1983)

HARBAGE, ALFRED, and SCHOENBAUM, S., *Annals of English Drama: 975–1700* (London: Methuen, 1964)

HART, ALFRED, *Stoln and Surreptitious Copies* (Melbourne: Melbourne Univ. Press, 1942)

HATTAWAY, MICHAEL, *Elizabethan Popular Theatre* (London: Routledge and Kegan Paul, 1982)

HAYASHI, TETSURO, *The Theory of English Lexicography 1530–1791* (Amsterdam: John Benjamins BV, 1978)

HIGHFILL, PHILIP, FR., BURNIM, KALMAN, and LANGHANS, EDWARD, *A Biographical Dictionary of Actors, Actresses, Musicians, Dancers, Managers & Other Stage Personnel in London, 1660–1800*, 12 vols. (Carbondale and Edwardsville, Ill.: Southern Illinois Univ. Press, 1973–1993)

HOLLAND, PETER, *The Ornament of Action* (Cambridge: CUP, 1979)

HONIGMANN, E. A. J., *The Texts of 'Othello' and Shakespearean Revision* (London and New York: Routledge, 1996)

HÖPFNER, ERNST, *Reformbestrebungen auf dem Gebiete der Deutsche Dichtung des XVI. und XVII. Jahrhunderts* (1886)

HOTSON, LESLIE, *The Commonwealth and Restoration Stage* (Cambridge, Mass.: Harvard Univ. Press, 1928)

HOUGHTON, NORRIS, *Moscow Rehearsals* (London: George Allen & Unwin Ltd., 1938)

HOWARD-HILL, T. H., *Ralph Crane and Some Shakespeare First Folio Comedies* (Charlottesville, Va.: Virginia Univ. Press, 1972)

HOWE, ELIZABETH, *The First English Actresses: Women and Drama* (Cambridge: CUP, 1992)

HOWELL, WILBUR SAMUEL, *Eighteenth Century British Logic and Rhetoric* (Princeton: Princeton Univ. Press, 1971)

HOY, CYRUS, Introductions, Notes, and Commentaries to Texts in *The Dramatic Works of Thomas Dekker*, 4 vols. (Cambridge: CUP, 1980–1)

HUGHES, LEO, *The Drama's Patrons* (Austin, Tex.: Univ. of Texas Press, 1971)

HUME, ROBERT D., *Henry Fielding and the London Theatre, 1728–37* (Oxford: Clarendon Press, 1988)

—— (ed.), *The London Theatre World, 1660–1800* (Carbondale and Edwardsville, Ill.: Southern Illinois Univ. Press, 1980)

—— *The Rakish Stage: Studies in English Drama, 1660–1800* (Carbondale, Ill.: Southern Illinois Univ. Press, 1983)

INGRAM, R. W. (ed.), *REED: Coventry* (Manchester: Manchester Univ. Press, 1981)

ISSACHAROFF, MICHAEL and JONES, ROBIN F. (eds.), *Performing Texts* (Philadelphia: Univ. of Pennsylvania Press, 1988)

JENKINS, HAROLD, *The Life and Work of Henry Chettle* (London: Sidgwick and Jackson Ltd., 1934)

JOHNSTON, ALEXANDRA F., and ROGERSON, MARGARET (eds.), *REED: York* (Manchester: Manchester Univ. Press, 1979)

JOSEPH, BERTRAM, *Elizabethan Acting* (London: OUP, 1951)
—— *Elizabethan Acting*, rev. edn. (London: OUP, 1964)
—— *The Tragic Actor* (London: Routledge & Kegan Paul, 1959)
KENDALL, ALAN, *David Garrick: A Biography* (London: Harrap, 1985)
KENNY, SHIRLEY STRUM (ed.), *British Theatre and Other Arts, 1660–1899* (Washington, DC: Folger Books, 1984)
KLAUSNER, DAVID N. (ed.), *REED: Herefordshire/Worcestershire* (Manchester: Manchester Univ. Press, 1990)
KNUTSON, ROSLYN LANDER, *The Repertory of Shakespeare's Company 1594–1613* (Fayetteville, Ark.: Univ. of Arkansas Press, 1991)
KRUTCH, J. W., *Comedy and Conscience after the Restoration* (New York: Columbia Univ. Press, 1924)
LAFLER, JOANNE, *The Celebrated Mrs Oldfield* (Carbondale and Edwardsville, Ill.: Southern Illinois Univ. Press, 1989)
LANGHANS, EDWARD A., *Restoration Promptbooks* (Carbondale and Edwardsville, Ill.: Southern Illinois Univ. Press, 1981)
—— *Eighteenth Century British and Irish Promptbooks: A Descriptive Bibliography* (New York: Greenwood Press, 1987)
LAWRENCE, W. J., *Those Nut-Cracking Elizabethans* (London: Argonaut Press, 1935)
LEE, SIDNEY, and ONIONS, C. T. (eds.), *Shakespeare's England*, 2 vols. (Oxford: Clarendon Press, 1917)
LENNOX-BOYD, CHRISTOPHER, SHAW, GUY, and HALLIWELL, SARAH, *Theatre: The Age of Garrick* (London: Christopher Lennox-Boyd, 1994)
LIMON, JERZY, *Gentlemen of a Company: English Players in Central and Eastern Europe, 1590–1660* (Cambridge: CUP, 1985)
LINK, FREDRICK M., *English Drama 1660–1800* (Detroit: Gale Research Company, 1976)
LOFTIS, JOHN (ed.), *Essays on the Theatre from Eighteenth-Century Periodicals* (Los Angeles: Univ. of California Press, 1960)
—— *Steele at Drury Lane* (Berkeley and Los Angeles; Univ of California Press, 1952)
—— *et al.* (eds.), *The Revels History of Drama in English*, v. 1660–1750 (London: Methuen, 1976)
LONSDALE, ROGER, *Dr. Charles Burney* (Oxford: Clarendon Press, 1965)
—— (ed.), *Sphere History of Literature: Dryden to Johnson* (London: Sphere Books, 1971)
LOSCH, PHILIPP, *Johannes Rhenanus, ein Cassele Poet des siebenzehnten Jahrhunderts* (1895)
LOWENSTEIN, F. E., *The Rehearsal Copies of Bernard Shaw's Plays* (London: Reinhardt & Evans, 1950)

LUERE, JEANE (ed.), *Playwright Versus Director: Authorial Intentions and Performance Interpretations* (Westport, Conn.: Greenwood Press, 1994)

LYNCH, JAMES J., *Box, Pit, and Gallery* (1953; Berkeley: Univ. of California Press, 1971)

MCGANN, JEROME J., *Critique of Modern Textual Criticism* (Chicago and London: Univ. of Chicago Press, 1983)

MCKENDRICK, MALVEENA, *Theatre in Spain 1490–1700* (Cambridge: CUP, 1989)

MACMILLAN, DOUGALD, *Catalogue of the Larpent Plays in the Huntington Library* (San Marino, Calif.: Huntington Library Lists, 1939)

—— *Drury Lane Calendar 1747–1776* (Oxford: Clarendon Press, 1938)

MCMILLIN, SCOTT, *The Elizabethan Theatre & the Book of Sir Thomas More* (Ithaca, NY and London: Cornell Univ. Press, 1987)

—— and MACLEAN, SALLY-BETH, *The Queen's Men and their Plays* (Cambridge: CUP, 1998)

MAGUIRE, NANCY KLEIN, *Regicide and Restoration* (Cambridge: CUP, 1992)

MANN, DAVID, *The Elizabethan Player* (London and New York: Routledge, 1991)

MARSHALL, NORMAN, *The Producer and the Play*, 3rd edn. (1957; London: Davis-Poynter, 1975)

MICHAEL, IAN, *The Teaching of English* (Cambridge: CUP, 1987)

MILES-BROWN, JOHN, *Directing Drama* (London: Peter Owen, 1980)

MILHOUS, JUDITH, *Thomas Betterton and the Management of Lincoln's Inn Fields* (Carbondale and Edwardsville, Ill.: Southern Illinois Univ. Press, 1979)

—— and HUME, ROBERT D., *Producible Interpretation* (Carbondale and Edwardsville, Ill.: Southern Illinois Univ. Press, 1985)

MITTER, SHOMIT, *Systems of Rehearsal* (London: Routledge, 1992)

MOLINARI, CESARE, *Theatre through the Ages* (London: Cassell, 1975)

MORRISON, HUGH, *Directing the Theatre*, 2nd edn. (London: Adam and Charles Black, 1984)

MOTTER, T. H. VAIL, *The School Drama in England* (London: Longman's, Green and Co., 1929)

MURRAY, JOHN TUCKER, *English Dramatic Companies, 1558–1642*, 2 vols. (London: Constable and Company Ltd., 1910)

NAGLER, A. M., *A Source Book in Theatrical History* (New York: Dover Publications, Inc., 1952)

NASHE, THOMAS, *The Works of Thomas Nashe* (ed.) R. B. McKerrow, 2nd edn., rev. F. P. Wilson, 5 vols. (Oxford: Basil Blackwell, 1958)

NELSON, ALAN H., *Early Cambridge Theatres* (Cambridge: CUP, 1994)

—— (ed.), *REED: Cambridge* 1 vol. in 2 (Manchester: Manchester Univ. Press, 1990)

NICOLL, ALLARDYCE, *The Development of the Theatre* (London, Toronto, Wellington, Sydney: George G. Harrap & Co. Ltd., 1927)

—— *The Garrick Stage* (Manchester: Manchester Univ. Press, 1980)

—— *A History of English Drama*, 3 vols. (1923; Cambridge: CUP, 1952)

—— *The Theatrical Public in the Age of Garrick* (New York: King's Crown Press, 1954)

NUNGEZER, EDWIN, *A Dictionary of Actors* (New Haven: Yale Univ. Press, 1929)

OLIVER, H. J., *Sir Robert Howard* (Durham, NC: Duke Univ. Press, 1963)

ORDISH, T. FAIRMAN, *Early London Theatres* (1894; London: White Lion Publishers Ltd., 1971)

ORGEL, STEPHEN, *Impersonations* (Cambridge: CUP, 1996)

PEARSON, JAQUELINE, *The Prostituted Muse* (New York and London: Harvester-Wheatsheaf, 1988)

PEDICORD, HARRY WILLIAM, *The Theatrical Public in the Time of Garrick* (New York: King's Crown Press, 1954)

PENNINGTON, MICHAEL, *Hamlet: A User's Guide* (London: Nick Hern Books, 1996)

PHIPPS, CHRISTINE, *Buckingham: Public and Private Man* (New York and London: Garland Publishing Inc., 1985)

PRICE, CECIL, *Theatre in the Age of Garrick* (Oxford: Basil Blackwell, 1973)

PRICE, CURTIS A., *Henry Purcell and the London Stage* (Cambridge: CUP, 1984)

RENNERT, HUGO ALBERT, *The Spanish Stage in the Time of Lope de Vega* (New York: Dover Publications, 1909)

RICHARDS, KENNETH, and THOMSON. PETER (eds.), *Essays on The Eighteenth-Century English Stage* (London: Methuen, 1972)

ROACH, JOSEPH R., *The Player's Passion* (Newark, Del.: Univ. of Delaware Press, 1985)

ROBERTS, DAVID, *The Ladies: Female Patronage of Restoration Drama* (Oxford: Clarendon Press, 1989)

ROSENFELD, SYBIL, *Strolling Players and Drama in the Provinces, 1660–1765* (Cambridge: CUP, 1939)

RUBIN, LEON, *The Nicholas Nickleby Story* (London: Heinemann, 1981)

RUTTER, CAROL CHILLINGTON (ed.), *Documents of the Rose Playhouse* (Manchester: Manchester Univ. Press, 1984)

SALGADO, GAMINI, *Eyewitnesses of Shakespeare* (London: Chatto & Windus for Sussex Univ. Press, 1975)

SCHÄFER, JÜRGEN, *Early Modern English Lexicography: I* (Oxford: Clarendon Press, 1989)

SCOLNICOV, HANNA, and HOLLAND, PETER (eds.), *Reading Plays* (Cambridge: CUP, 1991)

SELBOURNE, DAVID, *The Making of A Midsummer Night's Dream* (London: Methuen, 1982)

SHAPIRO, MICHAEL, *Children of the Revels* (New York: Columbia Univ. Press, 1977)

SLATER, ANN PASTERNAK, *Shakespeare the Director* (Sussex: Harvester Press, 1982)

SMITH, DANE FARNSWORTH, *The Critics in the Audience* (Albuquerque, N. Mex.: Univ. of Mexico Press, 1953)

—— *Plays about the Theatre in England from The Rehearsal in 1671 to the Licensing Act in 1737* (London and New York: OUP, 1936)

—— and LAWHON, M. L., *Plays about the Theatre in England, 1737–1800* (New Jersey: Associated Univ. Presses, 1979)

SMITH, DAVID L., STRIER, L., and BEVINGTON, DAVID (eds.), *The Theatrical City: Culture, Theatre and Politics in London, 1576–1649* (Cambridge: CUP, 1995)

SMITH, G. C. MOORE, *College Plays Performed in the University of Cambridge* (Cambridge: CUP, 1923)

SMITH, WILLIAM, *The Early Irish Stage* (Oxford: Clarendon Press, 1955)

SOMERSET, J. ALAN B. (ed.), *REED: Shropshire* (Manchester: Manchester Univ. Press, 1994)

SOUTHERN, RICHARD, *Changeable Scenery* (London: Faber and Faber, 1952)

SPRAGUE, ARTHUR COLBY, *The Stage and the Page* (Berkeley: Univ. of California Press, 1981)

—— and KAHRL, GEORGE M., *David Garrick: A Critical Biography* (Carbondale and Edwardsville, Ill.: Southern Illinois Univ. Press, 1979)

STAFFORD-CLARK, MAX, *Letters to George: The Account of a Rehearsal* (London: Hern, 1989)

STARNES, D. T., *Renaissance Dictionaries* (Austin, Tex.: Univ. of Texas Press, 1954)

STERNE, RICHARD L., *John Gielgud Directs Richard Burton in Hamlet* (New York: Random House, 1967)

STERNFELD, F. W., *Music in Shakespearean Tragedy* (London: Routledge and Kegan Paul, 1963)

STONE, G. W., *The Stage and the Page: London's 'Whole Show' in the Eighteenth Century Theatre* (Berkeley: Univ. of California Press, 1981)

STREITBERGER, W. R., *Edmond Tyllney, Master of the Revels and Censor of Plays* (New York: AMS Press, 1986)

STROUP, THOMAS B., *Microcosmos* (Lexington, Ky.: Univ. of Kentucky Press, 1965)

STURGESS, KEITH, *Jacobean Private Theatre* (New York and London: Routledge and Kegan Paul, 1987)

STYAN, J. L., *Restoration Comedy in Performance* (Cambridge: CUP, 1986)

—— *The Shakespeare Revolution* (Cambridge: CUP, 1977)

SOMERSET, J. A. B. (ed.), *REED: Shropshire* (Manchester: Manchester Univ. Press, 1994)

SUMMERS, MONTAGUE, *The Restoration Theatre* (London: Kegan Paul and Trench, 1934)

TAYLOR, GARY, *Reinventing Shakespeare* (London: Vintage, 1989)

—— and JOWETT, JOHN, *Shakespeare Reshaped* (Oxford: Clarendon Press, 1993)

TAYLOR, GEORGE, *Players and Performances in the Victorian Theatre* (Manchester: Manchester Univ. Press, 1989)

THALER, ALWIN, *Shakespeare to Sheridan* (Cambridge, Mass.: Harvard Univ. Press, 1922)

THOMAS, DAVID (ed.), *Theatre in Europe: Restoration and Georgian England, 1660–1788* (Cambridge: CUP, 1989)

THOMPSON, MARVIN and RUTH (eds.), *Shakespeare and the Sense of Performance* (Newark, Del.: Univ. of Delaware Press, 1989)

THOMSON, PETER, *Shakespeare's Theatre*, 2nd edn. (London and New York: Routledge, 1992)

—— *Shakespeare's Professional Career* (Cambridge: CUP, 1992)

TROUBRIDGE, ST VINCENT, *The Benefit System in the British Theatre* (Leicester: Blackfriars Press Ltd., 1967)

VAN LENNEP, W. B. *et al.*, (eds.), *The London Stage, 1660–1800, A Calendar of Plays* etc., 5 parts in 11 vols. (Carbondale, Ill.: Southern Illinois Univ. Press, 1960–9)

WARK, ROBERT R., *Drawings by Thomas Rowlandson in the Huntington Collection* (San Marino, Calif.: Huntington Library, 1975)

WASSON, JOHN (ed.), *REED: Devon* (Manchester: Manchester Univ. Press, 1986)

WELLS, STANLEY, *Re-editing Shakespeare for the Modern Reader* (Oxford: Clarendon Press, 1984)

—— and TAYLOR, GARY, *William Shakespeare: A Textual Companion* (Oxford: Clarendon Press, 1987)

WEST, SHEARER, *The Image of the Actor* (London: Pinter Publishers, 1991)

WESTFALL, SUZANNE R., *Patrons and Performance: Early Tudor Household Revels* (Oxford: Clarendon Press, 1990)

WHITE, PAUL WHITFIELD, *Theatre and Reformation* (Cambridge: CUP, 1993)

WICKHAM, GLYNNE, *Early English Stages 1300–1600*, 3 vols. in 4 (London: Routledge and Kegan Paul, 1959–81)

WILES, DAVID, *Shakespeare's Clown: Actor and Text in the Elizabethan Playhouse* (Cambridge: CUP, 1987)

WILSON, JOHN HAROLD, *All the King's Ladies. Actresses of the Restoration* (Chicago: Univ. of Chicago Press, 1958)

—— *The Court Wits of the Restoration* (1948)

—— *Mr Goodman the Player* (Pittsburgh: Univ. of Pittsburgh Press, 1964)

—— *A Preface to Restoration Drama* (Cambridge, Mass: Harvard Univ. Press, 1968)

—— *A Rake and His Times* (London: Frederick Muller Ltd., 1954)

WOOD, H. HARVEY (ed.), *The Plays of John Marston,* 3 vols. (London: Oliver and Boyd, 1934)

WOODS, LEIGH, *Garrick Claims the Stage* (Westport, Conn.: Greenwood Press, 1984)

# Index

Lightning Source UK Ltd.
Milton Keynes UK
UKOW02f1158171015

260785UK00001B/8/P